ON THE ROAD TO PERMANENCY

AN EXPANDED DATA BASE FOR SERVICE TO CHILDREN IN FOSTER CARE

David Fanshel

Published in collaboration with
the Columbia University School of Social Work
by
Child Welfare League of America, Inc.
67 Irving Place, New York, New York 10003

HV
883
.N7
F36
1982

Library of Congress Cataloging in Publication Data

Fanshel, David.
  On the road to permanency.

  "Parental visiting of foster children, the
availability and capacities for service
involvement of parents of foster children,
foster parents and their foster children:
adoption perspectives."
  Includes bibliographical references.
  1. Foster home care—New York (State)
2. Child Welfare—New York (State)—Administration—Data processing. I. Title.
HV883.N7F36   1982   362.7'33'09747   82-12832

Child Welfare League of America
67 Irving Place, New York, NY 10003

Copyright © 1982 by the Child Welfare League of America, Inc.

ALL RIGHTS RESERVED. Neither this book nor any part may
be reproduced or transmitted in any form or by any means,
electronic or mechanical, including photocopying,
microfilming, and recording, or by any information storage
and retrieval system, without permission in writing from
the publisher.

Current printing (last digit)
10 9 8 7 6 5 4 3 2 1

Printed in the United States of America

THE AUTHOR

David Fanshel received his doctoral degree in Social Welfare at Columbia University in 1960 and has been a professor at the Columbia University School of Social Work for almost 20 years; he is currently chairman of the doctoral program. His work experience since obtaining his master's degree in social work at Columbia has included 4 years as a caseworker at the Jewish Child Care Association of New York, 3 years of research at Cornell University Medical College in a study of the elderly of New York City, 4 years as research director of the Family and Children's Service in Pittsburgh, and 5 years as the research director of the Child Welfare League of America.

Dr. Fanshel is well known nationally for directing a major longitudinal study of foster children in New York City, focused upon 624 children whose progress was followed for 5 years (*Children in Foster Care*, co-author Eugene B. Shinn, Columbia U. Press 1978). His other books include *Far From the Reservation* (a 5-year followup study of American Indian children adopted transracially in 15 states), *Foster Parenthood: A Role Analysis*, and *How They Fared in Adoption* (with Benson Jaffee). He has also been a student of advanced social work practice and is known for the volumes *Playback: A Marriage in Jeopardy Examined* (with Freda Moss) and *Therapeutic Discourse* (with the linguist William Labov).

Dr. Fanshel's recent work has involved the development of standard computerized reports for the New York State Department of Social Service for all children in foster care in the state (he is author of the familiar "Fanshel-Grundy" reports issued quarterly to every voluntary agency and public social service district in the state). He is completing a contract with the Department to develop techniques for using routinely gathered computerized data to enable the state to carry out utilization review procedures for foster care services for children, as mandated by the New York State Child Welfare Reform Act.

Dr. Fanshel is principal investigator of a 3-year study funded November 1, 1981 (by the Robert Sterling Clark Foundation and the William T. Grant Foundation as a joint grant) designed to evaluate the services of the Lower East Side Family Union, an agency seeking to prevent family breakdown and the necessity for children to enter foster care.

Dr. Fanshel has served as consultant for federal agencies and has visited Sweden, Yugoslavia, Poland, Israel, and Canada in a consultant role. He has testified before the U.S. Congress on child welfare policy matters.

ACKNOWLEDGMENTS

The project described here encompasses three field surveys carried out in cooperation with Child Welfare Information Services (CWIS), a computerized management information system covering children in foster care in New York City. Some of the data analyzed in each study derive from the CWIS data files. A considerable amount of additional information was provided by the 20 to 33 agencies identified for each study. The cooperation of these agencies in testing new data modules is greatly appreciated.

The work of the investigator was supported by Project Grant No. IVB: C93996 from the New York State Department of Social Services. The interpretation of the data is that of the author and does not necessarily reflect the views of CWIS, the New York State Department of Social Services or the cooperating agencies.

The author wishes to acknowledge with thanks the major contributions to the project made by John Grundy, senior research associate, and Ann Gerlock, research assistant. Sheila Beatty was most helpful in the coding and editing of the data.

CONTENTS

INTRODUCTION

I PARENTAL VISITING OF FOSTER CHILDREN
1 Parents' Contact with Their Children in Care
2 Background Characteristics of the Sample
3 Frequency of Contact Between Family Members and the Children in Care
4 Qualitative Aspects of the Visiting Phenomenon
5 Factors Related to Frequency of Parental Visiting
6 Index Scores: Composite Measures of Parental Visiting
7 Conclusions
Notes
Appendix
The Questionnaire

II THE AVAILABILITY AND CAPACITIES FOR SERVICE INVOLVEMENT OF PARENTS OF FOSTER CHILDREN
1 Service to Parents of Foster Children
2 Availability of Natural Parents for Service Contacts
3 Further Perspectives on Parental Service Needs and Service Contacts
4 Prospects for Discharge
5 Creation and Analysis of Service-Related Index Scores
6 Summary of Findings and Implications
Notes
The Questionnaire

III FOSTER CHILDREN AND THEIR FOSTER PARENTS: ADOPTION PERSPECTIVES
1 Foster Children and Their Foster Parents
2 Characteristics of the Foster Families
3 The Children in Foster Family Care
4 Discharge Objectives and the Issue of Adoption by Foster Parents
5 Assessing the Child's Relationships to the Natural Family and to the Foster Family
6 What Lies Ahead for the Child?
7 Evaluative Ratings of the Foster Parents
8 Creation of Composite Indexes
9 Multiple Regression Analysis of the Index Scores
10 Movement Toward Permanency: A Validity Test
11 Summary of Findings and Implications
Notes
Appendixes
The Questionnaire

CONCLUSION

INTRODUCTION

This volume reports upon three related "mini-projects" that were carried out in 1976–77 with the cooperation of voluntary child welfare agencies in New York City. The number of agencies participating in each study ranged from 20 to 33. The aim of the investigator was to perform a field trial of new data modules representing informational domains which seemed likely candidates for inclusion in an expanded data base. The effort was designed to build upon the management information system currently in place in New York City known as Child Welfare Information Services (CWIS). The areas represented by the studies focus upon three phenomena: (1) parents' visiting of their children in care; (2) service contacts with parents and the ability of the latter to establish working relationships with their social workers; and, (3) the child's foster home as a potential permanent abode in the event of parental failure to resume care of the child.

An important feature of these trial runs of data modules is that they have been linked to the existing CWIS data base. Information was already being collected at the time these data were being tested and our efforts sought to go further in illuminating the foster care phenomenon. The agencies cooperating in these studies had already gone far in organizing their processes to conform with the demands made by the computerized system. Their responses to the additional data demands made on behalf of the "mini-projects" thus came from the perspective of a sector of the social services already exposed to the new computer technology.

The available CWIS data base made it possible to sample cases from each agency's caseload in a systematic way. Equally important, it made it possible to follow children for whom experimental forms had been filled out over the course of a year or more to determine whether measures developed from the data modules were predictive of status changes such as the discharge of the children to their parents. This type of testing of the predictive validity of the data is normally not possible in a one-time research effort such as reported here.

Background

The introduction of computer technology into the world of social work is beginning to take place in various service fields. This is especially true for child welfare agencies offering foster care services. There is fairly widespread acceptance of the fact that computerization of essential information will make possible a higher level of managerial efficiency in the delivery of services. At the same time, computerization will make it possible to achieve greater accountability of service from providers in assuring the public that they are performing their service missions in a responsible manner.

Attempting to harness the new information technology on behalf of children in foster care has been a difficult task in the State of New York and its major metropolitan area. New York City has had the unenviable distinction for many years of having more children in foster care than any state in the union outside of New York State itself. On December 31, 1980, there were 39,718 children in foster care in New York State; of these, 23,866 represented the New York City caseload and 15,852 the upstate figure.

After a number of unsuccessful efforts to design a computerized management information system relevant to foster children on a statewide basis, the establishment in 1972 of the Child Welfare Information Services (CWIS) in New York City represented a considerable advance. A strenuous effort was required by all the parties involved, such as public social service officials, voluntary agency board members and executives, and the staff hired to execute the plans. To bring about an operating system capable of tracking such large numbers of children in care was a major achievement.

The writer was privileged to participate in the developmental phase of the CWIS effort by being invited to create a report series which permitted feedback of summarized data to agencies about the children in their care. In collaboration with John Grundy (serving as computer programmer), a software capability was brought into being which made it possible to access each agency's data file and to generate organized reports containing about 75 statistical tables. This capacity to easily summarize information has been found useful to various service entities in the State of New York for the past seven years. Reid has observed that the ability to produce such organized information on a routine basis has profound implications for all social work research that makes use of data on agency clients and services. He feels that an information system can obviate the need for many special research projects.[1]

Current Information Services in New York State

Under legislative mandate enacted by the New York State Legislature in 1976, the Child Care Review Service (CCRS) was brought into being with the ultimate objective of creating a statewide management information system covering all children in care. Two stages of development were provided for. In stage one, the service would be implemented with respect to all children in foster care with an authorized agency. Stage two provided for an expanded data base and would be applicable to children in full-time care with an agency providing foster care or for whom the New York State Department of Mental Hygiene or the New York State Division for Youth was providing full-time care away from their homes. Children being considered for care would be included in the system as well as those in care.

The CCRS system was first brought into operation in all of New York State outside of New York City by simply taking the CWIS system and replicating it upstate. A contract between the New York State Department of Social Services and CWIS resulted in a successful technology transfer, with the latter organization being given the responsibility for training staff in the public social service districts throughout the state in the initial phase of implementation of the system. By 1981, almost all operations involving children in foster care, in New York City and upstate, had been fully transferred from CWIS to CCRS. In addition, the implementation of the second stage of CCRS involving an expanded data base was well under way throughout the state.

Why an Enriched Data Base?

The aim of enriching the data base for the management of child welfare services as presented in this volume is not motivated by a desire to engage in an evaluative characterization of agencies. In other words, it is the writer's view that one need not gather such data in order to be able to pin a label on an agency as "good" or "bad" in its performance. Two such evaluation-oriented systems have already been developed in New York State and New York City using the CWIS/CCRS data base.[2]

An enriched data base can serve the purpose of enhancing management functioning in the delivery of service to children in care and their families in the interest of promoting permanency. This requires that administrators such as commissioners of public social service districts, directors of voluntary agencies, and those at the middle management level in either type of organization be in a position to know "what is going on" in their caseloads so that essential programmatic thrusts can be developed.

Sifting such data for a district with, say, about a thousand children in care, a commissioner can make the following types of probes:

> Who are the foster children in my district who have a discharge plan of returning home but have not seen their parents or relatives in about a year? What do we know about the family's visiting behavior? What has been done in an effort to stimulate such visiting? How viable is the parental home in each case? For those parents who show little likelihood of actually providing a home for their children, what has been the nature of service contacts with them? Has consideration been given to the possibility of seeking termination of parental rights and adoption by the foster parents?

The data base should provide opportunities for administrators to scan their caseloads to determine which children are at risk and to make it possible for them to organize efforts to overcome barriers standing in the way of accomplishing system goals. In the long run this is likely to have evaluative implications. Such data as are contained in the mini-projects presented here can be organized in a variety of evaluation-oriented schemes. The primary aim, however, is to help social service organizations to identify soft spots in their service delivery efforts so that they can move into action to remedy dysfunctional organizational performance that is responsible for children languishing in care.

Trying to capture the phenomenological complexity of the situations surrounding children in foster care by the creation of expanded data sets is of course constrained by the limitations of the social service enterprise. Demands made upon social workers to fill out forms must take into account the fact that these staff members are often carrying sizable caseloads and they are called upon regularly to respond to emergencies that may arise in their cases. They show a natural tendency to resist "paper work," with the associated imagery of a mindless bureaucracy making seemingly ceaseless and irrational demands.

What Kind of Information to Gather?

One must also keep in mind Hunt's admonition about the limitations of social workers as processors of information. Asking for an endless series of judgments about a case runs counter to the ability of informants to store all kinds of information in their heads.[3] All of which lends validity to the notion that data collection requirements be kept to an essential minimum and that data elements be as simple or straightforward as possible.

Yet, complete closure on the kinds of data elements required to bring a system like the foster care of children under statistical control, i.e., accounting for major amounts of variance in outcomes such as status changes and length of time in care, is a state unlikely to be achieved. There are, no doubt, significant informational domains which an enterprising staff could promulgate in the form of data elements and could probably justify as additions to a management information system. These could include topics such as: (1) the child rearing patterns shown by the child's parents with respect to affection, health supervision, discipline, intellectual stimulation, and so forth; (2) the personality of the child and the kind of behavioral adjustment shown in the foster home or institution, his performance, relationship to adult authority, talents and friendship patterns; and (3) the social treatment offered by social workers to the child and his response to such efforts. Whether new, seemingly compelling data modules will soon be developed and absorbed in child welfare information systems will likely be determined by the degree of success achieved in adding the new data elements already being proposed, such as presented in this volume.

What Is Done with the Data Collected?

The issue of expanding the data base is also influenced by factors that go beyond the ability of social workers to respond to the demand for information. Something must be *done* with the data provided. There must be available an analytic capacity to organize the data into meaningful summary statements that eventually make possible an organized intelligence about the system. Further, there must be a disposition on the part of any agency's leadership to utilize the information in the operation of services. A cadre of management personnel is required that can read statistical tables and can relate findings to service tasks. The utilization of organized information is as demanding a task as the original promulgation of the data-gathering effort.

Routine Data Gathering in the Context of Service Operations

It is important to keep in mind the fact that circumstances surrounding the repetitive and routine collection of data in the midst of the service operations of a social agency constrain the kinds of data that can be gathered in the direction of simplicity. These circumstances make the experience different from an effort that is essentially undertaken to meet research interests or one that is designed to add to the repertoire of psychometric test procedures available for clinical assessment purposes. These special features include the following:

1. The scale of operations in the tens of thousands of cases is much larger than the samples developed in typical social research projects. The sheer volume of cases and the data-processing tasks associated with it give one pause about adding any data elements to the system that are not absolutely necessary. In other words, parsimony is most essential.

2. Aside from the matter of scale, there is a feature of data collection in this instance that creates special concern. A single worker may have to provide information for every child in his or her caseload. Under the present CWIS/CCRS system, information is required on a foster child every six months. A social worker is thus likely to be required to fill out the form 50 or 60 times during a single year. We know little about the effects of such repeated experiences in rating cases upon the manner in which the staff person responds to the task. It is possible that a fatigue factor can set in leading to what has been called "instrument decay."[4] When a social worker fills out a data-gathering form about a case differently the second time than the first we need be concerned that the change may be in the observer rather than the observed.

3. There is some uncertainty as to whether variations in training among those filling out the forms will be reflected in the manner in which they respond to the informational items. In the third mini-project study dealing with the role of foster parents in the lives of children in care, 46 percent of the workers filling out the forms had graduate degrees in social work (MSW's), 12 percent had other graduate training and 41 percent were limited to undergraduate degrees. It seems obvious that those responsible for creating data elements for a management information system suitable for diverse informants must be mindful that the skill demand has to be set at a level suitable for the least trained staff.

4. Finally, we have the special feature that in gathering data about social service systems we are asking for information from involved actors. We are asking social workers to attempt to be objective about cases in which they are participating.

The mini-projects that follow should be reviewed with the following questions in mind: Do the new data elements add useful information about factors affecting permanency for children in care? Do the proposed new data elements have appeal on a common sense basis, i.e., does it seem valid to make such inquiry of social workers?

Notes

1. William J. Reid, "The Social Agency as a Research Machine," *Journal of Social Service Research*, 2: 1 (Fall 1978), 11-23.

2. The Child Welfare Monitoring Project was developed at the New York State Board of Social Welfare in the fall of 1975. A second approach, a Program Assessment System, was designed and developed by Special Services for Children of the New York City Human Resources Administration, further developed in a joint effort with the State of New York, and first implemented in October 1980.

3. J. McVicker Hunt, "On the Judgment of Social Workers as a Source of Information in Social Work Research," *Use of Judgments as Data in Social Work Research* (New York: National Association of Social Workers, 1958), 39.

4. Donald T. Cambell and Julian C. Stanley, "Experimental and Quasi-experimental Designs for Research on Teaching," in *Handbook of Research on Teaching*, ed. by N.L. Gage (Chicago: Rand McNally & Co., 1963), 179.

I Parental Visiting of Foster Children

CONTENTS

1 Parents' Contact with Their Children in Care . . . 7
Introduction . . . 7
Parental Visiting: A Multifaceted Phenomenon . . . 8
The Sample . . . 8
The Questionnaire . . . 10

2 Background Characteristics of the Sample . . . 11
Introduction . . . 11
Characteristics of the Sample . . . 11
Age and Time in Care . . . 14
Location of Parents . . . 14
Present Understanding of Parental Visiting . . . 19
Ethnicity and Visiting . . . 19
Parental Contact and Discharge Objectives . . . 19
Comments . . . 19

3 Frequency of Contact Between Family Members and the Children in Care . . . 23
Introduction . . . 23
The Visited and Unvisited . . . 23
Visiting Patterns . . . 26
Last Contact with Parents . . . 26
Current Tendency to Visit . . . 30
Visiting Tendencies and Adoptive Planning . . . 30
Shifts in Visiting Frequency . . . 30
Site of Visitation . . . 36
Letters, Telephone Calls and Gifts . . . 36
Summary . . . 41

4 Qualitative Aspects of the Visiting Phenomenon . . . 44
Introduction . . . 44
Has the Parent Been Responsible in Visiting? . . . 44
Termination of Rights . . . 44
Parental Behavior During Visits . . . 47
Quality of Parental Contact . . . 51
Child's Reaction to Parental Visits . . . 60
Child's Reaction to Parent's Failure to Visit . . . 60
Summary Comments . . . 65

5 Factors Related to Frequency of Parental Visiting . . . 67
Introduction . . . 67
Factors Affecting Visting . . . 67
Sub-Groups of Mothers . . . 70
Factors Affecting Fathers . . . 70
Other Factors Accounting for Lack of Visitation . . . 73
Agency Efforts to Increase Parental Visits . . . 73
Parental Responses to Agency Efforts . . . 73
Contacts Prohibited or Restricted? . . . 80
Summary Comments . . . 80

6 Index Scores: Composite Measures of Parental Visiting ... 82
Introduction ... 82
Frequency of Visiting ... 82
Quality of Contact ... 82
Visiting Problems ... 85
Patterns of Parental Visiting and Index Scores ... 85
Predicting Later Contact ... 94
Predicting the Discharge of Children to Their Parents ... 94
Commentary ... 97

7 Conclusions ... 99
Perspectives on Visiting ... 99
Time in Care as a Factor ... 100
Reliability and Validity Considerations ... 100
Program Directions to Further Family-Child Contact ... 101

Notes ... 102

Appendix ... 103

The Questionnaire ... 107

LIST OF TABLES

Table

1. Agencies Participating in Mini-Projects 1 and 2: Total Questionnaires Sent and Returned. 9
2. Selected Characteristics of Sample According to Adoption Planning Objectives 12
3. Mean Age and Years in Care of Subjects According to Adoption Planning Objectives 15
4. Location of the Child's Mother According to Adoption Planning Status 16
5. Location of the Child's Father According to Adoption Planning Status 17
6. Location of the Child's Parent (Mother or Father) According to Adoption Planning Status 18
7. Total Parental Contact by Child's Current Age and Years in Care 20
8. Parental Contact with Children in Foster Care By Race-Ethnicity 21
9. Parental Contact with Children in Foster Care by Discharge Objective 22
10. Percent of Parents, Relatives or Non-Related Persons Reported to Have Visited Child in Foster Care in Past Six Months According to Years in Care 24
11. Indication That Children Had Any Visitors in the Previous Six Months According to Years Children Had Been in Care 25
12. Visiting Patterns of Children According to Adoption Planning 27
13. Last Contact Between Mother and Child According to Adoption Planning Objectives for Child . . 28
14. Last Contact Between Father and Child According to Adoption Planning Objectives for Child . . . 29
15. Caseworker's Characterization of the Mother's Current Tendency to Visit Child According to Years in Care 31
16. Caseworker's Characterization of the Father's Current Tendency to Visit Child According to Years in Care 32
17. Caseworker's Characterization of Mother's Current Tendency to Visit According to Adoption Planning Objectives for Child 33
18. Caseworker's Characterization of Father's Current Tendency to Visit According to Adoption Planning Objectives for Child 34
19. Changes in Frequency of Contact Between Mother and Child According to Adoption Planning Objectives for Children 35
20. Changes in Frequency of Contact Between Father and Child According to Adoption Planning Objectives for Children 37
21. Site of Visitation Between Mother and Child According to Adoption Planning Objectives for Children 38
22. Frequency of Visitation at Different Sites Between Mother and Child 39
23. Letters, Telephone Calls and Other Types of Contact Between Mother and Child Over Past Six Months According to Years in Care 40
24. Letters, Telephone Calls and Other Types of Contact Between Father and Child Over Past Six Months According to Years in Care 42
25. Sum of Other Parental Contacts (Telephone Calls, Letters, Cards and Gifts) for Visited and Non-Visited Children According to Adoption Planning Status 43
26. Social Worker's Characterization of Whether Mother Has Been Responsible in Visiting Child According to Adoption Planning Objectives for Child 45
27. Social Worker's Characterization of Whether Father Has Been Responsible in Visiting Child According to Adoption Planning Objectives for Child 46
28. Social Worker's Characterization of Mother's Visiting Behavior and Whether It Has Implications for Termination of Parental Rights According to Adoption Planning Objectives for Child 48
29. Social Worker's Characterization of Father's Visiting Behavior and Whether It Has Implications for Termination of Parental Rights According to Adoption Planning Objectives for Child 49
30. Problems Shown by Mothers When Visiting Children According to Adoption Planning Objectives for Children 50
31. Problems Shown by Fathers When Visiting Children According to Adoption Planning Objectives for Children 52
32. Number of Problems Shown by Mothers When Visiting Children According to Adoption Planning Objectives for Children 53
33. Number of Problems Shown by Fathers When Visiting Children According to Adoption Planning Objectives for Children 54

34. Social Worker's Perception of Quality of Mother's Contact with Child During Visits According to Adoption Planning Objectives for Children ... 56
35. Social Worker's Perception of Quality of Father's Contact with Child During Visits According to Adoption Planning Objectives for Children ... 57
36. Quality of Mother's Relatedness to Child During Visits According to Years in Care ... 58
37. Social Worker's Perception of the Degree to Which Mother Tries to Make Visits with Child Enjoyable According to Adoption Planning Objectives for Children ... 59
38. Social Worker's Perception of the Degree to Which Father Tries to Make Visits with Child Enjoyable According to Adoption Planning Objectives for Children ... 61
39. Child's Typical Reaction to Contact with Mother According to Adoption Planning Objectives for Children ... 62
40. Child's Typical Reaction to Contact with Father According to Adoption Planning Objectives for Children ... 63
41. Child's Reaction to Mother's Failure to Visit According to Adoption Planning Objectives for Children ... 64
42. Child's Reaction to Father's Failure to Visit According to Adoption Planning Objectives for Children ... 66
43. Problems of Mothers Rated by Caseworkers as Tending to Lower Frequency of Visiting: For Children Not Freed for Adoption ... 68
44. Proportions of Classes of Cases Where Factors Affecting Visiting by Mothers Have Been Identified by Social Workers (Percent Rated "Very Much" or "Somewhat" as a Problem ... 69
45. Problems of Fathers Rated by Caseworkers as Tending to Lower Frequency of Visiting: For Children Not Freed for Adoption ... 71
46. Proportions of Classes of Cases Where Factors Affecting Visitation by Fathers Have Been Identified by Social Workers (Percent Rated "Very Much" or "Somewhat" as a Problem ... 72
47. Factors Contributing to Lack of Parental Contact with Child for Children Not Freed for Adoption ... 74
48. Factors Contributing to Lack of Parental Contact with Child for Children Not Freed for Adoption: For Visited and Non-Visited Children ... 75
49. Degree of Effort Exercised by Agency to Influence Mothers and Fathers to Visit for Children Not Freed for Adoption ... 76
50. Efforts Made by Agency to Increase Visiting of Mothers and Fathers for Cases Where Children Not Freed for Adoption ... 77
51. Number of Types of Agency Efforts to Increase Visiting of Mothers and Fathers for Children Not Freed for Adoption ... 78
52. Nature of Parental Response to Agency Efforts to Increase Visiting for Children Not Freed for Adoption ... 79
53. Reported Necessity of Agency to Restrict or Prohibit Mother from Having Contact with Child According to Adoption Planning Objectives for Children ... 81
54. Index of Parental Contact Frequency ... 83
55. Index of Quality of Parental Contact with Child ... 86
56. Index of Sum of Problems Associated with Parental Visiting ... 88
57. Item-Criterion Correlations for Three Indexes of Visiting ... 90
58. Mean Scores on Index of Frequency of Contact for Children Not Freed for Adoption According to Groups of Cases Classified by Patterns of Parental Visitation ... 91
59. Mean Scores on Index of Quality of Parental Visiting for Children Not Freed for Adoption According to Patterns of Parental Visitation ... 92
60. Mean Scores on Index of Sum of Problems Associated with Parental Visiting for Children Not Freed for Adoption According to Patterns of Parental Visitation ... 93
61. Predicting Frequency of Parental Contact with Children Over 21-Month Period for Children Not Freed for Adoption ... 95
62. Status of Cases of Children Not Freed for Adoption 21 Months After Data Collection for Visited and Non-Visited Children ... 96
63. Predicting the Discharge of Children to Natural Parents Over a 21-Month Time Span for Children Not Freed for Adoption ... 98
A-1. Respondents' Knowledge of the Child's Mother According to Years Child Has Been in Care ... 104
A-2. Respondents' Knowledge of the Child's Father According to Years Child Has Been in Care ... 105
A-3. Reports of Social Workers About Difficulty in Providing Requested Data According to Years in Care ... 106

1 Parents' Contact with Their Children in Care

Introduction

The decision to focus upon parental visiting of foster children as a likely area for expansion of the CWIS/CCRS data base was influenced by several factors. First, there was the awareness derived from the longitudinal study conducted by the author and his colleagues at Columbia University that parental visiting was a quite strong predictor of the discharge of children from foster care.[1] Thus, 66 percent of the youngsters who received no visiting early in their placement experience were found to be remaining in care five years later. This contrasted with only 27 percent of those children who received frequent visiting shortly after their placement. It was further found that 57 percent of the children remaining in care at the end of the study were no longer in contact with their parents.[2]

The interest in parental visiting was also stimulated by the finding in the longitudinal study that ongoing contact between parents and children was linked to developmental progress in the children. That is, children who continued to see their parents seemed to fare better in a number of areas in which they were assessed compared to youngsters whose parents had essentially abandoned them after their entry into care.[3]

In its current version, the CWIS/CCRS system contains three simple data elements that deal with the visiting phenomenon. They appear in the following manner on CWIS Form B (Case Identifying Information) which is the form filled out every six months by the social worker assigned to the child by the under-care agency:

NUMBER OF PARENTAL CONTACTS
WITH CHILD
(*Since Last Review*)

See Table 7

In Placement Facility	At Natural Parents Home	At Other Setting
_____	_____	_____
(56)	(57)	(58)

The response categories for these elements are contained on the back of Form B; social workers providing the information are requested to select one of the response categories for each data element. The choices are as follows:

TABLE 7
Number of Parental Contacts with Child

A 1
B 2-5
C 6-12
D More than 12 visits
Z None

When the CWIS data on parental visiting of foster children were first aggregated, the results tended to be in accord with the dismal picture that had emerged from the earlier longitudinal investigation. That is, for close to twenty thousand children in care who had not been freed for adoption, more than half had not been seen by their parents in the six-month period covered by Form B.[4]

More recent CWIS reports provide information on children not freed for adoption as having a somewhat smaller proportion of unvisited children than portrayed by early CWIS reports; about 42 percent are so characterized.[5] The reason for the decline in reported unvisited children is not clear. It may be explained by the fact that the reports four or five years earlier were less reliable. As the computerized system was being implemented, "static and noise" were apt to be contaminating the data being collected, reflecting the process whereby the reporting social workers became initiated to the requirements of the system. A second explanation to be considered is that there has been a real decline in the proportion of unvisited children as the visiting phenomenon has received greater emphasis in the New York child welfare system.[6]

The phenomenon of parental abandonment looms particularly large for black children and those who have been in care for extended periods. Despite the modest decline in unvisited children noted, the need to firmly monitor parental visiting continues to be essential for any child welfare agency that takes seriously its professional mandate to safeguard the welfare of the children entrusted to its care.

Parental Visiting: A Multifaceted Phenomenon

Parents of children in foster care are known to include within their ranks many sorely troubled individuals. This fact no doubt accounts for the gross failure of many to fulfill the expectation that they will show interest in their children when they enter foster care, and will visit them.

Our sense of the marginality of the parents is reinforced by an examination of the CWIS quarterly reports which show that at least 80 to 85 percent of the children are in placement because of parental failures in adult functioning of one form or another. Thus, the aggregated CWIS data for March 31, 1979 show 26,865 children in care in New York City with the following parent-related factors as reasons for the children being in care:

	Number	Percent of Children in Care
Death	1,281	4.8
Mentally defective	866	3.2
Physically ill	967	3.4
Alcoholic	1,589	5.9
Drug addicted	1,622	6.0
Arrested or in prison	613	2.3
Abandoned child	2,261	8.4
Abused child	1,222	4.5
Neglected child	4,050	15.1
Unable to cope	10,291	38.3
Mentally ill	1,993	7.4
Parental conflict	1,403	5.2
Parent-child conflict	3,065	17.3

There were 4,655 children in care (17.3 percent) because of their own home behavior.[7] It should be observed, however, that even where children required placement away from their homes because of adjustment difficulties, the inability of the parents to be effective in their efforts to impose discipline was usually an important causal factor in the situation which made placement necessary. The overall impression from examination of the CWIS data and from the reports of many seasoned child welfare practitioners is that the parents show massive disability in their functioning and present a considerable challenge as targets of treatment intervention.

The present CWIS data system provides a limited range of information about the frequency of parental contacts with their children over the six-month reporting periods covered by CWIS Form B. There have been fairly frequent protests by social workers that the aggregated visiting information unfairly portrays the performance of agencies in a poor light. From this point of view, the amount of contact children have with their families is underestimated because of the following reasons:

- The form only accounts for visiting by parents and does not cover visiting by other relatives and unrelated persons.
- The form does not provide for information about contacts between parents and children other than through in-person visitation. Data are not collected about telephone calls, cards, letters, or mailed personal gifts.
- The CWIS questionnaire is not informative as to whether the parent is free to visit. Some parents may be hospitalized or incarcerated in prison and thus may not be in a position to have contact with their children. Their failure to visit should not be used to cast doubt about the quality of an agency's service to the children in its care.

In addition to the matter of frequency of contact, there are other kinds of information about the phenomenon of parental visitation which would appear to be of interest to those concerned with improving the delivery of services to foster children. For example, what factors in the living circumstances of the parents serve to interfere with their ability to see their children? Employment hours, responsibility for the care of other children, or lack of funds for travel might serve as a barrier for some parents with respect to visiting their children. Such information can bring into bold relief the areas in which help might be rendered to parents to enhance their capacity to visit.

It would be illuminating to secure information about what steps an agency has undertaken to facilitate contact between parents and children. It is also conceivable that in some instances agencies have restricted visitation by parents or have insisted that contacts between parents and children be supervised by the agency. Some parents may be highly disturbed adults whose contacts with their children are fraught with danger or have the potential of wreaking havoc with the child's current living arrangement. These are important elements in the phenomenon of parental visiting.

The questionnaire shown in the Appendix contains the data elements culled by the writer from his earlier studies of foster care that are likely candidates for the expansion of the CWIS/CCRS data base. The questionnaire was put to trial use by the 20 agencies that volunteered to participate in this exploratory project.

The Sample

Of the 20 agencies included in this study, 16 were private agencies and 4 were direct care borough offices of New York City's Social Service Department (Human Resources Administration) operating under its child care division, Special Services for Children (see Table 1). The agencies involved in the study represented about one-third of those approached. No pressure was put on any of the agencies to participate and it was expected that among the package of six miniprojects described in a letter soliciting participation, agencies would select one or two that came closest to their interests.[8]

A sampling procedure was developed to vary the number of cases randomly selected from each agency according to the size of the child population served. The largest agencies were asked to fill out forms for as many as 105 cases while the smaller agencies had samples as low as 47. The samples were randomly selected from the cases in each agency's active CWIS data file.

Of 1,704 forms sent to 20 participating agencies, 1,642 were returned, constituting a 96.4 percent response rate. After inspection, the number of usable forms was reduced to a size of 1,251. Of the 391 cases not used, a high percentage

TABLE 1

AGENCIES PARTICIPATING IN MINI-PROJECTS 1 AND 2:*
TOTAL QUESTIONNAIRES SENT AND RETURNED

Sent		Agency	Returned	
MP1	MP2		MP1	MP2
98	98	Abbott House	90	90
--	105	Brooklyn Bureau of Community Services	--	105
56	56	Brookwood Child Care	55	55
105	105	Catholic Guardian Society - Brooklyn	101	101
105	105	Catholic Home Bureau	105	105
105	105	Children's Aid Society	103	103
105	105	Edwin Gould Services for Children	91	89
47	47	Green Chimneys	45	45
103	103	Jewish Child Care Association	93	94
100	--	Leake and Watts Children's Home	96	--
--	105	Lt. Kennedy Home	--	105
--	105	Little Flower Children's Services	--	105
--	105	Mission of the Immaculate Virgin	--	103
105	105	New York Foundling Hospital	104	105
--	28	Ottilie Home for Children	--	28
--	98	St. Cabrini Home	--	98
103	103	St. Dominic's Home	92	92
--	24	St. Germaine's Home	--	24
104	104	St. Joseph's Home - Peekskill	101	101
51	51	Sisters of the Good Shepherd	51	51
105	105	Spence Chapin	105	105
101	101	Windham Child Care	101	101
90	90	Talbot Perkins Children's Services	90	90
55	55	Special Services for Children - Bronx	54	54
56	56	Special Services for Children - Brooklyn	55	55
56	56	Special Services for Children - Manhattan/Richmond	56	56
54	54	Special Services for Children - Queens	54	54
1704	2174	TOTAL	1642	2114

*A total of 20 agencies participated in MP1; 26 agencies in MP2.

of the children, almost two-thirds, were reported to be already discharged from care at the time the form was received. In a smaller number of instances, about twelve, the form had been filled out for a person other than a parent. The remaining cases involved returns with no information because the parents were totally unknown to the agency.

The Questionnaire

The research booklet used in the study contained questions with fixed-alternative responses (see Questionnaire).

The content of the items included in the booklet reflected the interests and concerns about the visiting phenomenon indicated earlier. They covered such topics as the frequency of visitation of various family members and non-relatives, other forms of contact between the parents and the children (e.g., letters, telephone calls, and gifts), barriers to parental visiting, agency restrictions upon parental contacts and agency efforts to increase parental involvement with the child. Items were also included which dealt with parental behavior while visiting and the reaction of the children to parental contacts or the failure of their parents to visit.

In the material that follows, descriptive information will be provided about aggregation of the data for the sample as a whole and for subgroups of the children organized according to stages of adoption planning, years in care, and other variables of interest. As with the other miniprojects, there is reported an approach to developing parsimonious measures of key phenomena through index construction procedures. There is also an attempt to predict later discharge of the children using the parental visiting information, among other predictors.

The general strategy of the undertaking reported here is to provide the reader with exposure to the data elements considered by the author to be useful in understanding the visiting behavior of parents and to examine the distribution of responses by the social workers. The aim is to see in what way the foster care phenomenon is illuminated by the information provided. The reliance upon face validity and to some extent, predictive validity, puts this study in the context of relatively "soft" measurement procedures. We say this without any sense of apology since we do not see the data collection requirements of a management information system in a child welfare service program as equivalent to the task of constructing objective tests for research purposes. Our efforts are more related to what Kogan has termed "logical or theoretical validity" than what has traditionally been called "empirical or statistical validity."[9]

It should be noted that while the primary source of data made available in this report is the questionnaire developed by the writer, the analysis was not restricted to this data set. It was possible to relate the questionnaire data to the information routinely collected by CWIS as part of its normal operations. We were thus able to probe the relationship of the new visiting data to the information provided by social workers covered by the March 31, 1977 and December 31, 1978 CWIS Report Series (informally known as the "Fanshel-Grundy Reports"). As indicated, this permitted an analysis of the predictive strength of visiting variables in accounting for the departure of children from care over a 21-month period.

2 Background Characteristics of the Sample

Introduction

In this chapter, we describe the 1,238 children who make up our sample with respect to their background characteristics and—except for information about the availability of the parents—the kind of information already obtainable from the CWIS/CCRS data system. We also present several of the tables available from the *Special Report Series* on a quarterly basis with respect to parental contact with their children. For these tables the sample is somewhat enlarged to incorporate the combined samples of Miniprojects No. 1 and 2. Subsequent chapters will focus upon new kinds of information obtained from the survey reported here.

Characteristics of the Sample

The sample of 1,238 children was selected from the CWIS files of the 20 agencies participating in Miniproject No. 1. Selected characteristics are shown for the total sample as well as for three subgroups classified by adoption planning status on the CWIS Form B as follows:

	Number	Percent
Child Freed for Adoption	331	26.7
Action Under Way to Free Child	200	16.2
Child Not Freed for Adoption	707	57.1
Total	1,238	100.0

Sex. With respect to the variable of sex of child, we observe that 54.8 percent of the children are males and 45.2 percent are females. There is little variation from this division for the three adoption planning groups.

Ethnicity. There is a heavy representation of black children; they constitute 61.6 percent of the total sample. They are even more strongly represented among the children freed for adoption. White children make up 16.0 percent of the sample and Hispanic children, mainly Puerto Rican, are an even larger presence, constituting 21.1 percent of the sample.

Reason for Placement. CWIS Form B permits selection of family reasons and child-related reasons for placement. A social worker can select three such reasons so that the categories are not mutually exclusive and hence do not add up to 100 percent in a frequency distribution. The aggregation of data is shown in Table 2. These can be compared with the distribution of reasons for placement of all children in care shown in Chapter 1.

Inability of the parent to cope with parental tasks is the most frequently cited reason for placement, accounting for almost a third of the cases (32.5 percent). It is most frequently identified with the cases of children not freed for adoption (37.2 percent).

Parental neglect of the child, abandonment, mental illness and alcoholism are leading reasons for placement. Although other reasons are not outstanding with respect to numbers, they do reflect serious impairments among the parents.

Child-related reasons account for modest percentages of cases. Misbehavior at home is a reason for placement in about one case in ten for the sample and is a factor in 15.8 percent of the cases where the children have not been freed for adoption.

Service to Families. Table 2 shows the percent of contacts between families and social workers around general service as well as in the form of counseling. Almost a third of the families received direct service (34.5 percent) and a similar proportion (38.7 percent) received counseling on family problems. Receiving either form of attention accounted for 47.4 percent of the total cases and almost three-fifths (59.7 percent) of the cases where the children were not freed for adoption. It is noteworthy nevertheless that no family service of any kind was reported for the remaining two-fifths of the cases.

Parental Contact with Children. This crucial variable is obviously of central interest given the focus of the Miniproject No. 1 study reported here. The visiting variable available from the existing CWIS data base was collapsed into a dichotomy to simply indicate whether a child was visited or not in the prior six-month period. If either his mother or father visited at least once, the variable was coded to indicate he had been visited.

Table 2 shows that 32.0 percent of the children were reported to have had contact with a parent while the overwhelming majority, 68.0 percent, failed to experience even a single visit. For the most relevant group, children not freed for adoption, the situation appears somewhat better: 47.7 percent of the children had some visitation with a parent while 52.3 did not. Despite this modification of the

TABLE 2

SELECTED CHARACTERISTICS OF SAMPLE
ACCORDING TO ADOPTION PLANNING OBJECTIVES

Adoption Status	Child Freed for Adoption	Action Under Way to Free Child	Child Not Freed for Adoption	Total
	(Percent)			
Characteristic:				
Ethnicity				
% Black	69.5	58.5	58.9	61.6
% White	13.0	13.5	18.1	16.0
% Hispanic	16.6	27.0	21.5	21.1
% Other	0.9	1.0	1.5	1.3
Sex				
% Male	53.5	55.3	55.3	54.8
% Female	46.5	44.7	44.7	45.2
Reason for Placement				
Parent Reasons:				
% Death	4.2	6.0	7.4	6.3
% Mentally Defective	3.3	4.5	5.0	4.5
% Physically Ill	1.5	4.0	7.0	5.0
% Alcoholic	6.3	7.0	11.6	9.5
% Drug Addicted	9.7	9.5	6.4	7.8
% Arrested or in Prison	2.1	3.0	2.4	2.4
% Other Confinement	0.9	2.5	2.6	2.1
% Surrendered Child	13.9	1.0	1.0	4.5
% Abandoned Child	13.0	14.0	8.5	10.6
% Abused Child	3.3	2.5	5.8	4.6
% Neglected Child	10.3	21.0	16.1	15.3
% Unable to Cope	28.1	23.0	37.2	32.5
% Inadequate Housing	6.0	5.5	6.4	6.2
% Inadequate Finances	6.3	2.5	3.6	4.1
% Mentally Ill	7.6	12.0	12.6	11.2
% Family Emergency	2.1	3.0	5.3	4.0
% Parental Conflict	4.5	5.0	7.4	6.2
% Parent-child Conflict	2.4	1.5	10.1	8.6
Number of Cases	(331)	(200)	(707)	(1238)

(Continued)

TABLE 2 (Continued)

SELECTED CHARACTERISTICS OF SAMPLE
ACCORDING TO ADOPTION PLANNING OBJECTIVES

Adoption Status	Child Freed for Adoption	Action Under Way to Free Child	Child Not Freed for Adoption	Total
	(Percent)			
Child Reasons				
% School Behavior	2.1	1.0	12.5	7.9
% Home Behavior	3.0	4.0	15.8	10.4
% Community Behavior	1.2	0.5	4.0	2.7
% Physical Problem	2.1	2.5	1.3	1.7
% Mental Problem	1.5	2.0	5.8	4.0
Service to Families				
% Family Service Provided	15.4	35.0	43.3	34.5
% Family Counseling Provided	13.0	38.5	50.5	38.7
Family Service or Counseling Provided:				
% Yes	14.5	20.5	25.3	21.6
% Both	6.9	26.5	34.4	25.8
Parental Contact with Child				
% Some Visitation	6.6	18.5	47.7	32.0
% No Visitation	93.4	81.5	52.3	68.0
Number of Cases	(331)	(200)	(707)	(1238)

grim picture posed by the total sample, the fact that more than half of the children in the category of children not likely to be adopted are unvisited must occasion dismay.[10]

Age and Time in Care

Our sample consists of somewhat older children, most of whom came into care when they were quite young. This is another way of saying that they have been in care for a relatively long period of time. They are about one year older than the entire population of children who were in care in New York City as of March 31, 1977.[11] This is accounted for by the fact that a criterion for sample selection in the present study was that the children were to have been in care for at least one year at the time of the survey. Removal of the group of children in care under one year from our concern serves to boost the average age of the sample and the average of the years spent in care.

In Table 3, we show the average current age of the sample, the average age at the time of admission to foster care and the mean years in care for the three groups of children categorized according to adoption planning status. For each of the measures there is significant variation in the means shown for the three groups identified by adoption planning status.

For the entire sample of Miniproject No. 1 subjects, the average current age of the children is 12.50 years. This is a relatively older group, many of whom are on the brink of adolescence. The oldest among them are the children not freed for adoption, who show a mean of 13.67 years. The youngest are the children where it has been indicated that action is under way to free the children; their mean age is 10.22 years. A one-way analysis of variance shows the differences in ages to be statistically significant ($p < .001$).

When mean age at initial placement is examined we see that for the entire sample, the figure is 5.27 years. Interestingly, the group freed for adoption came in at the youngest average age of the three groups with a mean of 2.09 years, followed closely by the group where action was under way to free the child; this group showed an average age at placement of 3.65 years. The group not freed for adoption was the oldest upon being placed in care. Their mean age at entry was 7.24 years.

The mean years in care for the total sample was 5.17 years.[12] Most illuminating is the finding that children already freed for adoption show a very much greater average length of time in care, a mean of 9.27 years compared to the other two groups. The group for whom steps were reportedly being taken to free them for adoption had a mean of 6.52 years in care and for those children who were not freed for adoption the mean was 6.44 years. The finding that it takes such a very long time to secure the adoption of foster children is a serious one and begs further understanding.

Many critics of the foster care system point to such findings as reflecting a basic flaw in service delivery. Some have even charged that agencies maintain children in care rather than releasing them for adoption because they have financial incentives to do so. Indeed it is this view that has stimulated the emphasis upon achieving early permanency for children as the most basic problem in foster care.

Location of Parents

To fully understand the chapters that follow, it is important to develop a picture of the availability of the child's parents. Obviously if a child's mother is deceased, or her whereabouts are unknown, or she is in a mental hospital, this severely constrains parental visiting from this source. If the mother is unavailable, the question naturally arises as to whether there is an identified father, whether his location is known and whether he has visited the child.

In Tables 4 and 5 we display this information with respect to the mothers of the children and the fathers. In Table 6, we combine the parental availability information in order to make clear the proportions of children who do not have a mother or a father whose location is known and who has visited the children. The three tables are organized according to the specified adoption planning objectives set forth by the social workers.

Table 4 presents information about the mothers of the children. The information is hierarchically ordered in a prescribed fashion so that a child is assigned to only one category. Cases subsumed under the category "mother's location known" are those where in addition to her whereabouts being known, the mother has seen the child within the past two years, and is otherwise available, i.e., is not deceased or in a mental hospital.

Table 4 shows that 10.4 percent of the sample involve cases where the mother is deceased. When these are excluded another 29.1 percent of the total sample concern situations in which the mother's whereabouts are not known. Excluding these, we are left with 13.9 percent of the cases where the mother had not been seen in two years, followed by 3.8 percent where she was reported to be in a mental hospital. Through this process of exclusion, we find that cases in which the mother's location is known and where she is available constitute 42.8 percent of the sample.

The mother's availability is most crucial for the class of cases involving children not freed for adoption. Sixty percent of these cases are such that the mother's location is specified as known and she is described as available. This compares with 35.5 percent of the cases where action was under way to free the child and 10.6 percent of those where the child had already been freed for adoption.

Table 5 shows the same information as applied to the fathers. The data show that it is much more unlikely for the fathers to be available than is true for the mothers. After 8.4 percent of the cases are removed because the father is deceased, fully 63.9 percent of the total sample involve situations in which the father's whereabouts is unknown. Only 16.0 percent of the cases involve a father whose location is known and who is otherwise available. The situation is somewhat better for the cases where the children have not been freed for adoption; 22.4 percent are identified positively with respect to the availability of the fathers.

In Table 6 we consolidate the information about the parents in order to ascertain whether fathers are available in the absence of mothers. We thus see that 51.1 percent of the sample show the availability of at least one parent. For cases of children not freed for adoption, the percentage climbs to 70.0 percent. The remaining cases are a source

TABLE 3

MEAN AGE AND YEARS IN CARE OF SUBJECTS
ACCORDING TO ADOPTIVE PLANNING OBJECTIVES

		Mean	Standard Deviation	N
A. Current Age (Years)				
Group 1	Child Freed for Adoption	11.37	3.93	331
Group 2	Action Under Way to Free Child	10.22	4.23	199
Group 3	Child Not Freed for Adoption	13.67	4.30	704
	Total	12.50	4.42	1234
	F-Test = 68.729　p < .001			
B. Age at Initial Placement (Years)				
Group 1	Child Freed for Adoption	2.09	3.04	330
Group 2	Action Under Way to Free Child	3.65	3.50	198
Group 3	Child Not Freed for Adoption	7.24	4.65	697
	Total	5.27	4.70	1225
	F-Test = 195.174　p < .001			
C. Years in Care				
Group 1	Child Freed for Adoption	9.27	4.16	330
Group 2	Action Under Way to Free Child	6.53	4.13	198
Group 3	Child Not Freed for Adoption	6.44	5.10	696
	Total	7.22	5.87	1224
	F-Test = 42.744　p < .001			

TABLE 4

LOCATION OF THE CHILD'S MOTHER
ACCORDING TO ADOPTION PLANNING STATUS[a]

Adoption Status	Mother's Location					Total
	Deceased	Whereabouts Unknown	Not Seen in Two Years	In Mental Hospital	Mother's Location Known	
	(percentaged across)					
Freed for Adoption	8.8	60.1	18.4	2.1	10.6	26.7 (331)
Action Under Way to Free Child	11.5	30.5	16.5	6.0	35.5	16.2 (200)
Not Freed for Adoption	10.9	14.1	11.0	4.0	60.0	57.1 (707)
Percent Total	10.4 (129)	29.1 (360)	13.9 (172)	3.8 (47)	42.8 (530)	100.0 (1238)

[a]The information about parental location is hierarchically ordered so that a child is assigned to a single category. If the mother's location is known, she has seen the child within the past two years and is available, case is assigned to the category indicating her location is known. Otherwise cases are assigned according to the following priority: in mental hospital, not seen in two years, whereabouts unknown and deceased.

TABLE 5

LOCATION OF THE CHILD'S FATHER
ACCORDING TO ADOPTION PLANNING STATUS[a]

Adoption Status	Father's Location					Total
	Deceased	Whereabouts Unknown	Not Seen in Two Years	Father Incarcerated	Father's Location Known	
	(percentaged across)					
Freed for Adoption	4.5	78.9	12.1	0.6	3.9	100.0 (331)
Action Under Way to Free Child	8.0	69.0	8.0	1.5	13.5	100.0 (200)
Not Freed for Adoption	10.3	55.0	10.9	1.4	22.4	100.0 (707)
Percent Total	8.4 (104)	63.7 (788)	10.7 (133)	1.2 (15)	16.0 (198)	100.0 (1238)

[a] See footnote shown in Table 4.

TABLE 6

LOCATION OF THE CHILD'S PARENT (MOTHER OR FATHER)
ACCORDING TO ADOPTION PLANNING STATUS[a]

Adoption Status	Parent's Location						Total
	Mother Deceased	Mother's Whereabouts Unknown	Mother Not Seen in Two Years	Mother in Mental Hospital	Father's Location Known	Mother's Location Known	
	(percentaged across)						
Freed for Adoption	7.6	59.8	16.6	1.8	2.1	12.1	26.7 (331)
Action Under Way to Free Child	9.0	28.5	11.5	5.5	6.0	39.5	16.2 (200)
Not Freed for Adoption	8.5	10.9	7.6	3.0	8.3	61.7	57.1 (707)
Percent Total	8.3 (103)	26.8 (332)	10.7 (132)	3.1 (38)	6.3 (78)	44.8 (555)	100.0 (1238)

[a] The information about parental location is hierarchically ordered so that a child is assigned to a single category. If the mother's location is known, she has seen the child within the past two years and is available, case is assigned to this category indicating location is known; if not, and the father's location is known and he has seen the child within the last two years and is available, case is assigned to this category. If neither parent is available, case is assigned according to the following priority: mother in mental hospital, mother not seen in two years, mother's whereabouts unknown, and mother deceased.

of concern, however. That 30 percent of such children have neither an available mother or father gives some idea of the fairly massive abandonment of children in care.

Present Understanding of Parental Visiting

Another way in which the CWIS/CCRS data system already has the capacity to illuminate the phenomenon of parental contact with foster children is through the *Special Report Series* routinely produced every three months for all of the public social service districts and many of the voluntary social agencies in New York State. A special series within these reports, Series C, is exclusively devoted to an aggregation of information about the extent of parental contact with their children in care. The writer has previously reported the kind of information available from this source for all of the children in care in New York City.[13]

We here present some of the information available through use of the software program which creates the *Special Report Series* tables. We have applied the software program to an enlarged sample of cases derived from Miniprojects No. 1 and 2 samples combined.[14]

In Table 7 we show one of the tables routinely produced in the *Special Report Series*. It is a three-variable table which seeks to explain frequency of parental visiting as obtained for each subject from the CWIS data file of March 31, 1977 by introducing the explanatory variables of age and length of time in care.

Table 7 shows that the longer the children have spent in foster care, the higher the proportion of non-visited children among them. When the same age category is followed to cover the various lengths of time children can be in care, the phenomenon becomes quite clear. Thus, if one takes the oldest group of children, 10 to 21 years of age, the following proportions of unvisited children emerge:

Years in Care	Percent Unvisited
Under 2 Years	37.1
2 to 5 Years	50.6
6 to 9 Years	66.1
10 to 21 Years	84.9

The table also shows that when length of time in care is kept constant, the older children tend to show smaller proportions of unvisited youngsters than the younger ones. Thus when we look at the group of children in care under two years, we get the following percentages of unvisited children:

Current Age	Percent Unvisited
Under 2 Years	52.6
2 to 5 Years	46.5
6 to 9 Years	50.0
10 to 21 Years	37.1

The data tend to support the view that older children hold a greater claim on the commitment of their parents than do younger children.

Ethnicity and Visiting

Another way in which the CWIS/CCRS data system already has the capacity to illuminate the phenomenon of parental contact with foster children is to show the relationship between race-ethnicity and frequency of contact. We generated such a table for the combined samples of Miniprojects No. 1 and 2.

In Table 8, we see that black, white and Hispanic children suffer fairly heavy loss of contact with their parents, more than half for each group.[15] The black children appear to be faced with the maximum deprivation of contact with parents; 69.6 percent had no contact with their parents in the six-month reporting period covered by the forms they submitted to CWIS. The white children suffered 15 percent fewer situations in which there was no parental contact; 54.6 percent of the white children were so described. The Hispanic children were in the middle with 61.5 percent having had no parental contact.

Parental Contact and Discharge Objectives

Another tabular presentation from the combined Miniproject 1 and 2 samples shows the relationship of frequency of parental contact with the children and the discharge objectives specified by the social workers on the CWIS form. This is shown in Table 9. We see that the greatest volume of parental contact with the children is shown for those subjects who are reported to be destined to be returned to their own parents. Only 37.4 percent of these children are reported to have had no parental contact during the past six months. This compares with 65.1 percent of the children slated to be discharged to their own responsibility upon reaching adulthood, and 89.4 percent of those children for whom adoption is identified as the discharge objective. What causes concern is the fact that children slated to return home are a relatively small group within the total sample.

Comments

This chapter makes visible the fact that our sample is composed of children who have, on the average, experienced extended tenure in care. We must nevertheless keep in mind the fact that almost 43 percent have either been freed for adoption or are slated to be freed. Of special concern are those not freed for adoption.

We have seen that the present capability of the CWIS/CCRS system to produce an intelligence about the visiting of parents is significant. It shows that there are many unvisited children within the sample, that age and length of time in care are important predictors of whether children are visited, as is the discharge objective specified for each child. On a more modest level, age-ethnicity is also an important predictive variable.

We now move to our next chapter in which we present data about frequency of contact between foster children and their families, gathered in Miniproject No. 1 as a trial effort to enrich the data base.

TABLE 7

TOTAL PARENTAL CONTACT BY CHILD'S CURRENT AGE AND YEARS IN CARE[a]
(N = 1833)

Years in Care:	Under 2 Years				2 to 5 Years				6 to 9 Years		10 to 21 Years
Current Age:	Under 2 Years	2 to 5 Years	6 to 9 Years	10 to 21 Years	2 to 5 Years	6 to 9 Years	10 to 21 Years		6 to 9 Years	10 to 21 Years	10 to 21 Years
					(Percent)						
All Parental Contacts:											
None	52.6	46.5	50.0	37.1	76.5	75.8	50.6		85.6	66.1	84.9
One	--	6.9	--	1.9	2.6	3.0	4.2		3.2	5.0	2.1
2 to 5	10.5	11.6	11.1	17.5	11.3	14.1	18.1		8.8	14.4	8.5
6 to 12	5.3	16.3	22.2	12.6	6.9	5.0	15.0		2.4	10.4	2.9
More Than 12 Visits	15.8	4.6	5.5	13.1	2.6	2.0	9.9		--	3.6	1.3
Not Reported	15.8	13.9	11.1	17.5	--	--	2.1		--	0.3	0.2
Percent Total	100.0 (19)	100.0 (43)	100.0 (54)	100.0 (205)	100.0 (115)	100.0 (99)	100.0 (425)		100.0 (125)	100.0 (278)	100.0 (470)

[a] Data reflect combination of study samples of Miniprojects No. 1 and 2. Table is from D. Fanshel and J. Grundy, CWIS Special Report Series, Series C; Table 3 produced by special computer run for March 31, 1977 data file.

TABLE 8

PARENTAL CONTACT WITH CHILDREN
IN FOSTER CARE BY RACE-ETHNICITY[a]
(N = 1770)

Frequency of Contact	Race-Ethnicity		
	Black	White	Hispanic
	(Percent)		
None	69.6	54.6	61.5
One Visit	3.2	2.6	3.8
Two to Five Visits	12.2	18.5	13.3
Six to Twelve Visits	6.9	15.5	11.4
More than Twelve Visits	5.0	5.1	6.7
Not Reported	3.1	3.7	3.3
Percent Total	100.0 (1055)	100.0 (270)	100.0 (445)

[a]Source: CWIS data file of March 31, 1977. Data reflect combination of study samples of Miniprojects No. 1 and 2.

TABLE 9

PARENTAL CONTACT WITH CHILDREN IN FOSTER CARE BY DISCHARGE OBJECTIVE[a]
(N = 1851)

| All Parental Contacts | Discharge Objective ||||||||
	To Parents	To Relative	To Own Responsibility	Adoption	To Adult Custodial Care	Unknown	Not Reported
				(Percent)			
None	37.4	56.3	65.1	89.4	80.9	70.8	60.1
One Visit	1.9	2.8	5.2	2.1	--	4.8	0.5
Two to Five Visits	21.8	21.1	15.7	6.3	14.3	13.9	2.1
Six to Twelve Visits	24.1	9.8	9.0	1.7	4.8	6.9	2.1
More Than Twelve Visits	14.7	9.8	4.7	0.4	--	3.4	2.1
Not Reported	--	--	0.1	--	--	--	32.9
Percent Total	100.0 (353)	100.0 (71)	100.0 (611)	100.0 (463)	100.0 (21)	100.0 (144)	100.0 (188)

[a]Source: CWIS data file of March 31, 1977. Data reflect combination of study samples of Mini-projects No. 1 and 2.

3 Frequency of Contact Between Family Members and the Children in Care

In this chapter, we focus attention upon what is the heart of our concern as we examine the phenomenon of parental visiting of children in foster care, viz, the frequency of contact between parents and children. We also address the issue of whether other family members, in addition to the parents, have maintained contact with the children. Further elaboration of concern with the frequency of visitation leads us to ask when the child last had contact with his family. We also inquire into the frequency of contacts that do not depend on in-person visitation: the use of telephone calls and the mails for sending letters, cards, and gifts. The chapter also surveys such issues as whether the visitation of the parents has declined or increased since the child first entered foster care and whether visitation tends to take place in the parental home, the foster family home or institution, or in the agency office.

Introduction

Parents are obviously the persons whose visits to foster children potentially carry the most significance. Whether or not they keep in touch with their offspring has been shown to be predictive of their ability to arrange for the latter's return home on a permanent basis.[16] The well-being of foster children has also been linked to the issue of whether or not they maintain contact with their parents.[17] However, there are also other persons of potential significance to the child whose visits should be accounted for by social agencies responsible for the foster care services being rendered. These relevant others include maternal and paternal grandparents, siblings, uncles and aunts, cousins and unrelated persons who are friends of the child's family. Indeed, some agency staff members have complained that the failure to include opportunities to record such visiting in the CWIS system produced an exaggerated view of the total abandonment of children.[18]

In Table 10, we attempt to account for all of the in-person contacts experienced by the children in our sample during the six-month period preceding the completion of the research form. Inspection of the table does confirm that a fairly substantial amount of visiting is done by persons other than the parents of the children.

The data in Table 10 are organized according to the years the children have been in care (under two years/two to five years/six years or more). There is a clearly discernible association, inverse in nature, between the length of time children have spent in care and the quantity of visiting they have experienced within most of the various categories of visitors as seen from the perspective of aggregated data. For example, some 39.5 percent of all the children had seen their mothers during the past six months but this was true for only 23.3 percent of those in care six years or more. This compares with 51.1 percent of the children who had been in care two to five years and 70.1 percent of those in care less than two years. Almost ten percent of those in care for the longest period had seen their fathers, a very small group indeed, while this was true for more than twice the proportion of those in care for the shorter periods.

Almost a third of the entire sample had had contact with a sibling and this was true of 42.8 percent of the children who had been in care under two years. Other relatives, such as uncles, aunts and cousins, visited one out of five children in the sample and the proportion was almost double (36.8 percent) for children in care under two years. Maternal grandparents, particularly grandmothers, made a modest contribution to the visitation phenomenon; the latter accounted for 8.7 percent of all children and 18.9 percent of those in care under two years.

Stepfathers visited 7.4 percent of all the children and 10.0 percent of those in care for the shortest period. Stepmothers were less prominent in the overall visiting phenomenon but accounted for 4.5 percent of the group in care under two years.

Non-relatives constituted a fair-sized group of visitors. Almost 15 percent of all the children received such visitation and this was true of 28.4 percent of those in care under two years. Inspection of the questionnaires revealed that the unrelated visitor was frequently a male friend of the mother, who was either unmarried or separated or divorced from the child's father.

The Visited and Unvisited

In Table 11, the data have been aggregated in a form to highlight the answer to a simple question: Has the child had contact with *any* member of his family, or non-related friend of the family, during the past six months? The data are shown according to length of time in care as well as for all the children. We note that 56.2 percent of the children

TABLE 10

PERCENT OF PARENTS, RELATIVES OR NON-RELATED PERSONS REPORTED TO HAVE VISITED CHILD IN FOSTER CARE IN PAST SIX MONTHS ACCORDING TO YEARS IN CARE[a]
(N = 1225)[b]

| Years in Care | Categories of Visitors ||||||||| Total |
	Mother	Father	Step-Mother	Step-Father	Sibling	Maternal Grandmother	Maternal Grandfather	Paternal Grandmother	Paternal Grandfather	Other Relatives	Other Non-Relatives	
	(Percent)										
Under Two Years	70.1	23.4	4.5	10.0	42.8	18.9	7.5	6.0	1.5	36.8	28.4	16.4 (201)
Two to Five Years	51.1	22.1	2.9	10.4	35.4	10.9	2.9	4.3	1.6	26.3	17.0	30.7 (376)
Six Years or More	23.3	9.9	0.9	4.9	29.3	4.3	1.1	1.1	0.2	11.1	9.0	52.9 (648)
Percent of All Children	39.5	15.8	2.1	7.4	33.4	8.7	2.7	2.9	0.8	20.0	14.6	100.0
Total Visitors	(484)	(194)	(26)	(91)	(409)	(107)	(33)	(35)	(10)	(245)	(179)	(1225)

[a] Inquiry posed to respondents was: "What persons have seen the child during the past six months (or since the child entered care if duration of placement is less than six months)?" The categories of visitors displayed in the table were shown with the instruction, "check all that apply." Percentages shown reflect proportion of each category where visitation had taken place; percent not visiting, or where the category is not applicable, are not shown in the table. Each column is discrete and independent of other columns.

[b] Thirteen cases omitted because years in care could not be determined.

TABLE 11

INDICATION THAT CHILDREN HAD ANY VISITORS IN THE PREVIOUS SIX MONTHS
ACCORDING TO YEARS CHILDREN HAD BEEN IN CARE

Age of Child	Child Was Visited	Child Was Not Visited	Information Unknown	Not Applicable	Total
		(percentaged across)			
Under Two Years	85.6	12.9	0.5	1.0	16.4 (201)
Two to Five Years	66.0	33.0	0.3	0.7	30.7 (376)
Six Years or More	41.6	44.1	0.6	13.7	52.9 (648)
Percent Total	56.2 (689)	35.6 (436)	0.5 (6)	7.7 (94)	100.0 (1225)

had some visitation contact connected with the family of origin. This was true of 85.6 percent of the children in care under two years, 66.0 percent in care two to five years, and 41.6 percent of those in care for six years or more.

Visiting Patterns

In Table 12, we explore the patterns of visitation to the child according to three categories of adoption planning status: (1) freed for adoption, (2) action under way to free the child, and (3) not free for adoption. We note that the majority of the subjects (57.1 percent) fall within the third category. We would naturally expect that children already freed for adoption would receive minimal visiting from biological family members while those not free would be recipients of much more visiting.

An important feature of Table 12 is the way the data are organized. Unlike the preceding table, the visitation reported for a child has been assigned to only one category of visitor even though he might have experienced contacts with several of the types of persons shown in the table. Here, the assignment to a single category is according to a prescribed order as shown in Table 12. Thus a child visited by both parents would be classified within that category since it was assigned the highest priority. Visitation by mothers only was given the next highest priority, followed by fathers only, and so forth. The fact that a child had been assigned to the column indicating visitation by the grandparents, for example, signifies that he received no visiting from either his mother or father. The table thus affords a consolidated view of the visiting situation of the children.

Table 12 enables us to state definitively what proportion of the children in care have had contact with at least one of their parents. For the entire sample, we observe that 46.2 percent had contact with a parent, most often with the mother alone (29.3 percent). Slightly more than one child in ten (11.1 percent) had the advantage of the more normal situation, i.e., contact with both parents, and 5.8 percent with the father alone.

As might be anticipated, the children who had already been freed for adoption were lowest in the proportion of those still having contact with either or both of their parents. Only 7.2 percent were reported to have such contact. This contrasted with 30.5 percent of those children where the social workers indicated that action was under way to free the child.

For children where adoption was not being considered, contact was maintained with at least one parent in 68.9 percent of the cases. Such children had visits with both parent in 17.4 percent of the cases, with the mother alone in 43.4 percent of the cases, and 8.1 percent where the father was seen alone. Such children had visitation from an adult relative—but not with a parent—in 5.5 percent of the cases. An additional 8.2 percent had no contact with adult relatives, but were in contact with at least one sibling. The children being considered for adoption also had contact with siblings in similar proportions of cases.

Perhaps the most significant column in Table 12 is the one bearing the sad label, "Not Visited." For the entire sample, 40.2 percent of the children were faced with the absence of contact with any family member or friend. When one excludes siblings (8.2 percent) it is clear that almost half of the sample (49.1 percent) had no contact with an adult relative.

For children freed for adoption, 80.4 percent were reported to have no visitation of any kind and 90.2 percent failed to see any adult relative, i.e., a person who is not a sibling. For those children where action was under way to free the child, 56.0 percent had no visitation from any source and 64.0 percent had no contact with an adult relative.

The group for whom visitation from families and others can be deemed most crucial is the one identified as being not free for adoption. Table 12 shows that 16.8 percent of these children were totally unvisited and 25.6 percent had no contact with an adult relative. Although the visiting situation of these children appears decidedly better than the two other groups, concern might well be expressed about the possibility that one in four of the subjects not slated for adoption appear to be in limbo, facing foster care as their mode of life until achieving majority.

Last Contact with Parents

Another perspective that can provide insight about the nature of a foster child's relationship with his parents is provided by asking the question: "When did the child last see his mother and his father?" This information is shown in Table 13 for the mothers and Table 14 for the fathers. The data are organized according to the adoptive planning categories specified in each case.

We observe in Table 13 that 39.5 percent of the children had not had contact with their mothers since birth or from the very beginning of placement shortly after birth. For these children, it would seem that the mothers could only take on the quality of some abstract being. The situation was most severe for children already freed for adoption; 82.8 percent of them had no contact with their mothers since birth. This was true of 45.0 percent of those children where action was under way to free them for adoption and 17.7 percent of those not freed for adoption.

Almost one child in ten (11.7 percent) had not seen his mother in over two years and an additional 9.2 percent had seen their mothers 6 months to 24 months earlier. Another 13.9 percent of the children had seen their mothers two to five months earlier, while one child in four (25.7 percent) had seen his mother within the past month.

If we were to stretch the notion of an acceptable interval of time since the child had been seen to five months, indicating that he had not been abandoned, the data would show that 39.6 percent of the cases met this minimum standard. For children freed for adoption, 5.1 percent of the cases were so described, while this was true for 24.0 percent of the cases where action was under way to free the child.

Most fortunately situated were the children not freed for adoption; 60.1 percent of the youngsters had seen their mothers within the past five months, the majority within the past month. Nevertheless concern arises because 17.7 percent of the children had not seen their mothers since birth and 12.4 percent had not seen them within the past two years, both categories accounting for 30.1 percent of the cases. Neither defined as being headed for adoption

TABLE 12

VISITING PATTERNS OF CHILDREN ACCORDING TO ADOPTION PLANNING[a]

Adoption Status	Both Parents Visit	Mother Only Visits	Father Only Visits	Grand-parents Visit	Other Relative Visits	Sib-lings Visit	Non-relative Visits	Not Visited	Total
				(percentaged across)					
Freed for Adoption	0.6	4.5	2.1	1.8	0.6	8.8	1.2	80.4	26.7 (331)
Action Underway to Free Child	6.0	20.5	4.0	2.0	3.5	7.5	0.5	56.0	16.2 (200)
Not Free for Adoption	17.4	43.4	8.1	1.0	4.5	8.2	0.6	16.8	57.1 (707)
Percent Total	11.1 (137)	29.3 (363)	5.8 (72)	1.4 (17)	3.3 (41)	8.2 (102)	0.7 (9)	40.2 (497)	100.0 (1238)

[a] Categories of visitation maximized to the left. Children were included in a category of visitation only if they could not be classified under a previous category.

TABLE 13

LAST CONTACT BETWEEN MOTHER AND CHILD
ACCORDING TO ADOPTION PLANNING OBJECTIVES FOR CHILD

Time of Last Contact	Freed for Adoption	Action Under Way to Free Child	Not Freed for Adoption	Total
	(Percent)			
No Contact Since Birth of Child (or Since Placement)	82.8	45.0	17.7	39.5
Over Two Years Ago	8.8	14.0	12.4	11.7
Six to 24 Months Ago	3.3	17.0	9.8	9.2
Two to Five Months Ago	2.4	16.5	18.5	13.9
Within Past Month	2.7	7.5	41.6	25.7
Percent Total	100.0 (331)	100.0 (200)	100.0 (707)	100.0 (1238)

TABLE 14

LAST CONTACT BETWEEN FATHER AND CHILD
ACCORDING TO ADOPTION PLANNING OBJECTIVES FOR CHILD

Time of Last Contact	Freed for Adoption	Action Under Way to Free Child	Not Freed for Adoption	Total
	(Percent)			
No Contact Since Birth of Child (or Since Placement)	90.1	74.5	57.6	69.1
Over Two Years Ago	5.7	11.0	11.6	9.9
Six to 24 Months Ago	1.5	6.0	6.1	4.8
Two to Five Months Ago	1.2	4.0	8.6	5.9
Within Past Month	1.5	4.5	16.1	10.3
Percent Total	100.0 (331)	100.0 (200)	100.0 (707)	100.0 (1238)

nor in touch with their mothers, these children reflect cases which would appear to need careful sifting with permanency planning objectives in mind.

In Table 14, we show the same type of data, in this instance related to the child's last contact with the father. As might be expected, paternal contact with the children is considerably more attenuated than was the case for the mothers. Almost seven children in ten (69.1 percent) had not seen their fathers since birth, with this fact more likely to be characteristic of children freed for adoption (90.1 percent) or where action was under way to free the child (74.5 percent) than for children not freed for adoption (57.6 percent).

Only 16.2 percent of the children had seen their fathers during the past six months. For the children not slated for adoption, 24.7 percent had such recent contact. This contrasts with 2.7 percent of the children freed for adoption and 8.5 percent of those where there was action under way to free them.

Current Tendency to Visit

The social workers were asked to characterize the current tendency of the child's parents to visit the child. This may perhaps strike the reader as somewhat redundant, given the fact that actual visiting frequencies had already been obtained. However, the writer considered it important to make explicit the overall view of the social worker of the parent's visiting tendencies at the time of the survey. It seemed conceivable, for example, that recent parental visiting behavior was atypical due to temporal circumstances such as illness and that prospects for future visiting might be better than current behavior would indicate.

The characterization of the mother's visiting is shown in Table 15 according to the years the children have been in care. For all of the children, the perspectives of the social workers is rather dismal. More than half the mothers (54.4 percent) are said to *never* visit their children and 13.8 percent rarely; thus 68.2 percent, or about two-thirds of the children, appear cut off from their mothers. An additional 9.3 percent of the mothers are described as seeing their children infrequently. Only about one child in ten is said to see his mother regularly or often and another 13.1 percent are described as seeing her fairly regularly.

Length of time in care is again obviously a major factor in discriminating among the children. Thus, for example, children in care six years or more show 71.0 percent of the mothers never visiting compared to 41.1 percent of those in care two to five years and 25.9 percent of those who entered the system less than two year earlier.

The situation with respect to the fathers appears even more bleak. About four-fifths (80.7 percent) of the children are said to never see their fathers and an additional 6.3 percent see them rarely. Only 3.4 percent of the children are reported as seeing their fathers fairly regularly. Thus, less than one child in ten is characterized as being in regular contact with his father. The situation is slightly better for children who have been in care for shorter periods, but not appreciably so. (See Table 16.)

Visiting Tendencies and Adoptive Planning

We continue to be concerned with the social worker's characterization of the visiting tendencies of the parents. As has previously been shown, dividing the children into three groups according to their adoption planning status introduces a factor that discriminates quite sharply with respect to parental visiting behavior. This occasions no surprise since common sense would lead one to expect that surrendered children would have almost no contact with their parents. Yet the data presented in Table 17 do provide further illumination of the visiting phenomenon that serves to create disquiet.

We observe that 60.6 percent of the children were in situations where the social worker indicated that the mother *never* visited and in another 7.6 percent of the cases, she was said to visit *rarely*. In only 9.3 percent of the cases was the mother described as visiting regularly or often and in another 13.1 percent her visiting was fairly regular. Less than one child in four is apparently visited with any regularity.

What emerges as the most serious finding reported in Table 17 is that for the children most affected by parental visiting, i.e., not freed for adoption, only 15.4 percent were said to see their mothers regularly and another 19.8 percent saw them fairly regularly. Thus, almost two-thirds (64.8 percent) of the children who were not destined to be adopted either never saw their mothers (41.6 percent), saw them rarely (10.3 percent) or infrequently (12.9 percent). The implications for permanency planning seem quite obvious: most of these children will remain in foster care until they can be discharged to their own responsibility.

The characterization of the visitation tendencies of the fathers of the children presents a much more grim scene of parental abandonment than the one described for the mothers. The vast majority of the children (83.9 percent) were *never* seen by their fathers. Only 3.4 percent were seen regularly and 5.1 percent fairly regularly. The children not freed for adoption were only slightly better off than those who had been surrendered or where action was under way to free them (Table 18).

Shifts in Visiting Frequency

The social workers were asked to report upon changes in the frequency of parental contact since the child had entered care. Had there been a decline in visiting or had it remained stable over time? Perhaps with the change of circumstances faced by the parent or with the effort of the agency to change parental behavior, parental visiting had increased. Information in this domain would give indication as to where cases were heading and provide added clues as to what could be expected of parents.

Table 19 provides the aggregated information about changes in frequency of parental visiting for the mothers of the children. The data are shown separately for three categories of adoption planning objectives as well as for the total sample of children. For all the children, we observe there has been some decline in visiting by the mother in 27.5 percent of the cases; major decline was noted in 13.5 percent of the cases. There were also cases where social workers reported increases in visiting, 12.5 percent in all. Major increases were reported for 4.3 percent of the cases.

It is perhaps not surprising that cases classified as "action under way to free child" with reference to adoption

TABLE 15

CASEWORKER'S CHARACTERIZATION OF THE MOTHER'S CURRENT TENDENCY
TO VISIT CHILD ACCORDING TO YEARS IN CARE

Years in Care	Frequency of Visitation[a]					Total
	Never	Rarely	Infrequently or Occasionally	Fairly Regularly	Regularly or Often	
	(percentaged across)				
Under Two Years	25.9	13.4	10.0	30.8	19.9	16.4 (201)
Two to Five Years	41.1	17.3	13.6	16.0	12.0	30.7 (376)
Six Years or More	71.0	11.9	6.6	6.0	4.5	52.9 (648)
Percent Total	54.4 (667)	13.8 (169)	9.3 (114)	13.1 (161)	9.3 (114)	100.0 (1225)

[a] "Rarely" was defined as once a year or less, "infrequently" as once in 6 months or less, "occasionally" as once in 4 to 6 months, "fairly regularly" as once in 1 to 3 months, "regularly" as at least twice a month, and "often" as at least once a week.

TABLE 16

CASEWORKER'S CHARACTERIZATION OF THE FATHER'S CURRENT TENDENCY
TO VISIT THE CHILD ACCORDING TO YEARS IN CARE

Years in Care	Frequency of Visitation[a]					
	Never	Rarely	Infrequently or Occasionally	Fairly Regularly	Regularly or Often	Total
			(percentaged across)			
Under Two Years	69.7	7.0	8.0	8.5	7.0	16.4 (201)
Two to Five Years	73.9	8.8	5.1	7.2	5.1	30.7 (376)
Six Years or More	88.0	4.6	3.2	2.8	1.4	52.9 (648)
Percent Total	80.7 (988)	6.3 (77)	4.6 (56)	5.1 (62)	3.4 (42)	100.0 (1225)

[a] "Rarely" was defined as once a year or less, "infrequently" as once in 6 months or less, "occasionally" as once in 4 to 6 months, "fairly regularly" as once in 1 to 3 months, "regularly" as at least twice a month, and "often" as at least once a week.

TABLE 17

CASEWORKER'S CHARACTERIZATION OF MOTHER'S CURRENT TENDENCY TO VISIT
ACCORDING TO ADOPTION PLANNING OBJECTIVES FOR CHILD

Adoption Planning Status	Frequency of Visitation[a]					Total
	Never[b]	Rarely	Infrequently or Occasionally	Fairly Regularly	Regularly or Often	
	(percentaged across)					
Freed for Adoption	94.5	1.8	2.1	1.2	0.3	26.7 (331)
Action Under Way to Free Child	72.0	7.5	9.0	9.0	2.5	16.2 (200)
Not Freed for Adoption	41.6	10.3	12.9	19.8	15.4	57.1 (707)
Percent Total	60.6 (751)	7.6 (73)	9.4 (116)	13.1 (162)	9.3 (109)	100.0 (1238)

[a] "Rarely" was defined as once a year or less, "infrequently" as once in 6 months or less, "occasionally" as once in 4 to 6 months, "fairly regularly" as once in 1 to 3 months, "regularly" as at least twice a month, and "often" as at least once a week.

[b] Includes cases where mother was reported as deceased or not available because of confinement.

TABLE 18

CASEWORKER'S CHARACTERIZATION OF FATHER'S CURRENT TENDENCY TO VISIT ACCORDING TO ADOPTION PLANNING OBJECTIVES FOR CHILD

Adoption Planning Status	Frequency of Visitation[a]					Total
	Never	Rarely	Infrequently or Occasionally	Fairly Regularly	Regularly or Often	
			(percentaged across)			
Freed for for Adoption	97.2	0.9	0.9	--	0.9	26.7 (331)
Action Under Way to Free Child	91.5	2.0	3.0	2.5	1.0	16.2 (200)
Not Freed for Adoption	75.4	4.4	6.8	8.2	5.3	57.1 (707)
Percent Total	83.9 (1038)	3.0 (38)	4.6 (57)	5.1 (63)	3.4 (42)	100.0 (1238)

[a] "Rarely" was defined as once a year or less, "infrequently" as once in 6 months or less, "occasionally" as once in 4 to 6 months, "fairly regularly" as once in 1 to 3 months, "regularly" as at least twice a month, and "often" as at least once a week.

TABLE 19

CHANGES IN FREQUENCY OF CONTACT BETWEEN MOTHER AND CHILD
ACCORDING TO ADOPTION PLANNING OBJECTIVES FOR CHILDREN

Adoption Planning Status	Major Decline	Moderate Decline	Slight Decline	No Change	Slight In- crease	Moderate In- crease	Major In- crease	Not Relevant (No visiting, deceased, etc.)	Total
				(percentaged across)					
Freed for Adoption	10.3	1.2	3.6	5.4	1.2	--	0.3	78.0	26.7 (331)
Action Under Way to Free Child	21.5	3.5	9.0	13.5	2.5	1.5	2.5	46.0	16.2 (200)
Not Freed for Adoption	12.7	8.5	10.3	34.9	6.6	6.1	6.6	14.3	57.1 (707)
Percent Total	13.5 (167)	5.7 (71)	8.3 (103)	23.5 (291)	4.5 (56)	3.7 (46)	4.3 (53)	36.5 (451)	100.0 (1238)

planning show the highest proportion where a major decline is reported to have taken place in the parental visiting; this was the social worker's report in 21.5 percent of the cases. It would seem likely that the decision to undertake steps to free the children was strongly influenced by the increasing failure of the mothers to visit.

Concern would be appropriately expressed for the situation facing children not freed for adoption. One hopes such children would eventually be restored to their families. Yet, decline in visiting by the mothers is reported in 31.5 percent of the cases as contrasted with 19.3 percent where visiting has increased. The question might well be asked: If there is a decline in visiting, do we have any basis for anticipating that children can be restored to their families? Optimism about the return of the children would not seem indicated.

In Table 20, the same data about changes in frequency of parental visitation is shown for the fathers of the children in the study. In previous tabular presentations in this chapter, it has been shown quite clearly that many of the fathers can be seen as being totally out of the picture. In the table presented here, this impression of "being out of it" is reinforced by the fact that for almost half of the cases (49.0 percent) the issue of "change" in visiting frequency is considered not relevant because of such factors as the fathers not acknowledging paternity, never visiting since the birth of the child, or since the child's placement in the foster home.

For an additional 18.8 percent of the cases, the reports of the social workers indicated a decline in frequency of visiting by the fathers while in only 5.1 percent of the cases, an increase was reported. For children not slated for adoption, the decline in frequency of visitation covered 23.2 percent of the children while increases in visiting was reported in only 7.8 percent of the cases. The picture that thus emerges about the father's role with respect to foster children is not reassuring.

Site of Visitation

Questions were directed to the social workers about the location of visits. This seemed to have some implication for the way the child could relate to his parents. Did the parents bring their children home for visits? Did they simply pick the children up for a day's outing, perhaps taking them to the movies, the circus, or to visit with a friend? Did they visit them at the site of placement, i.e., the foster home or institution? How often did the contact between parents and children take place in the agency office?

Table 21 shows the frequency of visitation of the mothers according to the various sites where such contacts might take place. It is of interest that visiting in the mother's home turns out to be the most frequent site of contact with 28.1 percent of the children seeing the parent in the home at least sometimes. Visiting in the agency office is the next most frequent way mother and child are able to get together (at least sometimes), accounting for 20.9 percent of the children.

It is of interest that visiting in the foster home is a relatively rare occurrence, accounting for only 9.4 percent of the children. Visiting in institutions is reported for 11.2 percent of the cases.

In Table 22 information is again provided about site of visitation by the mothers, this time set forth by adoption planning objectives. The data are presented in hierarchical fashion so as to maximize the order shown, i.e., visiting in parental home first, day's outing second. Visiting at a site was coded positively if the social worker indicated that such visitation took place "sometimes," "often," or "always."

Of most significance is the information about sites of contact with the child by mothers in the instances where the children were not freed for adoption, and where they were designated as not likely to be freed. Somewhat less than half the children (44.6 percent) saw their mothers in their homes. This reflects a fairly substantial group who are able to remain connected with a community-based place of family residence. This is no guarantee, however, that the housing occupied by the mother offered accommodations that eventually could absorb the child as a resident. Indeed some of the mothers were living in furnished rooms that could not serve as future homes for the children.

The site next most often used for the mother-child contact was the agency office. For the children not freed for adoption, this appeared to be the only place for meetings with the mother for 5.1 percent of the children. Not much has been written about the nature of parent-child visitation in offices of agencies. For the writer, such a site seems quite limited because it is not a place where natural interaction can take place between mother and child. If the aim of visiting is to reinforce the parent-child tie, this hardly seems the most likely way to do this.

Given the overall apparent abandonment of the children by their fathers, previously described, no effort will be made here to provide a description of the site of visitation for the small group who were reported to maintain contact with their children. When data are broken down by site of visitation, the information becomes relatively trivial.

Letters, Telephone Calls and Gifts

In reporting the frequency of contact between parents and children living under foster care arrangements, we have until this point stayed exclusively within the domain of in-person contacts. We now focus our attention upon other forms of contact: telephone calls, letters, postal cards and gifts. The social workers were asked to indicate for each child covered in the survey whether there were "occasional" or "quite a few" contacts between parents and children through such communication opportunities. The aggregated information in this regard is shown in Table 23.

Table 23 shows the information relative to the mothers according to the years the children have been in care. In every category, whether it be telephone calls, letters, cards or gifts, the longer a child has been in care, the more attenuated is his communication with his parents.

With respect to telephone calls, we observe that one child in four (25.9 percent) is reported to be the recipient of telephone calls. For children in care under two years, the number in telephone communication with their mothers is fairly large, 43.8 percent, while this is true for only 15.6 percent of those in care six years or more.

Letters and cards are apparently resorted to infre-

TABLE 20

CHANGES IN FREQUENCY OF CONTACT BETWEEN FATHER AND CHILD
ACCORDING TO ADOPTION PLANNING OBJECTIVES FOR CHILDREN

Adoption Planning Status	Major Decline	Moderate Decline	Slight Decline	No Change	Slight In-crease	Moderate In-crease	Major In-crease	Not Relevant (No visiting, deceased, etc.)	Total
				(percentaged across)					
Freed for Adoption	6.6	0.3	2.1	9.7	0.6	--	0.3	80.4	26.7 (331)
Action Under Way to Free Child	10.5	1.5	7.5	26.0	1.0	--	1.5	52.0	16.2 (200)
Not Freed for Adoption	11.6	3.3	8.3	35.5	3.0	2.5	2.3	33.5	57.1 (707)
Percent Total	10.1 (125)	2.2 (27)	6.5 (81)	27.1 (335)	2.0 (25)	1.5 (18)	1.6 (20)	49.0 (607)	100.0 (1238)

TABLE 21

SITE OF VISITATION BETWEEN MOTHERS AND CHILD
ACCORDING TO ADOPTION PLANNING OBJECTIVES FOR CHILDREN[a]

Adoption Planning Objective	Location						Total
	Parental Home	Day's Outing	Foster Home	Institution	Agency Office	Other	No Visiting	
	(percentaged across)							
Freed for Adoption	2.7	--	2.4	--	2.1	0.6	92.2	26.7 (331)
Action Under Way to Free Child	12.0	0.5	4.5	2.0	15.5	--	65.5	16.2 (200)
Not Freed for Adoption	44.6	1.4	5.1	2.5	15.1	1.8	29.5	57.1 (707)
Percent Total	28.1 (348)	0.9 (11)	4.3 (53)	1.8 (22)	11.7 (145)	1.2 (15)	52.0 (644)	100.0 (1238)

[a] Data shown to indicate one category of visiting per child maximized in the order shown, e.g., parental home visiting first, day's outing, second, etc. Visiting at a site encompasses categories of "sometimes," "often," or "always."

38

TABLE 22

FREQUENCY OF VISITATION AT DIFFERENT SITES BETWEEN MOTHER AND CHILD

Site	Sometimes	Often	Always	Never/ Not Applicable	Total
	(percentaged across)				
Visiting in Parental Home	12.8	9.6	5.7	71.9	100.0 (1238)
Day's Outing (Mother picks up child and goes elsewhere)	5.7	1.1	0.2	92.8	100.0 (1238)
Visiting in Foster Home	5.8	1.9	1.7	90.6	100.0 (1238)
Visiting in Institution	7.8	2.7	0.7	88.8	100.0 (1238)
Visiting in Agency Office	11.2	1.9	7.8	79.1	100.0 (1238)
Other Site for Parent-Child Contact	1.1	0.4	0.3	98.2	100.0 (1238)

TABLE 23

LETTERS, TELEPHONE CALLS AND OTHER TYPES OF CONTACT BETWEEN MOTHER AND CHILD
OVER PAST SIX MONTHS ACCORDING TO YEARS IN CARE

Years in Care	Telephone Calls None	Telephone Calls Occa-sional	Telephone Calls Quite a Few	Letters None	Letters Occa-sional	Letters Quite a Few	Cards None	Cards Occa-sional	Cards Quite a Few	Gifts None	Gifts Occa-sional	Gifts Quite a Few
						(percentaged across)						
Under Two Years	56.2	23.9	19.9	84.6	10.9	4.5	77.1	15.4	7.5	67.1	26.9	6.0
Two to Five Years	66.0	23.4	10.6	85.9	11.7	2.4	81.9	14.6	3.5	77.9	17.6	4.5
Six Years or More	84.4	12.7	2.9	94.3	4.5	1.2	92.0	6.0	2.0	92.4	6.2	1.4
Percent Total	74.1 (908)	17.8 (218)	8.1 (99)	90.1 (1104)	7.8 (95)	2.1 (26)	86.5 (1059)	10.2 (125)	3.3 (41)	83.8 (1027)	13.1 (160)	3.1 (38)
	(N = 1225)			(N = 1225)			(N = 1225)			(N = 1225)		

quently, with 9.9 percent of the children reported to receive letters, mostly on an occasional basis, and 13.5 percent reported to receive cards. We again observe that time in care is an important correlate of the number of children reported as recipients of such mail.

While 16.2 percent of the children were identified as receiving gifts from their mothers, mostly on an occasional basis, this form of contact was particularly strong for children in care under two years. Almost a third of the youngsters (32.9 percent) were identified as receiving gifts, minimally on an occasional basis.

In Table 24, the same type of information about contacts, other than those of an in-person nature, is provided with reference to the fathers of the children.

The number of cases where such contact has taken place is less than was true of the mothers. This is not a surprise given what has already been learned about the total unavailability of most of the fathers. However, it is noteworthy that 10.0 percent of the children did receive telephone calls from their fathers and this was true of 15.0 percent of the children in care under two years and 13.9 percent of those in care two to five years. We also observe that 15.4 percent of the children in care under two years were recipients of gifts from their fathers.

A rather crucial question relative to forms of child-parent contact other than through in-person visits, is whether children we have heretofore identified as abandoned, totally without visitation of any kind, do in fact have communication with family members in the form of telephone calls, letters, cards or gifts. In order to ascertain this information, we divided the subjects into two groups: children who had contact with at least one family-connected member (e.g., parent, grandparent, uncle, sibling or family friend) and those who had no in-person contact of any kind. There were 698 children in the first group (56.4 percent) and 540 children in the second group (43.6 percent).

For the mothers of the children already experiencing some form of visitation, the aggregated information shows the following:

Telephone calls: 14.3 percent received quite a few calls
                  28.9 percent received occasional calls
                  56.8 percent received no calls

Letters: 3.6 percent received quite a few letters
                  12.4 percent received occasional letters
                  84.0 percent received no letters

Cards: 5.6 percent received quite a few cards
                  17.0 percent received occasional cards
                  77.4 percent received no cards

Gifts: 5.4 percent received quite a few gifts
                  22.1 percent received occasional gifts
                  72.5 percent received no gifts

When we examined the aggregated data for the mothers of children who had absolutely no in-person contacts with their families, we found the following information:

Telephone calls: 0.2 percent received quite a few calls
                  3.3 percent received occasional calls
                  96.5 percent received no calls

Letters: 0.2 percent received quite a few letters
                  1.7 percent received occasional letters
                  98.1 percent received no letters

Cards: 0.4 percent received quite a few cards
                  1.3 percent received occasional cards
                  98.3 percent received no cards

Gifts: 0.0 percent received quite a few gifts
                  1.3 percent received occasional gifts
                  98.7 percent received no gifts

For the visited children, the cases where children often had contact with their mothers through telephone calls, letters and gifts, were the ones where the children were not destined to be adopted. For the unvisited children, one has to be struck by the very low frequency of contact between mothers and children through mail or telephone.

The data gathered about mail and telephone contacts with the fathers is similar to that reported for the mothers but is not presented here because of space limitation. Instead, we provide an overall summary in Table 25 which aggregates the information about "parents" and their use of mail and telephone. The data reflect either the mother's activity alone or, if she is out of the picture, the father's, if he is available. If both parents are available, the information reflects the sum of both parents' activities. The cross-tabulation deals with three variables: visited vs. non-visited children, by adoption planning status, with the dependent variable being the sum of the "other" (non-visiting) forms of contact.

The data in Table 25 make it clear that much of the indirect, i.e., not in-person, contact between parents and children is taking place in those cases where they are already seeing each other in person. Thus, 61.6 percent of the children who have the label "visited" had had at least one form of mail or telephone contact and this is true of 67.9 percent of those not slated to be adopted. This was true of 6.0 percent of the "non-visited" children although the group not freed for adoption contained 15.9 percent of cases where there was at least one contact by mail or telephone. We thus see some reduction, modest in nature, in the percentages of children who appear to have lost total contact with their parents. This additional information has some value in planning for children in foster care and ought to be monitored.

Summary

This chapter has constituted a multidimensional examination of the visiting phenomenon. We have probed such issues as how often a foster child sees his parents, how often he sees other relatives as well as non-related persons connected with his family, when he last had contact with his parents, and how often contact took place through other than in-person visits. This information was examined from the perspective of the length of time children had spent in care as well as from the point of view of adoption planning. We regard the information as critical for any agency or public social service district that wishes to seriously address the issue of permanency planning.

TABLE 24

LETTERS, TELEPHONE CALLS AND OTHER TYPES OF CONTACT BETWEEN FATHER AND CHILD OVER PAST SIX MONTHS ACCORDING TO YEARS IN CARE

Years in Care	Telephone Calls			Letters			Cards			Gifts		
	None	Occa-sional	Quite a Few	None	Occa-sional	Quite a Few	None	Occa-sional	Quite a Few	None	Occa-sional	Quite a Few
	(percentaged across)
Under Two Years	85.0	8.5	6.5	95.5	2.5	2.0	94.0	3.5	2.5	84.6	11.4	4.0
Two to Five Years	86.1	10.4	3.5	95.2	2.7	2.1	93.3	4.3	2.4	89.9	7.4	2.7
Six Years or More	93.8	4.8	1.4	98.3	1.4	0.3	97.6	1.9	0.5	97.5	1.9	0.6
Percent Total	90.0 (1103)	7.1 (87)	2.9 (35)	96.9 (1187)	2.0 (24)	1.1 (14)	95.7 (1173)	2.9 (35)	1.4 (17)	93.1 (1140)	5.1 (63)	1.8 (22)
	(N = 1225)			(N = 1225)			(N = 1225)			(N = 1225)		

TABLE 25

SUM OF OTHER PARENTAL CONTACTS (TELEPHONE CALLS, LETTERS, CARDS AND GIFTS)[a]
FOR VISITED AND NON-VISITED CHILDREN ACCORDING TO ADOPTION PLANNING STATUS
(N = 1238)

Adoption Planning Status	Frequency of Other Parental Contacts						Total
	None	One	Two or Three	Four or Five	Six or More		

(percentaged across)

Visited Children

Adoption Planning Status	None	One	Two or Three	Four or Five	Six or More	Total
Freed for Adoption	73.4	13.3	10.0	3.3	--	8.6 (60)
Action Under Way to Free Child	56.1	19.5	22.0	--	2.4	11.7 (82)
Not Freed for Adoption	32.1	22.8	26.4	13.1	5.6	79.7 (556)
Percent Total	38.4 (268)	21.6 (151)	24.5 (171)	10.7 (75)	4.7 (33)	100.0 (698)

Non-Visited Children

Adoption Planning Status	None	One	Two or Three	Four or Five	Six or More	Total
Freed for Adoption	99.2	0.4	0.4	--	--	50.1 (271)
Action Under Way to Free Child	94.1	2.5	1.7	1.7	--	21.9 (118)
Not Freed for Adoption	84.1	8.6	6.0	1.3	--	28.0 (151)
Percent Total	94.0 (507)	3.1 (17)	2.2 (12)	0.7 (4)	--	100.0 (540)

[a] The Visited Children category reflects cases where the child had at least one in-person contact in the past six months with a family-connected person (parent, grandparent, step-parent, aunt or uncle, sibling, cousin or friend of the family). The Non-Visited Children did not have even one such contact. "Parental Contact" in the title of the table reflects the sum of contacts of the mothers and fathers, if both visit, or the sum of contacts of either parent.

4 Qualitative Aspects of the Visiting Phenomenon

Introduction

Until this point, we have been primarily concerned with the issues of frequency and recency of contact between the child and his family. We now address the more qualitative aspects of the visiting phenomenon. We inquire into such matters as the degree of responsibility shown by the parents for their children in care as reflected by their visiting behavior. We probe for any problematic behavior the parents display while in contact with their children. Beyond this, we seek to determine the quality of relatedness the parents extend to their offspring while visiting and the degree to which they seek to make the occasions enjoyable. To round out the picture, we seek information about the reactions of the children to encounters with their parents. We have interest in determining whether parental visits appear to engender enjoyment in their youngsters or whether the latter manifest anxiety or otherwise show that they are upset about the contact.

Has the Parent Been Responsible in Visiting?

The social workers were asked to characterize the parents' current visiting behavior with respect to the degree of responsibility shown. When the assessment was applied to the mothers, it turned out that 17.0 percent of the entire sample of cases were characterized as "parent responsible." The percentage was somewhat higher for the category of cases where the issue was most important, i.e., the cases where the children were obviously not going to be considered for adoption. For these children, 27.2 percent were receiving visiting from the mothers with a level of frequency and in a manner that was regarded as reflecting responsible parent behavior (Table 26).

What occasions concern is the fairly large proportion of cases in which the mother's approach to visiting was characterized as irresponsible. For the sample as a whole, 10.8 percent were rated as being "somewhat irresponsible" while 16.3 percent were characterized as being completely "irresponsible." For the group not freed for adoption, the proportions were even higher; 16.3 percent were rated as "somewhat irresponsible" and 20.2 percent as "irresponsible." Thus, more than a third of the mothers were not living up to agency expectations with regard to visiting.

For 12.8 percent of the cases, the social workers indicated that they could not make a judgment about the responsibility shown by the mothers because of circumstantial factors that did not permit them to visit, e.g., hospitalization. This was true in 14.1 percent of the cases where the children were not freed for adoption.

In a major proportion of the cases, the question was rated as "not applicable," presumably because the child had already been surrendered, plans were under way to initiate such surrender, or because the mother was otherwise out of the picture. More than a third of the cases (37.5 percent) were characterized in this manner and this was true of 15.1 percent of the cases where the child had not been freed for adoption.

With respect to the responsibility shown by the fathers, one is struck by the fact that so many of the cases could not be meaningfully rated because the father was totally out of the picture. This was true of more than half of the sample (52.2 percent) and applied to 37.6 percent of the cases where the children had not been freed for adoption. An affirmative indication of responsible visiting behavior was possible in only 6.2 percent of the cases and irresponsible behavior in another 19.7 percent. Fathers of children not freed for adoption were characterized as responsible in 9.3 percent of the cases in contrast with a rating of irresponsibility in 26.6 percent of the cases (Table 27).

Termination of Rights

The social workers were asked to consider whether the quality of the parent's visiting behavior, or the failure to visit, raised the issue of whether parental rights should be terminated. If a parent failed to visit his or her child in care, what was left of any notion of a relationship with the child? Of any sense of a future between them?

Less than one case in ten (8.8 percent) was characterized as clearly reflecting such dereliction of parental responsibility in the area of visiting as to lead the social worker to assert that parental rights should be terminated. For the most significant group of children, i.e., those not destined to be adopted, only 5.8 percent were rated as justifying such action against the parents. This contrasts with 27.5 percent of the cases where action was under way to free the child.

A small group of cases, 4.4 percent, were rated as

TABLE 26

SOCIAL WORKER'S CHARACTERIZATION OF WHETHER MOTHER HAS BEEN RESPONSIBLE IN VISITING CHILD ACCORDING TO ADOPTION PLANNING OBJECTIVES FOR CHILD[a]

Adoption Planning Status	Parent Responsible	Parent Somewhat Irresponsible	Parent Irresponsible	Not Applicable (Circumstances Do Not Permit Visiting)	Other Characterization	Not Applicable	Total
			(percentaged across)				
Freed for Adoption	0.3	1.2	5.7	10.9	3.3	78.6	26.7 (331)
Action Under Way to Free Child	8.5	7.5	20.0	11.5	4.0	48.5	16.2 (200)
Not Freed for Adoption	27.2	16.3	20.2	14.1	7.1	15.1	47.1 (707)
Percent Total	17.0 (210)	10.8 (115)	16.3 (202)	12.8 (159)	5.6 (69)	37.5 (464)	100.0 (1238)

[a] Question posed to the social worker: "How would you characterize the parent's current visiting behavior in meeting the needs of the child?"

TABLE 27

SOCIAL WORKER'S CHARACTERIZATION OF WHETHER FATHER HAS BEEN RESPONSIBLE IN VISITING CHILD ACCORDING TO ADOPTION PLANNING OBJECTIVES FOR CHILD[a]

Adoption Planning Status	Parent Responsible	Parent Somewhat Irresponsible	Parent Irresponsible	Not Applicable (Circumstances Do Not Permit Visiting)	Other Characterization	Not Applicable	Total
	(percentaged across)						
Freed for Adoption	0.9	0.6	5.7	8.5	3.3	81.0	26.7 (331)
Action Under Way to Free Child	4.0	2.5	15.0	14.5	7.0	57.0	16.2 (200)
Not Freed for Adoption	9.3	7.5	19.1	14.1	12.4	37.6	57.1 (707)
Percent Total	6.2 (77)	4.8 (60)	14.9 (184)	12.7 (157)	9.1 (113)	52.2 (647)	100.0 (1238)

[a]Question posed to the social worker: "How would you characterize the parent's current visiting behavior in meeting the needs of the child?"

possibly being suitable for action to be taken against the parents, providing the parent's poor visiting performance remained unchanged.

A rating indicating that parental visiting behavior was satisfactory was made in only 18.3 percent of the cases. Showing the largest proportion of such cases were the youngsters not slated to be considered for adoption; 29.8 percent were characterized in this positive fashion. This contrasted with less than one percent of those freed for adoption and 6.0 percent of those where action was under way to free the child (Table 28).

It is significant that about a third of the cases involving children not freed for adoption (33.7 percent) were characterized as involving circumstances affecting the parent's ability to visit and therefore did not justify termination of parental rights. This is a sizable proportion of the cases and the phenomenon is associated with philosophical dispute.[19] For example: Do we seek to terminate the rights of parents who are patients residing in mental hospitals? Advocates on behalf of the rights of mental patients would strongly resist a policy designed to terminate the parental rights of mentally ill persons on grounds that this was in the best interests of the children. Yet there are those whose concern for the rights of children would lead them to urge creating a condition of permanency for the children if they have lived, for example, in the same foster homes for several years.

In Table 29, we present the same data regarding the visiting behavior, or failure to visit, of the fathers. In 8.4 percent of the cases, the concern of the social workers is sufficient to cause them to advocate termination of the rights of such parents. In 7.2 percent of the cases, the father's visiting was described as satisfactory.

Among the 707 children for whom adoption was not planned, there were 556 children who received visiting from at least one family-connected person. Within this latter group, there were 454 mothers who could be rated on the issue of termination of parental rights. There were 249 fathers who also could be rated on the same issue.

For the mothers, the distribution of ratings with respect to the question, "Should termination of rights be considered?" was as follows:

No, visiting is satisfactory.........	45.6%
No, circumstances affect ability to visit............................	41.0%
Somewhat, if visiting behavior is not changed......................	7.9%
Yes, termination of rights should be considered...................	5.5%

We thus can see that a sizable proportion of this most relevant group of mothers is defined as satisfactory in their visiting behavior. Over two out of five cases, however, are seen as involving low maternal visiting because of circumstantial factors. These cases pose the dilemma of whether action can be taken against the rights of the parents when their inability to have normal contact with their children stems from circumstances outside of their control.

There is a fair-sized group of mothers (13.4 percent) who are rated quite negatively; either their behavior has to change or termination of parental rights will be required,

or the behavior is beyond change. Termination of rights in these cases seems a likely prospect.

For the cases where children were not visited by anyone, there were ratings for 81 mothers of children not freed for adoption. The distribution is as follows:

No, visiting is satisfactory.........	4.9%[20]
No, circumstances affect ability to visit............................	64.2%
Somewhat, if visiting behavior is not changed......................	11.1%
Yes, termination of rights should be considered...................	19.8%

It is of interest that the overwhelming proportion of cases involve what social workers considered to be circumstantial factors preventing the parents from visiting.

The ratings for the 249 fathers who visited was as follows:

No, visiting is satisfactory.........	30.9%
No, circumstances affect ability to visit............................	49.4%
Somewhat, if visiting behavior is not changed......................	6.4%
Yes, termination of rights should be considered...................	13.3%

The distribution shows that half the fathers are seen as being unable to visit because of circumstances and almost a third are rated as satisfactory in their visiting. Almost one case in five (19.7 percent) is rated as having implications for termination of parental rights.

Parental Behavior During Visits

The matter of how the parent conducts himself or herself when contact takes place with the child is a matter of some importance. Indeed, the writer has often heard foster parents and staff workers of child welfare agencies assert that some parents create more havoc in the lives of their children when they visit than when they simply absent themselves. While the writer has helped produce evidence to support the opposite point of view, there is no question that parents' behavior while visiting their children ought to be monitored.[21]

To secure information germane to this issue, the questionnaire provided a list of potential problem behaviors that parents might show in connection with their visiting. The social workers were asked to indicate whether any of the behaviors had been manifested during the past six months. Table 30 displays the aggregated information in this area of inquiry, again displayed according to the familiar three categories of adoption planning objectives.

There is no problem which stands out in the reports of the informants. One needs to keep in mind, however, that since many of the parents did not visit at all, the behavior could not be reported for many of them.

The most frequently reported dysfunctional parental behavior associated with visiting is the report that the parent relates to the child in a superficial manner. This was indicated in 11.6 percent of all cases and was as high

TABLE 28

SOCIAL WORKER'S CHARACTERIZATION OF MOTHER'S VISITING BEHAVIOR AND WHETHER IT HAS IMPLICATIONS
FOR TERMINATION OF PARENTAL RIGHTS
ACCORDING TO ADOPTION PLANNING OBJECTIVES FOR CHILD[a]

Adoption Planning Status	Should Termination of Rights Be Considered?					Total
	No, Visiting is Satisfactory	Yes, Termination of Rights Should be Considered	Somewhat, If Visiting Behavior Unchanged	No, Circumstances Affect Ability to Visit	Other	Not Applicable (or Unknown)	
	(percentaged across)						
Freed for Adoption	0.9	3.9	--	6.6	9.4	79.2	26.7 (331)
Action Under Way to Free Child	6.0	27.5	4.5	8.5	6.5	47.0	16.2 (200)
Not Freed for Adoption	29.8	5.8	6.4	33.7	6.9	17.4	57.1 (707)
Percent Total	18.3 (226)	8.8 (109)	4.4 (54)	22.4 (277)	7.5 (93)	38.7 (479)	100.0 (1238)

[a] Question posed to the caseworker: "Does parent's quality of visiting behavior or failure to visit have implications for termination of parent's rights?"

TABLE 29

SOCIAL WORKER'S CHARACTERIZATION OF FATHER'S VISITING BEHAVIOR AND WHETHER IT HAS IMPLICATIONS
FOR TERMINATION OF PARENTAL RIGHTS
ACCORDING TO ADOPTION PLANNING OBJECTIVES FOR CHILD[a]

Adoption Planning Status	Should Termination of Rights Be Considered?					
	No, Visiting is Satisfactory	Yes, Termination of Rights Should be Considered	Somewhat, If Visiting Behavior Unchanged	No, Circumstances Affect Ability to Visit	Other	Not Applicable (or Unknown)	Total
	(percentaged across)						
Freed for Adoption	0.9	4.2	0.3	4.5	6.6	83.4	26.7 (331)
Action Under Way to Free Child	3.5	23.0	1.0	2.5	9.5	60.5	16.2 (200)
Not Freed for Adoption	11.2	6.2	2.7	20.2	11.3	48.4	57.1 (707)
Percent Total	7.2 (89)	8.4 (104)	1.8 (22)	13.2 (163)	9.8 (121)	59.6 (739)	100.0 (1238)

[a] Question posed to the caseworker: "Does parent's quality of visiting behavior or failure to visit have implications for termination of parent's rights?"

TABLE 30

PROBLEMS SHOWN BY MOTHERS WHEN VISITING CHILDREN
ACCORDING TO ADOPTION PLANNING OBJECTIVES FOR CHILDREN[a]

Problems Associated With Visiting	Adoption Planning Status			Total (1238)
	Freed for Adoption (N=331)	Action Under Way to Free Child (N=200)	Not Freed for Adoption (N=707)	
	(Percent Showing Problems)			
Relates to Child in a Superficial Manner	2.4	11.5	15.8	11.6
Visits Are Too Brief	0.3	4.0	3.4	2.7
Creates Disturbance	0.9	4.5	6.9	4.9
Appears Intoxicated or Under Influence of Drugs	1.2	3.5	6.2	4.4
Brings Inappropriate Strangers	0.6	2.0	3.5	2.5
Behavior Appears Bizarre or Seriously Divergent from Normal	0.3	6.5	5.4	4.2
Visits at Inappropriate Times	--	0.5	2.1	1.3
Other Problems	--	2.0	3.7	2.4

[a] Instructions to the social worker: "Please indicate if any of the following problems have been manifested in the past six months in connection with the visiting of parents."

as 15.8 percent for the group of children who were not destined to be adopted. It would appear that such parents related to the child in a perfunctory manner devoid of warmth and genuine concern.

The remaining categories of behavior affected less than one in twenty children, with slightly higher percentages applying to the children not freed for adoption. For this group, 6.9 percent of the mothers were said to create disturbances while visiting, 6.2 percent were intoxicated or under the influence of drugs, and 5.4 percent behaved in a bizarre manner.

The data about the fathers also showed small percentages where problematic behavior was evidenced. It was even more true of the fathers, however, that the large number of non-visitors among them served as a ceiling on the number of behavior problems that could be reported (see Table 31).

In Table 32, we provide a count of the number of problems reported for the mothers. For the total sample, 21.8 percent were reported to manifest at least one problem. Nine percent showed two or more problems.

Mothers of children not freed for adoption showed higher percentages of problematic behavior associated with their visiting. Almost a third (31.1 percent) showed at least one problem while 12.1 percent manifested two or more problems.

The number of problems manifested by the fathers was quite small for the whole sample. The ratings of the social workers indicated that 8.9 percent showed at least one type of problem in visiting while this was true of 13.0 percent of the fathers of children not freed for adoption.

When we isolated the 707 cases where there was indication that there was no plan under way to free the child for adoption and further narrowed our purview to the children who had experienced visiting from some source for the past six months, we had a group of 556 children. Of these, 415 (74.6 percent) received visiting from their mothers and these children became the focus of our attention. We asked ourselves: How many of these mothers displayed problems when visiting their children? Our findings for this most relevant group are as follows:

Relates to child in a superficial manner	26.0%
Visits are too brief	5.8%
Creates disturbance	11.1%
Appears intoxicated or under the influence of drugs	10.4%
Brings inappropriate strangers	6.0%
Behavior appears bizarre or seriously divergent from normal	8.7%
Visits at inappropriate times	3.6%
Comes late or misses appointments	2.4%
Other problems	5.8%

A sense of the prevalence of problems among these visiting mothers can be derived from a simple tabulation of the sum of problems:

No problem	50.1%
One problem	29.6%
Two problems	13.3%
Three problems	4.8%
Four problems	1.2%
Five problems	1.0%

We thus see that half of the visiting mothers of children not freed for adoption exhibited at least one problem. About a fifth of them (20.3 percent) were rated as showing two or more problems. This appears to reflect a quite sizable group and is an indication of the need for professional monitoring and the potential service investment associated with the visiting of the parents.

Out of the 556 children not freed for adoption and visited by someone connected with their families, 165, or 29.7 percent, received visitation from their fathers in the six-month period prior to the filling out of the research forms. The distribution of problems reported for these visiting fathers is as follows:

Relates to child in a superficial manner	26.1%
Visits are too brief	9.7%
Creates disturbance	10.9%
Appears intoxicated or under the influence of drugs	9.1%
Brings inappropriate strangers	2.4%
Behavior appears bizarre or seriously divergent from normal	6.1%
Visits at inappropriate times	5.5%
Comes late or misses appointments	2.4%
Other problems	7.3%

When the problems were summed for each father, we had the following distribution:

No problem	50.9%
One problem	32.2%
Two problems	9.1%
Three problems	4.2%
Four problems	1.8%
Five problems	1.8%

We are struck by the fact that the proportion of visiting fathers who show problems fairly closely approximates that shown for the visiting mothers. Thus 49.1 percent show at least one of the mentioned problems compared to 49.9 percent of the mothers (Table 33).

Quality of Parental Contact

Aside from the matter of disturbed or disruptive behavior that might be shown by the parent, there was also interest in obtaining a picture of the overall quality of his or her relationship to the child. The questionnaire posed the following request: "We are interested in your impression of the quality of the parent(s) contact during visiting oc-

TABLE 31

PROBLEMS SHOWN BY FATHERS WHEN VISITING CHILDREN
ACCORDING TO ADOPTION PLANNING OBJECTIVES FOR CHILDREN[a]

Problems Associated With Visiting	Freed for Adoption (N=331)	Action Under Way to Free Child (N=200)	Not Freed for Adoption (N=707)	Total (1238)
	Adoption Planning Status			
	(Percent Showing Problems)			
Relates to Child in a Superficial Manner	0.9	3.5	6.4	4.4
Visits Are Too Brief	--	1.0	2.4	1.5
Creates Disturbance	--	1.0	3.0	1.9
Appears Intoxicated or Under Influence of Drugs	0.3	0.5	2.3	1.5
Brings Inappropriate Strangers	--	--	0.6	0.3
Behavior Appears Bizarre or Seriously Divergent from Normal	--	0.5	1.6	1.0
Visits at Inappropriate Times	--	1.0	1.3	0.9
Other Problems	0.6	1.0	2.3	1.6

[a] Instructions to the social worker: "Please indicate if any of the following problems have been manifested in the past six months in connection with the visiting of parents."

TABLE 32

NUMBER OF PROBLEMS SHOWN BY MOTHERS WHEN VISITING CHILDREN
ACCORDING TO ADOPTION PLANNING OBJECTIVES
FOR CHILDREN

Adoption Planning Status	No Problems Reported (Including Non-visiting Parents)	One	Two	Three	Four	Five	Total
	(percentaged across)						
Freed for Adoption	96.4	1.2	2.1	0.3	--	--	26.7 (331)
Action Under Way to Free Child	81.0	10.5	4.0	2.5	1.0	1.0	16.2 (200)
Not Freed for Adoption	68.9	19.0	8.1	2.8	0.7	0.6	57.1 (707)
Percent Total	78.2 (968)	12.8 (159)	5.8 (72)	2.1 (26)	0.6 (7)	0.5 (6)	100.0 (1238)

TABLE 33

NUMBER OF PROBLEMS SHOWN BY FATHERS WHEN VISITING CHILDREN
ACCORDING TO ADOPTION PLANNING OBJECTIVES
FOR CHILDREN

Adoption Planning Status	No Problems Reported (Including Non-visiting Parents)	One	Two	Three	Four	Five	Total
	(percentaged across)						
Freed for Adoption	97.9	2.1	--	--	--	--	26.7 (331)
Action Under Way to Free Child	93.5	4.0	2.5	--	--	--	16.2 (200)
Not Freed for Adoption	87.0	8.8	2.3	1.1	0.4	0.4	57.1 (707)
Percent Total	91.1 (1126)	6.2 (77)	1.7 (21)	0.6 (8)	0.2 (3)	0.2 (3)	100.0 (1238)

casions. Would you say that the parent appears well-related to the child during visits?"

Table 34 provides the distribution of the responses of the social workers to this question as it applies to the mothers of the children. For less than one in ten cases (8.9 percent) the response was "very much," indicating a good quality of relatedness. For another 23.0 percent the rating was the more equivocal "somewhat." A flatly negative indication, "not at all" characterized 8.6 percent of the answers. For almost three-fifths of the cases (59.5 percent) the quality of the mother's relatedness during visiting was regarded as an estimate that could not be given by the respondent because the mother did not visit or because the quality of contact was unknown.

For the category of cases where parental visiting was most germane to the issue of permanency planning for foster children, i.e., those not destined to be adopted, the proportion of mothers characterized as well-related to their children during visits was somewhat higher. Almost fifteen percent (14.9 percent) were characterized as "very much" with respect to how well-related they were to their children. Another 33.8 percent were rated "somewhat" well-related to their children. For one case in ten (10.2 percent), the social worker chose the doleful "not at all" as the response to the question. For an additional 41.1 percent, the question of quality of visiting was considered not applicable as an issue or unknown.

Perhaps the most thought-provoking impression one can get from Table 34 is that only 15 percent of the mothers in the cases where adoption is not planned evoke unqualified positive responses in the workers. These cases would appear to have strength with respect to parent-child ties. The fact that a third of the cases reflect marginal behavior on the part of the mothers and another ten percent show an inability to relate to the child at all must cause concern. The challenge to an agency inherent in the situation is to undertake to modify the behavior of the parents, if indeed their inability to relate adequately to their children is changeable, or to move in the direction of terminating rights. Either direction obviously poses a demand for skilled work on the part of the social work practitioner.

Table 35 shows the aggregation of social worker ratings as applied to the visiting behavior of the fathers. Meaningful judgments could only be made in a small minority of cases because almost 85 percent of the cases involved situations where the father did not visit or his behavior was not known to the social worker. Thus only 4.2 percent of the cases received affirmative ratings ("very much") indicating the father was related to the child during visits and 8.3 percent were rated as "somewhat" related. The proportion of fathers who visited but who were not related at all during visits was 3.1 percent.

For cases of children not slated to be adopted, 23 percent were rated with respect to the visiting behavior of the fathers. Rated as "very much" related were 6.6 percent of the cases, compared to 12.2 percent marginal cases ("somewhat") and 4.2 percent rated negatively ("not at all").

An additional way of looking at the same phenomenon is to organize the information about parental relatedness to the child when visiting according to the years the latter has been in care. The matter might be put in the form of a question: Do the parents of children who have experienced long tenure in substitute living arrangements have more attenuated relationships with their offspring than those who are more recent arrivals to the foster care system? Are they less likely to keep in touch with their children?

In Table 36 we present in aggregated form the responses of the social workers to the question of how well-related to their children the mothers were when visiting according to the number of years the children have been in care. The analysis is restricted to 497 cases where the mother's visiting behavior could be rated and omits 47 children where the informants were unable to do so.

Table 36 shows that the quality of the mother's relatedness varies according to the years the children have been in care. The split appears to be at the five-year mark, with twice as many of the mothers of children in care five years or less rated as well-related to their children compared to mothers of children in care six years or more. Twenty-six percent of the mothers of children in care under two years and 25.9 percent for cases reflecting two to five years of care were rated "very much so" indicating a good quality of relatedness. This compared with 13.9 percent of the cases where the children had been in care six years or more. This category of cases also had twice the proportion rated "not at all," indicating the most attenuated relationships with the children.

Another approach to assessing the quality of parental visiting was to pose the following question to the social workers participating in the study: "Does the parent make an effort to make the contact an enjoyable occasion for the child?" Table 37 shows the distribution of responses with respect to the mothers according to adoption planning status.

Only 40 percent of the sample of cases permitted rating of the mothers on the dimension. This is understandable since in order to make such a rating there must be an available mother in the case who visits. Given this, there were some 86 cases (6.9 percent) where the social workers checked the response "not at all" indicating a very negative perception of the mother's visiting behavior. For 254 cases (20.5 percent), the response category checked was "somewhat," suggesting some modest effort to make the visit enjoyable. The most positive category, "very much," was checked for 162 cases (13.1 percent), indicating behavior in which the mother invested positively in the visit.

For children not freed for adoption, the ratings were more frequently positive. One in five cases (20.1 percent) were rated "very much" and 30.4 percent as "somewhat." Thus at least half the cases were rated as involving a mother who made some effort to make the visiting occasion an enjoyable occasion between herself and her child. Less than one case in ten (8.5 percent) was identified in the most negative terms.

There were 382 cases from among the 707 children not freed for adoption where the mother visited and the social worker was able to rate the degree to which the mother sought to make her visits enjoyable for the child. The distribution of ratings for these most relevant cases was as follows:

Very much	36.4%
Somewhat	50.2%
Other	2.9%
Not at all	10.5%

TABLE 34

SOCIAL WORKER'S PERCEPTION OF QUALITY OF MOTHER'S CONTACT WITH CHILD DURING VISITS ACCORDING TO ADOPTION PLANNING OBJECTIVES FOR CHILDREN[a]

Adoption Planning Status	Parent Well-Related to Child?				Total
	Very Much	Some-what	Not at All	Not Applicable/ Does Not Visit (or Unknown)	
	(percentaged across)				
Freed for Adoption	--	3.6	2.7	93.7	26.7 (331)
Action Under Way to Free Child	2.5	17.0	12.5	68.0	16.2 (200)
Not Freed for Adoption	14.9	33.8	10.2	41.1	57.1 (707)
Percent Total	8.9 (110)	23.0 (285)	8.6 (106)	59.5 (737)	100.0 (1238)

[a] Question posed to social worker: "We are interested in your impression of the quality of the parents' contact during visiting occasions. Would you say that the parent appears well-related to the child during visits?"

TABLE 35

SOCIAL WORKER'S PERCEPTION OF QUALITY OF FATHER'S CONTACT WITH CHILD DURING VISITS ACCORDING TO ADOPTION PLANNING OBJECTIVES FOR CHILDREN[a]

Adoption Planning Status	Parent Well-Related to Child?				Total
	Very Much	Some-what	Not at All	Not Applicable/ Does Not Visit (or Unknown)	
	(percentaged across)				
Freed for Adoption	--	1.8	0.6	97.6	26.7 (331)
Action Under Way to Free Child	2.5	5.5	3.0	89.0	16.2 (200)
Not Freed for Adoption	6.6	12.2	4.2	77.0	57.1 (707)
Percent Total	4.2 (52)	8.3 (103)	3.1 (38)	84.4 (1045)	100.0 (1238)

[a]Question posed to social worker: "We are interested in your impression of the quality of the parents' contact during visiting occasions. Would you say that the parent appears well-related to the child during visits?"

TABLE 36

QUALITY OF MOTHER'S RELATEDNESS TO CHILD DURING VISITS
ACCORDING TO YEARS IN CARE[a]
(N = 497)[b]

Years in Care	Parent Well-Related to Child?				Total
	Very Much So	Somewhat	Other	Not at All	
	(percentaged across)				
Under Two Years	26.0	60.3	1.5	12.2	26.4
Two to Five Years	25.9	57.5	3.6	13.0	38.8
Six Years or More	13.9	54.3	6.4	25.4	34.8
Percent Total	21.7 (108)	57.2 (284)	4.0 (20)	17.1 (85)	100.0 (497)

[a] Inquiry posed to respondents was: "We are interested in your impression of the quality of the parent(s)' contact during visiting occasions. Would you say that the parent appears well-related to the child during visits?"

[b] Does not include 681 children where mother was reported as not visiting and 47 children where rating on variable was not available.

TABLE 37

SOCIAL WORKER'S PERCEPTION OF THE DEGREE TO WHICH MOTHER TRIES
TO MAKE VISITS WITH CHILD ENJOYABLE
ACCORDING TO ADOPTION PLANNING OBJECTIVES FOR CHILDREN[a]

Adoption Planning Status	Tries to Make Visits Enjoyable?				Total
	Very Much	Some-what	Not at All	Not Applicable/ Does Not Visit (or Unknown)	
	(percentaged across)				
Freed for Adoption	0.9	3.3	2.1	93.7	26.7 (331)
Action Under Way to Free Child	8.5	14.0	9.5	68.0	16.2 (200)
Not Freed for Adoption	20.1	30.4	8.5	41.0	57.1 (707)
Percent Total	13.1 (162)	20.5 (254)	6.9 (86)	59.5 (736)	100.0 (1238)

[a] Question posed to the social worker: "Does the parent make an effort to make the contact an enjoyable occasion for the child?"

We thus see that when we zero in on that portion of the caseload for which parental visiting behavior is most significant—children not slated for adoption—and further restrict our focus to mothers who actually visited, only slightly more than a third of the cases (36.4 percent) evoke firm positive responses from the social workers. Perhaps some comfort can be derived from the fact that only about ten percent of the mothers' visits are characterized in the most negative terms.

The ratings of the father's visiting behavior was, of course, restricted to an even smaller group who actually visited their children. For 84.6 percent, the ratings were not applicable, mainly because the fathers did not visit. The data are shown in Table 38. For the children not freed for adoption, one child in five (19.5 percent) had a father who was rated as trying very much (7.5 percent) or somewhat (12.0 percent) to make the visits enjoyable. Only 3.3 percent were rated "not at all" in their efforts.

There were 149 fathers among the 707 children not freed for adoption who visited their children and whose behavior could be rated by the social workers. The distribution of ratings of their efforts to make their contacts wiht their children enjoyable is as follows:

Very much	33.6%
Somewhat	55.0%
Other	4.0%
Not at all	7.4%

This distribution of ratings is not markedly different from the one presented for the mothers.

Child's Reaction to Parental Visits

There has been recent interest in the child welfare literature about potential conflicts experienced by foster children who must relate to two sets of parental figures, their own parents and their foster parents.[22] In this sense, continued contact with his own parents might serve to arouse anxiety in the child. A question posed to the social workers sought to address this phenomenon. They were asked: "How has the child typically reacted to the contact with the parent(s)?"

Table 39 shows the distribution of the ratings applied to the visiting of the mothers. Ratings about the child's reactions could be ascertained for 45.9 percent of the total study population and 66.3 percent of the children not freed for adoption. The cases subsumed under the column heading "not applicable" are overwhelmingly those where the mother was out of the picture and thus had no contact with her children.

An examination of Table 39 shows an almost equal balance between the proportions of children showing positive reactions and those seen as guarded or anxious in their reactions to seeing their mothers. On the positive side, 18.3 percent appeared to the social workers to enjoy the visits of their mothers and another 4.1 percent were rated as being initially shy and then warming up.

About one child in five was said to show what might be considered a strained reaction to contact with his mother. Those appearing cautious, uncomfortable or embarrassed constituted 14.3 percent of the sample. Even more strain was apparently evidenced by 6.3 percent of the children who were rated as anxious or upset. A small group of youngsters, 3.8 percent of the sample, were rated as showing no overt reaction.

For children not freed for adoption, 29.0 percent were rated as appearing to enjoy the contact with their mothers while another 5.1 percent were seen as being initially shy and then warming up. On the more strained side of the ratings, 20.8 percent were rated as being cautious, uncomfortable or embarrassed in the presence of their mothers and another 8.1 percent were seen as overtly anxious or upset. A small group, 3.3 percent, were rated as showing no overt reaction.

Of the 707 children not freed for adoption, 556 received some form of visiting, parental or otherwise. Of this latter group, 141 were identified as receiving no visiting from their mothers, but visiting from other persons, leaving 415 children for whom the rating of the child's reaction to maternal visitation applied. For these children, the percentages in each category were as follows:

Appears to enjoy visits	47.8%
Initially shy and then warms up (or shows no reaction)	12.1%
Cautious, uncomfortable or embarrassed	32.1%
Anxious or upset	8.0%

Less than one child in five (18.6 percent) could be rated in reaction to the visits of their fathers. For this small group of children the spread of reactions was similar to that reported for the mothers. The same could be said for the children freed for adoption.

There were 169 children who were not freed for adoption and had contact with their fathers. The distribution of ratings concerning the child's reaction to such contact is as follows:

Appears to enjoy visits	48.0%
Initially shy and then warms up (or shows no reaction)	18.3%
Cautious, uncomfortable, or embarrassed	25.4%
Anxious or upset	8.3%

The distribution of ratings is similar to that found for the mothers (Table 40).

Child's Reaction to Parent's Failure to Visit

The failure of the parent to visit would appear to have serious emotional ramifications for a child treated in this fashion. Most mental health professionals recognize the profound rejection implicit in such behavior. Nevertheless, it does not make sense to assume that children react in uniform fashion to total parental absence from their lives, at least in their surface behavior. Informal reports to the writer from social workers who have witnessed this phenomenon indicate that some children openly show their agitation and feelings of upsetness while others show mild

TABLE 38

SOCIAL WORKER'S PERCEPTION OF THE DEGREE TO WHICH FATHER TRIES
TO MAKE VISITS WITH CHILD ENJOYABLE
ACCORDING TO ADOPTION PLANNING OBJECTIVES FOR CHILDREN[a]

Adoption Planning Status	Tries to Make Visits Enjoyable?				Total
	Very Much	Some-what	Not at All	Not Applicable/ Does Not Visit (or Unknown)	
	(percentaged across)				
Freed for Adoption	0.6	1.2	0.3	97.9	26.7 (331)
Action Under Way to Free Child	2.5	6.0	3.0	88.5	16.2 (200)
Not Freed for Adoption	7.5	12.0	3.3	77.2	57.1 (707)
Percent Total	4.8 (60)	8.2 (101)	2.4 (30)	84.6 (1047)	100.0 (1238)

[a] Question posed to the social worker: "Does the parent make an effort to make the contact an enjoyable occasion for the child?"

TABLE 39

CHILD'S TYPICAL REACTION TO CONTACT WITH MOTHER
ACCORDING TO ADOPTION PLANNING OBJECTIVES FOR CHILDREN[a]

Adoption Planning Status	Appears to Enjoy Visits	Initially Shy, Then Warms Up	No Overt Reaction	Cautious, Uncomfortable or Embarrassed	Anxious or Upset	Not Applicable (No Visits, Deceased, Other)	Total
	(percentaged across)						
Freed for Adoption	1.8	0.6	1.2	2.1	2.4	91.9	26.7 (331)
Action Under Way to Free Child	8.0	6.5	4.0	11.5	6.5	63.5	16.2 (200)
Not Freed for Adoption	29.0	5.1	3.3	20.8	8.1	33.7	57.1 (707)
Percent Total	18.3 (227)	4.1 (51)	2.8 (35)	14.3 (177)	6.3 (78)	54.1 (670)	100.0 (1238)

[a] Question posed to the social worker: "How has the child typically reacted to the contact with the parent(s)?"

TABLE 40

CHILD'S TYPICAL REACTION TO CONTACT WITH FATHER
ACCORDING TO ADOPTION PLANNING OBJECTIVES FOR CHILDREN[a]

Adoption Planning Status	Appears to Enjoy Visits	Initially Shy, Then Warms Up	No Overt Reaction	Cautious, Uncomfortable or Embarrassed	Anxious or Upset	Not Applicable (No Visits, Deceased, Other)	Total
			(percentaged across)				
Freed for Adoption	1.5	0.3	--	0.9	1.2	96.1	26.7 (331)
Action Under Way to Free Child	3.5	2.0	2.0	2.5	2.0	88.0	16.2 (200)
Not Freed for Adoption	12.2	2.1	2.5	6.4	4.1	72.7	57.1 (707)
Percent Total	7.9 (98)	1.6 (20)	1.8 (22)	4.3 (53)	3.0 (37)	81.4 (1008)	100.0 (1238)

[a] Question posed to the social worker: "How has the child typically reacted to the contact with the parent(s)?"

TABLE 41

CHILD'S REACTION TO MOTHER'S FAILURE TO VISIT
ACCORDING TO ADOPTION PLANNING OBJECTIVES FOR CHILDREN[a]

Adoption Planning Status	Strong Negative Reaction	Moderate Negative Reaction	Mild Negative Reaction	No Reaction	Appears to Prefer No Visits	Not Relevant (Visits, Reaction Unknown, Deceased, Other)	Total
			(percentaged across)				
Freed for Adoption	0.3	1.2	2.7	6.3	4.8	84.7	26.7 (331)
Action Under Way to Free Child	2.5	1.0	5.0	17.5	7.5	66.5	16.2 (200)
Not Freed for Adoption	4.1	5.5	9.8	13.2	8.6	58.8	57.1 (707)
Percent Total	2.8 (35)	3.6 (45)	7.1 (88)	12.0 (149)	7.4 (92)	67.1 (829)	100.0 (1238)

[a] Instruction posed to the social worker: "If parent does not visit, please describe child's overt reaction to parent's failure to visit."

reactions or even manifest a surface veneer of equanimity.

The question posed to the respondents took the form: "If parent does not visit, please describe the child's overt reaction to parent's failure to visit." Table 41 shows the responses of the social workers with reference to the children's reactions to the failure of mothers to visit. The data are again organized by the three adoption planning categories.

For two-thirds of the cases, the response has to be classified as "not relevant" because the mother does visit, or because she is deceased or hospitalized, or because the child's reaction is unknown. Where the rating is available, we see that few children are identified as showing a strong negative reaction. Only 2.8 percent are so identified while 3.6 percent are described as showing a moderate negative reaction and 7.1 percent are said to show a mild negative reaction. Thus 13.5 percent are rated as showing some degree of negative reaction.

The ratings indicate that 12.0 percent of the children show no reaction and 7.4 percent actually appear to prefer no visits, perhaps related to the quality of parental behavior when visiting. For the children not freed for adoption, 19.4 percent are rated as showing some negative reaction, 13.2 percent as showing no reaction, and 8.6 percent as appearing to prefer no visits by the parents.

The data for ratings of the reactions to failure of the fathers to visit are shown in Table 42. There is a much heavier concentration of children in the category "no reaction" than was true with respect to the ratings applied to the absence of mothers. This may perhaps be another reflection of the degree to which the fathers are seen as being "out of it," i.e., relatively insignificant in the lives of their children.

In an effort to secure a firmer sense of the reactions of the children to the mother's failure to visit, we restricted our analysis to children not freed for adoption and divided them into two groups: (1) 180 cases where the mother's failure to visit had been identified as a problem for children who nevertheless had received some kind of visitation from a relative or non-relative, and (2) 86 children for whom non-visitation of mothers had been identified as a problem and who received no visiting of any kind from other persons.

The distribution of ratings for the first group of children visited by persons other than the mothers showed the following reactions to the failure of the mother to visit:

Strong negative reaction............	15.5%
Moderate negative reaction	17.8%
Mild negative reaction.............	20.0%
No reaction	30.0%
Appears to prefer no visits........	16.7%

For the second group of children who received no visits from any family-connected source, the distribution of ratings was as follows:

Strong negative reaction...........	1.2%
Moderate negative reaction	8.1%
Mild negative reaction.............	9.3%
No reaction	45.4%
Appears to prefer no visits........	36.0%

It is of interest that the children who have experienced total loss of contact with their families appear to be more resigned to the failure of their mothers to keep in touch with them, with only 18.6 percent showing some form of negative reaction. The children who have retained some contact with their families, but not with their mothers, include 53.3 percent who appear to show overt negative reaction to the absence of their mothers, almost three times the proportion of the earlier group.

The findings we present here are provocative and suggest that children totally removed from their families of origin show a kind of surface behavior which suggests resolution of their problems of separation from their mothers, or that the problem has been submerged, whereas those with some kind of family contact show more surface effects. There is the possibility, of course, that some spurious element in the data is accounting for the difference and that it will wash away when further analysis is undertaken, perhaps with a richer data base.

Summary Comments

We have earlier seen evidence that a large proportion of parents do not visit their children or otherwise keep in touch with them. Even among those who do visit, there are sizable numbers who show problematic behavior, that is, who do not appear well-related to the youngsters. For some of the children, contact with the parents appears to arouse anxiety and is not an unalloyed source of pleasure. These instances are of course counterbalanced by equally large groups of cases where the parents display their commitment to their children and where their visiting is a source of obvious comfort to the latter. The range of behaviors and qualities displayed by the parents clearly requires monitoring by the staff of child welfare agencies so that professional efforts can be made to influence the behavior when required. On the face of it, the quality of parental visiting appears to have important implications for an agency's ability to restore a child to his own home.

TABLE 42

CHILD'S REACTION TO FATHER'S FAILURE TO VISIT
ACCORDING TO ADOPTION PLANNING OBJECTIVES FOR CHILDREN[a]

Adoption Planning Status	Strong Negative Reaction	Moderate Negative Reaction	Mild Negative Reaction	No Reaction	Appears to Prefer No Visits	Not Relevant (Visits, Reaction Unknown, Paternity Unknown, etc.)	Total
	(percentaged across)						
Freed for Adoption	--	0.6	3.0	9.1	3.6	83.7	26.7 (331)
Action Under Way to Free Child	1.0	1.5	4.0	24.0	4.5	65.0	16.2 (200)
Not Freed for Adoption	2.3	3.5	8.1	26.4	5.2	54.5	57.1 (707)
Percent Total	1.5 (18)	2.4 (30)	6.1 (75)	21.4 (265)	4.7 (58)	63.9 (792)	100.0 (1238)

[a] Instruction posed to social worker: "If parent does not visit, please describe child's overt reaction to parent's failure to visit."

5 Factors Related to Frequency of Parental Visitation

Introduction

In this chapter, we look at the personal circumstances of parents that serve to constrain the frequency with which they have in-person contact with their children. Such phenomena as the parent's physical distance from the child's agency, other child care responsibilities and lack of finances for travel seemed likely to inhibit visitation and these topics were included in the questionnaire. From another perspective, we seek to learn about any steps taken by the agencies to stimulate parental visiting and the reactions of parents to such efforts. Our intention is to go beyond the simple frequency count of parental contacts as developed in Chapter 3 in order to probe the forces at play that serve to lower or enhance visitation.

Factors Affecting Visiting

In Tables 43 and 44 we show the distribution of circumstantial and other problems identified by the social workers as possibly serving to inhibit parental visiting. For these analyses, we focus upon only those cases where the children were not freed for adoption and where there was no action under way to free them. There were 707 children in the residual non-adoption group. Table 43 shows the data reported for the mothers. We see that a number of problem areas appear to affect modest-sized groups. Other child care responsibilities, for example, are said to be a factor that lowers visitation in 16.9 percent of the cases (4.2 percent rated as "very much" a factor and 12.7 percent as "somewhat" a factor). Employment hours of the mother are not a factor for any but a small number of cases, 7.2 percent are rated as "very much" or "somewhat."

Lack of funds for travel or babysitters is identified as an inhibiting factor in 16.0 percent of the cases (3.3 percent "very much" and 12.7 percent "somewhat"). More frequently cited is the problem of the distance the parent has to travel to the child's placement. Identified as "very much" a problem were 8.9 percent of the cases and an additional 19.8 percent as "somewhat" a problem. Almost three cases in ten were thus identified as problematic because the physical distance between the parent and child served to lower the frequency of parental visitation.

The mental illness of the mother was cited as "very much" a factor in 14.6 percent of the cases and "somewhat" in another 10.0 percent. Thus in one of four cases, the mother's mental illness was linked to her visiting behavior. Many of the social workers wrote brief narratives on the survey booklets that clearly indicated that mental illness was an important source of explanation of parental visiting behavior:

> Mother is encouraged to visit weekly and does at the group home. When mental illness or alcohol problem interferes, she does not come. Because of these problems, however, home visits are supervised by social worker. Mother is usually sober and appropriate when she comes to group home, and then staff does not supervise visits.
>
> * * * *
>
> Child is institutionalized, so there is no point in terminating rights. The agency has not encouraged mother to visit child. We have encouraged the father to send cards, letters, gifts, but he has not followed through. Mother is seriously mentally and emotionally disturbed, has no connection with child. Child doesn't know either parent. Father is busy with his other children who he feels can benefit from his support and contact.
>
> * * * *
>
> Frequent visiting in foster home restricted, as mother has periods of mental illness and sometimes has been using drugs. Child sees mother under worker's supervision, usually for a pleasant outing away from agency. Child is not always interested in visiting with mother and may refuse. Mother's mental health varies—at times behaves impulsively and immaturely with child. Mother has attended weekly joint therapeutic sessions with psychiatrist and child for four months during 1976.
>
> * * * *
>
> Mother is seemingly psychotic, has no interest in child, deserted child 3 1/2 years ago; her present whereabouts is unknown. However, the long-range plan for child is not adoption, therefore mother's rights need not be terminated. Father cannot provide suitable home for child because of employment and no extended family, but has meaningful relationship with child.
>
> * * * *
>
> Father has a history of schizophrenia and needs aid that I cannot give as a caseworker, but he refuses ongoing treatment. Consequently my work has come down to arranging visits and reinforcing the reality of what the conditions are for a return and the conditions for continued foster care.
>
> * * * *
>
> Visits by mother no longer permitted, as we are ter-

TABLE 43

PROBLEMS OF MOTHERS RATED BY CASEWORKERS
AS TENDING TO LOWER FREQUENCY OF VISITING:
FOR CHILDREN NOT FREED FOR ADOPTION[a]
(N = 707)

Factors Affecting Parent's Visiting	Has Factor Tended to Lower Visitation?			
	Very Much	Some-what	Hardly/ Not at All	Not Applicable or Unknown
	(percentaged across)			
Other Child Care Responsibilities	4.2	12.7	43.8	39.3
Employment Hours	1.4	5.8	47.1	45.7
Lack of Funds (e.g., for Carfare, Babysitter)	3.3	12.7	41.9	42.1
Distance from Child's Placement Address	8.9	19.8	33.7	37.6
Physical Illness of Parent	6.2	12.6	37.5	43.7
Mental Illness of Parent	14.6	10.0	33.5	41.9
Mental Retardation of Parent	2.1	2.3	47.4	48.2
Low Motivation (Lack of Relatedness to Child)	18.4	17.1	26.2	38.3

[a] Instruction to social worker: "Please indicate if any of the following factors have served to lower the frequency of parental visiting."

TABLE 44

PROPORTIONS OF CLASSES OF CASES WHERE FACTORS AFFECTING VISITATION BY MOTHERS HAVE BEEN IDENTIFIED BY SOCIAL WORKERS (PERCENT RATED "VERY MUCH" OR "SOMEWHAT" AS A PROBLEM)

Classes of Cases:	Total Sample (N=1238)	Children Not Freed for Adoption			Not Applicable/ Unrated Cases Removed	
		All Children Not Freed for Adoption (N=707)	Visited Children (N=556)	Non-Visited Children (N=151)	Visited (Percentage Base)	Non-Visited (Percentage Base)
	%	%	%	%	%	%
Factors Affecting Mother's Visiting:						
Other Child Care Responsibilities	11.6	16.9	18.3	11.9	27.3 (373)	32.1 (56)
Employment Hours	4.9	7.2	8.6	2.0	14.2 (338)	6.5 (46)
Lack of Funds (e.g., for Carfare, Babysitter)	11.5	16.0	17.5	10.6	27.2 (356)	20.2 (53)
Distance from Child's Placement Address	18.9	28.7	31.7	17.9	46.4 (379)	43.5 (62)
Physical Illness of Parent	13.3	18.8	21.6	8.6	34.9 (344)	24.1 (54)
Mental Illness of Parent	18.1	24.6	24.8	23.8	39.4 (350)	59.0 (61)
Mental Retardation of Parent	3.8	4.4	4.6	4.0	7.9 (315)	11.8 (51)
Low Motivation (Lack of Relatedness to Child)	27.1	35.5	35.2	36.4	53.6 (366)	78.6 (70)

minating her rights in court to free child for adoption. Natural mother is sociopathic individual with no ability to care for child and no motivation to do so. On occasion of mother's sole visit in May of 1975, child had violent negative reaction to visit. Child does not want to see mother. This is a virulently hostile client who is known to a multitude of social service agencies, all of whom have found her to be absolutely impossible to work with. Her hostility, negative attitude, and outright refusal to cooperate with agencies render any kind of positive intervention fruitless. She has been violently abusive towards her own mother, her sister, and the child in care, who needs to be protected from her.

Physical illness of the parent was a fairly frequent factor, accounting for lower visitation in 18.8 percent of the cases (6.2 percent "very much" and 12.6 "somewhat a problem"). Mental retardation, on the other hand, was rarely cited and was indicated as a major or moderate factor in only 4.4 percent of the cases.

The most frequently cited reason was the matter of the mother's low motivation to see her child and a lack of relatedness to her offspring. In almost one case in five (18.4 percent) this was seen as "very much" a factor and for a similar-sized group (17.1 percent) this was checked by the social workers as "somewhat" a factor. Thus, more than a third of the cases (35.5 percent) of the children not freed for adoption were viewed as being in situations where their mothers showed low motivation to see the child.

Given the fact that a high percentage of the cases were coded as "not applicable" or information to make the rating was unavailable, fully 38.3 percent, this left only little more than a quarter of the cases (26.2 percent) where the social workers made an affirmative judgment that the mother's motivation to see her child was not a problem, or hardly one.

Sub-Groups of Mothers

In Table 44, we look at the same list of factors that might serve to lower the visitation of mothers, setting forth the percentages where the social workers chose the ratings "very much" and "somewhat," indicating the relevancy of the factors. We attempt to determine how relevant the factors are for:

(1) The entire sample
(2) The sub-class of children not freed for adoption
(3) The children in (2) divided into visited and non-visited children[23]
(4) The children in (3) with the removal of the cases where the mother is out of the picture ("Not Applicable") or where the social worker was unable to make a rating ("Unknown")

As one moves from the total sample to smaller groups of children where the saliency of the ratings is more apparent, the list of factors affecting the visitation of the mothers looms larger. That is, by successively pruning away the cases of children where adoption is planned and then those where the mother is deceased or there are other reasons for the social worker choosing the category "Not Applicable" and eliminating the cases where the information was rated "Unknown," we come to the groups of visited and unvisited children where the ratings are most informative. We thus see that among the visited children, the distance of the mother from the child's placement residence is rated as a factor in 46.4 percent of the cases; the same factor is rated as affecting 43.5 percent of the non-visited children.

Other child care responsibilities and lack of funds for carfare or a babysitter affect almost three out of ten cases among the visited and non-visited children. These factors appear to be among those where agency programmatic activity can be mobilized to facilitate visiting by the mothers. While mental illness of the mother and low motivation to see the child are more frequently cited factors, they seem less amenable to agency efforts to prod the mother's visiting.

Factors Affecting Fathers

We already know that the fathers of the children tend to be more peripheral figures on the foster care scene. Many have not acknowledged paternity and their whereabouts are unknown. Even larger numbers have simply dropped out of the lives of their children. For the minority of cases in which a father is in the picture, no more than one case in five, the relationship with the social worker appears to vary so that the gathering of information about their visiting behavior relative to the child is marked with uncertainty. We thus present data about the fathers in the two tables that follow with some sense of uncertainty of their value. We say this because the percentages describing the distributions of ratings are based upon a small minority of available fathers.

Table 45 shows the distribution of ratings for the group of 707 children who have not been freed for adoption. The percentage of cases affected is small for each category because so many cases are not applicable. The three factors that stand out as most often inhibiting the visits of fathers—that is, rated "very much" or "somewhat" a problem—are employment hours (9.4 percent), distance required to travel to the child's placement (10.3 percent) and low motivation to visit (17.1 percent).

In Table 46, we show the percentage of fathers who were rated as being constrained in their visiting behavior by the kinds of problems listed. Perhaps the most meaningful column is the one that specifies the class of cases where the children were not freed for adoption with "not applicable" and "unknown" cases pruned away. For the visited children, i.e., those who received at least one visit from a family-related person, the father's employment hours, distance from the child's placement and low motivation to visit were again the outstanding factors. The motivational factor loomed particularly large and was a factor in more than half the cases.

For the non-visited children, there were very few cases left after those designated "not applicable" or "unknown" were removed. For the small groups of residual cases, the percentage of fathers rated as affected by the three factors of employment hours, distance from the child's placement and low motivation to visit were as high as those shown for the visited children.

TABLE 45

PROBLEMS OF FATHERS RATED BY CASEWORKERS
AS TENDING TO LOWER FREQUENCY OF VISITING:
FOR CHILDREN NOT FREED FOR ADOPTION[a]
(N = 707)

Factors Affecting Parent's Visiting	Has Factor Tended to Lower Visitation?			
	Very Much	Some-what	Hardly/ Not at All	Not Applicable or Unknown
	(percentaged across)			
Other Child Care Responsibilities	0.8	2.4	22.2	74.6
Employment Hours	2.3	7.1	16.8	73.8
Lack of Funds (e.g., for Carfare, Babysitter)	0.7	2.7	21.2	75.4
Distance from Child's Placement Address	3.1	7.2	17.7	72.0
Physical Illness of Parent	1.1	2.4	21.1	75.4
Mental Illness of Parent	1.6	1.7	21.1	75.6
Mental Retardation of Parent	0.7	0.4	23.5	75.4
Low Motivation (Lack of Relatedness to Child)	11.3	5.8	14.0	68.9

[a] Instruction to social worker: "Please indicate if any of the following factors have served to lower the frequency of parental visiting."

TABLE 46

PROPORTIONS OF CLASSES OF CASES WHERE FACTORS AFFECTING VISITATION BY FATHERS HAVE BEEN IDENTIFIED BY SOCIAL WORKERS (PERCENT RATED "VERY MUCH" OR "SOMEWHAT" AS A PROBLEM)

Classes of Cases:	Total Sample (N=1238)	Children Not Freed for Adoption			Not Applicable/ Unrated Cases Removed	
		All Children Not Freed for Adoption (N=707)	Visited Children (N=556)	Non-Visited Children (N=151)	Visited (Percentage Base)	Non-Visited (Percentage Base)
	%	%	%	%	%	%
Factors Affecting Father's Visiting:						
Other Child Care Responsibilities	3.2	3.3	3.1	4.0	10.8 (157)	26.1 (23)
Employment Hours	9.4	8.9	10.6	4.6	36.0 (164)	33.3 (21)
Lack of Funds (e.g., for Carfare, Babysitter)	3.4	3.4	3.4	3.3	12.4 (153)	23.8 (21)
Distance from Child's Placement Address	10.3	10.3	11.5	6.0	36.6 (175)	39.1 (23)
Physical Illness of Parent	3.5	3.7	4.1	1.3	14.8 (155)	10.5 (19)
Mental Illness of Parent	3.4	3.3	3.8	1.3	13.8 (152)	10.0 (20)
Mental Retardation of Parent	1.1	1.4	0.9	2.0	3.3 (151)	13.0 (23)
Low Motivation (Lack of Relatedness to Child)	17.1	18.5	17.4	15.9	51.3 (189)	77.4 (31)

Other Factors Accounting for Lack of Visitation

The failure of parents to visit their children involves such a basic failure in fulfilling societal expectations that one naturally searches for simple explanations beyond those we have already presented. The identity of a father may be unknown. Another may have never acknowledged paternity. A mother may not have lived with a child since birth. Another may have been institutionalized for years, and so forth.

In Table 47, we set forth the percentage of cases among those where the children were not freed for adoption where such factors prevailed for either the mothers or fathers. We see that in a tenth of the cases, the mother's whereabouts is unknown. Fourteen percent of the cases involve situations where the identity of the father is unknown; in a similar proportion (13.9 percent), paternity has not been acknowledged. A small proportion of the mothers have never lived with their children (4.2 percent) in contrast to a much larger percentage of the fathers (18.1 percent). Some of the mothers (5.4 percent) and the fathers (6.1 percent) live outside the state in which the child resides.

In Table 48, we show the same data for two sub-groups: visited children and non-visited children. The latter have not had a single visit from any family-related person while the former received at least one such visit. As might be expected, the cases of the non-visited children are more affected by some of the specified factors. Thus 24.5 percent of the mothers in these cases have disappeared from the view of the agency and their whereabouts are unknown. This compares with 6.1 percent of the visited children. We also observe that 11.3 percent of the mothers of the non-visited children never had the experience of living with their offspring compared to 2.3 percent of the visited children.

Agency Efforts to Increase Parental Visits

Stimulating parents to visit their children, up to their fullest capacity, is obviously a major responsibility of an agency providing foster care for children. The social workers were asked to characterize the degree to which the agency had attempted to influence the parents to visit during the past six months. Their responses as applied to cases of children not freed for adoption are shown in Table 49.

For the mothers of 28.1 percent of the children, it was reported that it was not necessary for the agency to invest any special effort in stimulating visitation because the mothers were already visiting. This was true of 10.0 percent of the fathers. Some effort to prod mothers was reported for 30.4 percent of the cases, divided among "major effort" (8.9 percent), "moderate effort" (13.2 percent) and "slight effort" (8.3 percent). In 25.0 percent of the cases, the agencies reported no effort to stimulate maternal visiting. For 12.0 percent of the cases the issue was considered "not applicable" because the mother was out of the picture.

For the fathers, it was reported in 14.0 percent of the cases that the agency made some investment in seeking to stimulate visiting. However, there was no effort made in 35.2 percent of the cases and the category of "not applicable" applied in 32.5 percent of the cases. The investment by the agencies in stimulating visitation of the fathers appears quite minimal.

The visited and unvisited categories of cases were compared with respect to agency investment to spur visitation by the mother. We found that according to the reports of social workers, 20.1 percent of the cases in the visited category involved no effort to promote parental visiting; this compared with 43.0 percent of the cases where the children were totally unvisited by any family-related person.

In Table 50, an itemized list of efforts made by the agencies to increase visiting is set forth. Percentages are shown for reported efforts for mothers and for fathers treated separately. The most frequently reported activity is the agency advice to parents of the need to visit, 27.2 percent for the mothers and 11.2 percent for the fathers. Next in frequency is the provision of funds for travel costs, 21.8 percent for the mothers and 4.8 percent for the fathers. Direct provision of transportation service is provided on a relatively minor scale, 4.4 percent for mothers and only 1.4 percent of the fathers.

In Table 51, we provide a frequency count of the sum of the types of efforts to increase visiting reported for the mothers and fathers. The range is from zero to four. Almost sixty percent (59.7 percent) of the sample of mothers involve no effort to increase their visiting; of these, almost half (28.1 percent) do not require agency effort because the mother's visiting frequency is deemed satisfactory. Almost twenty percent of the cases (19.5 percent) involve two or more different actions by the agencies. For the fathers, agency effort of any kind, e.g., one to three different kinds of action, account for only 18.1 percent of the cases.

When the cases of the visited and non-visited children not freed for adoption were compared, the aggregated data showed that 21.8 percent of cases involving the former involved at least one kind of effort to spur visitation of the mothers. This compared with 34.4 percent of the cases involving unvisited children. This is some indication that more effort is being directed at the cases most in need of agency activity.

Parental Responses to Agency Efforts

Given the severe personal problems faced by many of the parents leading to the need for placement of the children, it was not expected that the social workers would report many success stories about the results of their efforts to increase parental visiting. This is borne out by Table 52. For the mothers, 16.1 percent were reported to be essentially unresponsive to the exhortations and attempted assistance of the social workers. Their visiting behavior was not improved. Another 6.4 percent were somewhat responsive and their visiting was only slightly improved. The group of mothers reported to be responsive constituted only 6.5 percent of the sample.

The reports of the responses of the fathers were quite dismal as shown in Table 52. The responsive group was distinctively trivial in size; 1.8 percent were rated as showing improved visiting behavior.

Cases were further segregated into visited and non-visited groups and cases where no effort was reported to increase parental visiting were excluded. For 177 visited

TABLE 47

FACTORS CONTRIBUTING TO LACK OF PARENTAL CONTACT WITH CHILD
FOR CHILDREN NOT FREED FOR ADOPTION[a]
(N = 707)

	Mother No.	Mother Percent	Father No.	Father Percent
Identity of Parent Is Unknown	4	0.6	99	14.0
Has Not Acknowledged Paternity	X X X X X X		98	13.9
Has Never Lived with Child	30	4.2	128	18.1
Lives out of State	38	5.4	43	6.1
Whereabouts Is Unknown	71	10.0	234	33.1
Parent Is Institutionalized	52	7.4	16	1.6
Other Factor	44	6.2	41	5.8

[a]Question posed to social worker: "Have any of the following factors been operating to explain the lack of contact between parent and child?" Data shown above reflects positive identification of problem factors.

TABLE 48

FACTORS CONTRIBUTING TO LACK OF PARENTAL CONTACT WITH CHILD
FOR CHILDREN NOT FREED FOR ADOPTION:
FOR VISITED AND NON-VISITED CHILDREN[a]

	Visited (N=556)		Non-Visited (N=151)	
	Mothers	Fathers	Mothers	Fathers
	%	%	%	%
Identity of Parent is Unknown	3.6	12.9	1.3	17.9
Has Not Acknowledged Paternity	X X X X	12.2	X X X X	19.9
Has Never Lived With Child	2.3	17.3	11.3	21.2
Lives Out of State	4.5	6.1	8.6	4.6
Whereabouts Are Unknown	6.1	31.7	24.5	38.4
Parent is Institutionalized	7.5	2.9	6.6	--
Other Factor	5.6	6.1	8.6	4.6

[a] Visited children have had at least one in-person visit from a family related person. Non-visited children have had none.

TABLE 49

DEGREE OF EFFORT EXERCISED BY AGENCY TO INFLUENCE MOTHERS AND FATHERS TO VISIT FOR CHILDREN NOT FREED FOR ADOPTION[a]

	Mother		Father	
	No.	Percent	No.	Percent
Parent Visits, No Special Effort Required	198	28.1	71	10.0
Major Effort to Get Parent to Visit	63	8.9	26	3.7
Moderate Effort to Get Parent to Visit	93	13.2	44	6.2
Slight Effort to Get Parent to Visit	59	8.3	29	4.1
No Effort to Get Parent to Visit	177	25.0	249	35.2
Other	24	3.4	25	3.5
Unknown	8	1.1	34	4.8
Not Applicable	85	12.0	229	32.5
Total	707	100.0	707	100.0

[a] Instruction posed to social worker: "Please characterize the degree to which the agency has attempted to influence parent(s) to visit during the past six months."

TABLE 50

EFFORTS MADE BY AGENCY TO INCREASE VISITING
OF MOTHERS AND FATHERS FOR CASES
WHERE CHILDREN NOT FREED FOR ADOPTION[a]
(N = 707)

	Mother		Father	
	No.	Percent	No.	Percent
Not Applicable, Parent Visits Frequently, No Need to Increase Visiting	195	27.6	65	9.2
Agency Advised Parent of Need to Visit	192	27.2	79	11.2
Agency Provided Funds to Pay for Travel Costs	154	21.8	34	4.8
Agency Provided Funds to Pay for Babysitter	13	1.8	3	0.4
Agency Provided Transportation for Visiting Child	31	4.4	10	1.4
Agency Telephoned or Sent Letters	16	2.3	16	2.3
Agency Sent Child Home	27	3.8	4	0.6
Agency Provided Other Forms of Encouragement of Visiting	33	4.7	28	4.0

[a] Question posed to the social worker: "Has the agency attempted to increase parental visiting of the child in care through any of the following measures?"

TABLE 51

NUMBER OF TYPES OF AGENCY EFFORTS
TO INCREASE VISITING OF MOTHERS AND FATHERS
FOR CHILDREN NOT FREED FOR ADOPTION

	\multicolumn{5}{c	}{Number of Types of Efforts}	Total
	Zero	One	Two	Three	Four	
	\multicolumn{5}{c	}{(percentaged across)}	
Mothers	59.7	20.8	13.6	5.8	0.1	100.0 (707)
Fathers	81.9	13.3	3.4	1.4	--	100.0 (707)

TABLE 52

NATURE OF PARENTAL RESPONSE TO AGENCY EFFORTS
TO INCREASE VISITING FOR CHILDREN NOT FREED FOR ADOPTION[a]

	Mother No.	Mother Percent	Father No.	Father Percent
Not Applicable, No Effort to Increase Visiting	376	53.2	322	45.6
Essentially Non-Responsive, Visiting Not Influenced	114	16.1	65	9.2
Somewhat Responsive, Visiting Slightly Improved	45	6.4	18	2.5
Responsive, Visiting Improved	46	6.5	13	1.8
Other	18	2.5	23	3.3
Unknown	15	2.1	49	6.9
Not Applicable	93	13.2	217	30.7
	707	100.0	707	100.0

[a] Question posed to the social worker: "How has the parent responded to agency efforts to increase visiting during the past six months?"

children where effort was reported to spur the parent's visiting, the breakdown of results showed 50.3 percent of the parents to be unresponsive, 23.7 percent somewhat responsive and 26.0 percent were described as responsive. Thus, about one case in four where effort was extended showed positive results. This is a sobering perspective and an indication of the challenge facing agencies.

Of the 151 cases of children not freed for adoption where there was no contact at all with family-related persons, only 28 cases were targets of agency efforts to increase visitation of mothers. Of these, 89.3 percent were totally unresponsive and 10.7 percent somewhat responsive. Again, this kind of outcome points up the obdurate nature of the parents' problems.

Contacts Prohibited or Restricted?

Given the awareness that many of the parents of the children in foster care suffer from mental illness or lead highly irregular and dysfunctional lives, one cannot assume that parental visiting can uniformly be encouraged by the agencies carrying responsibility for the children. Some parents are so disruptive in their visiting behavior that their visiting must be prohibited or restrained.

The following inquiry was addressed to the social workers who were the respondents in this study: "Has the agency ever found it necessary to restrict or prohibit a parent from having contact with the child?" The distribution of responses for the entire sample of mothers is shown in Table 53. Many cases are omitted (441) because the mother was not in the picture and the question therefore did not apply.

For about four out of every five rated cases (80.3 percent), it was reported that it had never been necessary to prohibit or restrict parental visiting. For 7.0 percent it had been necessary in the past but prohibition or restriction of visiting was no longer in force. For 6.6 percent, visiting was currently restricted and for 1.5 percent it was currently prohibited. There were only modest differences in percentages of restricted or prohibited cases among the three groups organized according to adoption planning status.

Although we show no table because of limitations in space, we can report that 88.7 percent of some 504 fathers for whom information was reported were never restricted in visiting their children or prohibited from seeing them at all. We also found only minor differences between cases of visited and non-visited children in this regard; this applied to both mothers and fathers.

One final kind of information should be noted. More than one case in five of visiting parents (21.7 percent) were reported to require supervision of their visits. The proportion of such cases among parents of children not freed for adoption was 26.5 percent. The disturbed or disruptive behavior of the parents was most often cited as the reason for the need to supervise visits.

Summary Comments

The reasons for parental failure to visit their children are rooted in a variety of circumstantial factors as well as those related to parental disturbance and low motivation to see their children. The problems sometimes create enormous barriers between the parents and their children and agency efforts to overcome them are exerted on a modest proportion with limited success. This is very difficult work.

TABLE 53

REPORTED NECESSITY OF AGENCY TO RESTRICT OR PROHIBIT MOTHER FROM HAVING CONTACT WITH CHILD ACCORDING TO ADOPTION PLANNING OBJECTIVES FOR CHILDREN[a]

Adoption Planning Status	No, Contact Never Prohibited or Restricted	Yes, in Past but Not Now	Yes, Now Restricted	Yes, Now Prohibited	Other	Un-known	Total
	(percentaged across)						
Freed for Adoption	65.2	4.3	5.8	8.7	7.2	8.7	8.7 (69)
Action Under Way to Free Child	77.0	5.3	12.4	3.5	1.8	--	14.2 (113)
Not Freed for Adoption	82.6	7.6	5.7	0.3	2.4	1.3	77.2 (615)
Percent Total	80.3 (640)	7.0 (56)	6.6 (53)	1.5 (12)	2.8 (22)	1.8 (14)	100.0 (797)

[a] Question posed to the social worker: "Has the agency ever found it necessary to restrict or prohibit a parent from having contact with the child?"

[b] 441 omitted cases--information not reported.

6 Index Scores: Composite Measures of Parental Visiting

Introduction

Given the relative wealth of information about the visiting phenomenon made available through the use of the special questionnaire, it seemed advisable to develop a relatively compact set of measures reflecting key dimensions of visiting. To accomplish this, the variables were sifted using the conventional techniques of factor analysis and subsequent index construction based upon our understanding of the dimensionality of the information revealed by the analysis. We have emerged with three indexes which appear to reflect essential aspects of visiting.

Frequency of Visiting

Our most important measure would appear to be the Index of Parental Contact Frequency. We based the measure on information made available about either the mother's or the father's visiting, or both. Visiting data were included in the index which reflected the maximum visiting available to the child with either parent.

The items that make up the index are shown in Table 54. The items are included in a form that results in a high index score signifying frequent visiting and a low score being an indication that the child is actually or close to being totally isolated from his parents.

The first item concerns frequency of contact and is a response to the question: "When did the child last have contact with a family-related person?" The range covers situations in which the child never had contact with a parent since birth or placement in foster care to contact within the past month. The second item deals with the question of the identity of visitors the child has had during the past six months, with visits by both parents given the highest weight, followed in importance by contact with either parent. The third item concerns frequency of communication between parents and child other than through in-person visits, e.g., telephone calls, mail, and gifts.

The fourth item is the social worker's overall characterization of the parent's current tendency to visit, ranging from never to twice or more a month. The fifth item concerns the matter of whether parental visiting has been declining and is based on the mean of the mother-related and father-related information. The item ranges from major decline to major increase in visiting.

The last item concerns the response of parents to agency efforts to increase their visiting. The item ranges from behavior which is considered non-responsive to that which is seen as indicating that parental visiting has been enhanced.

The intercorrelation of items reveals that they are moderately well-related to each other and, more importantly, show fairly good item-criterion correlations, i.e., correlations of the item with the modified total index scores.[24] The weakest item is the last, dealing with parental responsiveness to agency efforts to increase visiting. There are too many cases where the question of responsiveness is not relevant because there is no agency effort reported; either the parent is already visiting and needs no prod or the parents are so completely out of the picture that no pressure to visit can be brought to bear. It is the view of the writer that the information provided by the item is highly important but ought to be included in the index only when there is a homogeneous population being studied, i.e., parents who are targets of agency efforts to boost their visiting. The problem of defining the relevant population in measuring parental visiting behavior is a pervasive one and is not fully resolved in the writer's experience.

It should be noted that the measure of internal reliability of the index, Cronbach's Alpha, is fairly high (alpha = .893). We can thus say that the items "belong together," i.e., that they share a fairly high degree of common content.

Quality of Contact

Recognizing the primacy of the issue of whether or not the child has contact with his family after he enters foster care and how frequently such contact takes place, there are nevertheless other aspects of the visiting phenomenon that also loom large in the concerns of those responsible for service delivery in child welfare. What is the quality of the contact that takes place? Are the visits enjoyable for the child? Are they non-disruptive of the foster care arrangement? What does the quality of the parent's visiting behavior reveal about the degree of responsibility shown by the parent? Does the visiting behavior have implications for the key issue of whether termination of parental rights should be proposed by the agency to the appropriate court? There is also concern about non-visitation; how does this impact upon the child?

TABLE 54

INDEX OF PARENTAL CONTACT FREQUENCY

A. Question 4: When was the last in-person contact between the parent(s) and other relatives and the child?

    Responses:
- 0   Never (no contacts since birth or placement)
- 1   Over two years ago
- 2   6 to 24 months ago
- 3   2 to 5 months ago
- 4   Past month

(Maximized for most frequent visitation of mother and/or father.)

B. Question 2: What persons have seen the child during the past six months (or since the child entered care if duration of placement is less than six months)?

    Responses:
- 0   No visitor
- 1   Sibling
- 2   Other relative
- 3   Father or mother
- 4   Father and mother

C. Question 5: Has there been any contact during the past six months between parents and child other than through in-person visits (telephone calls, letters, cards (holidays and birthdays), gifts, other)?

    Responses:
- 0   None
- 1   One
- 2   Two or three
- 3   Four or five
- 4   Six or more

(Maximum for either mother or father.)

(Continued)

TABLE 54 (*Continued*)

INDEX OF PARENTAL CONTACT FREQUENCY

D. Question 6: How would you characterize the parent's current tendency to visit the child in care?

   Responses: 0 ___ Never
   1 ___ Yearly
   2 ___ Four to eleven months
   3 ___ One to three months
   4 ___ Twice or more a month

   (Maximum for either mother or father.)

E. Question 8: Has the frequency of parental contact changed since the child entered care?

   Responses: 0 ___ Major decline
   1 ___ Moderate or slight decline
   2 ___ No change
   3 ___ Moderate or slight increase
   4 ___ Major increase

   (Mean of mother and father response.)

F. Question 19: How has the parent responded to agency efforts to increase visiting during the past six months?

   Responses: 1 ___ Non-responsive
   3 ___ Somewhat responsive
   4 ___ Responsive
   (Others = blank)

   (Mean of mother and father.)

Intercorrelation of Items

	A	B	C	D	E	F
A	1.00	.85	.63	.84	.51	.40
B		1.00	.54	.70	.45	.30
C			1.00	.68	.38	.35
D				1.00	.59	.48
E					1.00	.47
F						1.00

Mean Index Score   = 1.638
Standard Deviation = 1.133
Cronbach Alpha   = .893

In Table 55, we show the constituent items of the composite measure we call Index of Quality of Parental Contact with the Child. It is based upon the five items shown. The intercorrelation of the items is moderately strong for the five items, averaging about .50, statistically significant but modest. The total score correlations are quite firm for the five items and average about .60. (See Table 57.)

The first item deals with a child's reaction to parental visiting with a high score indicating obvious enjoyment in having contact and a low score indicating no visiting is taking place or anxiety or upset is shown in connection with the parent's visits. The second item concerns the quality of the parent's relatedness while visiting, with a high score indicating positive relatedness and a low score indicating "not at all," i.e., a very poor level of relatedness. The third item concerns the apparent effort made by the parent to make the visit enjoyable, a high score signifying very much of a positive effort and a low score indicative of no effort being shown.

The fourth and fifth items involve a judgment by the social worker as to whether the parent is showing responsible behavior in visiting the child and meeting his needs and whether the behavior is sufficiently an indication of dereliction of responsibility to suggest that parental rights ought to be terminated. A low score on these items would signify irresponsible behavior and justification for moving toward termination of rights.

The Alpha coefficient for the index is .79, indicating a moderately strong level of internal reliability. However, the high correlation between Index of Quality of Parental Contact Scores and the Index of Parental Contact Frequency ($r = .76$) suggests that the content of both is strongly linked to whether or not the parents visit the child. In future use of these measures, it may be preferable to think of them as sub-components of one measure which simultaneously measures quantity and quality of visitation by the parents, a measure which deals with the *adequacy* of parental role performance.

Visiting Problems

The Index of Sum of Problems Associated with Parental Visiting has content which combines concern with circumstantial and personal factors which interfere with the ability of parents to visit and agency efforts to overcome these. It also covers agency necessity to restrict or prohibit visiting or to supervise the parent's visits by having a social worker present. The six-item index reflects the appropriateness of the parent's behavior when visiting. We present the index because our various analyses suggest that a multi-faceted composite measure is somehow embedded among all the variables we have included in the questionnaire. However, the index gives us pause because of the following serious limitations: low correlations between the items, low item-total score correlations and low internal reliability (Table 56).

We present the index to indicate where our first steps in measurement have taken us and not because we feel we have a finished product. We intend to work further on the task, perhaps going through alternative index construction routes with the same data. One small consideration in favor of the index is that there is little overlap with the first two indexes; the correlation with Parental Contact Frequency is .17 and with Quality of Contact is $-.14$.

Patterns of Parental Visiting and Index Scores

To probe the validity of the index scores a one-way analysis of variance was performed for each index to compare mean scores assigned to cases classified according to known patterns of visiting as characterized by the social workers. The children not freed for adoption constituted the source of five groups: (1) both parents visit, (2) mother only visits, (3) father only visits, (4) other visitor, and (5) child not visited. It was assumed that mean scores on the indexes could be expected to vary with classes of children so diverse in the sources of visitation. One added note: While there were 707 children who could be classified as not freed for adoption, the group was reduced to 467 cases by eliminating situations in which there was no parent free to visit the child for reason of being deceased or because of institutionalization.

Table 58 presents the mean scores for the five groups on the Index of Parental Contact Frequency. The highest mean scores are shown by the class of cases where both parents visit (Mean = 3.07), followed closely by the cases where the mother only was described as visiting (Mean = 2.76), and those where the father only visited (Mean = 2.66). Both groups of cases where neither parents visited, i.e., those that had other visitors such as adult relative or siblings, and those who had no visitors of any kind showed the same mean scores (Mean = 1.17). The children in these groups were thus very low in the scores assigned their cases on the Index of Frequency Contact. The mean scores assigned to the different groups are in accord with our expectations (Table 59).

The Index of Quality of Parental Visiting was treated in the same manner. The one-way analysis of variance showed the highest scores, reflecting good quality of visiting assigned to cases where both parents visited (Mean = 3.6) followed closely by cases where the mother only visited (Mean = 2.85) and where the father only visited (Mean = 2.82). All three categories of cases reflected higher quality of visiting behavior. The children who were not visited at all showed low scores on the index (Mean = 1.08) as well as those who received visits from persons other than their parents (Mean = 0.83). Again, this was in accord with our expectations.

The Index of Sum of Problems Associated with Parental Visiting shows the highest mean for the groups of cases where the mothers only visited (Mean = 9.03) followed closely by those where both parents visited (Mean = 8.75). The group of fathers who were the sole parents visiting also scored fairly high on this index (Mean = 8.47).

The group of unvisited children were in situations in which there were quite a few problems associated with parental visiting (Mean = 7.40). This compared with cases where children were visited by persons other than their parents where visiting problems were not as readily identified (Mean = 5.79) (Table 60).

TABLE 55

INDEX OF QUALITY OF PARENTAL CONTACT WITH CHILD

A. Question 9A: How has the child typically reacted to the contact with the parent(s)?

    Responses:
- 0 — No parental visits
- 1 — Appears anxious or upset
- 2 — Appears cautious, uncomfortable or embarrassed
- 3 — Appears shy or shows no reaction
- 4 — Appears to enjoy visits

(Maximized for mother and father.)

B. Question 11: We are interested in your impression of the quality of the parent(s)' contact during visiting occasions. Would you say that the parent appears well-related to the child during visits?

    Responses:
- 1 — Not at all
- 2 — Other
- 3 — Somewhat
- 4 — Very much so

(Mean of father and mother response.)

C. Question 12: Does the parent make an effort to make the contact an enjoyable occasion for the child?

    Responses:
- 1 — Not at all
- 2 — Other
- 3 — Somewhat
- 4 — Very much

(Mean of father and mother response.)

(Continued)

TABLE 55 (Continued)

INDEX OF QUALITY OF PARENTAL CONTACT WITH CHILD

D. Question 15: How would you characterize the parent's current visiting behavior in meeting the needs of the child?

    Responses: 0 ___ Irresponsible
                      2 ___ Somewhat irresponsible
                      4 ___ Responsible

(Mean of father and mother response.)

E. Question 16A: Does quality of parent's visiting behavior or failure to visit have implications for termination of parent's rights?

    Responses: 1 ___ Yes, termination of rights should be considered
                      2 ___ Yes, termination of rights should be considered if visiting behavior not corrected
                      3 ___ No, circumstantial factors affecting visiting, termination of rights need not be considered
                      4 ___ No, quality of visiting is satisfactory

(Mean of father and mother response.)

Intercorrelation of Items

	A	B	C	D	E
A	1.00	.44	.41	.49	.43
B		1.00	.65	.45	.39
C			1.00	.47	.37
D				1.00	.62
E					1.00

Mean Index Score   = 2.416
Standard Deviation = 0.943
Cronbach Alpha   = .790

TABLE 56

INDEX OF SUM OF PROBLEMS ASSOCIATED WITH PARENTAL VISITING

A. Question 13: Please indicate if any of the following factors have served to lower the frequency of parental visiting--very much/somewhat/hardly or not at all. (For: Other child care responsibilities, employment hours, financial limitations re carfare or babysitter, distance from child's placement, physical illness, mental illness, mental retardation, other incapacity, low motivation or other.)

    Responses: 1____One factor
                   2____Two or three factors
                   3____Four or five factors
                   4____Six or more factors

    (Maximum for father or mother.)

B. Question 17: Has the agency attempted to increase parental visiting of the child in care through any of the following (For: Advising parent of child's need for such visiting, providing funds for travel costs and/or babysitter, and other forms of encouragement.)

    Responses: Maximum number of agency efforts for father or mother.

C. Question 18A: Please characterize the degree to which the agency has attempted to influence parent(s) to visit during the past six months.

    Responses: 1____Parent visits, no special effort required
                   2____Slight effort to get parent to visit
                   3____Moderate effort to get parent to visit
                   4____Major effort to get parent to visit

    (Mean of mother and father response.)

D. Question 20A: Has the agency ever found it necessary to restrict or prohibit a parent from having contact with the child?

    Responses: 1____No, contact never restricted or prohibited
                   2____Yes, in past but not now
                   3____Yes, contact now restricted
                   4____Yes, contact now prohibited

    (Mean of mother and father response.)

(Continued)

TABLE 56 (Continued)

INDEX OF SUM OF PROBLEMS ASSOCIATED WITH PARENTAL VISITING

E. Question 21A: Has the agency found it necessary to supervise the parent's in-person visits with the child?

Responses: 1 ___ No, supervision not required
4 ___ Yes, supervision required

(Mean of mother and father response.)

F. Question 10: Please indicate if any of the following problems have been manifested in the past six months in connection with the visiting of parents. (For: creates disturbance, intoxicated or under influence of drugs, brings inappropriate strangers, behavior bizarre or seriously divergent from normal, visits are too brief, visits at inappropriate times, late or misses appointments, and other problems.)

Responses: 0 ___ None
2 ___ One
4 ___ Two or more

(Maximum of mother or father response.)

Intercorrelation of Items

	A	B	C	D	E	F
A	1.00	.18	.18	.01	.07	.09
B		1.00	.16	.00	.14	.07
C			1.00	-.08	.03	.18
D				1.00	.30	.15
E					1.00	.22
F						1.00

Mean Index Score = 1.538
Standard Deviation = 0.517
Cronbach Alpha = .436

TABLE 57

ITEM-CRITERION CORRELATIONS FOR THREE INDEXES OF VISITING

Index	Index 1	Index 2	Index 3
1. Parental Contact Frequency			
Item: A	.83	.63	.28
B	.60	.47	.15
C	.57	.57	.08
D	.80	.74	.20
E	.54	.50	-.01
F	.47	.51	.00
2. Quality of Contact			
Item: A	.70	.57	.14
B	.37	.60	-.23
C	.40	.59	-.18
D	.69	.66	-.19
E	.52	.58	-.23
3. Visiting Problems			
Item: A	.06	-.09	.21
B	.03	-.12	.27
C	.18	.09	.21
D	.11	-.02	.24
E	-.08	-.19	.28
F	.24	-.10	.31

Intercorrelations of Indexes

	Index 1	Index 2	Index 3
1. Parental Contact Frequency	1.00	.76	.17
2. Quality of Contact		1.00	-.14
3. Visiting Problems			1.00

TABLE 58

MEAN SCORES ON INDEX OF FREQUENCY OF CONTACT FOR CHILDREN
NOT FREED FOR ADOPTION ACCORDING TO GROUPS OF CASES
CLASSIFIED BY PATTERNS OF PARENTAL VISITATION

	Visiting Pattern	Mean Score	Standard Deviation	Number of Children
Group 1	Both Parents Visit	3.07	0.55	92
Group 2	Mother Only Visits	2.76	0.54	246
Group 3	Father Only Visits	2.66	0.61	30
Group 4	Other Visitor	1.17	0.42	42
Group 5	Child Not Visited	1.17	0.55	57
	TOTAL (Groups 1-5)	2.48	0.88	467

Analysis of Variance Table

	Mean Square	DF	F-Test	Significance
Among Groups	55.808	4	188.429	Under .001
Within Groups	0.296	462		

TABLE 59

MEAN SCORES ON INDEX OF QUALITY OF PARENTAL VISITING
FOR CHILDREN NOT FREED FOR ADOPTION
ACCORDING TO PATTERNS OF PARENTAL VISITATION

	Visiting Pattern	Mean Score	Standard Deviation	Number of Children
Group 1	Both Parents Visit	3.10	0.79	92
Group 2	Mother Only Visits	2.85	0.91	246
Group 3	Father Only Visits	2.82	0.95	30
Group 4	Other Visitor	0.83	0.76	42
Group 5	Child Not Visited	1.08	1.02	57
	TOTAL (Groups 1-5)	2.499	1.99	467

Analysis of Variance Table

	Mean Square	DF	F-Test	Significance
Among Groups	74.219	4	91.920	Under .001
Within Groups	0.807	462		

TABLE 60

MEAN SCORES ON INDEX OF SUM OF PROBLEMS
ASSOCIATED WITH PARENTAL VISITING FOR CHILDREN
NOT FREED FOR ADOPTION ACCORDING TO PATTERNS OF PARENTAL VISITATION

Visiting Pattern		Mean Score	Standard Deviation	Number of Children
Group 1	Both Parents Visit	8.75	3.92	92
Group 2	Mother Only Visits	9.03	3.92	246
Group 3	Father Only Visits	8.47	3.86	30
Group 4	Other Visitor	5.79	3.78	42
Group 5	Child Not Visited	7.40	3.60	57
	TOTAL (Groups 1-5)	8.45	3.99	467

Analysis of Variance Table

	Mean Square	DF	F-Test	Significance
Among Groups	113.266	4	7.501	Under .001
Within Groups	15.100	462		

Predicting Later Contact

An attempt was made to determine the predictive validity of the measures that had been composited into index form by determining their strength in predicting subsequent contact between parents and children. The CWIS data file of December 31, 1978, was accessed for our subjects. This was some 21 months after our survey. The frequency of parental contact was coded on the CWIS form so that the bottom of the scale represented no family visits over a six-month period while the top indicated twelve or more visits.

Treating the later information as the dependent variable, a multiple regression analysis was performed including the three visiting-related indexes as independent variables. Among other predictor variables included in the analyses were sex, years the child had been in care, ethnicity, whether there was parent-child contact in the parent's home, whether the placement was mandated by the court and whether the family had received any service during the past six months. It was also decided to include two measures from Miniproject No. 2, the Index of Viability of Natural Home as Resource for the Child and the Index of Mother's Capacity for Service Involvement. The latter decision was made possible by the considerable overlap between the samples included in both studies.

It is of interest to first take note of the zero-order correlations between the three visiting indexes and the dependent variable, i.e., the state of parental visiting about two years after the survey.

	r
Index of Parental Contact Frequency	.65
Index of Quality of Parental Contact	.59
Index of Sum of Problems	−.35

Obviously there is a fairly firm association between each of the indexes and the frequency of later parental visiting, particularly the first two. However, it should also be noted that the earlier CWIS visiting measure, a single item, shows an equally strong association with the dependent variable (r = .66). There are other significant predictors: the variable indicating that the child visits in the parent's home (r = .53), the years the child has been in care (r = −.33), and an indication that some service was rendered to the family during the prior six months (r = .42).

In addition there are fairly strong correlations between the two Miniproject No. 2 indexes and later visiting. The Index of the Viability of the Natural Parent Home as a Resource for the Child shows a correlation of .52 and the Index of the Mother's Capacity for Service Involvement is correlated fairly firmly with the later visiting measure (r = .45).

Table 61 shows the results of the multiple regression analysis in which we seek to account for the later variance in parental visiting by the information gathered in the survey some two years earlier. The analysis is restricted to children not freed for adoption and still in care after the passage of two years. The most important predictor, i.e., accounting for the most unique variance and having the highest beta weight (standardized regression coefficient) is the earlier CWIS visiting variable. The beta weight for this predictor is .41, and 13.1 percent of unique variance is accounted for.

Next most important as a predictor is the Index of Parent Contact Frequency, which shows a beta weight of .25 and accounts for 3.3 percent of unique variance. There are only two other variables that account for statistically significant percentages of variance: parent-child contact in the parent home (no/yes) and the Index of the Viability of the Natural Parent Home as a Resource for the Child. Their contributions are quite modest.

The two other indexes of parental visiting, Quality of Contact and Sum of Problems, make no special contribution to predicting later parental visiting in a child's career in foster care.

It should be noted that the multiple correlation for the set of predictors in Table 61 is .69, and 47 percent of variance is thus accounted for. It would appear within the resources of social planners analyzing caseloads of foster children to develop fairly strong predictions of the later course of cases with respect to visiting of children who are not able to be discharged to parents. If this is indeed the case, the planning task would be less formidable than has been the view until now.

Given the fact that the single CWIS visiting variable shows strength in predicting later CWIS information about parental visiting, question arises as to whether a richer amount of information such as contained in the Index of Parental Contact Frequency is required. Arguments about whether or not to adopt the six-item index would have to consider the following: (1) the high association between the two single-variable CWIS measures reflects to some extent the fact that using the same source and format for data collection tends to boost the level of association that one can get, an admitted plus; (2) a single-item measure, however, is ultimately not as solid a platform to predict future events as is a measure which is a composite of several items; (3) the six items included in the index are not particularly complex pieces of information and are relatively easy to gather.

Predicting the Discharge of Children to Their Parents

One of the important aims of collecting organized information in this area of practice is to bring the phenomenon of discharge of children to their parents under predictive control. This is one of the major purposes one would have in seeking to enrich the information system.

One way of examining the value of the information being tested is to examine its relation to actual discharge information such as we show in Table 62. We see that after the passage of 21 months—from March 31, 1977 to December 31, 1978—69.3 percent of the children not freed for adoption were still in care. This proportion was relatively the same for children we have assigned the label of "Visited" (68.8 percent) as opposed to those who did not experience a single in-person visit in the six-month reporting period, whom we call "Non-Visited" (70.8 percent).

The children in the Visited category show 16.4 percent who were discharged to their parents after the passage of 21 months. This compares with 2.0 percent of the Non-Visited group.

TABLE 61

PREDICTING FREQUENCY OF PARENTAL CONTACT WITH CHILDREN
OVER 21-MONTH PERIOD FOR CHILDREN NOT FREED FOR ADOPTION
(N = 489)[b]

Independent Variables[a]	Zero-order Correlation	Standardized Regression Coefficient	Percent Unique Variance Explained
1. Parental Contact (CWIS, 6/30/76)	.59***	.41***	13.1
2. Index Score (Parental Contact Frequency)	.55***	.25***	3.3
3. Parent-Child Contact in Parent Home	.42***	.12***	1.0
4. Index Score (Viability of Natural Parent Home as Resource for Child)	.41***	.10**	0.7
Multiple R		.69	
Multiple R^2		.47	

**p < .01   ***p < .001

Partial Correlations with Dependent Variable for Variables Not Entered:

Index Score (Quality of Parental Contact	-.01	Court Placement	.05
		Sex	.01
Index Score (Sum of Problems)	-.04	Family Service Received (CWIS, 6/30/76)	-.01
Years in Care	-.07	Index Score (Mother's Capacity for Service Involvement)	.06
Ethnicity-Black	.04		
Ethnicity-Hispanic	-.04		

[a] The independent variables reflect data collected within three months of March 31, 1977. The dependent variable covers the frequency of parental visiting on December 31, 1978 as reported to CWIS.

[b] Does not include 217 children no longer in care on December 31, 1978.

TABLE 62

STATUS OF CASES OF CHILDREN NOT FREED FOR ADOPTION 21 MONTHS
AFTER DATA COLLECTION FOR VISITED AND NON-VISITED CHILDREN[a]

Status of Cases	Visited Children No.	Visited Children %	Non-Visited Children No.	Non-Visited Children %	Total No.	Total %
Discharged to Parents or Relatives	91	16.4	3	2.0	94	13.3
Discharged To Self	60	10.8	30	19.9	90	12.7
Discharged to Adoption	1	0.2	1	0.7	2	0.3
Other (Military, Public Assistance, etc.)	21	3.8	10	6.6	31	4.4
Still in Care	382	68.8	107	70.8	489	69.3
Total	555	100.0	151	100.0	706[b]	100.0

[a] The time span covered by this analysis is from March 31, 1977, to December 31, 1978. Data were obtained from the CWIS data files of these dates. Categories of visited and non-visited children are based upon information at the beginning of the study as to whether child had at least one in-person contact with a family-related person (Visited) or no visit of any kind (Non-Visited) during the prior six months.

[b] One case omitted where follow-up information could not be ascertained.

Discharge to own responsibility upon reaching the age of majority accounts for 10.8 percent of the discharges of the children in the Visited category. Almost twice the proportion of the Non-Visited children, 19.9 percent, left care in this manner.

In Table 63, we show the results of a multiple regression of the discharge data, defining the dependent variable as children discharged to parents or relatives versus all other children.

Only two variables proved to be significant predictors: (1) the Index of the Viability of Natural Parent Home as Resource for the Child, and (2) years the child has been in care. The product-moment correlation between the index and the dependent variable is .37, indicating that a higher score is associated with a greater tendency to be discharged. Years in care is inversely related to discharge (r = −.28) showing that the children who have been in care for shorter periods are more likely to be returned to their parents.

The Index of Viability of Natural Parent Home as Resource for Child is the strongest predictor with a beta weight of .31 and 7.8 percent of unique variance accounted for in the discharge phenomenon. The variable of years in care is more modest in its overall contribution as a predictor; the beta weight is −.15 and the variable accounts for 1.9 percent of the variance in the dependent variable.

It should be noted that the overall amount of variance accounted for by the two significant predictors is modest, being only 16 percent. Of some importance here is the fact that the three visiting index measures do not emerge as significant in their contribution to understanding of the discharge phenomenon.

It may puzzle the reader to find that the visiting index scores do not emerge as significant predictors given our finding that children we gave the label of "Visited" showed 16.4 percent discharged to their parents or relatives over a two-year period compared to only 2.0 percent of those we assigned the label "Non-Visited." This can likely be explained by the fact that the three indexes measuring parental visiting behavior are significantly correlated with the Index of Viability of Natural Parent Home as a Resource for the Child:

	r
Index of Parental Contact Frequency	.62
Index of Quality of Parental Contact with Child	.64
Index of Sum of Problems Associated with Parental Visiting	−.32

We can also point out that the correlations between the three indexes measuring parental visiting and the dependent variable of discharge to parents, treated as a dichotomy, are also statistically significant:

	r
Index of Parental Contact Frequency	.31
Index of Quality of Parental Contact with Child	.31
Index of Sum of Problems Associated with Parental Visiting	−.15

It seems clear that in the regression analysis shown in Table 63, the Index of Viability of Natural Parent Home as a Resource for the Child, developed in Miniproject No. 2, has preempted the ability of the indexes measuring visiting behavior of the parents. They are largely redundant measures, i.e., strongly correlated, and each measure has some capacity to predict discharge.

Commentary

The effort to develop a parsimonious set of measures portraying the key dimensions of parental visiting has met with mixed success. It does seem clear that frequency and recency of contact are rather crucial dimensions of the visiting phenomenon that ought to be monitored. The six items included in the Index of Parental Contact Frequency have appeal because the information is obviously relevant.

The Index of Quality of Parental Contact also appears to tap important content but it is closely linked to the issue of whether or not parents visit and is therefore highly correlated with the first index.

It is the writer's view that the measurement task relative to visiting is very much linked to the need to define suitable measures for *appropriately defined populations*. Children in foster care can be divided according to three criteria: (1) freed for adoption vs. not freed for adoption; (2) parent in or out of the picture (deceased, institutionalized, or whereabouts unknown); and (3) parent visits vs. parent does not visit. The dimensionality of visiting appears highly influenced by the context within which the measurement effort takes place, i.e., how the subjects have been selected relative to the three criteria.

TABLE 63

PREDICTING THE DISCHARGE OF CHILDREN TO NATURAL PARENTS
OVER A 21-MONTH TIME SPAN FOR CHILDREN NOT FREED FOR ADOPTION
(N = 583)

Independent Variables[a]	Zero-order Correlation	Standardized Regression Coefficient	Percent Unique Variance Explained
1. Index Score (Viability of Natural Parent Home as Resource for Child)	.37***	.31***	7.8
2. Years in Care	-.28***	-.15***	1.9
Multiple R		.40	
Multiple R^2		.16	

***$p < .001$

Partial Correlations with Dependent Variable for Variables Not Entered:

Index Score (Parental Contact Frequency)	.05	Court Placement	.06
Parental Contact Frequency (CWIS 6/30/76)	.04	Sex	.01
Index Score (Quality of Parental Contact)	.04	Family Service Received (CWIS 6/30/76)	.04
Index Score (Sum of Problems)	-.02	Index Score (Mother's Capacity for Service Involvement)	.01
Ethnicity-Black	-.04		
Ethnicity-Hispanic	.00		

[a] The independent variables reflect data collected within three months of March 31, 1977. The discharge data were obtained from the CWIS data file as of December 31, 1978. Children who were discharged to their own responsibility, were adopted or were discharged to a mental institution are not included in this analysis.

7 Conclusions

We have engaged in a special effort to enrich the informational base underlying child welfare practice in the area of foster care services for children. The focus has been upon the visiting of the child by his parents and other family-related persons. What has started out as a seemingly simple subject has been shown to be phenomenologically complex. Establishing the frequency of family contact required documenting whether a child had had contact with his parents, grandparents, stepparents, uncles, aunts, cousins and siblings. We also included friends of the family in our survey. In addition to in-person contacts, we inquired into frequency of communication by telephone, letters, cards and gifts.

Our multidimensional look at the visiting behavior of the parents of foster children included an examination of the way they conducted themselves while in contact with their children and covered a variety of manifestations of disruptive and dysfunctional behaviors. We attempted to document the agency's perspectives about the significance of the visiting behavior of the parents, whether it reflected responsible role performance and, if markedly deficient or deviant, had any implications for recommending the termination of parental rights.

Our survey also focused upon the circumstantial factors that constituted barriers to visitation by the parents. The range of concerns covered parental illness, other child care responsibilities, lack of funds for travel or for the use of a babysitter, and distance from the child's placement setting. We inquired about the parent's lack of motivation to visit. We also explored the efforts made by the agency to stimulate parental visiting and inquired into the degree of responsiveness of the parents to such efforts.

We also report efforts to develop composite measures of central aspects of parental visiting and reveal mixed results in this regard. We emerge from this excursion with a sense of those data elements in our survey that ought to be included in an expanded data base. We also have no doubt that further exploration of the visiting phenomenon is warranted by the inconclusive nature of our results. Indeed, it occasions some surprise to grapple with what appears to be a relatively small subject such as parental visiting of foster children and to find that one has to travel on many byways in order to comprehend the explanatory factors at play.

Perspectives on Visiting

We have emphasized in Chapter 3 the need to gather information about in-person contacts a child might have with relatives and other non-related persons. For some children who are denied contact with both parents, a grandmother, sibling, uncle or family friend might be the only family-related person to show an interest in them. In a sense, the current CWIS/CCRS data system tends to present an exaggerated picture of the size of the group of children in foster care who have been abandoned by their families. This is due to the fact that data are only gathered about parental in-person contacts with the children.

In our sample of 1,238 children, 46.2 percent had an in-person contact with at least one parent during the prior six months, leaving 53.8 percent who would normally be classified as unvisited. If we restricted our attention to children not freed for adoption, the percent of non-visited children would drop to 31.1 percent. For the total sample the percentage of children seeing other persons, but not their parents, constitute 13.6 percent of the cases, reducing the proportion of unvisited children to 40.2 percent. For the children not freed for adoption, those seeing family-related persons other than their relatives constituted 14.3 percent of the sample; this reduced the proportion of unvisited children to 16.8 percent.

Aside from the issue of whether other relatives or friends compensate for the failure of parents to visit, there is quite a bit of visiting that supplements the in-person contacts of parents. Almost one child in three was reported to have had contact with a sibling and almost one child in ten saw a grandparent. Two children in ten saw uncles, aunts or cousins. Whether such visits serve to cement a child's ties to his own family is not completely known. On an intuitive basis, such contacts would appear to be a positive phenomenon, useful in reinforcing a child's sense of his own self-worth.

Our study has also examined the issue of whether contact is maintained with the foster children through use of the telephone, the mails and the sending of gifts. We found that while there was a fair amount of communication between parents and children through these channels, more often than not, it was the children already being visited who were the recipients of calls, letters and gifts. Almost

62 percent of the children being visited had at least one form of mail or telephone contact while this was true of only six percent of the unvisited children.

Despite the mitigation of the bleak picture held by many critics of the foster care system as involving the massive abandonment of children by their parents, there remains nevertheless a large group of children in our sample who have had absolutely no contact with a family-related person. About 40 percent of the sample had not had an in-person contact with anyone. While these abandoned children were mainly concentrated among the children slated to be adopted, 16 percent of the children not freed for adoption also were totally without family contact. An additional 14 percent had no contact with either of their parents. The situation of unvisited children in foster care remains worrisome although on a smaller scale than originally presented.

Time in Care as a Factor

It is important to keep in mind the fact that many of the children in our sample had been in care for an extended period of time. More than half had experienced foster care for at least six years. While other children had come and gone, they had remained as long-term wards of the system. They were the remnants of previously entered cohorts.

Our sample selection was based upon the criterion that children in care under one year were to be omitted. Our purpose was to study cases where the child's career in foster care was sufficiently extended to permit the social workers who were our informants to report on various aspects of family visiting behavior. We made this decision because in the CWIS reporting system which we helped to develop, it was typically reported that about 40 percent of the cases of children in care under two years were characterized as "not reported" with reference to total parental contact with the child; this compared with about four percent for children in care two to five years.

On March 31, 1977, the average length of time in care of 28,372 children in the New York City caseload was 5.17 years (standard deviation = 4.73 years).[25] The average number of years in care for our sample of 1,238 children was 7.22 years (standard deviation = 4.88 years). We thus see that the elimination of children in care under one year from eligibility for our sample had the consequence of boosting the mean length of time in care of the sample by two years.

It is the perspective of the writer that while a cross-sectional view of the visiting phenomenon for caseloads, as undertaken in the research reported here, is informative and should routinely be done, it does have a serious limitation. The cross-sectional approach to sampling garners cases that have been in foster care for a *long* time. The children have been in care so long that many of them have extremely attenuated relationships with their parents, if indeed there is a parent with whom they can relate.

We remind the reader that out of the 1,238 children in our sample, there was a report that the mother was deceased in 103 cases (8.3 percent), both parents' whereabouts were said to be unknown in 332 cases (26.8 percent), the mother had not been seen in two years in 132 cases (10.7 percent) and 38 mothers (3.1 percent) were in mental hospitals. A cross-sectional view of children in foster care thus presents an abysmal scene where parents are lost to their children in very large numbers.

It makes sense to emphasize the monitoring of the visiting frequency of parents and other family-related persons as soon as a child enters foster care. A strong case can be made for insisting upon an early definition of the adequacy of visiting and that this information should be kept in the forefront when planning goals are established for each case. Newly entering cohorts of children constitute the sectors of the caseload where timely intervention can be expected to have the most positive consequences in establishing permanency for children.

Developing composite measures of diverse aspects of parental visiting is easier to carry out and makes greater sense if the measurement work takes place at the time cases open and are continued over time. Data can then be aggregated for groupings of children who are members of the same cohort.

One of the difficulties we face in studying children who have been in care for very extended periods is that many of them are destined to be discharged to their own responsibility. In our study, 450 youngsters constituting 36.3 percent of the sample had this kind of discharge as the specified plan for the CWIS data file. For children in care six years or more, the plan of discharge to own responsibility accounted for 47.8 percent of the children.

While family visiting may well be in the best interest of the child's mental health—and something to be encouraged—it takes on different significance if it is clear that the child is destined to return home. Visiting in the interest of eventually returning the child to his home is a very different phenomenon from that which takes place when it is known that the parents will never restore the child to his family home.

Reliability and Validity Considerations

Much of the information gathered in our special survey is fairly factual in nature. Thus, a number of the questions in our survey would not appear to require complex judgments on the part of social workers reporting on cases. The following types of questions could be subsumed under this category: When did the mother last see the child? The father? What other family-related persons have seen the child in the last six months? Is the mother alive? Is her whereabouts known? Has the agency offered specific help to the parents to facilitate visiting? In what other ways has the agency communicated with the parents about the need to visit?

There are also questions in our survey which obviously call for more complex judgments on the part of social workers. For example: Has the mother been responsible in her visiting behavior? Has her behavior been such that termination of parental rights ought to be considered? Is the parent well related to the child when visiting? Does the child appear to enjoy contact with the parents? What is the child's reaction to the parent's failure to visit? And so forth.

Obviously, the gathering of data of this kind as a routine activity in a computerized information system such as CWIS/CCRS has outer limits as to the kind of qualitative assessments that can be demanded of social workers. The kinds of qualitative ratings included in our survey covered what we considered observable parental behavior relative to the visiting phenomenon. They represent the kind of behaviors already routinely being recorded in case records by social workers.

The use of multiple-item composite indexes dealing with quantity and quality of visiting does appear to offer some assurance of internal reliability. Future efforts will be required to test inter-rater reliability and other aspects of the reliability of the ratings. It should be emphasized, however, that the gathering of qualitative information about the nature of family visiting for a management information system in child welfare is not the same phenomenon as creating a psychometric test. The information is not intended to classify persons. Much of its value will be exploited in aggregated form to characterize the situation of classes of children. The purposes eventually served by such organization of data are likely to be in the area of program management, planning and evaluation. The data might well have the function of generating concern about classes of cases but the consequence of this may be to generate an audit of cases by those who have an oversight interest or monitoring responsibility.

The data are not intended to have any consequence on the level of the individual case different from what a social worker would record in the way of case narrative. This does not mean, however, that the composite measures do not need to be probed periodically, for their predictive validity as well as in the context of theory-testing situations in which their construct validity might be explored.

Program Directions to Further Family-Child Contact

The purpose of the research reported here is to provide guidance for the expansion of the data base used in tracking children in foster care. However, it is not possible to examine more than 1,200 cases, as we have here, without conjuring with the visiting phenomena in a substantive way that has implications for possible modification of the manner in which services for foster children are organized and delivered. The following speculative thoughts are offered out of the sense of the need to create innovations in meeting the challenge of the dreadful condition that covers the foster care system, the blight of masses of totally abandoned children.

1. When a child first comes into foster care, the visiting of parents and significant others should be carefully monitored. Very disciplined systems for recording the frequency of visitation should be developed—the visiting should be documented and known. Perhaps this requires a diary to be kept by foster parents or institutional personnel of all in-person contacts between the child and his family. Consider the fact that for 25 to 40 percent of the children in care under two years, the social workers filling out the CWIS forms were unable to report the frequency of visitation.

2. Agencies might consider the conduct of educational campaigns among parents and staff. Materials graphically portraying the significance of family contact for the child in the form of agency posters, pamphlets and film strips might be prepared in order to communicate the agency's commitment to further family-child contact.

3. Various kinds of expression of agency concern when parents fail to visit ought to be formulated and tested for effectiveness in a series of experiments. An experiment might include one group where parents received telegrams when they failed to visit, another group might receive a communication from the court, etc.

4. Passive agency acceptance of parental drop-out should be considered violation of one of the criteria employed in utilization review procedures to monitor performance and lead to disciplinary action against the agency.

5. Agencies might experiment with the use of agency-owned "weekend apartments" for permitting child and family to spend occasional short periods together experiencing the process of living together.

Notes

1. David Fanshel and Eugene B. Shinn, *Children in Foster Care: A Longitudinal Investigation* (New York: Columbia University Press, 1978), pp. 85-111.

2. *Ibid.*, pp. 88-89.

3. *Ibid.*, pp. 486-90.

4. David Fanshel, "Parental Visiting of Foster Children: A Computerized Study," *Social Work Research and Abstracts*, Vol. 13, No. 3 (Fall 1977), pp. 2-10.

5. See David Fanshel and John F. Grundy, *Special Report Series* (Quarterly Reports issued by CWIS and CCRS).

6. See "Policy Statement on Parental Visiting," by Carol J. Parry, Assistant Commissioner, New York City Department of Social Services, Special Services for Children, September 16, 1975.

7. David Fanshel and John F. Grundy, *op. cit.*, March 31, 1979, Series A, p. 6.

8. Close to 100 agencies and subdivisions of agencies participating in the CWIS systems were approached about participating in a series of six "mini-projects" designed to test data modules for possible later inclusion in the CWIS system. In addition to the three mini-projects for which reports have been issued, future efforts were to include: (1) follow-up inquiries to explain incongruous information submitted by the agencies about children (e.g., that the discharge objective for an infant was "discharge to own responsibility"), (2) a parent description module, and (3) a child description module. At the present time, there are no plans to execute these projects.

9. Leonard S. Kogan, "Validity, Reliability, and Related Considerations," in *Use of Judgments as Data in Social Work Research*, ed. by Ann W. Shyne (New York: National Association of Social Workers, 1959), p. 69.

10. The CWIS *Special Report Series* (Fanshel/Grundy) for March 31, 1977 shows that for the entire New York City caseload of children not freed for adoption (N = 25,489) 48.3 percent were reported to have received no visiting from either parent and 18.8 percent of the cases were such that visiting information was not reported.

11. The CWIS *Special Report Series* (Fanshel/Grundy) for March 31, 1977 shows a current mean age of 28,644 children in the system, representing the New York City foster care caseload, as 11.57 years (standard deviation = 11.57). The mean age at entry for these children was 6.38 years (standard deviation = 5.29).

12. The mean years in care for the entire New York City caseload on March 31, 1977 was 5.17 years (standard deviation = 4.73). source: CWIS *Special Report Series, Ibid*.

13. David Fanshel, "Parental Visiting of Foster Children," *Social Work Research and Abstracts*, 13: 3 (Fall, 1977), pp. 2-10.

14. Many of the participating agencies shown in Table 1 participated in both Miniprojects No. 1 and 2.

15. The group has not been differentiated to reflect the frequency of contact for children not freed for adoption where parental contact is most important as opposed to children slated for adoption. If the latter were removed, the proportion of children not being seen by their parents would be reduced significantly.

16. David Fanshel and Eugene B. Shinn, *Children in Foster Care: A Longitudinal Investigation, op. cit.*, pp. 123-30.

17. *Ibid.*, pp. 486-90.

18. In the expansion of the data base of the statewide Child Care Review Service (CCRS), which will replace CWIS in data gathering about the foster care phenomenon, it will be possible to include evidence of contacts with foster children by related and non-related persons in addition to the parents. Such revisions are expected to be in place statewide some time in 1982.

19. Joseph Goldstein, Anna Freud and Albert J. Solnit, *Beyond the Best Interests of the Child* (New York: The Free Press, 1973).

20. These cases were rated as satisfactory even though the mother had not visited during the past six months.

21. David Fanshel and Eugene B. Shinn, *Children in Foster Care: A Longitudinal Investigation, op. cit.*

22. Joseph Goldstein, et al., *Beyond the Best Interests of the Child, op. cit.*

23. "Visited" children are those who have received at least one visit from a family relative or friend during the six-month reporting period; "non-visited" children received no visits at all.

24. The items are removed from the total scores to avoid autocorrelation.

25. David Fanshel and John F. Grundy, *CWIS Special Report Series*, March 31, 1977 (New York: Child Welfare Information Services, March 31, 1977), Series C, Table 3.

Appendix

Table A-1   Respondents' Knowledge of the Child's Mother According to Years Child Has Been in Care

Table A-2   Respondents' Knowledge of the Child's Father According to Years Child Has Been in Care

Table A-3   Reports of Social Workers About Difficulty in Providing Requested Data According to Years in Care

TABLE A-1

RESPONDENTS' KNOWLEDGE OF THE CHILD'S MOTHER
ACCORDING TO YEARS CHILD HAS BEEN IN CARE*

Degree to Which Respondent Knows Mother	Under Two Years	Two to Five Years	Six Years or More	Total
	(percentaged)			
Very Well	17.4	18.9	6.9	12.3
Fairly Well	26.4	24.8	12.5	18.5
Slightly	16.9	12.5	9.6	11.7
Hardly At All	12.4	12.5	11.4	11.9
Not At All	19.4	25.0	38.6	31.3
Not Relevant[a]	7.5	6.4	21.0	14.3
Percent Total	16.4 (201)	30.7 (376)	52.9 (648)	100.0 (1225)

*The respondents were asked: "How well do you feel you know the mother of the child?"

[a] Respondents felt they could not provide meaningful information because of total parental absence.

TABLE A-2

RESPONDENTS' KNOWLEDGE OF THE CHILD'S FATHER
ACCORDING TO YEARS CHILD HAS BEEN IN CARE*

Degree to Which Respondent Knows Father	Under Two Years	Two to Five Years	Six Years or More	Total
	(percentaged)			
Very Well	4.5	5.1	1.5	3.1
Fairly Well	8.0	9.8	4.5	6.7
Slightly	8.0	7.7	3.7	5.6
Hardly At All	11.9	16.9	8.5	9.8
Not At All	57.6	58.2	60.2	59.2
Not Relevant[a]	10.0	8.3	21.6	15.6
Percent Total	16.4 (201)	30.7 (376)	52.9 (648)	100.0 (1225)

*The respondents were asked: "How well do you feel you know the father of the child?"

[a] Respondents felt they could not provide meaningful information because of total parental absence.

TABLE A-3

REPORTS OF SOCIAL WORKERS ABOUT DIFFICULTY
IN PROVIDING REQUESTED DATA ACCORDING TO YEARS IN CARE*

Degree of Difficulty	Under Two Years	Two to Five Years	Six Years or More	Total
	(percentaged)			
Very Difficult	3.5	4.3	4.8	4.4
Somewhat Difficult	26.4	22.6	15.1	19.3
Quite Easy	47.2	49.2	40.3	44.1
Very Easy	16.4	19.7	22.5	20.7
Not Applicable[a]	6.5	4.3	17.3	11.5
Percent Total	16.4 (201)	30.7 (376)	52.9 (648)	100.0 (1225)

*The respondents were asked: "How difficult was it for you to fill out this form?"

[a] Respondents felt they could not provide meaningful information because of total parental absence.

The Questionnaire

COLUMBIA UNIVERSITY SCHOOL OF SOCIAL WORK

Research and Demonstration Center
622 West 113 Street • New York, N.Y. 10025

EXPANDED DATA BASE FOR CHILD WELFARE

To Child Welfare Social Worker:

The New York State Department of Social Services has granted funds to Columbia University to conduct research designed to expand the data base of Child Welfare Information Services (CWIS). Your agency has agreed to participate in this research on a limited sample of the agency's children. Other agencies are also participating in this effort. The results of this work will make it possible to determine what kind of information can expeditiously be gathered to add to our knowledge about children in foster care. The aim of this effort is to improve service to children.

Your cooperation in filling out the enclosed form will facilitate our study greatly. For some of the items, it may be necessary to make an estimate based upon your most informed judgment. Please try to answer every item. You will later be contacted for your advice about the content of items and their wording. If you have any doubt about a reply, place a question mark next to the item.

The material you provide will be treated in the strictest confidence. Please return the form to _____who has been designated as your agency's contact person with our project.

Thank you very much for your help in this matter.

Sincerely yours,

David Fanshel, D.S.W.
Director
Research and Demonstration Center

CONFIDENTIAL

COLUMBIA UNIVERSITY SCHOOL OF SOCIAL WORK
Research and Demonstration Center
622 West 113 Street
New York, New York 10025

Trial Form on Parental Visiting of Foster Children

      This is a pre-test version of an information form about children in foster care. The form is designed to secure facts about the frequency and nature of parental contact with their children in care from the social worker who has responsibility for the case. The form is being tested for Child Welfare Information Services (CWIS). Your cooperation in filling out the form will make it possible to learn more about the kind of information that needs to be gathered for children in foster care in order to improve the delivery of service. Your care in filling out the form will be appreciated. The data will be kept confidential and a report will be made to your agency about the findings.

ID Name_____

SSC Number_____
            1-9/

Worker Code_____

Agency_____
         12-14/

[Card]: 10-11/(01)   (MP 1)

Q1. <u>Has the child had any visitors in the past six months?</u>   15/

        Yes   ___(1)

        No*   ___(2)

        Unknown* ___(3)

    *If <u>No</u> or <u>Unknown</u>, Skip to Q3.

Q2. <u>What persons have seen the child during the past six months (or since the child entered care if duration of placement is less than six months)?</u> (Check *all that apply*.)

	Yes (1)	No (2)	Unknown (3)	
a. Mother	___	___	___	16/
b. Father	___	___	___	17/
c. Stepmother	___	___	___	18/
d. Stepfather	___	___	___	19/
e. Sibling(s)	___	___	___	20/
f. Maternal grandmother	___	___	___	21/
g. Maternal grandfather	___	___	___	22/
h. Paternal grandmother	___	___	___	23/
i. Paternal grandfather	___	___	___	24/
j. Other relative(s)	___	___	___	25/
k. Other non-related person	___	___	___	26/

Q3. A. <u>Is the child free for adoption?</u>   27/

        Yes   ___(1)

        No, but action is being taken to free child ___(2)

        No*   ___(3)

        Unknown* ___(4)

        *If <u>No</u> or <u>Unknown</u>, Skip to Q4.

   B. <u>Will parent(s) continue to be involved with the child?</u>   28/

        Yes, will continue contact after adoption ___(1)

        Yes, until adoption, but not after ___(2)

        No* ___(3)

        Unknown ___(4)

        *If <u>No</u>, Skip to Q22.

Q4. <u>When was the last in-person contact between the parent(s) and other relatives and the child?</u> (*Check the most recent occasion.*)

	Mother 29-30/	Father 31-32/	Other Adult Relative 33-34/	Sibling 35-36/
Within past month	(1)	(1)	(1)	(1)
Within past 2-3 months	(2)	(2)	(2)	(2)
Within past 6 months	(3)	(3)	(3)	(3)
Within past year	(4)	(4)	(4)	(4)
Within past 2 years	(5)	(5)	(5)	(5)
Within past 3 years	(6)	(6)	(6)	(6)
Within past 4 years	(7)	(7)	(7)	(7)
Within past 5 years	(8)	(8)	(8)	(8)
Within past 6-10 years	(9)	(9)	(9)	(9)
More than 10 years ago	(10)	(10)	(10)	(10)
No contacts since birth of child	(11)	(11)	(11)	(11)
Other _____	(12)	(12)	(12)	(12)
Unknown	(13)	(13)	(13)	(13)
Not applicable	(14)	(14)	(14)	(14)

Q5. Has there been any contact during the past six months between parents and child other than through in-person visits? (Check for each category.)

MOTHER	None (1)	Occa- sional (2)	Quite a Few (3)	Un- known (4)	
a. Telephone calls	___	___	___	___	37/
b. Letters	___	___	___	___	38/
c. Cards (holidays and birthdays)	___	___	___	___	39/
d. Gifts	___	___	___	___	40/
e. Other (Specify) _____	___	___	___	___	41/

FATHER	None (1)	Occa- sional (2)	Quite a Few (3)	Un- known (4)	
a. Telephone calls	___	___	___	___	42/
b. Letters	___	___	___	___	43/
c. Cards (holidays and birthdays)	___	___	___	___	44/
d. Gifts	___	___	___	___	45/
e. Other (Specify) _____	___	___	___	___	46/

Q6. **How would you characterize the parent's current tendency to visit the child in care?** (Check *response that applies*.)

	Mother 47/	Father 48/
Never visits	(1)	(1)
Visits rarely (once a year or less)	(2)	(2)
Visits infrequently (once in 6 months or less)	(3)	(3)
Visits occasionally (once in 4 to 6 months)	(4)	(4)
Visits fairly regularly (once in 1 to 3 months)	(5)	(5)
Visits regularly (at least twice a month)	(6)	(6)
Visits often (at least once a week)	(7)	(7)
Other _____ _____	(8)	(8)
Unknown	(9)	(9)

Q7. **Where does contact between parent and child tend to take place?** (*Respond to each item.*)

MOTHER	Never (1)	Sometimes (2)	Often (3)	Always (4)	Not Applicable (5)	Unknown (6)	
a. Child visits parent's home	___	___	___	___	___	___	49/
b. Mother visits in foster home	___	___	___	___	___	___	50/
c. Mother visits in institution	___	___	___	___	___	___	51/
d. Mother visits in agency office	___	___	___	___	___	___	52/
e. Mother picks up child and goes elsewhere	___	___	___	___	___	___	53/
f. Other_____ _____	___	___	___	___	___	___	54/

FATHER	Never (1)	Sometimes (2)	Often (3)	Always (4)	Not Applicable (5)	Unknown (6)	
a. Child visits parent's home	___	___	___	___	___	___	55/
b. Father visits in foster home	___	___	___	___	___	___	56/
c. Father visits in institution	___	___	___	___	___	___	57/
d. Father visits in agency office	___	___	___	___	___	___	58/
e. Father picks up child and goes elsewhere	___	___	___	___	___	___	59/
f. Other_____ _____	___	___	___	___	___	___	60/

Q8. **Has the frequency of parental contact changed since the child entered care?** (Check appropriate category.)

	Mother 61/	Father 62/
Major decline in contact with child	(1)	(1)
Moderate decline in contact with child	(2)	(2)
Slight decline in contact with child	(3)	(3)
No change in contact with child	(4)	(4)
Slight increase in contact with child	(5)	(5)
Moderate increase in contact with child	(6)	(6)
Major increase in contact with child	(7)	(7)
Other: Mother_____ _____	(8)	
Father_____ _____		(8)
Unknown	(9)	(9)

Q9 A. How has the child typically reacted to the contact with the parent(s)? (Check appropriate response.)

	Mother 63/	Father 64/
Appears to enjoy visits	(1)	(1)
Initially shy, then warms up	(2)	(2)
Shows no overt reaction	(3)	(3)
Appears cautious, uncomfortable, or embarrassed	(4)	(4)
Appears anxious or upset	(5)	(5)
Reactions tend to vary	(6)	(6)
Not applicable, parent does not visit* (Answer Q9 B.)	(7)	(7)
Other (Specify) _____	(8)	(8)
Unknown	(9)	(9)

*Q9 B. If parent does not visit, please describe child's overt reaction to parent's failure to visit:

	Mother 65/	Father 66/
Strong negative reaction	(1)	(1)
Moderate negative reaction	(2)	(2)
Mild negative reaction	(3)	(3)
No reaction	(4)	(4)
Appears to prefer that parent not visit	(5)	(5)
Other (Specify) _____	(6)	(6)
Unknown	(7)	(7)

Q10. <u>Please indicate if any of the following problems have been manifested in the past six months in connection with the visiting of parents.</u> (Check *all* responses that apply.)

	Mother (1)	Father (2)	Both (3)	Neither (4)	
a. Not applicable, parent does not visit	___	___	___	___	67/
b. No apparent problems	___	___	___	___	68/
c. Relates to child in superficial manner	___	___	___	___	69/
d. Visits are too brief	___	___	___	___	70/
e. Creates disturbance	___	___	___	___	71/
f. Appears intoxicated or under influence of drugs	___	___	___	___	72/
g. Brings inappropriate strangers	___	___	___	___	73/
h. Behavior appears bizarre or seriously divergent from normal	___	___	___	___	74/
i. Visits at inappropriate times	___	___	___	___	75/

j. Other: *Mother*_____

_____ ___

*Father*_____

_____ ___ ___ ___ 76/

Q11. <u>We are interested in your impression of the quality of the parent(s)' contact during visiting occasions. Would you say that the parent appears well-related to the child during visits?</u>

	Mother 77/	Father 78/
Very much so	(1)	(1)
Somewhat	(2)	(2)
Not at all	(3)	(3)
Not applicable (does not visit)	(4)	(4)
Other	(5)	(5)
Unknown	(6)	(6)

Q12. <u>Does the parent make an effort to make the contact an enjoyable occasion for the child?</u>

	Mother 79/	Father 80/
Very much so	(1)	(1)
Somewhat	(2)	(2)
Not at all	(3)	(3)
Not applicable (does not visit)	(4)	(4)
Other	(5)	(5)
Unknown	(6)	(6)

[Card]: 10-11/(02)

Q13. Please indicate if any of the following factors have served to lower the frequency of _parental visiting_. _(Check appropriate category for each item.)_

	MOTHER					FATHER			
	Very much (1)	Some-what (2)	Hardly/ Not At All (3)	Un-known (4)		Very Much (1)	Some-what (2)	Hardly/ Not At All (3)	Un-known (4)
a. Other child care responsibilities	___	___	___	___ 12/		___	___	___	___ 22/
b. Employment hours	___	___	___	___ 13/		___	___	___	___ 23/
c. Financial limitations (lack of funds for carfare, babysitter)	___	___	___	___ 14/		___	___	___	___ 24/
d. Distance from child's placement address	___	___	___	___ 15/		___	___	___	___ 25/
e. Physical illness	___	___	___	___ 16/		___	___	___	___ 26/
f. Mental illness	___	___	___	___ 17/		___	___	___	___ 27/
g. Mental retardation	___	___	___	___ 18/		___	___	___	___ 28/
h. Other incapacity (_Specify_) _____	___	___	___	___ 19/		___	___	___	___ 29/
i. Low motivation (lack of re-latedness to child)	___	___	___	___ 20/		___	___	___	___ 30/
j. Other (_Specify_) _____	___	___	___	___ 21/		___	___	___	___ 31/

Q14. **Have any of the following factors been operating to explain the lack of contact between parent and child?** (Check *all that apply.*)

	Mother (1)	Father (2)	Both (3)	Neither (4)	
a. Identity of parent is unknown	___	___	___	___	32/
b. Has not acknowledged paternity	X X X	___	X X	X X	33/
c. Has never lived with child	___	___	___	___	34/
d. Has surrendered child	___	___	___	___	35/
e. Has expressed intention of surrendering child	___	___	___	___	36/
f. Parent lives out of state* (*Answer Q14 j.*)	___	___	___	___	37/
g. Parent's whereabouts are unknown** (*Answer Q14 k.*)	___	___	___	___	38/
h. Is institutionalized (*Type of institution*):	___	___	___	___	39/

   Mother _____

   Father _____

i. Other (*Specify*) _____

   _____ ___ ___ ___ ___ 40/

*j. Where does parent live? _____ 41-42/

**k. For how long a period have whereabouts been unknown? 43-44/
(*Please give the information in years and months*):

   Mother _____

   Father _____

Q15. How would you characterize the parent's current visiting behavior in meeting the needs of the child? (Check response that applies.)

	Mother 45/	Father 46/
Parent has been responsible in visiting child	(1)	(1)
Parent has been somewhat irresponsible in visiting child	(2)	(2)
Parent has been irresponsible in visiting child	(3)	(3)
Not applicable, circumstances do not permit parent to visit	(4)	(4)
Other (Specify) _____ _____	(5)	(5)
Unknown	(6)	(6)

Q16 A. Does parent's quality of visiting behavior or failure to visit have implications for termination of parent's rights? (Check response that applies.)

	Mother 47/	Father 48/
No, quality of visiting satisfactory (Skip to Q17.)	(1)	(1)
Yes, termination of rights should be considered on grounds of failure to visit	(2)	(2)
Somewhat, termination of parental rights should be considered if visiting behavior cannot be corrected	(3)	(3)
No, because of circumstantial factors effecting visiting, termination of parental rights need not be considered	(4)	(4)
Other (Specify) _____ _____	(5)	(5)
Unknown	(6)	(6)

Q16 B. Describe basis for characterization in Q16 A:

Mother: _____ 49-50/
_____

Father: _____ 51-52/
_____

Q17. **Has the agency attempted to increase parental visiting of the child in care through any of the following measures?** (Check *all* that apply.)

	Mother Only (1)	Father Only (2)	Both (3)	Neither (4)	
a. Not applicable, parent is not permitted to visit (*Skip to* Q20.)	_____	_____	_____	_____	53/
b. Not applicable, parent visits frequently, no need to increase visiting	_____	_____	_____	_____	54/
c. Advising the parent of the child's need for such visiting	_____	_____	_____	_____	55/
d. Providing funds to pay for travel costs	_____	_____	_____	_____	56/
e. Providing funds to pay for babysitter arrangements for other children	_____	_____	_____	_____	57/
f. Other forms of encouragement of visiting (*Specify*) _____ _____ _____	_____	_____	_____	_____	58/

Q18 A. <u>Please characterize the degree to which the agency has attempted to influence parent(s) to visit during the past six months.</u> (*Check appropriate responses.*)

	Mother 59/	Father 60/
Parent visits, no special effort required	(1)	(1)
Major effort to get parent to visit	(2)	(2)
Moderate effort to get parent to visit	(3)	(3)
Slight effort to get parent to visit* (*Answer* Q18 B.)	(4)	(4)
No effort to get parent to visit* (*Answer* Q18 B.)	(5)	(5)
Other (*Specify*) _____	(6)	(6)
Unknown	(7)	(7)

*Q18 B. <u>Are there any circumstances which have deterred the agency from exerting greater effort?</u>

Mother: _____

_____ 61-62/

Father: _____

_____ 63-64/

Q19. How has the parent responded to agency efforts to increase visiting during the past six months? (Check appropriate responses.)

	Mother 65/	Father 66/
Not applicable, no agency effort to increase visiting	(1)	(1)
Essentially non-responsive, visiting not influenced	(2)	(2)
Somewhat responsive, visiting slightly improved	(3)	(3)
Responsive, visiting improved	(4)	(4)
Other (Specify) _____ _____	(5)	(5)
Unknown	(6)	(6)

Q20 A. <u>Has the agency ever found it necessary to restrict or prohibit a parent from having contact with the child?</u> (*Check response that applies.*)

	Mother 67/	Father 68/
No, contact never restricted or prohibited (*Skip to* Q21.)	(1)	(1)
Yes, in past but not now*	(2)	(2)
Yes, contact now restricted*	(3)	(3)
Yes, contact now prohibited*	(4)	(4)
Other _____	(5)	(5)
Unknown	(6)	(6)

*Q20 B. <u>If visiting ever restricted or prohibited, please give details (including whether Court has issued directives restricting or modifying visiting opportunities of parents)</u>: 69-70/

_____
_____
_____
_____
_____

Q21 A. <u>Has the agency found it necessary to supervise the parent's in-person visits with the child?</u>
(*Check response that applies.*)

	Mother 71/	Father 72/
Yes, supervision required* (*Answer* Q21 B.)	(1)	(1)
No, supervision not required	(2)	(2)
Other (*Specify*) _____ _____ _____	(3)	(3)

*Q21 B. <u>Give reasons for supervision:</u> 73-74/

_____
_____
_____
_____

Q22. <u>Is there any information about the nature of service contacts with the parent(s) which you deem significant and has not been covered by the information already provided?</u>   75-76/

_____
_____
_____
_____
_____
_____
_____
_____

Q23 A. <u>How difficult was it for you to fill out this form?</u>   77/

    Very difficult*
    (Answer Q23 B.)   (1)

    Somewhat difficult*
    (Answer Q23 B.)   (2)

    Quite easy   (3)

    Very easy   (4)

*Q23 B. <u>What was the source of difficulty?</u>   78-79/

_____
_____
_____
_____
_____

Name of Rater_____ Telephone_____

Agency Position_____ 12-13/

Highest Professional Degree: 14/

    High school graduate (1)
    Some college (2)
    BSW (3)
    Other Bachelor's degree (4)
    MSW (5)
    Other Master's degree (6)
    DSW or Ph.D. in social work (7)
    Other doctoral degree (8)
    Other (9)

Years with Agency_____ 15-16/

What is the size of your caseload?

    Number of children_____ 17-18/
    Number of families_____ 19-20/

How well do you feel you know the MOTHER of the child? 21/

    Very well (1)
    Fairly well (2)
    Slightly (3)
    Hardly at all (4)
    Other (Specify)_____ (5)

How well do you feel you know the FATHER of the child? 22/

    Very well (1)
    Fairly well (2)
    Slightly (3)
    Hardly at all (4)
    Other (Specify)_____ (5)

II The Availability and Capacities for Service Involvement of Parents of Foster Children

CONTENTS

1 Service to Parents of Foster Children 135
Background 135
Sampling Methodology 135
The Questionnaire 136

2 Availability of Natural Parents for Service Contacts 138
Availability of Parents for Service Contacts 138
Characteristics of the Surveyed Cases 138
Frequency of Service Contacts 141

3 Further Perspectives on Parental Service Needs and Service Contacts 144
Need for Counseling 144
Parental Circumstances That Hinder Service Contacts 144
Family Problems or Conditions Serving to Keep Children in Care 148
Parental Behavior in the Client Role 151
Referrals to Other Agencies 151

4 Prospects for Discharge 159
Prospect for Return 159
Support or Opposition to Returning Child to Parents 162

5 Creation and Analysis of Service-Related Index Scores 164
Mother's Capacity for Service Involvement 164
Viability of Natural Parent Home 164
"Understanding" the Index Scores 171
An Attempt at Predictive Validation of the Index Scores: An Analysis of Discharge 171
Who Shall Be Served? 175

6 Summary of Findings and Implications 184
Major Findings Summarized 184
Discussion of Results of the Research 185
Service Tasks in Perspective 186
A Word of Caution 186
How Good Are the Data? 186
Feasibility of Routinized Data Collection 187
Scanning Caseloads: A Tool for Better Management of the Social Services 187

Notes 189

The Questionnaire 191

LIST OF TABLES

Table

1. Agencies Participating in Mini-Projects 1 and 2: Total Questionnaires Sent and Returned 137
2. Grouping of Parents According to Availability for Service Involvement. 139
3. Characteristics of Sample According to Availability of Parents for Service Involvement 140
4. Service Contact Information According to Availability of Parents for Service Involvement 142
5. Extent to Which Parents Require Counseling About Resumption of Care of Children According to Their Availability for Service Involvement 145
6. Circumstances Tending to Lower Frequency of Parental Service Contacts According to the Availability of Parents for Service Involvement 146
7. Problems or Conditions of Mothers of Children in Care Identified as Causal Factors Related to Keeping the Child in Foster Care 149
8. Reported Problems in Establishing Service Contacts with Parents. 152
9. Nature of Referral Needs for Major Problems or Conditions Affecting Mother. 155
10. Agency Discharge Plan for Child According to Availability of Parents for Service Involvement 160
11. Agency Perspectives on Potentiality of Child's Return Home According to Availability of Parents for Service Involvement. 161
12. Agency's Attitude Toward Possibility of Parent Taking Child Home According to Availability of Parents for Service Involvement. 163
13. Index of Mother's Capacity for Service Involvement. 165
14. Index of Viability of Natural Parent Home as Resource for Child (Mother Index) 168
15. Relation of Selected Independent Variables to Index of Mother's Capacity for Service Involvement . . . 172
16. Relation of Selected Independent Variables to Index of Viability of Natural Parent Home as Resource for Child. 173
17. Status of Subjects at Follow-up (June 30, 1978) According to Availability of Parents 174
18. Predicting the Discharge of Children to Natural Parents Over A Two-Year Time Span 176
19. Mean Scores on Index of Natural Parent's Home as a Resource for the Child According to Availability of Mothers and Discharge Status of Children on June 30, 1978. 177
20. Delivery of Services to Families 178
21. Family Services Provided as of June 30, 1978 by Current Location of Children According to Availability of Parents as of June 30, 1976. 181
22. Predicting the Delivery of Service to Families of Children Over a Two-Year Time Span 183
23. Reports of Social Workers About Difficulty in Providing the Requested Data According to the Availability of Parents for Service Involvement 188

1 Service to Parents of Foster Children

Background

Child welfare agencies responsible for the placement of children in foster homes and institutions have repeatedly been criticized for their failure to provide service to the parents of their wards. The problem has been identified as one that must be resolved if a greater measure of "permanency" for children separated from their parents is to be achieved. It must be recognized, however, that these parents present something of a puzzle for social planners and program managers. Taking on the task of serving them may be more complicated than it would seem at first glance. While it has been shown that the natural parents of foster children are the most likely resource for securing the discharge of the children from care, there are also very substantial numbers of parents who seem "out of it"; the children of such parents appear locked into foster placements on a permanent basis.[1]

Very little systematic attention has been given to the matter of determining what proportion of caseloads of foster children involve natural parents who have the potential for resuming responsibility for the care of their children and who can be worked with towards the goal of accomplishing a family reunion. The need for well-organized information in this area is readily apparent. It would otherwise be impossible to establish the parameters of service needs and to effectively manage the system. Such information is essential for developing appropriate program goals and for promulgating social policies and legislation designed to ameliorate the problems of children in foster care.

The report presented here is based upon data gathered from agencies providing foster care to children in New York City that agreed to participate in a project designed to augment the data normally gathered by Child Welfare Information Services (CWIS). This computerized management information system was established in New York City in 1973 and became fully operational in 1975. It has already become recognized as an important feature of child welfare service delivery in New York City.[2] CWIS has been identified by HHS as a most promising innovation in service delivery and is a likely prototype for other human services systems throughout the United States that have not yet been able to develop computerized informational systems.

The data to be discussed here concern current experiences and perspectives of child welfare agencies with respect to the rendering of service to parents. The purpose of such service is to restore the child's own home as a viable resource in lieu of remaining in foster care. The investigation is one of three "mini-projects" designed by the writer to test new data modules for potential inclusion in a computerized system such as CWIS.[3] The assumption underlying the study is that if the trial gathering of such data shows positive results in the form of useful information, and can easily be provided by the agencies, their incorporation in an expanded data base can be recommended.

Sampling Methodology

Agencies included in the CWIS system were approached about their willingness to be included in each of six proposed mini-projects. Cooperation with respect to the effort described here was received from 26 direct service agencies of which 22 were private agencies and four were direct care borough offices of New York City's Social Service Department (Human Resources Administration) operating under its child care division (Special Services for Children).[4]

Since agencies volunteered to participate in one or more projects according to their interests and work pressures at the time they were approached—and were not selected on a random basis—we can make no strong claim about the representativeness of the cases for which we have data. However, this limitation does not gainsay the fact that a wide range of agency types varying by size, religious auspice and child populations served were included in the study. Our sense is that these agencies are not markedly different in the kinds of service programs they run from the agencies not participating in the study.

The sampling procedure developed for the study was designed to vary the number of cases sampled from each agency according to the size of the child population served. The largest agencies were asked to fill out forms for as many as 105 cases while the smaller agencies had samples as low as 24. An interval selection procedure was used in sampling each agency's file in the computerized system maintained by CWIS. The total number of children cared for was divided by the number of cases desired for the agency sample, providing a basis for selecting every nth case from the agency's CWIS file for June 30, 1976.[5] The sample was limited to one sibling per family unit.

In Table 1, we show the agencies that participated in the first two "mini-projects." For the study which concerns us here, 2,174 research forms were sent to the 26 participating agencies and 2,114 were returned (97.2 percent). It was determined that 690 (32.6 percent) of the cases were children who had been discharged since the last semi-annual data collection designed to update each child's case file and therefore the research forms were not appropriate for filling out.[6] An additional 126 of the forms (6.0 percent) were not filled out by the agency staff because the parents were so completely unrelated to the child's situation for so long that the social workers felt they could not provide any meaningful information. The absence of these cases—although small in number—tends to give a somewhat more positive coloration to the overall picture regarding the availability of parents for service involvement.

We are thus left with a sample of 1,293 cases for which the data gathering form developed by the writer was appropriate. This provides a fairly substantial basis for a trial experience in using these new data elements.

The Questionnaire

The research booklets utilized for the study contained questions with fixed-alternative responses. An attempt was made to phrase the inquiries in a straightforward manner. Simplicity was an important consideration since the major purpose of the study was to explore new areas of data content for possible future expansion of the computerized data base. The trial utilization of the form was designed to determine whether the social workers would be able to respond to the questions without difficulty and to determine how useful the information was in illuminating problems of service delivery to parents of children in foster care.

The completed booklet was edited by the research staff to identify questions that were not answered and to account for inconsistencies and "trouble spots." Where the category "other" was used frequently, the responses were studied for the purpose of elaborating the list of fixed-alternative responses. Open-ended questions were coded to reflect major themes in the responses received.

In addition to the data secured in the survey, it was also possible to utilize the information available for the subjects in the CWIS data file. These data could be easily organized into tabular form through the use of the software programs developed by the writer and John F. Grundy in the earlier phase of the research.[7]

The analysis of the data took several forms, including: (1) the organization of the subjects into six groups according to the whereabouts and status of the parents, (2) the comparison of the groups for a number of service-related variables, (3) the creation of two indexes to reflect two major phenomenological domains, and (4) a study of the predictive validity of the indexes and other variables relative to the discharged status of the children after an elapse of two years.

TABLE 1

AGENCIES PARTICIPATING IN MINI-PROJECTS 1 AND 2:*
TOTAL QUESTIONNAIRES SENT AND RETURNED

Sent		Agency	Returned	
MP1	MP2		MP1	MP2
98	98	Abbott House	90	90
--	105	Brooklyn Bureau of Community Services	--	105
56	56	Brookwood Child Care	55	55
105	105	Catholic Guardian Society - Brooklyn	101	101
105	105	Catholic Home Bureau	105	105
105	105	Children's Aid Society	103	103
105	105	Edwin Gould Services for Children	91	89
47	47	Green Chimneys	45	45
103	103	Jewish Child Care Association	93	94
100	--	Leake and Watts Children's Home	96	--
--	105	Lt. Kennedy Home	--	105
--	105	Little Flower Children's Services	--	105
--	105	Mission of the Immaculate Virgin	--	103
105	105	New York Foundling Hospital	104	105
--	28	Ottilie Home for Children	--	28
--	98	St. Cabrini Home	--	98
103	103	St. Dominic's Home	92	92
--	24	St. Germaine's Home	--	24
104	104	St. Joseph's Home - Peekskill	101	101
51	51	Sisters of the Good Shepherd	51	51
105	105	Spence Chapin	105	105
101	101	Windham Child Care	101	101
90	90	Talbot Perkins Children's Services	90	90
55	55	Special Services for Children - Bronx	54	54
56	56	Special Services for Children - Brooklyn	55	55
56	56	Special Services for Children - Manhattan/Richmond	56	56
54	54	Special Services for Children - Queens	54	54
1704	2174	TOTAL	1642	2114

*A total of 20 agencies participated in MP1; 26 agencies in MP2.

2 Availability of Natural Parents for Service Contacts

Because of the serious problems faced by many of the families of the children placed in care, it is not unusual in the experience of agencies to find that parents are out of the picture and simply not available for service contacts. It is obviously important to first establish whether the mothers and/or fathers are in a position to be seen before exploring such matters as their attitudes towards service, the problems requiring referrals to other agencies, and so forth.

Availability of Parents for Service Contacts

The availability of parents for service involvement is directly considered in Table 2. The cases of children included in the survey are organized in sequential groups according to quite explicit criteria. All children whose mothers were essentially out of the picture with respect to their availability for service activity with the caseworkers assigned to the cases and whose fathers were also unavailable were placed in the first four groups in hierarchical, mutually exclusive order.

Group 1 consisted of children whose mothers were deceased; 8.8 percent of the sample was placed in this group. Group 2 was selected from the remaining cases and contained situations where the mothers' whereabouts were unknown; this grouping accounted for 17.3 percent of the cases.

From the remaining cases, the criterion for selection for Group 3 was that the mother had not been seen for at least two years; this condition characterized 11.1 percent of the sample. Group 4 consisted of mothers in mental hospitals; they represented 2.9 percent of the sample.

Groups 1 to 4 represent almost no potential with respect to service involvement. It is sobering to observe that the four groups collectively account for 40.1 percent of the sample. Some of the written comments of the social workers on the research forms make quite graphic the unavailability of the parents:

> Mother inaccessible. No address. Doesn't keep appointments.

> Although mother's whereabouts out of state is known, and she has been contacted by mail several times, she has not responded to these attempts, nor has she contacted child. Since from all reports she does not seem to be a resource for the child, and since child (an adolescent) has extremely negative feelings about mother, we have not pursued her any further than periodic mail contact. Father has only recently responded by mail to our efforts to engage him.

> In this case, mother moved out of state to Massachusetts. Recently phone contact was made. Mother is minimally involved at present time. Father is an unemployed, alcoholic, promiscuous individual. Situation could be termed dangerous for youngster. Mother has abandoned youngster and her message is evident. She does not want Pat and Pat is aware of her rejection.

Group 5 cases reflect situations where the mother was unavailable but where a father's presence was identified. If the child's father was identified, his whereabouts known and he had been seen by the agency's social worker during the past two years, the case was included in the group. Of the 104 cases meeting these criteria, there were 32 cases where the mother was deceased, 37 where her whereabouts was unknown, 19 where she had not been seen in two years and 11 cases where the mother was in a mental hospital. Five additional cases were also included where the mother was unavailable for other reasons.

Group 6 cases included those where the child's mother was alive, whereabouts known and had been seen within the past two years. The proportion of cases falling within this group was 41.9 percent. Although representing a majority of cases, they need not necessarily be viewed as promising prospects for service involvement given the minimal standard set by the criterion that they had been seen within the past two years. We shall subsequently provide information about *when* these mothers had last been seen as well as more qualitative information about their ability to respond to efforts seeking to involve them in a casework helping relationship designed to facilitate the child's return to his own home.

Characteristics of the Surveyed Cases

In Table 3 there are displayed descriptive data about the children covered by the survey. For all the children in Groups 1-4, the mean age is 14.3 years while those in Group 5 showed a somewhat older mean age (14.8 years). These children shared the common characteristic of not

TABLE 2

GROUPING OF PARENTS ACCORDING TO AVAILABILITY
FOR SERVICE INVOLVEMENT

			Number	Percent
Group 1	-	Mother Deceased	114	8.8
Group 2	-	Mother's Whereabouts Unknown	224	17.3
Group 3	-	Mother Not Seen in Two Years	144	11.1
Group 4	-	Mother in Mental Hospital	38	2.9
Group 5	-	Mother Out of Picture - Father Available*	104	8.0
Group 6	-	Mother Available**	669	51.9
		TOTAL	1293	100.0

*Group 5 cases were removed from Groups 1 to 4 if the child's father was identified and paternity acknowledged, his whereabouts known and he had been seen by the agency within the past two years.

**Group 6 includes cases where the child's mother was alive, whereabouts known and had been seen within the past two years.

TABLE 3

CHARACTERISTICS OF SAMPLE ACCORDING TO AVAILABILITY
OF PARENTS FOR SERVICE INVOLVEMENT

Characteristic	Groups 1-4 Combined (Mother Deceased, Whereabouts Unknown, Not Seen in Two Years or in Mental Hospital)	Group 5 (Mother Out of Picture; Father Available)	Group 6 (Mother Available)
Mean Current Age	14.3	14.8	13.3
Mean Years in Care	9.8	7.7	6.6
Ethnicity:			
% Black	58.4	42.5	54.1
% White	15.0	17.5	16.1
% Hispanic	21.6	33.7	26.3
Current Location:			
% Foster Home	74.2	61.2	56.5
% Group Home	9.0	16.2	16.9
% Institution	7.1	21.2	22.5
Reason for Placement:			
% Alcoholic	6.6	12.5	12.7
% Drug Addicted	6.6	10.0	7.6
% Abused Child	2.9	2.5	5.7
% Neglected Child	11.8	20.0	20.6
% Abandoned Child	16.6	8.8	6.5
% Mentally Ill	13.2	17.5	12.9
% Surrendered Child	4.2	1.2	1.2
% Intends to Surrender Child	1.3	--	0.4
Number of Children	(520)	(104)	(669)

having their mothers in the picture and available for service contacts. Group 6 children, whose mothers were identified as available, averaged at least a year younger (13.3 years). The more than 25,000 children included in the CWIS data file of June 1976 were somewhat younger; they averaged 11.4 years of age. It is presumed that the sample of children covered by the survey are somewhat older because of the criterion used in sample selection which stipulated that a child had been in care for at least a year.

The children in the study had been in care for substantial periods of time. For Groups 1-4 (Combined), the mean years in care was 9.8 years, while those with fathers available (Group 5) had experienced an average of 7.7 years of care and the large group whose mothers were available had averaged 6.6 years of foster care.

Black children formed the highest proportion in each of the groupings just cited. However, a sizable group of Hispanic children were among the children in Group 5 where the father was available despite the mother's absence. They constituted 33.7 percent of the group.

It is noteworthy that a higher proportion of the children who had neither mother nor father available (Groups 1-4 Combined) were in foster homes (74.2 percent) compared to those in Group 5 (61.2 percent) and Group 6 (56.5 percent). The latter two groups had higher proportions of children in group homes and institutions.

Higher proportions of the children in Groups 5 and 6 were in care related to problems of alcoholism in a parent and neglect by a parent. On the other hand, the proportion of abandoned children in Groups 1-4 (16.6 percent) was twice as high as reported for Group 5 (8.8 percent) and Group 6 (6.5 percent).

Frequency of Service Contacts

The frequency with which parents have service contacts with social workers representing agencies caring for their children is obviously a crucial matter. If there is no service contact at all over sustained periods of time, it is difficult to anticipate that the child can be returned home in the foreseeable future. A number of inquiries related to this matter were included in the survey and four of these are displayed in Table 4. The set include the following questions: (A) "How often has the parent been seen by a social worker over the past six months?"; (B) "Has there been any pattern to service contacts with the parent?"; (C) "When was the parent last seen by an agency social worker?"; and (D) "Has the trend of service contact with the parent declined since the child entered care?"

Table 4 shows that children in combined Groups 1-4 had parents who were almost uniformly out of touch with their social workers. Only 4.2 percent of the parents had had a contact with a social worker and such parents were subsequently deceased, their whereabouts had become unknown or they had entered a mental hospital. The almost uniform lack of contact reflects the basis upon which Groups 1-4 were constituted, i.e., mothers who were almost totally out of the picture. For almost 59 percent, the social workers indicated no contact had taken place and for another 36 percent, the idea of contact was not applicable since the mother was unavailable.

The mothers in Group 6 were considered the most available of all groups and, indeed, the data in Table 4 confirm this. Only about 15 percent were reported not to have had any contact with a social worker over the six month reporting period although almost half had three or fewer contacts. About one in five of these mothers had at least monthly contacts.

The fathers of the 104 children in Group 5 showed only 31 percent who had no contact with a social worker and about 51 percent who had three or fewer contacts.

About 85 percent of the combined Groups 1-4 were reported to show a pattern of no service contact (or almost never) and included a large group where the question of service was not applicable because of the total absence of the mother. A pattern of no service contacts was true of almost 20 percent of the mothers in Group 6 and 30 percent of the fathers in Group 5.

With respect to trends in frequency of service contacts, only 4.4 percent of the mothers in Groups 1-4 (Combined) showed an increase in such contacts compared to 22.1 percent of the fathers in Group 5 and 29.2 percent of the mothers in Group 6. It is important to note that relatively large groups of parents in each of the groups showed some decline: 28.5 percent of the mothers in Groups 1-4 (Combined), 35.6 percent of the fathers in Group 5 and 27.4 percent of the mothers in Group 6.

The service contact picture that emerges has a mixed quality but generally reflects the basis upon which the groups were organized by the investigator. Groups 1-4 are almost entirely out of the picture and many have not been seen for considerable periods. There has been more recent contact with the parents in Groups 5 and 6, but the contact has been relatively sparse for sizable proportions of these groups, with decline in trend of contact for more than a fourth of the mothers (Group 6) and more than a third of the fathers (Group 5).

TABLE 4

SERVICE CONTACT INFORMATION ACCORDING TO THE AVAILABILITY
OF PARENTS FOR SERVICE INVOLVEMENT

Service Contact Information	Groups 1-4 Combined (Mother Deceased, Whereabouts Unknown, Not Seen in Two Years or in Mental Hospital)*	Group 5 (Mother Out of Picture; Father Available)**	Group 6 (Mother Available)*
	(percentages)		
A. How often has the parent been seen by a social worker over the past six months?			
No Contact	58.6	21.2	13.9
1 Time	1.7	30.8	15.2
2-3 Times	1.5	20.2	31.0
4-5 Times	0.8	14.4	17.2
6-10 Times	--	6.7	12.9
11-20 Times	--	2.9	5.5
More than 20 Times	0.2	3.8	2.8
Other/Not Applicable	36.0	--	1.5
Unknown	1.2	--	--
Total	100.0	100.0	100.0
Number of Children	(520)	(104)	(669)
B. Has there been any pattern to service contacts with the parent?			
No Contact, Almost Never	42.2	25.0	10.8
Weekly	0.4	2.9	5.5
Bi-weekly	0.8	4.8	11.5
Monthly	3.1	18.3	27.4
Every Other Month	0.4	9.6	11.4
Occasional	9.2	33.6	24.6
Other/Not Applicable	43.1	4.8	8.5
Unknown	0.8	1.0	0.3
Total	100.0	100.0	100.0
Number of Children	(520)	(104)	(669)

*Refers to Mother's Service Contacts.

**Refers to Father's Service Contacts.

TABLE 4 (Continued)

SERVICE CONTACT INFORMATION ACCORDING TO THE AVAILABILITY
OF PARENTS FOR SERVICE INVOLVEMENT

Service Contact Information	Groups 1-4 Combined (Mother Deceased, Whereabouts Unknown, Not Seen in Two Years or in Mental Hospital)*	Group 5 (Mother Out of Picture; Father Available)**	Group 6 (Mother Available)*
	(Percentages)		
C. When was the parent last seen by an agency social worker?			
Within Past Month	1.5	45.2	47.9
Within Past 3 Months	0.8	19.2	29.0
Within Past 6 Months	2.7	18.3	10.0
Within Past Year	3.8	17.3	12.7
Within Past 2 Years	14.3	--	--
Within Past 3 Years	11.3	--	--
Within Past 4 Years	4.6	--	--
Within Past 5 Years	4.8	--	--
Within Past 6-10 Years	10.0	--	--
More than 10 Years Ago	7.5	--	--
No Contacts Since Birth of Child	9.0	--	--
No Contacts Since Placement of Child	10.2	--	--
Other/Not Applicable	16.4	--	0.4
Unknown	3.1	--	--
Total	100.0	100.0	100.0
Number of Children	(520)	(104)	(669)
D. Has the trend of service contact with the parent declined since the child entered care?			
Major Decline	23.5	13.5	13.3
Moderate Decline	2.5	15.4	7.8
Slight Decline	2.5	6.7	6.3
No Change	16.9	32.7	34.9
Slight Increase	1.3	6.7	10.0
Moderate Increase	1.2	7.7	8.4
Major Increase	1.9	7.7	10.8
Other/Not Applicable	48.5	5.8	7.0
Unknown	1.7	3.8	1.5
Total	100.0	100.0	100.0
Number of Children	(520)	(104)	(669)

*Refers to Mother's Service Contacts. **Refers to Father's Service Contacts.

3 Further Perspectives on Parental Service Needs and Service Contacts

We continue here to probe the nature of the service needs of the parents, the problems and conditions that serve to keep the children in foster care, and the degree to which the reporting agencies have been able to garner services for the parents from other human service delivery systems.

Need for Counseling

One estimate of the need of the parents for service contacts was arrived at by making the following inquiry of the social workers: "To what extent does parent require counseling help to clarify own feelings about resumption of care for child?" The responses shown in Table 5 are quite revealing.

The mothers in Group 6 are those most likely to be available for service contacts and might thus be regarded as the most promising of the parents with respect to their potential for restoring homes for their children. Yet, the social workers filling out the study forms rated 46.8 percent of these mothers as "very much" requiring counseling help and for another 23.0 percent the response was "somewhat." Thus seven out of ten of the mothers were seen as confused in their feelings about resumption of care. A positive identification that the parent did not require counseling help was made in only 15.1 percent of the cases.

The social workers are clearly less than sanguine about most of the 669 mothers in Group 6. They show a similar perspective about the available fathers (Group 5); almost 60 percent of these men are rated as requiring counseling help to clarify their feelings.

The children of the mothers classified as being "out of it" (Groups 1-4) are mainly seen as being beyond such counseling help. Close to 57 percent of the cases were rated "not applicable" and 11 percent "not at all."

Parental Circumstances That Hinder Service Contacts

The parents of children in foster care are likely to be individuals living under depressed social conditions.[8] They are apt to have little control over their lives. Such matters as keeping appointments at a social agency may make demands upon their resources for transportation, baby sitting funds, and so forth, which may be difficult for them to muster.

To determine whether circumstantial factors were operating to lower the participation of parents in service contacts with their social workers, a list of obstacles to service contacts was prepared. It included the following sources of difficulty: other child care responsibilities, employment hours, financial limitations, distance of the parent from the agency office, physical or mental illness, mental retardation, institutionalization of the parent and other unspecified factors. One item was included in the list that related to psychological rather than social factors: the low motivation of the parent to see the social worker.

In Table 6, there are presented in aggregated form the ratings made by the social workers according to the classification of the parents with respect to their overall availability. Of interest is the fact that for all groupings, the factor most frequently identified by the social workers as a hindrance to service contacts was the low motivation of the parents to see their social workers. Thus for mothers in Group 6, more than 30 percent were said to show this problem "very much" and another 24 percent, "somewhat." Only about 29 percent were rated as not manifesting a motivation problem. For the fathers in Group 5, over 40 percent showed the problem "very much" and 20 percent "somewhat," while 25 percent were rated as not evidencing this problem.

Some of the written comments of the social workers on the research forms are revealing of the motivational problems encountered in the parents:

> Neither mother nor mother's husband is willing to look at the problems which led to child's placement. Child was placed because of a parent-child conflict and because of problems in the marital relationship. Neither parent is willing to accept ongoing therapeutic treatment, which is needed in order for the child to return home. Both parents want the child to remain in care and will not accept responsibility for the situation, neither are they attempting to solve the problem within the family.

> Parents were adamant that they wanted very little if any casework contact. Intensive efforts were made with them from 1970-1973 to reach out to them. In 1974, court action began, resulting in termination of parental rights in 1976. The parents were seen occasionally in court during this time.

TABLE 5

EXTENT TO WHICH PARENTS REQUIRE COUNSELING ABOUT RESUMPTION OF CARE OF CHILDREN ACCORDING TO THEIR AVAILABILITY FOR SERVICE INVOLVEMENT*

Needs Counseling?	Groups 1-4 Combined (Mother Deceased, Whereabouts Unknown, Not Seen in Two Years or in Mental Hospital)	Group 5 (Mother Out of Picture; Father Available)	Group 6 (Mother Available)
	(Percentaged)		
Very Much	11.7	44.2	46.8
Somewhat	1.9	16.3	23.0
Not at All	11.0	19.3	15.1
Other/Not Applicable	56.9	14.4	12.0
Unknown	18.4	5.8	3.1
Total Number of Children	100.0 (520)	100.0 (104)	100.0 (669)

*Question posed to respondents was: "To what extent does parent require counseling help to clarify own feelings about resumption of care for child?"

TABLE 6

CIRCUMSTANCES TENDING TO LOWER FREQUENCY OF PARENTAL SERVICE CONTACTS
ACCORDING TO THE AVAILABILITY OF PARENTS FOR SERVICE INVOLVEMENT*

Circumstance	Groups 1-4 (Combined) (Mother Deceased, Whereabouts Unknown, Not Seen in Two Years or in Mental Hospital)					Group 6 (Mother Available)				
	Very Much	Some-what	Hardly/ Not at All	Un-known	Other/ Not Appli-cable	Very Much	Some-what	Hardly/ Not at All	Un-known	Other/ Not Appli-cable
	(Percentaged Across)										
Other Child Care Responsibilities	2.5	3.1	22.7	16.0	55.7	5.5	16.4	57.2	4.3	16.6
Employment Hours	0.8	1.9	22.3	18.1	56.9	4.2	9.6	61.4	4.9	19.9
Financial Limitations (Lack of Funds for Carfare, Babysitter)	0.6	2.5	21.0	19.2	56.7	3.6	12.7	60.1	4.2	19.4
Distance from Agency Office	5.4	4.8	20.6	15.2	54.0	8.7	23.5	48.6	2.5	16.7
Physical Illness	2.7	2.7	18.3	20.0	56.3	5.8	13.0	55.0	6.3	19.9
Mental Illness	14.6	3.8	13.8	16.0	51.8	13.9	10.5	50.9	6.9	17.8
Mental Retardation	2.1	1.3	22.1	17.9	56.6	2.8	4.0	61.0	7.8	24.4
Other Incapacity	1.9	0.2	13.3	17.9	66.7	2.7	1.0	34.7	8.0	53.5
Parent is Institu-tionalized	2.1	1.5	18.1	14.0	64.3	1.9	1.2	56.2	3.3	37.4
Low Motivation to See Social Worker	22.3	5.6	8.5	12.9	50.7	30.3	24.1	28.6	1.6	15.4
Number of Children	(520)					(669)				

*Question posed to respondents was: "Please indicate if any of the following circumstances have served to lower the frequency of parental contact with the social worker."

TABLE 6 (Continued)

CIRCUMSTANCES TENDING TO LOWER FREQUENCY OF PARENTAL SERVICE CONTACTS
ACCORDING TO THE AVAILABILITY OF PARENTS FOR SERVICE INVOLVEMENT

Circumstance	Group 5, 6 (Combined): Children Not Freed (Mother Out of Picture, Father Available; Mother Available)*					Group 5 (Mother Out of Picture, Father Available)**				
	Very Much	Some-what	Hardly/ Not at All	Un-known	Other/ Not Appli-cable	Very Much	Some-what	Hardly/ Not at All	Un-known	Other/ Not Appli-cable
	(Percentaged Across)										
Other Child Care Responsibilities	4.9	15.0	54.1	6.4	19.6	1.9	10.6	54.8	10.6	22.1
Employment Hours	4.0	9.6	56.5	7.1	22.8	9.6	24.0	37.6	11.5	17.3
Financial Limitations (Lack of Funds for Carfare, Babysitter)	3.7	12.3	55.4	6.5	22.1	3.8	6.7	54.9	12.5	22.1
Distance from Agency Office	8.7	22.2	44.8	4.9	19.4	9.6	16.3	50.1	7.7	16.3
Physical Illness	5.5	12.4	51.7	7.9	22.5	1.0	5.7	56.8	12.5	24.0
Mental Illness	13.8	9.8	47.5	8.0	20.9	7.7	1.9	55.8	10.6	24.0
Mental Retardation	2.1	3.3	57.4	9.3	27.9	--	1.9	53.0	16.3	28.8
Other Incapacity	2.1	0.9	33.9	9.2	53.9	2.9	--	30.8	11.5	54.8
Parent is Institutionalized	2.1	0.6	52.1	5.9	39.3	1.0	--	57.6	5.8	35.6
Low Motivation to See Social Worker	27.1	22.7	28.0	3.1	19.1	40.4	20.2	25.0	1.9	12.5
Number of Children	(675)					(104)				

*Refers to Mother's Circumstance.

**Refers to Father's Circumstance.

Workers make appointments to see mother at her home and arrive to find she is not at home. Unannounced visits also have been in vain. Mother is not home or is suspected to be home but unwilling to receive visit. Contacts by agency are made with children's eldest sister.

Extensive outreach by agency caseworker has occurred within one-and-a-half years of child's placement. Mother is resistant to engaging in contact focused on developing insight into child's special needs and her role. She remains quite defensive and is unable to accept that she is crucial in child's treatment.

"Other child care responsibilities" was a circumstance that was "very much" or "somewhat" a factor for 22 percent of the Group 6 mothers. Other problems for these women included "distance from the office" (32 percent), "mental illness" (24 percent), "physical illness" (19 percent) and "financial limitations" (16 percent). For the fathers in Group 5, "employment hours" was a noteworthy problem (34 percent) and "distance from the agency office" (26 percent).

The following case comments written by social workers on the research form make clear that circumstantial factors that inhibit service contacts are often intertwined with motivational aspects of parental orientations to service:

Mother can only be seen at home since she cannot keep office appointments. She has no baby sitter to care for her C.P. child. Her daughter refuses to do so. In order to service this woman, we have to go to her home in the Bronx.

On several occasions the mother has called to make arrangements to come. Carfare has been sent, child was notified but mother has subsequently not appeared. Mother is highly anxious, must travel with companion; afraid of own impulses and ability to handle child. Mother is severely mentally ill; is inconsistent about contact and visiting and child becomes extremely upset whenever mother reenters picture, which cannot be predicted.

Both parents hold 9-5 jobs. Mother resides in Queens and feels she has no time to come to worker's office during our office hours (9-5). She only is available for home visits during weekends and after 8:00 p.m. when she gets home. Father's situation similar to mother.

Extremely difficult to work with mother out of state and even child welfare worker in community where she lives has difficulty maintaining contact. When she is seen either there or here she insists she wants her son and is making concrete plans, but fails to follow through. If this continues, we will consider terminating parental rights.

Mother has moved three times in last year. Does not leave forwarding address or notify agency. Has no phone. Does not answer letters. Is not in when worker calls. Refuses to see child.

For the parents in Groups 1-4 (Combined), "low motivation to see the social worker" (28 percent) and "mental illness" (18 percent) were the most frequently identified barriers to service contacts. In the main, however, the social workers chose the category "not applicable" for most of the circumstances identified in the list, another indication that these mothers were almost totally "out of it."

For the most available parents in Groups 5 and 6 (Combined), we removed the children freed for adoption. For this most relevant group of parents, the leading barriers to the mother's involvement in service contacts were: "low motivation" (50 percent), "distance from the agency" (31 percent), "mental illness" (23 percent), and "other child care responsibilities" (20 percent).

Family Problems or Conditions Serving to Keep Children in Care

It is well known that the natural parents of children who have been placed in foster care are adults who suffer from a variety of disabling conditions. More often than not, they are individuals living under the most marginal social circumstances and they also tend to be afflicted with serious personal problems. Many of them are profoundly demoralized persons who have found life to be a struggle and their capacities for coping appear almost exhausted. Many have given up on the notion that they can establish normal family environments for their children. There is marked over-representation of minority groups and single-parent households among these families.[9]

A list of problems or conditions that might be causal factors serving to keep children in foster care was presented to the social workers participating in the study. The list is in Table 7 and is an adaptation of one used by Beck and Jones.[10] The social workers who were our respondents were requested to note each problem or condition listed and to rate whether it was a *major factor*, *minor factor*, or *not a factor* in preventing the child from returning home. The purpose of engaging in this line of inquiry was to shed some light upon the service needs of the parents in the caseload.

Table 7 presents the frequency distribution of the ratings on these factors made by the social workers in the 26 agencies that participated in the study. The data are presented separately for the four groupings previously identified.

When we examine the problems or conditions aggregated for Groups 1-4 (Combined), we oberve that the preponderant response for each category is *Other/Not Applicable*; usually over 50 percent of the ratings fell within this classification. This reflects the condition of total collapse in functioning of these parents with respect to the way in which they related to their maternal roles and to the agencies caring for their children. In the face of the massive failure of these women to maintain contact with their children and to perform the normal tasks of parenthood, most of the categories of problems or conditions presented to the social workers were apparently meaningless as potential targets of service intervention. Nevertheless, three areas are evidenced in which the caseworkers identified problems or conditions that were *major* or *minor factors* in keeping the children in care for at least 20 percent of the cases. These were: child rearing/child care practices, mental illness, and parent-child relationship problems.

Group 6 reflects the grouping of cases where a more well-defined picture of parental service needs can be established. Most of the mothers in this group were in contact

TABLE 7

PROBLEMS OR CONDITIONS OF MOTHERS OF CHILDREN IN CARE IDENTIFIED AS CAUSAL FACTORS
RELATED TO KEEPING THE CHILD IN FOSTER CARE*

Problem or Condition	Groups 1-4 (Combined) (Mother Deceased, Whereabouts Unknown, Not Seen in Two Years or in Mental Hospital)					Group 6 (Mother Available)				
	Major Factor	Minor Factor	Not a Factor	Unknown	Other/ Not Applicable	Major Factor	Minor Factor	Not a Factor	Unknown	Other/ Not Applicable
				(Percentaged)						
Inadequate Housing	7.5	7.3	13.1	20.0	52.1	20.8	26.0	36.5	3.9	12.9
Unemployment or Unsuitable Job	2.7	5.0	18.8	21.0	52.5	8.8	15.5	53.2	5.1	17.3
Poor Work Performance	1.3	2.9	19.8	22.7	53.3	3.1	4.6	58.9	12.1	21.2
Inadequate Income for Basic Needs	4.4	6.5	16.9	19.4	52.7	13.2	21.5	43.5	5.4	16.4
Health Problems, Physical Illness or Handicap	6.5	4.4	15.8	21.0	52.3	17.8	13.9	46.2	6.4	15.7
Child-rearing/ Child Care Practices	16.9	4.6	9.2	18.1	51.2	46.8	21.8	16.3	4.2	10.9
Marital Problem	5.8	3.8	17.9	19.8	52.7	13.0	12.9	47.8	8.8	17.5
Criminal Problem	2.5	1.7	21.5	20.8	53.5	2.2	2.2	66.1	8.5	20.9
Alcoholism	5.0	1.7	18.1	22.5	52.7	18.8	4.8	49.3	8.5	18.5
Drug Abuse	6.3	1.9	17.7	21.3	52.7	7.3	4.8	57.7	10.6	19.6
Mental Illness	20.2	2.9	11.7	16.3	48.8	24.5	6.3	44.7	9.0	15.5
Mental Retardation	2.5	2.1	22.3	20.0	53.1	5.5	4.2	61.7	8.5	20.0
Management of Home	7.9	7.9	13.1	19.0	52.1	22.3	21.5	33.8	7.0	15.4
Management of Money, Budgeting, etc.	4.8	6.3	13.3	22.5	53.1	17.5	17.8	38.7	9.7	16.3
Health Practices	4.4	4.4	15.2	21.9	54.0	6.3	10.2	51.4	11.1	21.1
Severe Personal Adjustment Problem: Depression	10.8	3.3	11.9	21.0	53.1	28.0	14.9	30.8	9.0	17.3
Severe Personal Adjustment Problem: Other	5.6	1.9	12.9	20.2	59.4	16.1	2.7	32.7	12.6	35.9
Parent-Child Relationship Problem	17.5	3.7	11.2	16.2	51.5	45.9	19.6	16.9	4.9	12.7
Other Condition	12.1	0.2	8.3	15.6	63.8	5.7	0.3	27.4	8.8	57.8
Number of Children	(520)					(669)				

*Question posed to respondents was: "Please indicate whether any of the following problems or conditions of the parent(s) are causal factors related to keeping the child in foster care. Is the condition a <u>major factor</u>, <u>minor factor</u> or <u>not a factor</u> in preventing the child from returning home?"

TABLE 7 (Continued)

PROBLEMS OR CONDITIONS OF PARENTS OF CHILDREN IN CARE IDENTIFIED AS CAUSAL FACTORS
RELATED TO KEEPING THE CHILD IN FOSTER CARE

Problem or Condition	Group 5, 6 (Combined): Children Not Freed (Mother Out of Picture, Father Available; Mother Available)*					Group 5 (Mother Out of Picture, Father Available)**				
	Major Factor	Minor Factor	Not a Factor	Unknown	Other/Not Applicable	Major Factor	Minor Factor	Not a Factor	Unknown	Other/Not Applicable
	(Percentaged)									
Inadequate Housing	19.9	22.7	35.3	6.2	16.0	19.2	18.3	33.7	9.6	19.2
Unemployment or Unsuitable Job	7.4	14.7	51.0	7.3	19.7	14.4	9.6	49.0	7.7	19.2
Poor Work Performance	2.5	4.9	56.3	13.3	23.0	6.7	10.6	38.5	17.3	26.9
Inadequate Income for Basic Needs	12.0	19.4	41.8	7.6	19.3	14.4	7.7	40.4	13.5	24.0
Health Problems, Physical Illness or Handicap	16.4	12.9	44.4	7.9	18.4	8.7	7.7	45.2	11.5	26.9
Child-rearing/Child Care Practices	43.0	21.0	16.0	6.1	13.9	41.3	15.4	16.3	10.6	16.3
Marital Problem	12.4	12.0	45.5	10.2	19.9	23.1	10.6	31.7	13.5	21.2
Criminal Problem	1.8	2.4	63.0	10.1	22.8	6.7	5.8	48.1	14.4	25.0
Alcoholism	16.7	4.4	47.4	10.5	20.9	15.4	12.5	38.5	11.5	22.1
Drug Abuse	5.9	4.4	56.3	12.0	21.3	4.8	1.0	52.9	15.4	26.0
Mental Illness	23.7	6.1	41.8	10.7	17.8	9.6	5.8	45.2	14.4	25.0
Mental Retardation	4.7	3.7	58.8	10.2	22.5	1.0	3.8	52.9	14.4	27.9
Management of Home	20.0	19.6	32.6	9.6	18.2	17.3	16.3	26.9	16.3	23.1
Management of Money, Budgeting, etc.	15.9	15.7	38.1	11.7	18.7	11.5	11.5	31.7	20.2	25.0
Health Practices	5.6	8.9	49.8	12.7	23.0	4.8	1.0	47.1	20.2	26.9
Severe Personal Adjustment Problem: Depression	26.4	14.2	29.9	10.1	19.4	10.6	6.7	40.4	17.3	25.0
Severe Personal Adjustment Problem: Other	13.9	2.5	32.3	14.2	37.0	13.5	1.0	31.7	19.2	34.6
Parent-Child Relationship Problem	42.7	18.7	16.1	7.1	15.4	35.6	18.3	16.3	11.5	18.3
Other Condition	4.6	0.3	26.7	10.2	58.2	9.6	--	17.3	14.4	58.7
Number of Children	(675)					(104)				

*Refers to Mother's Problem or Condition.

**Refers to Father's Problem or Condition.

with the agencies and presumably were available for service contacts. The data are interesting and point to two overall problem areas where the parents were seen as requiring help if their homes were to be restored: (1) conditions of social deprivation, and (2) problems of intrapsychic and interpersonal impairment or difficulty.

Almost 47 percent of these mothers were said to have inadequate housing to the extent that housing was identified as a *major* or *minor factor* in keeping the child in foster care. The table also shows that almost 35 percent of the women had inadequate income to meet basic needs. Problems of physical health were also identified in almost a third of the cases.

Problems in personal adjustment and interpersonal relationships were identified as afflicting many of these women. The caseworkers clearly saw them as inadequate in their parental functioning; more than two-thirds were identified as evidencing problems in their child-rearing or child care practices and a similar-sized group was identified as having parent-child relationship problems that were sufficiently serious to cause the children to remain in care. At least a fourth of the mothers were identified as having marital problems and larger proportions were said to have problems in the management of their homes (43.8 percent) and in the management of money (35.3 percent).

A large group of women were described as suffering from severe personal adjustment difficulties in the form of depression (42.9 percent) and almost a fourth suffered from alcoholism. All of these difficulties identified by the caseworkers were rated as *major or minor factors* in keeping the children in foster care.

The fathers of children whom we have located in Group 5 also showed a sizable proportion whose child rearing or child care practices were rated as problematic (66.7 percent) or who were involved in parent-child relationship problems (53.9 percent). Marital problems (33.7 percent) and alcoholism (27.9 percent) also loomed fairly large. Social factors tending to keep the children in care included housing (37.5 percent), unemployment (24.0 percent) and problems in management of the home (33.6 percent).

Parental Behavior in the Client Role

A group of items in the questionnaire were designed to gauge the behavior of the parents as potential recipients of casework service. Did they lend themselves to the helping process? Did they tend to break appointments, come late, or act defensively in the interviews with the social workers assigned to their cases? The items are shown in Table 8 where the aggregated responses are displayed separately for the four groupings of parents previously shown.

The mothers in Groups 1-4 (Combined) were most often so unavailable that the social workers often chose to check the category "not applicable" in response to all of the specified items. For each item of behavior, almost two-thirds of the responses were of this type. Where a more definitive response was possible, it invariably reflected problematic behavior shown by the mothers (Table 8).

For the mothers in Group 6, sizable proportions were reported to show problems for each type of behavior listed. Thus, over 50 percent were said to resist seeing the social worker (21.5 percent "very much" and 28.7 percent "somewhat"). Over 46 percent were described as failing to keep appointments and over 30 percent were late for appointments. Sizable groups were rated as being unable to discuss personal problems (52.3 percent), to be defensive about themselves (59.1 percent) or to be excessively dependent (51.3 percent).

The difficulty in serving the mothers because of their profound emotional instability was often cited by the social workers on the research forms:

> Mother is overwhelmed by many personal and concrete problems and is immobilized in terms of seeking relief from her dilemma. Her brief contacts with agency worker caused her much turmoil. Her only meeting with her son was quite a traumatic experience for her, which she dared not repeat.

> Mother has consistently refused all contacts with agency (to the point of hanging up the phone). Brief phone contacts with mother have demonstrated mother's considerable pathology and rigidity in refusing contact with child or agency.

> Parents are very willing to keep contact with agency as long as they're pleased and not inconvenienced. Once the agency demands some effort on their part to get to see the child, they refuse to work. They're very limited in terms of their capacity to deal with this child but fail to recognize it.

> Parents come from a multi-problem Puerto Rican family. They are suspicious and defensive to some extent. They are not oriented to casework on an ongoing basis but want help in crisis situations. They eventually came to rely heavily on me for specific help. I also spoke Spanish which was extremely important as mother spoke little English.

> Parents seem to lack interest in the child but would not be willing to surrender because of cultural values. They do not want to sacrifice too much or make too much effort to keep in contact or receive the services necessary to take child back.

Quite telling is the judgment of the social worker in 40 percent of the cases that the mother failed to show concern about her child (17.5 percent "very much" and 22.0 percent "somewhat"). The picture that emerges is that a large proportion of the caseload is composed of mothers whose maternal orientation is either undeveloped or distorted by the marginal existence they have experienced as individuals.

The fathers in Group 5 were rated as showing even more problematic behaviors than the mothers in Group 6. Almost 57 percent were rated as resisting seeing the social workers and more than half were characterized as having problems in keeping appointments. When Groups 5 and 6 were combined and the cases where the children had been freed for adoption were removed, the problems of service delivery to the mothers again loomed large.

Referrals to Other Agencies

Because of the many types of serious personal and social problems to be found among the families in the study, it would not be reasonable to expect that their service

TABLE 8

REPORTED PROBLEMS IN ESTABLISHING SERVICE CONTACTS WITH PARENTS*

Reported Problems	Groups 1-4 (Combined) (Mother Deceased; Whereabouts Unknown; Not Seen in Two Years; or in Mental Hospital)					Group 6 (Mother Available)				
	Very Much	Some-what	Not At All	Not Appli-cable	Un-known	Very Much	Some-what	Not At All	Not Appli-cable	Un-known
	(Percentaged Across)										
Resists Seeing Social Worker	21.0	5.2	1.5	64.8	7.5	21.5	28.7	30.3	17.4	2.1
Fails to Keep Appointments	17.9	5.0	1.3	68.1	7.7	21.8	24.5	28.6	22.6	2.5
Is Late for Appointments	6.0	4.6	2.1	75.6	11.7	10.6	19.6	32.0	33.8	4.0
Is Unable to Discuss Personal Problems	8.5	5.0	3.3	69.5	13.7	20.8	31.5	23.2	20.0	4.5
Is Defensive About Self	9.2	5.2	3.1	69.2	13.3	29.5	29.8	16.7	18.5	5.5
Fails to Show Concern About Child	17.7	6.5	2.9	63.9	9.0	17.5	22.0	37.3	20.2	3.0
Is Excessively Dependent	8.5	5.2	1.7	68.8	15.8	28.4	22.9	20.6	20.3	7.8
Other Problem	11.2	0.2	3.3	72.8	12.5	6.6	1.2	19.0	61.4	11.8
Number of Children	(520)					(669)				

*Question posed to respondents was: "Have any of the following problems been evidenced in attempting to establish an ongoing service contact with the parent?"

TABLE 8 (Continued)

REPORTED PROBLEMS IN ESTABLISHING SERVICE CONTACTS WITH PARENTS

Reported Problems	Groups 5, 6 (Combined): Children Not Freed (Mother Out of Picture, Father Available; Mother Available)*					Group 5 (Mother Out of Picture, Father Available)**				
	Very Much	Some- what	Not At All	Not Appli- cable	Un- known	Very Much	Some- what	Not At All	Not Appli- cable	Un- known
	(Percentaged Across)						(Percentaged Across)				
Resists Seeing Social Worker	18.4	27.4	28.2	22.7	3.3	33.7	23.1	24.0	16.3	2.9
Fails to Keep Appointments	18.7	22.7	27.4	27.3	3.9	29.8	21.2	26.9	18.3	3.8
Is Late for Appointments	9.5	17.5	30.4	37.4	5.2	14.4	11.5	35.7	28.8	9.6
Is Unable to Discuss Personal Problems	18.5	29.2	21.3	25.4	5.6	22.1	27.9	20.2	22.1	7.7
Is Defensive About Self	26.7	27.8	15.3	24.1	6.1	35.6	27.9	14.4	15.4	6.7
Fails to Show Concern About Child	13.2	20.9	36.4	25.5	4.0	26.9	13.5	36.5	18.3	4.8
Is Excessively Dependent	25.9	21.2	19.3	25.2	8.4	25.0	8.7	34.6	17.3	14.4
Other Problems	9.5	1.2	17.9	60.1	11.3	7.7	--	19.2	61.6	11.5
Number of Children	(675)					(104)				

*Refers to Mother's Problems.

**Refers to Father's Problems.

needs could exclusively be met within the programs and resources of the child welfare agencies. Indeed, the child care responsibilities of these agencies would understandably loom large in determining how staff and other programmatic resources would be allocated.

Referrals to other agencies with different service missions would represent a major way in which services could be garnered for parents. Thus, the drug abusing mother would likely have need of the treatment facilities of an addiction services agency. A chronically unemployed father might be a good candidate for a job training program. And so forth.

In Table 9, we present information about referral activity in cases—or the absence of referrals—as related to the same list of problems or conditions just considered in Table 7. For each problem or condition identified as a "major factor" in keeping the child in care, the respondent was asked whether this required a referral to another agency or service program. The respondent could indicate that a service contact had already been established, a referral was needed and planned, or a referral was needed but the service was unavailable. The respondent could also indicate that service was not required or that the parent was unwilling to pursue the service. The referral information is provided in Table 9 for Groups 1-4 (Combined), Group 5, Group 6 and for Groups 5 and 6 (Combined) with the children freed for adoption removed. It should be understood that if a problem or condition was not identified as a "major factor" in creating the need for the child's continued placement in foster care, referral information would not be required of the respondent and the case was coded as "not applicable" with respect to referral actively for the problem category.

For the mothers in Groups 1-4, the least available parents, there is very little, if any, referral activity reported. This, no doubt, reflects the overall condition of inertia and lack of activity in these cases and adds to the cumulative dismal and rather hopeless aura that surrounds them. The only exception to this picture is the indication that nine percent of the mothers have already achieved contact with agencies or service programs treating mental illness. Such service contacts were not necessarily established through the intervention of the child welfare agencies participating in the study.

For the 104 fathers in Group 5, the amount of referral activity or the expression of need for service is quite trivial. However, for the 669 mothers in Group 6, there is indication of a modest amount of actual or planned service contacts with other agencies—in the neighborhood of 15 percent—in the areas of housing conditions, health problems, mental illness, personal adjustment problems (depression) and parent-child relationship problems. The picture is the same when Groups 5 and 6 are combined and the cases where children have been freed for adoption are deleted.

The overall impression that emerges from the aggregated information is that almost no referral work is taking place in Groups 1-4 and with the available fathers (Group 5); a modest amount of service involvement is shown for Group 6. The garnering of services for parents—and helping them to utilize such resources—is obviously a critical matter that touches directly on the issue of "permanency" planning. If left to their own devices—that is to say, without help—many of these parents will be unable to restore homes for their children. Witness the fact that the children in Groups 1-4 have been in care for an average of 9.8 years (see Table 3).

TABLE 9

NATURE OF REFERRAL NEEDS FOR MAJOR PROBLEMS OR CONDITIONS AFFECTING MOTHER:*

GROUPS 1-4 (COMBINED):
(Mother Deceased; Whereabouts Unknown; Not Seen in Two Years; or in Mental Hospital)

Problems or Conditions Affecting Mother	Service Contact Already Established	Referral Needed and Planned	Referral Needed but Service Unavailable	Service Not Required	Parent Unwilling to Use Service	Un-known	Other/ Not Applicable
			(Percentaged)				
Inadequate Housing	1.2	0.2	0.6	6.9	3.8	10.2	77.1
Unemployment or Unsuitable Job	0.4	--	0.4	7.3	1.5	9.4	81.0
Poor Work Performance	--	0.2	0.2	6.5	016	9.4	83.1
Inadequate Income for Basic Needs	1.5	0.4	0.6	6.2	1.9	9.8	79.6
Health Problems, Physical Illness	4.0	0.2	0.2	5.8	1.9	9.0	78.8
Child-rearing/ Child Care Practices	1.7	0.4	0.4	6.0	6.5	11.2	73.8
Marital Problem	--	--	0.4	7.5	1.5	10.2	80.4
Criminal Problem	0.4	--	--	6.0	1.2	10.2	82.3
Alcoholism	1.2	0.4	--	6.3	3.7	8.7	79.8
Drug Abuse	2.9	--	0.2	5.8	2.5	9.4	79.2
Mental Illness	9.0	0.2	0.2	3.7	5.8	9.0	72.1
Mental Retardation	1.2	--	0.2	7.1	1.2	9.0	81.3
Management of Home	0.8	0.2	0.4	6.7	2.3	10.2	79.4
Management of Money, Budgeting, etc.	1.0	--	0.4	6.2	1.7	9.8	81.0
Health Practices	2.1	--	2.0	5.2	1.3	10.0	81.2
Severe Personal Adjustment Problem: Depression	4.0	0.2	0.2	4.6	4.6	916	76.7
Severe Personal Adjustment Problem: Other	1.2	0.2	0.2	4.2	2.9	8.8	82.5
Parent-Child Relationship Problem	1.3	--	0.2	6.9	7.9	8.8	74.8
Other	0.8	--	--	6.7	1.9	8.7	81.9
Number of Children				(520)			

*Question posed to respondents was: "Do any of the problems or conditions cited in the previous sections as 'major factors' require referral to another agency or service program?"

TABLE 9 (Continued)

NATURE OF REFERRAL NEEDS FOR MAJOR PROBLEMS OR CONDITIONS AFFECTING FATHER:

GROUP 5:
(Mother Out of Picture, Father Available)

Problems or Conditions Affecting Father	Service Contact Already Established	Referral Needed and Planned	Referral Needed but Service Unavailable	Service Not Required	Parent Unwilling to Use Service	Un-known	Other/ Not Applicable
			(Percentaged)				
Inadequate Housing	3.8	1.0	5.8	12.5	11.5	6.7	58.7
Unemployment or Unsuitable Job	1.9	--	2.9	16.3	7.7	4.8	66.3
Poor Work Performance	1.0	--	--	14.4	6.7	5.8	72.1
Inadequate Income for Basic Needs	3.8	--	2.9	17.3	3.8	6.7	65.4
Health Problems, Physical Illness	6.7	--	--	12.5	3.8	7.7	69.2
Child-rearing/ Child Care Practices	3.8	1.9	1.9	14.4	16.3	9.6	51.9
Marital Problem	2.9	--	--	15.4	10.6	7.7	63.5
Criminal Problem	3.8	1.0	--	12.5	2.9	8.7	71.2
Alcoholism	1.0	1.0	--	9.6	12.5	9.6	66.3
Drug Abuse	1.9	1.0	--	11.5	3.8	7.7	74.0
Mental Illness	4.8	--	--	12.5	4.8	7.7	70.2
Mental Retardation	--	--	--	15.4	--	8.7	76.0
Management of Home	1.9	1.0	1.9	12.5	7.7	9.6	65.4
Management of Money, Budgeting, etc.	1.9	--	1.0	14.4	10.6	5.8	66.3
Health Practices	1.0	1.0	--	12.5	3.8	8.7	73.1
Severe Personal Adjustment Problem: Depression	2.9	--	--	7.7	6.7	11.5	71.2
Severe Personal Adjustment Problem: Other	3.8	--	--	8.7	7.7	9.6	70.2
Parent-Child Relationship Problem	4.8	1.0	--	6.7	17.3	9.6	60.6
Other	1.0	1.0	1.0	3.8	1.9	8.7	82.7
Number of Children				(104)			

TABLE 9 (Continued)

NATURE OF REFERRAL NEEDS FOR MAJOR PROBLEMS OR CONDITIONS AFFECTING MOTHER:

GROUP 6:
(Mother Available)

Problems or Conditions Affecting Mother	Service Contact Already Established	Referral Needed and Planned	Referral Needed but Service Unavailable	Service Not Required	Parent Unwilling to Use Service	Un-known	Other/ Not Applicable
			(Percentaged)				
Inadequate Housing	9.4	4.5	3.7	15.7	5.8	1.9	58.9
Unemployment or Unsuitable Job	4.2	0.7	1.8	17.6	3.3	2.4	70.0
Poor Work Performance	0.7	0.6	0.4	17.6	1.3	3.4	75.8
Inadequate Income for Basic Needs	8.2	2.5	4.0	16.0	2.7	2.2	64.3
Health Problems, Physical Illness	14.9	0.7	--	13.9	3.6	3.1	63.7
Child-rearing/ Child Care Practices	11.8	3.3	1.2	14.9	19.1	3.1	46.5
Marital Problem	3.6	0.6	0.4	16.4	6.6	3.9	68.5
Criminal Problem	1.6	--	0.3	17.8	0.6	3.1	76.5
Alcoholism	7.6	0.3	0.1	14.6	10.0	3.1	64.1
Drug Abuse	5.5	0.4	0.3	17.0	2.8	3.3	70.6
Mental Illness	13.6	0.6	0.1	13.8	8.1	3.1	60.7
Mental Retardation	2.2	--	0.3	18.4	2.2	2.5	74.3
Management of Home	5.4	2.1	2.2	15.1	10.9	3.0	61.3
Management of Money, Budgeting, etc.	6.4	1.2	2.4	15.1	8.2	2.4	64.3
Health Practices	3.9	0.9	0.1	14.8	4.3	3.1	72.8
Severe Personal Adjustment Problem: Depression	13.2	2.5	0.3	9.7	11.7	4.2	58.4
Severe Personal Adjustment Problem: Other	4.9	1.5	0.3	8.4	8.1	3.4	73.4
Parent-Child Relationship Problem	13.2	2.5	0.4	14.2	18.4	3.1	48.1
Other	1.8	--	0.3	4.6	0.9	3.3	89.1
Number of Children				(669)			

TABLE 9 (*Continued*)

NATURE OF REFERRAL NEEDS FOR MAJOR PROBLEMS OR CONDITIONS AFFECTING MOTHER:

GROUP 5, 6 (COMBINED): CHILDREN NOT FREED
(Mother Out of Picture, Father Available; Mother Available)

Problems or Conditions Affecting Mother	Service Contact Already Established	Referral Needed and Planned	Referral Needed but Service Unavailable	Service Not Required	Parent Unwilling to Use Service	Un-known	Other/ Not Applicable
				(Percentaged)			
Inadequate Housing	8.1	4.3	4.3	14.5	5.3	3.3	60.1
Unemployment or Unsuitable Job	3.7	0.7	1.8	16.3	2.7	3.7	71.1
Poor Work Performance	0.6	0.6	0.3	16.4	1.2	4.4	76.4
Inadequate Income for Basic Needs	7.6	2.4	4.1	14.5	1.9	3.7	65.8
Health Problems, Physical Illness	13.6	0.7	0.1	12.6	2.8	4.1	65.9
Child-rearing/ Child Care Practices	10.7	3.3	1.0	14.1	16.6	4.6	49.8
Marital Problems	3.3	0.4	0.3	14.4	6.7	4.6	70.4
Criminal Problem	1.5	--	0.1	16.1	0.6	4.3	77.3
Alcoholism	7.0	0.3	0.1	13.6	8.7	4.4	65.8
Drug Abuse	4.3	0.4	0.3	15.7	2.4	4.4	72.4
Mental Illness	13.0	0.6	0.1	12.1	7.4	4.4	62.2
Mental Retardation	2.2	--	0.3	16.4	1.5	3.9	75.7
Management of Home	4.9	1.8	2.4	14.2	9.5	4.3	63.0
Management of Money, Budgeting, etc.	5.8	0.9	2.4	14.1	7.1	3.7	66.1
Health Practices	3.4	0.7	0.1	13.3	3.7	4.4	74.2
Severe Personal Adjustment Problem: Depression	12.0	2.4	0.3	8.4	11.1	5.5	60.3
Severe Personal Adjustment Problem: Other	4.7	1.2	0.3	7.1	6.5	4.7	75.4
Parent-Child Relationship Problem	12.4	2.4	0.4	12.9	16.4	4.6	50.8
Other	1.2	--	0.4	4.1	0.4	4.3	89.5
Number of Children				(675)			

4 Prospects for Discharge

The most specific question one might direct to an agency responsible for planning for a child in foster care would take the form: "What is the agency's discharge plan for this child?" In Table 10, the tabulated responses to this question for the almost 1,300 cases covered by the survey are set forth.

We observe the important finding that for all the children covered by the survey, less than one in five (18.5 percent) were destined to be discharged to their parents. An additional 3.9 percent of the children were reported to have a discharge plan calling for them to live in a relative's home. Thus, less than one child in four was said to be slated to be returned to his own parents or relatives.

The widespread unavailability of parents is highlighted by the fact that for a large proportion of the children, it was indicated that the children would be discharged to their own responsibility (35.6 percent) or would be placed for adoption (28.3 percent). In 13 percent of the cases, the reporting caseworkers were unable to specify a discharge plan.

As might be anticipated, the discharge planning of the agency appears conditioned by the availability of the parents. Table 10 shows that Groups 1 to 4, where the mother is out of the picture, are very rarely seen as potential resources in discharge planning. Only 1.3 percent of the 520 children included in the four groups have a discharge plan which would result in their eventual return to a parent. This dismal picture is not surprising since the groups were organized as research entities by criteria which specified the unavailability of the mothers and fathers for service contacts.

The prospects for discharge to parents is somewhat brighter for the children in the group where the father was available, but not the mother (Group 5) and for those children in the group where the mother was available for service contacts (Group 6). Almost a fourth of the former had a discharge plan to be returned home and this was true of almost a third of the latter group. The more positive picture is only relative, however, because substantial proportions of both groups were apparently slated to be discharged to their own responsibility (46.2 percent of Group 5 and 29.4 percent of Group 6) or to be adopted (16.3 percent of Group 5 and 17.0 percent of Group 6).

Prospect for Return

Social workers filling out the Mini-project 2 booklet were asked to respond to the global question: "What is the agency's perspective about the possibility of the child's return home to own parent(s)?" The response categories they could choose from included: *no prospect*, *slight prospect*, *moderate prospect*, *good prospect*, and *other*.

Table 11 displays the percentage distributions of the responses of the social workers according to the six groups organized by the availability of the parents for service involvement. For all children included in the study, we observe that for almost two-thirds (63.5 percent) there was *no prospect* seen for the child's return home. If we include the 6.3 percent where the response was *not applicable* because the parent was not available and the 10.5 percent where the response was *slight prospect*, we come to the summary conclusion that it is unlikely that four out of every five children in the study will ever return to their natural parents.

It is clear that the four groups where the mother was out of the picture because she was deceased, her whereabouts unknown, she had not been seen in two years or was confined in a mental hospital showed almost no prospects whatever for the return of the children to their parents. For the 520 children in the four groups combined, some 83.1 percent were perceived by the social workers as having *no prospect* for returning home and an additional 9.4 percent were rated as *not applicable* because there was no parent in the picture. An additional 4.2 percent of the cases had responses which indicated the prospects were unknown. Only 3.3 percent of the cases were rated as having any prospect for the child's return to the natural parents.

For the children in Group 5 whose mothers were out of the picture but where the fathers were available, the aggregated picture was somewhat better than for Groups 1 to 4. For 39.5 percent of the cases, it was indicated that there was *slight* (18.3 percent), *moderate* (13.5 percent) or a *good prospect* (7.7 percent) that the child would return home. But even for this group, a large number of children were said to have *no prospect* for return to a natural parent: this was true for 56.6 percent of the children.

As might be anticipated, the group where the mothers were identified as being in the picture showed the largest proportion where the social workers perceived *some pros-*

TABLE 10

AGENCY DISCHARGE PLAN FOR CHILD ACCORDING TO AVAILABILITY OF PARENTS FOR SERVICE INVOLVEMENT
(N = 1293)

Discharge Plan	Group 1 (Mother Deceased)	Group 2 (Mother's Whereabouts Unknown)	Group 3 (Mother Not Seen in Two Years)	Group 4 (Mother in Mental Hospital)	Groups 1 to 4 (Combined)	Group 5 (Mother Out of Picture; Father Available)	Group 6 (Mother Available)	TOTAL
				(Percentaged)				
To Parent	0.9	1.3	1.4	2.6	1.3	23.1	31.1	18.5
To Relative	5.3	1.3	1.4	7.9	2.7	4.8	4.6	3.9
To Own Responsibility	52.6	38.0	37.4	47.4	41.7	46.2	29.4	35.6
To Adoption	27.2	50.0	53.5	39.5	45.2	16.3	17.0	28.3
Other	--	1.8	--	--	1.0	--	0.6	0.7
Unknown	14.0	7.6	6.3	2.6	8.1	9.6	17.3	13.0
Total Number of Children	100.0 (114)	100.0 (224)	100.0 (144)	100.0 (38)	100.0 (520)	100.0 (104)	100.0 (669)	100.0 (1293)

TABLE 11

AGENCY PERSPECTIVES ON POTENTIALITY OF CHILD'S RETURN HOME ACCORDING TO AVAILABILITY OF PARENTS FOR SERVICE INVOLVEMENT*
(N = 1293)

Agency's Perspectives on Child's Return Home	Group 1 (Mother Deceased)	Group 2 (Mother's Whereabouts Unknown)	Group 3 (Mother Not Seen in Two Years)	Group 4 (Mother in Mental Hospital)	Groups 1 to 4 (Combined)	Group 5 (Mother Out of Picture; Father Available)	Group 6 (Mother Available)	TOTAL
				(Percentaged)				
No Prospect	74.5	88.1	81.2	86.9	83.1	56.6	49.5	63.5
Slight Prospect	4.4	1.3	2.8	2.6	2.5	18.3	15.5	10.5
Moderate Prospect	--	0.4	--	2.6	0.4	13.5	13.5	8.1
Good Prospect	--	0.4	0.7	--	0.4	7.7	15.1	8.7
Other/Not Applicable	9.7	7.6	13.9	2.6	9.4	2.9	4.2	6.3
Unknown	11.4	2.2	1.4	5.3	4.2	1.0	2.2	2.9
Total Number of Children	100.0 (114)	100.0 (224)	100.0 (144)	100.0 (38)	100.0 (520)	100.0 (104)	100.0 (669)	100.0 (1293)

*The case worker filling out the form was asked, "What is the agency's perspective about the possibility of the child's return home to own parent(s)?" The response categories provided included: no prospect, slight prospect, moderate prospect, good prospect and other.

pect for the reunification of the children and their families. This was true of 44.1 percent of the 669 children included in Group 6; these were almost evenly divided between those whose prospects were seen as *slight, moderate,* and *good.* It is sobering to note, however, that 49.5 percent of the children were rated as having *no prospect* for return home and an additional 4.2 percent were in situations where reunification planning was responded to as *not applicable.*

If the respondents indicated no prospect (or only a slight prospect) for the children's return home, they were requested to provide the reasons for such a viewpoint. Their comments reflect the high degree of disturbance and/or dysfunctional parental behavior observed by them:

> The natural father has faced the fact that he is incapable of providing love and care for this child. The natural mother refuses to surrender the child. She admits that she may not be ready now but hopes to be someday in the nebulous future.

> Child has been in care since 1966. Initial attempts to involve mother were futile. She was hospitalized for mental illness and it was determined she was incapable of caring for any of her 8 children. She does not wish involvement with any but her youngest child (born 1971). She refuses to release her children for adoption. Another agency has planning responsibility and is working on freeing the children.

> This client does not follow through with planning. She is very dependent on agencies and is involved with many. She is manipulative and able to confuse most situations to the point that she still ends up unserviced though she comes across as cooperative, making it difficult to help this woman plan.

> Client is virulently hostile toward everyone in contact with her. She is known to many social agencies, all of whom have found her absolutely impossible to work with due to her outright refusal to work cooperatively with staff. She is vituperative, antagonistic, and negative to all staff. Positive casework intervention is fruitless. Client has been violently abusive towards her own mother, her sister, and the child, who needs protection from her. Mother is sociopathic and visits have been terminated by agency. We are in court to free child for adoption.

The fact that less than ten percent of the almost 1,300 children covered by this survey are deemed to have good prospects for being reunited with their biological parents provides a perspective about the nature of the service delivery situation that is extremely important from a service planning perspective. If the caseworkers' judgments are valid, it would appear that a very large proportion of the parents of children in foster care are not promising targets for service intervention.

Support or Opposition to Returning Child to Parents

The social workers were asked to respond to the following inquiry: "Given the current situation, what would the likely attitude of the agency be if the parent(s) expressed the desire to take the child home?" The response categories provided included indications that agency would *strongly support, moderately support, moderately oppose,* or would *strongly oppose* the child's return home. The response frequencies are set forth in Table 12. They are quite revealing.

There is strong indication from the aggregation of responses that it is relatively rare for the worker to strongly support the possibility of the parent taking the child home and it is only in a modest percentage of the cases that even moderate support would be forthcoming. The lack of enthusiasm is, as might be expected, most pronounced for the four groups of children where the mother is unavailable for service contacts because she is entirely out of the picture (Groups 1-4). In only less than one percent of these cases is there indication of strong support for return and in only four percent does the prospect arouse even moderate support. The overwhelming response tendency is to strongly oppose the return (41.5 percent) or to rule it out as not applicable since there is no viable parental home to consider (25.6 percent).

Of considerable importance is the fact that the social workers indicated in almost 42 percent of the cases where the mother was presumably available for service (Group 6) that they would strongly oppose having the parent take the child home and in 16 percent of the cases they responded that they would moderately oppose such a step. In only 12.4 percent of the cases would they strongly support the move and in almost 19 percent of the cases, they would offer only moderate support for return. This is an extremely bleak picture. The situation can be put into bold relief: (1) In 40 percent of the cases, the mother is out of the picture and so is the father. Less than five percent of these cases would garner even moderate support for the child's return to his parents. (2) In 60 percent of the cases, either the mother or the father is in the picture but in less than a third of these cases would the parents receive even moderate support from the agency if they indicated the desire to take their children home.

TABLE 12

AGENCY'S ATTITUDE TOWARD POSSIBILITY OF PARENT TAKING CHILD HOME ACCORDING TO AVAILABILITY OF PARENTS FOR SERVICE INVOLVEMENT*
(N = 1293)

Agency's Likely Attitude	Group 1 (Mother Deceased)	Group 2 (Mother's Whereabouts Unknown)	Group 3 (Mother Not Seen in Two Years)	Group 4 (Mother in Mental Hospital)	Groups 1 to 4 (Combined)	Group 5 (Mother Out of Picture; Father Available)	Group 6 (Mother Available)	Groups 5 and 6 (Combined)
				(Percentaged)				
Strongly Support	0.9	0.5	1.4	--	0.8	13.5	12.4	12.6
Moderately Support	4.4	4.0	4.9	5.3	4.4	18.3	18.8	18.7
Moderately Oppose	5.3	4.9	9.0	7.9	6.4	17.3	16.0	16.2
Strongly Oppose	21.9	42.8	48.5	65.7	41.5	34.5	41.7	40.7
Other/Not Applicable	20.2	28.6	29.2	10.5	25.6	14.4	8.7	9.4
Unknown	8.8	8.9	3.5	5.3	7.1	1.0	2.2	2.1
No Parents to Care for Child	38.5	10.3	3.5	5.3	14.2	1.0	0.2	0.3
Total Number of Children	100.0 (114)	100.0 (224)	100.0 (144)	100.0 (38)	100.0 (520)	100.0 (104)	100.0 (669)	100.0 (773)

*The caseworker filling out the form was asked: "Given the current situation, what would the likely attitude of the agency be if the parent(s) expressed the desire to take the child home?" The response categories provided included: strongly support, moderately support, moderately oppose, and strongly oppose.

5 Creation and Analysis of Service-Related Index Scores

When the content of the items created by the investigator for the survey questionnaire (shown in the appendix) is examined by the reader, it should be readily apparent that they reflect a number of relatively identifiable phenomenological domains. Two subject areas stand out as particularly important and these are now singled out for special consideration and treatment. Two indexes were created to reflect these domains.

Mother's Capacity for Service Involvement

One of these measures is a composite of nine Likert-type scale items. It has been given the name *Index of Mother's Capacity for Service Involvement*.[11] It is designed to measure the parent's typical behavioral stance with regard to involvement with the agency's social worker, particularly around efforts designed to make it possible for the child to return to a restored parental home.

The second index is based upon four Likert-type scale items. It has been titled *Index of Viability of Natural Parent's Home as Resource for Child*. Conceptually, the index is designed to measure the social worker's orientation as to whether the natural home can be expected to be restored as a permanent home for the child.

From a methodological standpoint, the approach to index construction utilized here was fairly routine and familiar to survey analysts.[12] The items were composited upon the basis of their manifest content and their relevance to two practice concerns: (a) the ability of the agency to involve the parents in the helping process so as to be able to more effectively overcome the problems and conditions causing the ongoing need for the child's placement, and (b) the degree to which the child's home appeared restorable. *Process* and *outcome* are the areas of interest reflected in the two indexes.

It was considered desirable that the items be fairly highly intercorrelated and that each item be firmly correlated with the composite of the other items included in the same index (with the item itself excluded to correct for autocorrelation). In addition, it was hoped that the internal reliability of each index, as measured by Cronbach's alpha, would show that the items "belonged" in the composite group to which they were assigned, that is, that they showed qualities of internal consistency.[13]

The intercorrelations among the nine items included in the Index of the Mother's Capacity for Service Involvement is shown in Table 13 for the total group and for those cases included in Group 6 only. The items are all clearly related to each other in content. In addition, it should be noted that each item is substantially correlated with total scores.[14]

The internal reliability measure (alpha) is quite high for the entire group (.937) and was also found to be high when calculated for each of the separate groupings.[15]

When the mean scores of the six groups were compared, the one-way analysis of variance showed them to be significantly different (p<.001) with Group 6 showing a considerably higher mean score than all the other groups ($\bar{X}$ = 15.205) and mothers in mental hospitals showing the next highest mean score ($\bar{X}$ = 6.935).

Viability of Natural Parent Home

The Index of the Viability of the Natural Parent Home as a Resource for Child was based upon responses to the four questions shown in Table 14. The content of these cover the agency's discharge plan, the parent's attitude toward taking the child home, the agency's perspective on the prospect for the child's return and the likely attitude of the agency if the parent expressed a desire to take the child home.

The intercorrelation of items and the item-total correlations are fairly substantial but more modest in size than for those reported for the previous index. The alpha for the total group is .835 and for Group 6 alone is .830 indicating a fairly substantial degree of internal consistency.

The one-way analysis of variance was calculated to test the difference of mean scores for the six groups. The result was significant (p<.001) and Groups 5 and 6 were clearly seen in more positive terms as resources for their children.

The one criterion which the two indexes were not clearly established to meet is the matter of their orthogonality. The issue of whether the indexes tapped two separate domains was dealt with in a less than rigorous manner. Instead of using a factor analysis to empirically determine the grounds for compositing variables, the investigator preferred to rely upon an understanding of the importance of the two domains for the realities of service delivery in this practice area. This orientation may of course be open to question.

TABLE 13

INDEX OF MOTHER'S CAPACITY FOR SERVICE INVOLVEMENT

Items

Question 21: Have any of the following problems been evidenced in attempting to establish an ongoing service contact with the parent? (7 items)

    a. Resists seeing social worker
    b. Fails to keep appointments
    c. Is late for appointments
    d. Is unable to discuss personal problems
    e. Is defensive about self
    f. Fails to show concern about child
    g. Is excessively dependent

    Responses: 3   Not at all
                  2   Somewhat
                  1   Very much
                  0   Not applicable

Question 12: Please indicate if any of the following circumstances have served to lower the frequency of parental contact with the social worker?

    j. Low motivation to see social worker

    Responses: 3   Not at all
                  2   Somewhat
                1   Very much
                0   Not applicable

Question 22: How would you characterize the quality of the working relationship between the parent and the social worker as it has manifested itself over the past six months?

    Responses: 5   Good
                  4   Fairly good
                  3   Mixed or average
                  2   Fairly poor
                  1   Very poor
                  0   No relationship

(*Continued*)

TABLE 13 (Continued)

INDEX OF MOTHER'S CAPACITY FOR SERVICE INVOLVEMENT

	A	B	C	D	E	F	G	H	I	Total	Group 6 Only
A	--	.75	.67	.66	.65	.67	.48	.48	.44	.87	.80
B	.84	--	.80	.62	.59	.66	.51	.40	.38	.85	.78
C	.76	.85	--	.62	.57	.64	.53	.40	.35	.82	.75
D	.77	.75	.75	--	.72	.68	.56	.40	.36	.85	.75
E	.77	.72	.70	.82	--	.62	.58	.37	.42	.83	.74
F	.80	.78	.74	.79	.75	--	.53	.40	.31	.84	.73
G	.67	.66	.68	.71	.72	.70	--	.32	.33	.76	.62
H	.58	.53	.51	.53	.51	.54	.48	--	.33	.61	.50
I	.65	.59	.57	.60	.62	.57	.56	.50	--	.68	.46

Columns A–I under "Intercorrelation Among Items[a]"; Total and Group 6 Only under "Corrected Item - Total Correlation[b]".

[a] Correlations above the diagonal are based upon 668 children's cases in Group 6 (available mothers); correlations below the diagonal are based upon all cases in the study (N = 1290).

[b] Correlation is between each item and the sum of all other items in the index with the item itself deleted to correct for auto-correlation.

Internal Reliabilities

		Alpha	Standardized Item Alpha
Group 2	Whereabouts Unknown	.918	.919
Group 3	Not Seen in 2 Years	.889	.896
Group 4	In Mental Hospital	.904	.936
Group 5	Father Known	.903	.930
Group 6	Mother Known	.894	.908
	TOTAL	.937	.948

(Continued)

TABLE 13 (Continued)

MOTHER'S CAPACITY FOR SERVICE INVOLVEMENT ACCORDING TO PARENT AVAILABILITY GROUPINGS

		Mean	Standard Deviation	Number of Children
Group 1	Deceased	0.412	1.099	114
Group 2	Whereabouts Unknown	2.603	4.428	224
Group 3	Not Seen in 2 Years	4.427	5.501	143
Group 4	In Mental Hospital	6.935	7.666	38
Group 5	Father Known	3.125	5.251	104
Group 6	Mother Known	15.205	8.127	669
	TOTAL (Groups 1-6)	9.290	9.152	1292

Analysis of Variance Table

	Mean Square	DF	F-test	Significance
Among Groups	10012.082	5	221.433	Under .001
Within Groups	45.215	1286		

TABLE 14

INDEX OF VIABILITY OF NATURAL PARENT HOME
AS RESOURCE FOR CHILD (MOTHER INDEX)

Items

Question 14: What is the agency's present discharge plan for the child?

    Responses:
- 5   To parents
- 3   To relatives
- 1   To own responsibility
- 1   To adoption
- 0   Unknown

Question 17: What is the parent's attitude toward child's return home?

    Responses:
- 5   Eager for child's return
- 3   Moderately interested in child's return
- 2   Moderately disinterested in child's return
- 1   Opposed to child's return
- 1   Plans to surrender child
- 0   Has surrendered child
- 0   Not applicable, unknown

Question 18A: What is the agency's perspective about the possibility of the child's return to own parent(s)?

    Responses:
- 5   See good prospect for child's return
- 3   See moderate prospect for child's return
- 2   See slight prospect for child's return
- 1   See no prospect for child's return to parent in foreseeable future
- 0   Not applicable, unknown

Question 19A: Given the current situation, what would the likely attitude of the agency be if the parent(s) expressed the desire to take the child home?

    Responses:
- 5   Would strongly support return
- 4   Would moderately support return
- 2   Would moderately oppose return
- 1   Would strongly oppose return
- 0   Not applicable, unknown

(Continued)

TABLE 14 (Continued)

INDEX OF VIABILITY OF NATURAL PARENT HOME
AS RESOURCE FOR CHILD (MOTHER INDEX)

	Intercorrelations Among Items[a]				Corrected Item - Total Correlations[b]	
	A	B	C	D	Total	Group 6 Only
A	--	.72	.55	.47	.68	.68
B	.50	--	.68	.54	.59	.79
C	.72	.57	--	.44	.80	.65
D	.54	.49	.68	--	.65	.55

[a] Correlations above the diagonal based upon 668 children's cases in Group 6 (available mothers); correlations below the diagonal are based upon all cases in the study (N = 1290).

[b] Correlation is between each item and the sum of all other items in the index with the item itself deleted to correct for autocorrelation.

Internal Reliabilities

		Alpha	Standardized Item Alpha
Group 1	Deceased	.364	.394
Group 2	Whereabouts Unknown	.370	.395
Group 3	Not Seen in 2 Years	.719	.759
Group 4	In Mental Hospital	.420	.504
Group 5	Father Known	.630	.623
Group 6	Mother Known	.830	.839
	TOTAL	.835	.847

(Continued)

TABLE 14 (Continued)

VIABILITY OF NATURAL PARENT HOME AS RESOURCE FOR CHILD
ACCORDING TO PARENT AVAILABILITY GROUPINGS

		Mean	Standard Deviation	Number of Children
Group 1	Deceased	2.386	1.536	114
Group 2	Whereabouts Unknown	2.866	1.631	224
Group 3	Not Seen in 2 Years	3.357	2.378	143
Group 4	In Mental Hospital	3.921	2.132	38
Group 5	Father Known	6.144	4.096	104
Group 6	Mother Known	8.580	5.718	669
	TOTAL (Groups 1-6)	6.139	5.186	1292

Analysis of Variance Table

	Mean Square	DF	F-test	Significance
Among Groups	1857.023	5	93.772	Under .001
Within Groups	19.804	1286		

The lack of independence between the scores (r = .58) suggests one overall content domain constituting a more global evaluation of the parents covering *both* their ability to participate in the helping process and the degree to which the home had the potential of ever being restored as a source of family permanency for the child.

"Understanding" the Index Scores

In order to prove the sources of variation in the two indexes, multiple regression analyses were performed using selected background variables as predictors of index scores. The results are shown in Tables 15 and 16. For the Index of Mother's Capacity for Service Involvement, the best source of explained variance was the dummy variable indicating whether or not the child was slated to be placed for adoption. This variable explained 4.7 percent of the unique variance. The results indicated, as one might expect, that a case being designated as suited for adoption planning was one in which the mother tended to be seen as a poor candidate for service involvement.

The child's current age and location in a foster home as opposed to group homes or institutions emerged as the next best predictors. The direction of our correlations indicated that parents of older children and those placed in institutions were seen as more available for service contacts while parents of infants, almost always placed in foster homes, were perceived as more elusive candidates for service intervention.

From the other significant predictors, it emerges that characteristics of cases that are linked to more promising prospects for service availability are: abandonment *not* being a reason for placement, placement for reason of the parent's alcoholism or the child's uncontrolled behavior at home, and the child *not* being placed through court action.

The multiple correlation for the eight variables included in the regression analyses was .41. The amount of variance accounted for was 17 percent.

When we scrutinize the results of the multiple regression analysis shown in Table 16, we find that children were more likely to be perceived as having a viable natural parent home to return to if the following conditions obtained: (1) the children had been in care for lesser periods of time; (2) adoption had *not* been specified as a discharge plan; (3) the children were in institutions or group homes rather than in foster family care; (4) they were younger; (5) they had *not* been placed because of abandonment or because of neglect; (6) they had *not* been placed through the courts; and (7) they were males.

The multiple correlation for the predictors cited was .52, accounting for 27 percent of the variance. We observe that an indication that adoption is being planned for the child accounted for 6.9 percent of unique variance in the index scores, a quite sizable amount.

An Attempt at Predictive Validation of the Index Scores: An Analysis of Discharge

An opportunity to test the validity of the index scores was available by virtue of the fact that CWIS maintained an ongoing data file for all children in care. With continuous updating by agencies of information on the status of the children, it was possible to determine whether the subjects in the study were still in foster placements almost two years after the mini-project's research forms had been filled out.

Information about discharge status provided an opportunity for predictive validation of the two indexes. It was recognized, however, that this criterion variable was more related in manifest content to the Index of the Viability of the Natural Parent Home as a Resource for the Child than it was to the Index of the Mother's Capacity for Service Involvement. The ability to become involved in service activity was, however, seen as a potentially important consideration for some parents if they were ever to overcome the problems preventing them from taking their children home.

The discharge status of the subjects as of June 30, 1978 is shown in Table 17. After the passage of almost two years from the time of the initial gathering of data for the project, 64.2 percent of the children were still in foster care. About 18 percent had been discharged to their parents or relatives while 5.6 percent were adopted. Being discharged to their own responsibility accounted for 6.6 percent of the children in the sample.

The differences in discharge status for the children in the six groups organized around the availability of the parents for service contacts was relatively minor, i.e., the percentage of children remaining in care after two years was fairly similar across groups, ranging from 61.4 percent of the children in Group 6 (mother available) to 71.3 percent of those in Group 2 (mother's whereabouts unknown). However, there are important differences among the groups with respect to the destinations of the children who left care. Thus, the subjects in Group 6 (mother available) show the largest proportion going to the homes of parents or relatives (26.9 percent) with Group 5 (father available) the next largest group (16.3 percent). This was only true of 11.4 percent of the children in Group 1 (mother deceased), 4.5 percent of those in Group 2 (mother's whereabouts unknown) and 9.1 percent of the youngsters in Group 3 (mother not seen in over two years).

Very few of the children whose mothers and fathers were available were discharged to their own responsibility, while this accounted for twice the proportions of those in the first four groups where mothers and fathers were both unavailable for agency service contacts. On the other hand, adoption tended to be a phenomenon primarily associated with Group 2 (mother's whereabouts unknown) and Group 3 (mother not seen in more than two years).

For the purpose of testing the predictive validity of the index scores, a decision was made to remove from the analysis the subjects who had departed from foster care via the route of adoption, discharge to own responsibility, or by being transferred to an institution outside of the foster care system, e.g., mental hospitals or correctional institutions. Their discharge was clearly not a positive outcome related to the viability of the parental home or the parent's service involvement.

Treating *discharge vs. remaining in care* as a dichotomous dependent variable, it was possible to undertake a multiple regression analysis using the two index scores as

TABLE 15

RELATION OF SELECTED INDEPENDENT VARIABLES
TO INDEX OF MOTHER'S CAPACITY FOR SERVICE INVOLVEMENT
(N = 1290)

Independent Variables[a]	Zero-order Correlation	Standardized Regression Coefficient	Percent Unique Variance Explained
1. Discharge Plan: Adoption (no/YES)	-.25***	-.25***	4.7
2. Years in Foster Care	-.24***	-.05	0.1
3. Reason Placed: Parental Abandonment (no/YES)	-.15***	-.10***	1.0
4. Child's Current Age	-.09**	-.22***	2.5
5. Current Location (others/FOSTER HOME)	-.22***	-.15***	1.5
6. Reason Placed: Parental Alcoholism (no/YES)	.10***	.09***	0.8
7. Reason Placed: Child's Home Behavior (no/YES)	.16***	.06*	0.3
8. Court Adjudication (no/YES)	-.10***	-.05*	0.3
Multiple R		.41	
Multiple R^2		.17	

*p < .05   **p < .01   ***p < .001

[a] Independent variables were entered to meet the criterion of "best prediction." The first variable selected was the one with the highest correlation with the dependent variable. The next variable selected is the variable with the maximum partial correlation with the dependent variable, relative to the independent variable that has already been entered into the equation, and so forth. This produces a solution which is "stepwise" in the usual sense, meaning that the best variable was entered at each step.

TABLE 16

RELATION OF SELECTED INDEPENDENT VARIABLES TO INDEX OF VIABILITY
OF NATURAL PARENT HOME AS RESOURCE FOR CHILD
(N = 1290)

Independent Variables[a]	Zero-order Correlation	Standardized Regression Coefficient	Percent Unique Variance Explained
1. Years in Care	-.37***	-.16***	1.5
2. Discharge Plan: Adoption (no/YES)	-.31***	-.30***	6.9
3. Current Location (others/FOSTER HOME)	-.31***	-.23***	3.4
4. Current Age of Child	-.13***	-.23***	2.8
5. Reason Placed: Abandonment (no/YES)	-.12***	-.07**	0.4
6. Reason Placed: Neglect (no/YES)	-.03	-.07**	0.4
7. Court Placement (other/YES)	-.09***	-.06*	0.3
8. Sex of Child (male/FEMALE)	-.07**	-.05*	0.3
Multiple R		.52	
Multiple R^2		.27	

*$p < .05$ **$p < .01$ ***$p < .001$

[a] Independent variables were entered to meet the criterion of "best prediction" criterion as discussed in the note shown in Table 14.

TABLE 17

STATUS OF SUBJECTS AT FOLLOW-UP (JUNE 30, 1978) ACCORDING TO AVAILABILITY OF PARENTS
(N = 1290)

Status of Subjects	Group 1 (Mother Deceased)	Group 2 (Mother's Whereabouts Unknown)	Group 3 (Mother Not Seen in Two Years)	Group 4 (Mother in Mental Hospital)	Group 5 (Mother Out of Picture; Father Available)	Group 6 (Mother Available)	TOTAL
			(Percentaged)				
In Care	63.1	71.3	63.6	71.1	67.3	61.4	64.2
Discharged to Parent or Relative (Including Trial Discharge)	11.4	4.5	9.1	5.3	16.3	26.9	18.2
Adopted	5.3	12.1	14.7	2.6	4.8	1.8	5.6
Discharged to Own Responsibility	13.2	8.1	8.4	18.4	5.8	4.0	6.6
Transferred to Other Institution	--	0.9	--	--	--	0.1	0.2
Other	3.5	0.9	1.4	--	1.0	1.2	1.3
Out of Care/ Location Unknown[a]	3.5	2.2	2.8	2.6	4.8	4.6	3.9
Total Number of Children	100.0 (114)	100.0 (223)	100.0 (143)	100.0 (38)	100.0 (104)	100.0 (668)	100.0 (1290)

[a] At follow-up these children (49 in number) were no longer in the CWIS data file, but their discharge destination was not retrieved.

predictors along with other selected variables. The results of the multiple regression analysis are shown in Table 18.

It should be pointed out that the independent variables were entered in the usual stepwise manner without predetermining the order of entry. Rather, the computer option used called for the entrance of variables in the order of their ability to predict variance at each computational stage.

Table 18 demonstrates that the scores derived from the Index of the Viability of the Natural Parent Home as a Resource for the Child is the most important predictor of discharge. The product-moment correlation between the index score and the discharge status of the subjects was the highest for all predictor variables ($r = .38$; $p < .001$). The standardized regression coefficient was more substantial than those reported for other regressor variables (beta = .31; $p < .001$) and the percent of unique variance explained was fairly high (7.6 percent).

Table 18 shows that only two other variables were significant predictors: the dummy variable depicting the child's home behavior as a reason for placement (yes/NO) and the years a child had spent in foster care. Children entering care because of behavior difficulties were more likely to have intact homes to which they could be returned. It was also likely that the longer a child had been in care, the less likely he/she was to return home. The predictive power of this last variable, however, was very modest.

It is important to note that about a dozen variables were excluded from the regression analysis after the first six variables had been entered because their partial correlations with the dependent variables were trivial. These included information about the child's age, current location (foster home vs. other care facilities), court involvement, the child's sex, ethnicity and selected reasons for placement (in dummy variable form).

Attention should be given to the fact that scores derived from the Index of the Mother's Capacity for Service Involvement showed a very small partial correlation with discharge status ($r = .02$). The triviality of this index as a predictor variable can likely be accounted for by two facts: (1) the content of the index is more closely related to the behaviors and attitudes of the mothers vis-a-vis the relationship with the social worker than it is to discharge, and (2) the index's relatively high correlation with the index dealing with the viability of the child's home resulted in its predictive variance being preempted by the latter because of the order in which the variables were entered. The Index of Viability is clearly more closely related in content to the phenomenon of discharge status.

We observe that the multiple correlation for the six predictive variables shown in Table 18 was .42 and about 18 percent of the variance in discharge was thus explained.

Another way of looking at the information provided by the index characterizing the viability of the natural parent's home is shown in Table 19. The children were divided into four groups: (a) discharged children where the mothers were not available, (b) discharged children where the mothers were available, (c) children still in care where the mothers were not available, and (d) children still in care where the mothers were available. Mean index scores were determined for the four groups and an analysis of variance was computed covering the two factors of mother availability and discharge status.

The analysis shows the groups to be well discriminated with respect to their mean scores. We observe that the group which showed the highest scores were the 74 children whose mothers were available for service and who had been discharged (Mean = 13.5). The group with the lowest scores were the 366 children whose mothers were not available and who were still in care at the end of two years (Mean = 3.85). The group of children whose mothers were available but were still in care showed a mean score significantly lower than children of the same type of mothers who had been discharged (Mean = 7.50). For the small group of ten children whose mothers were not available for service but who nevertheless were discharged to a parent or relative, the mean score was fairly high (Mean = 8.0). While both factors being tested showed significant differences in mean scores, the interaction of these factors was not statistically significant.

Who Shall Be Served?

Another cogent issue we sought to address was the matter of service contacts with the parents subsequent to the original data gathering for the project. This constituted another basis upon which the validity of the index scores could be assessed. For this purpose, we again turn to the standard CWIS reports of June 30, 1978.

In Table 20, we display the service data reported for our subjects from the CWIS data files. The children discharged over the two years since the earlier data had been collected are not included in this analysis. The data are displayed by groupings according to the availability of the parents for service involvement. Groups 1-4 have been combined to reflect the cases where the mothers were out of the picture and the fathers were also uninvolved. Almost 80 percent of the cases had not had any services provided to the family of the child during the six months covered by the social workers' reports and almost 12 percent of the cases had responses that indicated the information was unknown or that questions about service to the parents were not applicable.

The mothers included in Group 6 included 40.4 percent who were reported to receive no service. It is noteworthy that 21 percent of the mothers needed psychiatric therapy and service was planned and 11.6 percent had received such service during the review period. For almost 20 percent of the cases, the social workers indicated that the question of service contacts with the parents did not apply.

The fathers included in Group 5 show a pattern similar to the one reported for the mothers in Group 6. They included 43.7 percent who had received no service and 31.2 percent for whom service was no longer an appropriate issue. The amount of service provided, as reported by the social workers, was extremely modest in each category provided.

In Table 21, we show the information about service delivered to the families in a somewhat different form. If the family, as distinct from the child, received any service, including family counseling, the case was categorized as "received service"; otherwise, it was categorized as "did not receive service." This dichotomized information is shown for the six groups of children—mother deceased, whereabouts unknown, etc.—for three categories of chil-

TABLE 18

PREDICTING THE DISCHARGE OF CHILDREN TO NATURAL PARENTS
OVER A TWO-YEAR TIME SPAN
(N = 971)

Independent Variables[a]	Zero-order Correlation	Standardized Regression Coefficient	Percent Unique Variance Explained
1. Index Score (Viability of Natural Parent Home as Resource for Child)	.38***	.31***	7.6
2. Reason Placed: Child's Home Behavior (no/YES)	.24***	.14***	1.7
3. Years in Care	-.22***	-.07*	0.4
4. Reason Placed: Alcoholic Parent (no/YES)	-.03	-.05	0.2
5. Discharge Plan: Adoption (no/YES)	-.15***	-.03	0.1
6. Reason Placed: Abandoned (no/YES)	-.08*	-.03	0.1
Multiple R		.42	
Multiple R^2		.18	

*p < .05   ***p < .001

Partial Correlations with Dependent Variable for Variables Not Entered:

Current Age	.01	Parental Contact	-.01
Current Location	-.02	Reason Placed-Drugs	-.02
Court Placement	.01	Reason Placed-Neglect	.01
Court Adjudication	.00	Reason Placed-Abuse	.02
Sex	-.02	Index Score (Mother's Capacity for Service Involvement)	.02
Ethnicity-Black	-.03		
Ethnicity-Hispanic	-.01		

[a]The independent variables reflect data collected within three months of June 30, 1976. The discharge data were obtained from the CWIS data file as of June 30, 1978. Children who were discharged to their own responsibility were adopted or were discharged to a mental institution are not included in this analysis. In the multiple regression performed here, independent variables were entered to meet the criterion of "best prediction."

TABLE 19

MEAN SCORES ON INDEX OF NATURAL PARENT'S HOME AS A RESOURCE
FOR THE CHILD ACCORDING TO AVAILABILITY OF MOTHERS
AND DISCHARGE STATUS OF CHILDREN ON JUNE 30, 1978[a]
(N = 892)

		Discharged	In Care	Row Marginals
Mother Not Available[b]	Mean S.D. N	8.00 6.43 10	3.85 2.75 366	5.93
Mother Available	Mean S.D. N	13.15 5.90 74	7.50 5.15 442	10.33
Column Marginals	Mean	10.57	5.68	8.13

Analysis of Variance

Source	Sum of Squares	DF	Mean Square	F-Test	Significance
(A) Mother Availability	653.63	1	653.63	33.426***	Under .001
(B) Discharge to Parents	809.85	1	809.85	41.415***	Under .001
A x B	18.889	1	18.888	0.966	.326
Unit	17364.605	888	19.555		

---

[a] 398 Children discharged to own responsibility, placed for adoption or leaving care to unknown destination not included in this analysis.

[b] Includes children whose mother was deceased, whereabouts unknown, not seen in two years, or was in a mental hospital.

TABLE 20

DELIVERY OF SERVICES TO FAMILIES*

GROUPS 1-4 (COMBINED):
(Mother Deceased; Whereabouts Unknown; Not Seen in Two Years; or in Mental Hospital)

Service Delivery	Services Needed and Planned	Services Needed But Unavailable	Services Needed But Refused	Services Provided in Review Period
	(Percentaged Across)			
Family Counseling	0.5	--	--	0.8
Psychiatric Therapy	4.2	1.3	3.9	2.6
Medical/Dental	1.3	0.5	--	1.1
Financial Assistance	1.1	0.3	--	0.5
Homemaker	0.3	--	--	0.3
Day Care	0.3	0.3	--	0.3
Employment	0.5	0.3	0.5	--
Job Training	1.3	0.5	0.5	0.8
Housing	1.1	1.6	0.3	0.3
Drug Related	0.3	--	1.1	--
Alcohol Related	1.1	0.3	0.5	--
Supportive Casework	1.3	--	--	2.4
Family Planning	2.4	0.8	0.5	1.1
Legal Service	1.6	--	0.8	1.6
Maternity Shelter Care	0.3	--	--	0.3
Other	5.3	0.3	1.6	5.3
Unknown	12.6	16.3	23.2	6.3
None	66.1	75.0	65.5	79.5
Number of Cases	(380)	(380)	(380)	(380)

*These data were obtained from the CWIS data files of June 30, 1978 maintained for the children included in the survey. Reports on service cover six month reporting periods.

TABLE 20 (Continued)

DELIVERY OF SERVICE TO FAMILIES

GROUP 6:
(Mother Available)

Service Delivery	Services Needed and Planned	Services Needed But Unavailable	Services Needed But Refused	Services Provided in Review Period
	(Percentaged Across)			
Family Counseling	1.6	0.4	--	0.6
Psychiatric Therapy	21.0	3.9	14.5	11.6
Medical/Dental	7.3	1.0	1.8	5.9
Financial Assistance	3.9	1.2	0.2	3.7
Homemaker	2.0	1.6	0.4	0.8
Day Care	1.0	0.4	0.4	0.2
Employment	4.9	2.4	0.8	1.0
Job Training	7.1	2.4	2.5	2.9
Housing	13.5	4.1	2.7	6.9
Drug Related	2.0	0.2	1.2	2.7
Alcohol Related	8.0	1.0	5.9	4.7
Supportive Casework	4.5	1.4	--	4.9
Family Planning	9.2	1.2	1.6	4.5
Legal Service	1.4	0.2	--	2.0
Maternity Shelter Care	0.2	--	--	0.2
Other	12.2	2.4	4.5	19.6
Unknown	3.7	6.9	17.1	2.9
None	31.4	70.4	54.1	40.4
Number of Cases	(510)	(510)	(510)	(510)

TABLE 20 (Continued)

DELIVERY OF SERVICE TO FAMILIES

GROUP 5:
(Mother Out of Picture, Father Available)

Service Delivery	Services Needed and Planned	Services Needed But Unavailable	Services Needed But Refused	Services Provided in Review Period
	(Percentaged Across)			
Family Counseling	1.2	--	--	--
Psychiatric Therapy	11.3	3.7	7.5	3.7
Medical/Dental	7.5	--	--	8.8
Financial Assistance	2.5	--	--	2.5
Homemaker	2.5	1.2	--	--
Employment	5.0	3.7	--	3.7
Job Training	3.7	2.5	2.5	1.2
Housing	12.5	2.5	3.7	3.7
Drug Related	1.2	--	1.2	--
Alcohol Related	3.7	--	2.5	1.2
Supportive Casework	1.2	--	--	1.2
Family Planning	1.2	--	1.2	3.7
Legal Service	--	--	--	1.2
Other	18.7	--	2.5	31.2
Unknown	7.5	6.2	17.5	2.5
None	42.5	82.5	66.2	43.7
Number of Cases	(80)	(80)	(80)	(80)

TABLE 21

FAMILY SERVICES PROVIDED AS OF JUNE 30, 1978 BY CURRENT LOCATION OF CHILDREN
ACCORDING TO AVAILABILITY OF PARENTS AS OF JUNE 30, 1976[a]
(N = 1290)

Child's Status on June 30, 1978	Group 1 (Mother Deceased)	Group 2 (Mother's Whereabouts Unknown)	Group 3 (Mother Not Seen in Two Years)	Group 4 (Mother in Mental Hospital)	Groups 1 to 4 (Combined)	Group 5 (Mother Out of Picture; Father Available)	Group 6 (Mother Available)
			(Percentaged)				
Still in Care:							
Received service	12.5	11.3	16.5	55.6	16.3	57.1	61.6
Did not receive service	87.5	88.7	83.5	44.4	83.7	42.9	38.4
(N = 828)	(72)	(159)	(91)	(27)	(349)	(70)	(409)
Final Discharge							
Received service	13.8	11.5	18.9	--	13.5	50.0	53.7
Did not receive service	86.2	88.5	81.1	100.0	86.5	50.0	46.3
(N = 265)	(29)	(52)	(37)	(8)	(126)	(18)	(121)
Trial Discharge, Suspended Payment or Discharge Status Unknown:[b]							
Received service	--	--	26.7	66.7	14.0	50.0	61.6
Did not receive service	100.0	100.0	73.3	33.3	86.0	50.0	38.4
(N = 197)	(13)	(12)	(15)	(3)	(43)	(16)	(138)

[a]Family service is treated as a dichotomy; if family received any service including family counseling, case was categorized as "received service." If no service of any kind was received, case was categorized as "did not receive service." Service to children is not included in these considerations.
Source: CWIS data file for June 30, 1978 (covers six month reporting period).

[b]Suspended payment covers children not in care because they may have been hospitalized, AWOL, sent to a detention facility or special school, have overstayed a weekend visit, etc. There were 83 children on trial discharge, 65 children on suspended payment and 49 out of care under undetermined circumstances.

dren: 828 children still in care after the passage of two years, 265 discharged children and 197 who were on trial discharge, suspended payment or out of care with the conditions of the child's departure undetermined because the information was not captured in the data files available.[16]

For the children still in care, Table 21 shows that for Groups 1-4, representing situations in which the parents were unavailable when the data were collected in 1976, very little service was rendered subsequently. Almost 87 percent received no service whatever. Only the small number of cases where the mothers were in mental hospitals received some kind of family service; this was true for 56.6 percent of such cases.

The cases in Group 6 (mothers available) showed the highest proportion where at least some service was rendered to parents (61.6 percent). This was true for 57.1 percent of the cases in Group 5 (fathers available).

For the cases where final discharge of the child was accomplished and for those where trial discharges, suspended payments, and undetermined departures took place, the patterns are the same as reported for the cases where the children were still in care. Very few cases in Groups 1-4 received any service, about 14 percent for each group. More sizable proportions of families in Groups 5 and 6 did receive service of some kind, presumably around discharge preparations.

An effort to predict the service delivered to the families over a two-year time span was carried through. As shown in Table 22, a multiple regression analysis was executed for all cases in the sample (N = 1290) treating the service variable as a dichotomy: the family having received some specified service or none at all. Two predictors emerged as quite strong: (1) an indication that the parent had maintained contact with the child through visiting (beta = .28; 6.5 percent unique variance explained), and (2) the score assigned the case on the Index of the Mother's Capacity for Service Involvement (beta = .25; 5.0 percent variance explained).

Two modest but statistically significant predictors were an indication that adoption was a discharge plan and the number of years the child had spent in care. Adoption as a plan was associated with minimal contact with the parent. The results also indicate that children who were in care for lesser periods of time were more likely to have parents who were recipients of service.

The multiple regression analysis was repeated restricting the analysis to the cases of children still in care on June 30, 1978 (N = 828). The results were essentially the same as those reported for the entire sample except that the Index of the Mother's Capacity for Service Involvement was a somewhat stronger predictor and ethnicity was not a significant predictor.

TABLE 22

PREDICTING THE DELIVERY OF SERVICE TO FAMILIES OF CHILDREN
OVER A TWO-YEAR TIME SPAN
(N = 1290)[a]

Independent Variables	Zero-order Correlation	Standardized Regression Coefficient	Percent Unique Variance Explained
1. Parental Contact with Child (none/SOME)	.44***	.28***	6.5
2. Index Score (Mother's Capacity for Service Involvement)	.40***	.25***	5.0
3. Discharge Plan: Adoption (no/YES)	-.29***	-.14***	1.9
4. Years in Care	-.23***	-.08**	0.5
5. Sex of Child (male/FEMALE)	-.08**	-.06*	0.4
6. Reason Placed: Neglect (no/YES)	.09**	.07**	0.4
7. Ethnicity: Black (no/YES)	-.08**	-.05*	0.3
Multiple R		.55	
Multiple R^2		.30	

*p <.05 **p <.01 ***p <.001

<u>Partial Correlations with Dependent Variable for Variables Not Entered:</u>

Current Age	-.04	Reason Placed-Alcoholic	.03
Current Location	-.02	Reason Placed-Drugs	.02
Current Placement	.01	Reason Placed-Abuse	.01
Court Adjudication	-.02	Reason Placed-Abandoned	-.03
Ethnicity-Hispanic	.00	Reason Placed-Home Behavior	.03

[a] The dependent variable is a dichotomy as specified in Table 21.

6 Summary of Findings and Implications

Major Findings Summarized

There are a number of important perspectives provided by the data analyzed in this report. It is necessary to keep in mind, however, the fact that the cases sampled reflect what one will find in a cross-sectional view of a caseload of children in foster care for at least one year rather than newly arrived youngsters. The children are remnants of previously entered cohorts and have been in care for an average of eight years. If the focus of attention were to shift to new arrivals to the foster care system, the proportion of "workable" parents would likely be quite higher.

It is also important to recall that the representativeness of the sample is somewhat distorted by the absence of 126 cases (6.0 percent) where the social workers could not fill out any meaningful information about the parent's capacity to be involved in service contacts because they were so totally out of contact with the agency that there was no basis for making judgments about the parent.

Some of the major findings provided by the analyses of the data include the following:

1. There was a sizable group of cases where the parents were totally unavailable for service contacts. About 40 percent of the cases involved situations in which the mother was either deceased, her whereabouts unknown or she had not been seen in at least two years; there was also a small group of mothers in mental hospitals. For these four groups, accounting for 520 children, the fathers were also out of the picture. A fifth group contained 104 children where the fathers acknowledged paternity and where some contact with the child care agency was possible.

The largest group of children were the 669 (51.9 percent) whose mothers were alive and whereabouts known, who had been seen within the past two years and were not patients in mental hospitals.

In much of the data presented in this report, it is clear that the first four groups of cases have almost no potential for involvement in a service relationship designed to restore the natural parent home for the foster child. For these children, in care for an average of 9.8 years, permanency in living arrangements could only be contemplated for those fortunate to be living with foster parents sufficiently committed to them to entertain the idea of adoption.

While there are more cases in Group 5 and Group 6 than in Groups 1-4 where there is potential for service involvement, they nevertheless constitute a relatively small minority within these groups. The overall potential for rehabilitation of the parents is soberingly limited, almost dismal.

2. The mothers in Group 6 have a relatively high proportion who have broken down in parental functioning. The majority of the children have come into care because of parental neglect or abuse of the child, alcoholism, drug addiction, abandonment, or parental mental illness. They are a group of parents whose lives are replete with the most stark kind of personal and social problems.

3. Almost none of the parents in Groups 1-4 had been seen for service contacts in a six-month reporting period, and this was true of only 21 percent of the fathers in Group 5 and the mothers in Group 6. At least three-fourths of the latter had been seen within the past six months.

4. Almost two-thirds of the mothers in Group 6 were seen to be in need of counseling help to help clarify their feelings about resumption of care for their children.

5. At least half of the mothers in Group 6 were characterized as having a low motivation to see the agency's social worker and at least a third of them had some problem in keeping appointments related to their distance from the agency's office. While the mothers in Group 6 were seen as representing the most promising cases in the sample, there were nevertheless high proportions among them who resisted seeing the social workers, failed to keep appointments and/or were late for them, were unable to discuss personal problems, were defensive about themselves and appeared to be excessively dependent. Over forty percent showed evidence of lack of concern about their children. The fathers in Group 5 showed a similar pattern in the way they related to agency efforts to involve them in service contacts. In sum, many of the parents appeared unpromising as candidates for service intervention.

6. All of the families, including the more "promising" parents in Groups 5 and 6 had a variety of social and personal problems and conditions which contributed to the need for the child remaining in foster care. For example, almost half the mothers in Group 6 were reported to have housing problems and for one case in five, it was a major factor in keeping the child in care. Relatively large proportions of these mothers had severe personal adjustment problems in the form of chronic depression and other problems and in almost two-thirds of the cases, parent-child relationship problems were seen as factors keeping

the child in foster care. The need of the parents for skilled service intervention seems readily apparent.

7. For the entire sample of 1,293 children, less than one-fifth had a declared agency discharge plan calling for their return to the home of a parent. Almost 36 percent were destined to be discharged to their own responsibility upon reaching adulthood and for 28 percent the declared plan was that the child be adopted. The social workers who filled out the questionnaires indicated in only 8.7 percent of the cases that there was a good prospect that a child would return to his parents and in 63.5 percent of the cases, they checked the category indicating that there was no prospect of such a return. Even in Group 6, the most promising grouping of cases, almost half the children were said to have no prospect of return home; this was true of 56.6 percent of the children in Group 5.

8. Particularly telling was the report of 41.7 percent of the social workers in Group 6 cases, that the agency would strongly oppose the return of a child home, if the parents expressed such a desire.

9. An eight-item Index of the Mother's Capacity for Service Involvement was created which showed high internal reliability and good discrimination among the six groups that had been created as research entities. Best predictors of scores on this index included such variables as the agency's planning vis-a-vis adoption (no/YES), the number of years the child had been in foster care, history of parental abandonment, and the child's current age.

10. A four-item index was created called Index of Viability of the Natural Parent's Home as a Resource for the Child. It too showed good internal reliability and discriminated well among the groupings of parents. The best predictors of the scores based upon the four items were: years in care, discharge planning for adoption, the location of the child (others/FOSTER HOME) and the current age of the child.

11. After the passage of almost two years, 64.2 percent of the subjects were still in care; 18.2 percent had been discharged to their parents. The best predictor of such a discharge was the index score measuring the viability of the parent's home.

12. After the passage of almost two years, the picture of service being rendered to the families of the children was that about 85 percent of those in Groups 1-4 were not receiving service of any kind while this was true of less than half of the fathers in Group 5. A majority of the mothers in Group 6 had at least one area in which service was being rendered to them. The best predictors of whether families had some service being rendered to them were: (1) information that the parents were in contact with their children, and (2) the scores assigned cases on the Index of the Mother's Capacity for Service Involvement.

Discussion of Results of the Research

An expanded data base for child welfare practice is a necessary next phase in the development of management information systems such as CWIS. The foster care of children is so phenomenologically complex as to require that multiple perspectives be built into the descriptive capability of the computerized system. These perspectives must focus upon such key actors in the placement situation as the child, the natural parents and the foster parents (for children in foster family care).

The research effort described here was designed to enrich the data base of CWIS on an exploratory basis. The existing capacity to describe parents was recognized as quite limited and hardly took into account the central role of parents in the foster care drama. Knowing that the vast majority of children entered foster care because of the breakdown in functioning of their parents, it appeared necessary to have a richer picture than currently available about the availability of the parents for contact with the agency social workers and their service needs.

A test of whether a computerized management information system such as CWIS should add to its data base by including data elements such as used in this miniproject is whether the information obtained is useful for the management of service programs and/or for social planning purposes. Unless the data make possible useful new insights, it would hardly be justified to impose further reporting activity on the social workers responsible for providing service. The "paper work" problem is sufficiently serious to dampen any enthusiasm for reporting activity for its own sake.

It may help the reader to gain some perspective on the issue of whether or not to expand the foster care data base by examining the questions that can be answered by the data collected in this effort:

- Is the mother alive? If not, is the father in the picture?
- Are the whereabouts of the parents known to the agency?
- Is the mother in a mental hospital or other source of confinement that may interfere with her participation in a service relationship with a social worker?
- When was the parent last seen by an agency social worker?
- How often has each parent been seen by a social worker over the past six months? Has there been a pattern to the service contacts? What has been the trend of contacts (e.g., decline)?
- What problems or conditions are currently faced by the parents that serve to keep the child in care? Have any of these required referral to another service agency?
- Have there been circumstances in the lives of the parents (e.g., other child care responsibilities, distance from the agency, etc.) which have served to lower their contact with the agency's social worker?
- What is the agency's discharge plan for the child? When is it likely to take place?
- What is the parent's attitude toward taking the child home?
- Does the agency see any likelihood that the child will return to the parent(s)?
- Would the agency approve if the parent desired to take the child home?
- To what extent do the parent(s) need counseling help to resolve their feelings about resuming care of the child?

- Do the parents resist seeing the social worker? When they do have contact, do they use the time effectively? Can they talk about their problems? Deal with the issues that have prevented them from caring for their children?

For the writer, these questions are fundamental and quite telling about a child's prospects for return home. Each question touches upon some facet of the service delivery situation with respect to parents of children in foster care. Such information should be available in a form that permits aggregation, so that entire agency caseloads can be analyzed.

Service Tasks in Perspective

The overall impression that can be distilled from the data analyzed in this report is that the parents of children in care are often difficult persons to involve in a treatment effort. At least this is true if one studies a cross-sectional sample of parents whose children have been in care at least one year, as was done in this instance, rather than restricting one's purview to children who are new arrivals to the system. Presumably the parents of children who have experienced care for shorter periods—who have left the system and are not available for scrutiny—are more promising targets for treatment involvement.

The fact that a large number of the parents are totally unavailable for any kind of service contact and that among those who are in the picture there are many who are resistant to efforts to involve them in meaningful service contacts is a sobering discovery. Perhaps it comes as no surprise to those who have dealt with these phenomena in their everyday practice. It occurs to the writer that the suggestions often made to agencies that they "treat" the families of the children has a cavalier ring and ought to be tempered by an appreciation for the severity of the problems experienced by the families.

It is difficult to determine how many of the parents can be helped to achieve a higher level of functioning which would be sufficient to enable them to provide homes for their children. Our survey has documented the fact that discharge plans specified by the social workers call for children to return to parents in less than one case in five for the entire caseload and for only 31 percent of the available mothers. Less than ten percent of the cases are seen as having a good prospect for return home and in only 13 percent of the cases would the agency strongly support such a return.

A Word of Caution

Nothing in the data we have presented casts light upon the question of the skill that may be required when the social worker seeks to help restore the parent to some level of adequate functioning. We have been concerned with the difficult prior task of the agency making a service connection with the parents and getting them involved in a working relationship.

There is no doubt that even when the parents are able to keep appointments with their social workers, one cannot be assured that positive transformations in the family's living circumstances can be effected. Bearing in mind the fact that the necessity for placement is often brought about because of serious parental problems such as mental illness, alcoholism, drug abuse, mental retardation and abuse or neglect of the children, and given the widespread ambivalence about resumption of care experienced by the parents in our study, the challenge of the service task should not be underestimated.

Many of the parents were reported to show difficulties in the quality of the relationships with their children; after years of separation, the children often manifested mixed loyalties and the parents showed uncertainty about their commitments to their offspring. Many of the mothers were also reported to have serious personal adjustment difficulties including quite a few who showed problems of depression. These interpersonal and intrapsychic problems must be seen against a backdrop of pressing social needs in the areas of housing, income support and health.

The service task, if well executed, would appear to require skill in dealing with complex family relationship problems and those in the area of personal adjustment. The social worker would also, no doubt, be called upon to serve as advocate for the family with other human service delivery systems in the areas of housing, addiction services, income maintenance, health, education, and so forth. Indeed, it is well known that the foster care system inherits the failures of other human service systems.

In addition to the responsibility for tending to the service needs of the parents and the children, the social workers must help formulate the agency's plan for achieving permanency for the children. If the effort to engage the parent in a service relationship proves unsuccessful, the agency may well have to consider undertaking legal steps to terminate parental rights so that the child can be placed for adoption. This is particularly the case when very young children are left in a state of limbo by their parents.[17]

It should thus be clear that the tasks facing social workers attempting to serve the families of children in foster care are highly demanding and ought to be respected for the challenges they represent. A series of diverse skills are required. (1) There is the cognitively complex requirement to determine where the case is going with respect to permanency planning. (2) There is need for skill in interpersonal transactions helping demoralized parents to "get their act together." (3) There is need for skill in garnering social supports for families and serving as advocates with other human service systems.

If social workers are to be effective in carrying out these tasks, they would likely require good preparatory educational backgrounds and in-service training to enhance their skills in the areas mentioned. They would also likely require an appropriate ceiling on the number of cases assigned to them.[18] Back-up consultative support from psychiatrists and other skilled professionals would also seem a necessity.

How Good Are the Data?

The observer who is skeptical of data provided by participants of the service delivery system—on grounds that these individuals might have a stake in seeing the system in a certain way and therefore are biased observers—might well inquire about the validity of the data reported here. Taking into account the fact that many of the respondents lacked formal training in social work,[19] is it not possible that more skilled staff would perceive and take better advantage of opportunities to serve the parents? Does the pessimistic view of the potentiality of the parents for service involvement reflected here arise out of the bias of inexperienced and untrained social workers overwhelmed by the problems shown by them? Unfortunately, an examination of the data according to the educational backgrounds of the reporting social workers does not change the view of this caseload as one that is replete with formidable challenges. Trained staff are as dubious as those who are untrained about the prospects for restoring the parental homes.[20]

Because of the importance of the issues involved, it may well be useful in future efforts to attempt to validate appraisals made by social workers who carry service responsibilities for the cases by research that introduces an independent audit covering the same phenomena.

Of some concern is the fact that 18.2 percent of the respondents in Group 6 reported that they knew the natural mothers only "slightly" and 13.2 percent reported that they knew them "hardly at all."[21]

Despite the lack of validation of the perspectives presented here, we are left with two compelling facts: (1) the social workers who were our respondents do in fact take a major responsibility for the direction taken in cases and their attitudes are the most influential in determining whether an effort is made to serve the parents. If their views are biased, the consequences are acted out in real-life decisions. And, (2) the indexes created from the responses of the social workers were fairly strong predictors of two phenomena occurring after the passage of two years: the discharge of children to the parents and services offered to the families. Thus, some evidence of predictive validity has already been established.

Feasibility of Routinized Data Collection

Whether the items included in this special research can be collected on a routine basis is of course a matter that requires consideration by the board and staff responsible for the further development of CWIS/CCRS. In this regard, one aspect of the data collection experience is noteworthy: the degree of difficulty reported by the responding social workers in filling out the form. Table 23 shows the responses of the reporting social workers to the inquiry: "How difficult was it for you to fill out this form?" Their answers are shown according to the availability of the parents for service involvement.

In each of the groupings, almost two-thirds of the respondents indicated that filling out the form was "quite easy" or "very easy." Only seven percent in each grouping reported the task "very difficult" and about 25 percent found it "somewhat difficult." From their written comments, it would appear that the only source of difficulty was the fact that a sizable number of parents were totally "out of it" so that answering individual items about working with them seemed pointless. It would thus seem quite feasible to collect the information such as reported here on a routine basis.

Scanning Caseloads: A Tool for Better Management of the Social Services

The research presented here could well be described as an exercise in "caseload scanning," a term coined by the writer for characterizing the process of aggregating information about service tasks for entire caseloads. It is envisioned that such a process could well become a generic management tool for social service delivery systems. While each social worker in an agency must be concerned with understanding the individual case, the commissioner of a public department or the director of a voluntary agency is faced with the task of understanding the service needs presented by the entire clientele being served by the department or agency. The distinction between the idiographic approach which emphasizes the uniqueness of the individual and the nomethetic approach to research which seeks general laws of behavior through the study of groups has its parallel in the differences in understanding of service delivery tasks required of the practitioner dealing with individual cases and the administrator responsible for the entire agency enterprise.

It is presently very difficult for administrators of social programs to adequately manage their organizations because they do not secure for themselves essential information about their program operations. At the direct service level, social workers often make decisions about handling cases which can have major consequences in the allocation of a service program's resources in a given case. For example, the failure of a social worker to work aggressively to involve natural parents in planning for their child's future care, on the grounds that such parents are not "workable," may result in extended years of foster care with public outlays amounting to tens of thousands of dollars for the individual case. The administrators of large agencies find it difficult to intervene at the case level to determine the validity of commitments of resources being made because organized information about caseloads is usually not now available to them. Without such information flowing from caseworker to agency directors, it is almost impossible to manage an agency effectively.

Data about the availability and capacities of parents of children in foster care for service involvement clearly have important implications for the evaluation of agency programs. It is not likely that the children are distributed to the agencies on a random basis. Some agencies may have more difficult caseloads than others and this can be seen from the aggregated data describing the parents. Their inability to discharge large groups of children may, in part, be "explained" by such data rather than being attributed to their failures in the delivery of service. Commissioners of large public welfare agencies such as the one in New York City require the capacity to "understand" the performance of agencies with the children entrusted to their care by having available aggregated descriptive information about the clientele served by each agency. Agencies can then be held accountable for their performance in more valid ways.

TABLE 23

REPORTS OF SOCIAL WORKERS ABOUT DIFFICULTY
IN PROVIDING THE REQUESTED DATA ACCORDING TO THE AVAILABILITY
OF PARENTS FOR SERVICE INVOLVEMENT*
(N = 1293)

Degree of Difficulty	Groups 1-4 (Combined)	Group 5 (Mother Out of Picture; Father Available)	Group 6 (Mother Available)
	(Percentaged)		
Very Difficult	7.3	6.7	6.7
Somewhat Difficult	25.8	26.0	25.0
Quite Easy	48.6	55.7	53.2
Very Easy	15.2	7.8	12.9
Not Applicable	3.1	3.8	2.2
Total Number of Cases	100.0 (520)	100.0 (104)	100.0 (669)

*The caseworkers were asked: "How difficult was it for you to fill out this form?"

Notes

1. David Fanshel, "Children Discharged from Foster Care in New York City: Where to—When—At What Age?" *Child Welfare*, 57: 8 (September/October 1978), pp. 467–483; also: David Fanshel, "Preschoolers Entering Foster Care in New York City: The Need to Stress Plans for Permanency," *Child Welfare*, 58: 2 (February 1979), pp. 67-80.

2. David Fanshel, "Computerized Information Systems and Foster Care: The New York City Experience with CWIS," *Children Today*, 5: 6 (November 1976), pp. 14-18, 44.

3. The other two "mini-projects" reported in this volume concern (1) an expanded view of factors related to parental visiting of children in care, and (2) the nature of the relationship of children to their foster parents and prospects for the foster homes becoming transformed into adoptive homes.

4. Close to 100 agencies and sub-divisions of agencies participating in the CWIS system were approached about participating in a series of six "mini-projects" designed to test data modules for possible later inclusion in the CWIS system. In addition to the three mini-projects cited, future efforts were to include (1) follow-up inquiries to explain incongruous information submitted by the agencies about children (e.g., that the discharge objective for an infant was "discharge to own responsibility"), (2) a parent description module, and (3) a child description module.

5. Some additional cases later had to be drawn from some of the smaller agencies and these were selected from the CWIS data files as of September 30, 1976.

6. In the course of a year, about 28 percent of the children who were in care at the beginning of the year tended to leave care with the passage of a year's time. See: *CWIS Special Report Series* developed by David Fanshel and John F. Grundy.

7. *Ibid.*

8. Shirley Jenkins and Elaine Norman, *Filial Deprivation and Foster Care* (New York: Columbia University Press, 1972); see also, by same authors, *Beyond Placement: Mothers View Foster Care* (New York: Columbia University Press, 1975).

9. *Ibid.*

10. Dorothy Fahs Beck and Mary Ann Jones, *Progress on Family Problems: A Nationwide Study of Clients' and Counselors' Views on Family Service* (New York: Family Service Association of America, 1973).

11. Where an effort is made to describe the situations of father of children, the index may be called *Index of Father's Capacity for Service Involvement*.

12. Claire Selltiz, Lawrence S. Wrightsman and Stuart W. Cook, *Research Methods in Social Relations* (3rd ed.; New York: Holt, Rinehart and Winston, 1976), pp. 418-421.

13. Lee J. Cronbach, "Coefficient Alpha and the Internal Structure of Tests," *Psychometrica*, Vol. XVI (1951), pp. 297-334.

14. Item-total correlations have been corrected for auto-correlation by removing the tested item from the total score.

15. Group 1 consisted of deceased mothers and no alpha was calculated for this group since service involvement was not a relevant issue in these cases.

16. See note included in Table 20.

17. David Fanshel, "Pre-Schoolers Entering Foster Care in New York City: The Need to Stress Plans for Permanency," *op. cit.*

18. For the 609 cases in Group 6, the reporting social workers reported a caseload whose mean was 20.916 children (S.D. = 10.390) and 13.987 families (S.D. = 7.153).

19. About 59 percent of the respondents had graduate degrees in social work.

20. The trained respondents were compared with those who were untrained with respect to the scores generated from their ratings of cases for the two indexes created for the study. The differences, as tested by t-test, were not statistically significant.

21. Some of the responses indicating the respondents had only limited knowledge of the natural mothers was related to the fact that the forms were sometimes filled out by supervisors or administrators. For Group 6, this accounted for about 70 cases.

The Questionnaire

COLUMBIA UNIVERSITY SCHOOL OF SOCIAL WORK
Research and Demonstration Center
622 West 113 Street ● New York, N.Y. 10025

EXPANDED DATA BASE FOR CHILD WELFARE

To Child Welfare Social Worker:

The New York State Department of Social Services has granted funds to Columbia University to conduct research designed to expand the data base of Child Welfare Information Services (CWIS). Your agency has agreed to participate in this research on a limited sample of the agency's children. Other agencies are also participating in this effort. The results of this work will make it possible to determine what kind of information can expeditiously be gathered to add to our knowledge about children in foster care. The aim of this effort is to improve service to children.

Your cooperation in filling out the enclosed form will facilitate our study greatly. For some of the items, it may be necessary to make an estimate based upon your most informed judgment. Please try to answer every item. You will later be contacted for your advice about the content of items and their wording. If you have any doubt about a reply, place a question mark next to the item.

The material you provide will be treated in the strictest confidence. Please return the form to _____ _____ who has been designated as your agency's contact person with our project.

Thank you very much for your help in this matter.

Sincerely yours,

David Fanshel, D.S.W.
Director
Research and Demonstration Center

CONFIDENTIAL

COLUMBIA UNIVERSITY SCHOOL OF SOCIAL WORK
Research and Demonstration Center
622 West 113 Street
New York, New York 10025

Trial Form on Parental Service Contact Information

     This is a pre-test version of an information form about children in foster care. The form is designed to secure facts about the nature of service contact information from the social worker who has responsibility for the case. The form is being tested for Child Welfare Information Services (CWIS). Your cooperation in filling out the form will make it possible to learn more about the kind of information that needs to be gathered for children in foster care in order to improve the delivery of service. Your care in filling out the form will be appreciated. The data will be kept confidential and a report will be made to your agency about the findings.

ID Name _____

SSC Number _____
              1-9/

Worker Code _____

Agency _____
           12-14/

[Card]: 10-11/(04)

(MP 2)

Q1. Does your agency have primary casework responsibility for this child? (Check response that applies.)

        Yes _____

        No* _____

*If No, Do Not Respond to Remaining Questions.

Q2 A. Are the parents' whereabouts known to the agency? (Check response that applies.)

	Mother 15/	Father 16/
Whereabouts known	(1)	(1)
Whereabouts unknown* (Answer Q2 B.)	(2)	(2)
Other (Specify) _____ _____	(3)	(3)
Not applicable, parenthood not established	X X X	(4)

*Q2 B. For how long a period have whereabouts been unknown?

    Mother: _____ 17/

    Father: _____ 18/

Q3. When was the parent last seen by an agency social worker? (Select most recent category for mother and father.)

	Mother /19-20/	Father /21-22/
Within past month	(1)	(1)
Within past 3 months	(2)	(2)
Within past 6 months	(3)	(3)
Within past year	(4)	(4)
Within past 2 years	(5)	(5)
Within past 3 years	(6)	(6)
Within past 4 years	(7)	(7)
Within past 5 years	(8)	(8)
Within past 6-10 years	(9)	(9)
More than 10 years ago	(10)	(10)
No contacts since birth of child	(11)	(11)
Other _____	(12)	(12)
Unknown	(13)	(13)

Q4. <u>How often has the parent been seen by a social worker for in-person interviews over the past six months?</u> (*Check appropriate response.*)

	Mother 23/	Father 24/
No contact	(1)	(1)
1 time	(2)	(2)
2-3 times	(3)	(3)
4-5 times	(4)	(4)
6-10 times	(5)	(5)
11-20 times	(6)	(6)
More than 20 times	(7)	(7)
Unknown	(8)	(8)
Not relevant: Identity unknown or paternity not acknowledged	X X X	(9)

Q5. <u>Has there been any pattern to service contacts with the parent?</u> (*Check appropriate response.*)

	Mother 25/	Father 26/
No contact/almost never	(1)	(1)
Weekly	(2)	(2)
Bi-weekly	(3)	(3)
Monthly	(4)	(4)
Every other month	(5)	(5)
Occasional	(6)	(6)
Other (*Specify*) _____ _____	(7)	(7)
Unknown	(8)	(8)
Not relevant: Identity unknown or paternity not acknowledged	X X X	(9)

Q6. Has the trend of service contact with the parent declined since the child entered care? (Check appropriate category.)

	Mother 27/	Father 28/
Major decline in service contacts	(1)	(1)
Moderate decline in service contacts	(2)	(2)
Slight decline in service contacts	(3)	(3)
No change in frequency of service contacts	(4)	(4)
Slight increase in service contacts	(5)	(5)
Moderate increase in service contacts	(6)	(6)
Major increase in service contacts	(7)	(7)
Other: Mother_____	(8)	
Father_____		(8)
Unknown	(9)	(9)

Q7. Where do caseworker contacts with the parents take place? (Check *all* that apply.)

	Mother (1)	Father (2)	Both (3)	
a. Agency office	___	___	___	29/
b. Parent home	___	___	___	30/
c. Foster home	___	___	___	31/
d. Institution	___	___	___	32/
e. Other place (*Specify*)_____ _____	___	___	___	33/
f. Not applicable	___	___	___	34/
g. Unknown	___	___	___	35/

Q8. **Please indicate whether any of the following problems or conditions of the parent(s) are causal factors related to keeping the child in foster care. Is the condition a major factor, minor factor or not a factor in preventing the child from returning home?** *(Check appropriate category for each item)*

PROBLEM OR CONDITION	AFFECTING MOTHER					AFFECTING FATHER				
	Major Factor (1)	Minor Factor (2)	Not a Factor (3)	Unknown (4)		Major Factor (1)	Minor Factor (2)	Not a Factor (3)	Unknown (4)	
a. Inadequate housing	___	___	___	___	36/	___	___	___	___	55/
b. Unemployment or unsuitable job	___	___	___	___	37/	___	___	___	___	56/
c. Poor work performance	___	___	___	___	38/	___	___	___	___	57/
d. Inadequate income for basic needs	___	___	___	___	39/	___	___	___	___	58/
e. Health problems, physical illness or handicap	___	___	___	___	40/	___	___	___	___	59/
f. Child-rearing/ child care practices	___	___	___	___	41/	___	___	___	___	60/
g. Marital problem	___	___	___	___	42/	___	___	___	___	61/
h. Criminal problem	___	___	___	___	43/	___	___	___	___	62/
i. Alcoholism	___	___	___	___	44/	___	___	___	___	63/
j. Drug abuse	___	___	___	___	45/	___	___	___	___	64/
k. Mental illness	___	___	___	___	46/	___	___	___	___	65/
l. Mental retardation	___	___	___	___	47/	___	___	___	___	66/
m. Management of home	___	___	___	___	48/	___	___	___	___	67/
n. Management of money, budgeting, etc.	___	___	___	___	49/	___	___	___	___	68/
o. Health practices	___	___	___	___	50/	___	___	___	___	69/
p. Severe personal adjustment problem: depression	___	___	___	___	51/	___	___	___	___	70/
q. Severe personal adjustment problem: Other *(Specify)*:										
Mother:	___	___	___	___	52/					
Father:						___	___	___	___	71/
r. Parent-child relationship problem	___	___	___	___	53/	___	___	___	___	72/
s. Other condition *(Specify)*:										
Mother:	___	___	___	___	54/					
Father:						___	___	___	___	73/

Q9. <u>Do any of the problems or conditions cited in the previous sections as "major factors"</u> <u>require referral to another agency or service program?</u> (Check appropriate category for each item.)

Problems or Conditions Affecting MOTHER	Service Contact Already Established (1)	Referral Needed and Planned (2)	Referral Needed but Service Unavailable (3)	Service Not Required (4)	Parent Unwilling to Use Service (5)	Unknown (6)	
a. Inadequate housing	____	____	____	____	____	____	74/
b. Unemployment or unsuitable job	____	____	____	____	____	____	75/
c. Poor work performance	____	____	____	____	____	____	76/
d. Inadequate income for basic needs	____	____	____	____	____	____	77/
e. Health problems, physical illness	____	____	____	____	____	____	78/
f. Child-rearing/child care practices	____	____	____	____	____	____	79/
g. Marital problem	____	____	____	____	____	____	80/
h. Criminal problem	____	____	____	____	____	____	12/
i. Alcoholism	____	____	____	____	____	____	13/
j. Drug abuse	____	____	____	____	____	____	14/
k. Mental illness	____	____	____	____	____	____	15/
l. Mental retardation	____	____	____	____	____	____	16/
m. Management of home	____	____	____	____	____	____	17/
n. Management of money, budgeting, etc.	____	____	____	____	____	____	18/
o. Health practices	____	____	____	____	____	____	19/
p. Severe personal adjustment problem: depression	____	____	____	____	____	____	20/
q. Severe personal adjustment problem: Other (Specify): _____	____	____	____	____	____	____	21/
r. Parent-child relationship problem	____	____	____	____	____	____	22/
s. Other (Specify) _____	____	____	____	____	____	____	23/

[Card]: 10-11/(05)

Q10. <u>Do any of the problems or conditions cited in the previous sections as "major factors" require referral to another agency or service program?</u> *(Check appropriate category for each item.)*

Problems or Conditions Affecting FATHER	Service Contact Already Established (1)	Referral Needed and Planned (2)	Referral Needed but Service Unavailable (3)	Service Not Required (4)	Parent Unwilling to Use Service (5)	Unknown (6)	
a. Inadequate housing	____	____	____	____	____	____	24/
b. Unemployment or unsuitable job	____	____	____	____	____	____	25/
c. Poor work performance	____	____	____	____	____	____	26/
d. Inadequate income for basic needs	____	____	____	____	____	____	27/
e. Health problems, physical illness	____	____	____	____	____	____	28/
f. Child-rearing/ child care practices	____	____	____	____	____	____	29/
g. Marital problem	____	____	____	____	____	____	30/
h. Criminal problem	____	____	____	____	____	____	31/
i. Alcoholism	____	____	____	____	____	____	32/
j. Drug abuse	____	____	____	____	____	____	33/
k. Mental illness	____	____	____	____	____	____	34/
l. Mental retardation	____	____	____	____	____	____	35/
m. Management of home	____	____	____	____	____	____	36/
n. Management of money, budgeting, etc.	____	____	____	____	____	____	37/
o. Health practices	____	____	____	____	____	____	38/
p. Severe personal adjustment problem: depression	____	____	____	____	____	____	39/
q. Severe personal adjustment problem: Other *(Specify)* _____	____	____	____	____	____	____	40/
r. Parent-child relationship problem	____	____	____	____	____	____	41/
s. Other *(Specify)* _____	____	____	____	____	____	____	42/

Q11. <u>Please indicate if any of the following agency factors have served to lower the frequency of contact between the social worker and parent.</u> (Check *all that apply*.)

Agency Factors	Yes, Is A Factor (1)	No, Is Not A Factor (2)	
a. Case has been uncovered by a caseworker* (*Answer* Q11f.)	_____	_____	43/
b. Case has recently been transferred to another caseworker	_____	_____	44/
c. Time not available to see parent** (*Answer* Q11g.)	_____	_____	45/
d. Other (*Specify*) _____ _____ _____	_____	_____	46/
e. Unknown	_____	_____	47/

f. For how many months has case been uncovered? _____

_____ 48-49/

g. Please amplify: _____ 50-51/

_____

_____

Q12. **Please indicate if any of the following circumstances have served to lower the frequency of parental contact with the social worker.** (Check appropriate category for each item.)

MOTHER	Very Much (1)	Some- what (2)	Hardly/ Not At All (3)	Un- known (4)	
a. Other child care responsibilities	___	___	___	___	52/
b. Employment hours	___	___	___	___	53/
c. Financial limitations (lack of funds for carfare, babysitter)	___	___	___	___	54/
d. Distance from agency office	___	___	___	___	55/
e. Physical illness	___	___	___	___	56/
f. Mental illness	___	___	___	___	57/
g. Mental retardation	___	___	___	___	58/
h. Other incapacity (Specify)_____ _____	___	___	___	___	59/
i. Parent is institution- alized (Type of insti- tution):_____ _____	___	___	___	___	60/
j. Low motivation to see social worker	___	___	___	___	61/
k. Other (Specify)_____ _____	___	___	___	___	62/

(Continued)

Q13. <u>Please indicate if any of the following circumstances have served to lower the frequency of parental contact with the social worker.</u> (*Check appropriate category for each item.*)

(*Continued*)

FATHER	Very Much (1)	Some- what (2)	Hardly/ Not At All (3)	Un- known (4)	
a. Other child care responsibilities	___	___	___	___	63/
b. Employment hours	___	___	___	___	64/
c. Financial limitations (lack of funds for carfare, babysitter)	___	___	___	___	65/
d. Distance from agency office	___	___	___	___	66/
e. Physical illness	___	___	___	___	67/
f. Mental illness	___	___	___	___	68/
g. Mental retardation	___	___	___	___	69/
h. Other incapacity (*Specify*) _____ _____	___	___	___	___	70/
i. Parent is institution- alized (*Type of insti- tution*): _____ _____	___	___	___	___	71/
j. Low motivation to see social worker	___	___	___	___	72/
k. Other (*Specify*) _____ _____	___	___	___	___	73/

Q14 A. What is the agency's present discharge plan for the   74/
child? (Check appropriate response.)

    Discharge to parent*   (1)

    Discharge to relative*   (2)

    Discharge to own responsibility
    (Skip to Q15.)   (3)

    Discharge to adoption*   (4)

    Unknown (Skip to Q15.)   (5)

*Q14 B. When is discharge likely to take place?   75/

    Within six months   (1)

    Within a year   (2)

    Within two years   (3)

    Within three years or more
    from now   (4)

    Other (Specify) _____
    _____ (5)

    Unknown   (6)

Q15. When was the plan last discussed with the mother or
father of the child? (Check appropriate response.)

	Mother 76/	Father 77/
Not discussed	(1)	(1)
Within past 3 months	(2)	(2)
Within past 6 months	(3)	(3)
Within past year	(4)	(4)
More than a year ago	(5)	(5)
Other (Specify): Mother_____	(6)	
Father_____		(6)
Unknown	(7)	(7)

204

Q16. What is the parent's attitude toward child's return home?
(Check appropriate categories.)

	Mother 78/	Father 79/
Eager for child's return	(1)	(1)
Moderately interested in child's return	(2)	(2)
Moderately disinterested in child's return	(3)	(3)
Opposed to child's return	(4)	(4)
Plans to surrender child	(5)	(5)
Has surrendered child	(6)	(6)
Other (Specify)_____	(7)	(7)
Not applicable	(8)	(8)
Unknown	(9)	(9)

Q17. If child's mother or father is living with a partner other than the child's natural parent, what is the attitude of that partner to the child's return to his or her household? (Check appropriate categories.)

	Mother's Partner 12/	Father's Partner 13/
Eager for child's return	(1)	(1)
Moderately interested in child's return	(2)	(2)
Moderately disinterested in child's return	(3)	(3)
Opposed to child's return	(4)	(4)
Other (Specify)_____	(5)	(5)
Not applicable	(6)	(6)
Unknown	(7)	(7)

[Card]: 10-11/(06)

Q18 A. What is the agency's perspective about the possibility   14/
of the child's return home to own parent(s)? (Select
appropriate category.)

    See no prospect for child's return to parent
    in foreseeable future.* (Answer Q18 B.)   (1)

    See slight prospect for child's return
    home.* (Answer Q18 B.)   (2)

    See moderate prospect for child's return
    home.   (3)

    See good prospect for child's return home.   (4)

    Other (Specify) _____

    _____ (5)

    Unknown   (6)

*Q18 B. What are some of the reasons for the perspective   15-16/
designated above?

_____
_____
_____
_____

Q19 A. Given the current situation, what would the likely attitude of the agency be if the parent(s) expressed the desire to take the child home? (Select appropriate category.) 17/

    Would strongly support return   ___(1)

    Would moderately support return   ___(2)

    Would moderately oppose return* (Answer Q19 B.)   ___(3)

    Would strongly oppose return* (Answer Q19 B.)   ___(4)

    Other (Specify) _____

    _____ ___(5)

    Unknown   ___(6)

*Q19 B. What is the basis for opposition to the child's return? 18-19/

_____

_____

_____

_____

Q20. To what extent does parent require counseling help to clarify own feelings about resumption of care of child? (Check appropriate response for father and mother.)

	Mother 20/	Father 21/
Very much	(1)	(1)
Somewhat	(2)	(2)
Not at all	(3)	(3)
Other (Specify) _____ _____ _____	(4)	(4)
Unknown	(5)	(5)

Q21. Have any of the following problems been evidenced in attempting to establish an ongoing service contact with the parent? (Check appropriate item for each category.)

MOTHER	Very Much (1)	Some- what (2)	Not At All (3)	Not Applic- able (4)	Un- known (5)	
a. Resists seeing social worker	___	___	___	___	___	22/
b. Fails to keep appointments	___	___	___	___	___	23/
c. Is late for appointments	___	___	___	___	___	24/
d. Is unable to discuss personal problems	___	___	___	___	___	25/
e. Is defensive about self	___	___	___	___	___	26/
f. Fails to show concern about child	___	___	___	___	___	27/
g. Is excessively dependent	___	___	___	___	___	28/
h. Other (Specify)_____ _____	___	___	___	___	___	29/

FATHER						
a. Resists seeing social worker	___	___	___	___	___	30/
b. Fails to keep appointments	___	___	___	___	___	31/
c. Is late for appointments	___	___	___	___	___	32/
d. Is unable to discuss personal problems	___	___	___	___	___	33/
e. Is defensive about self	___	___	___	___	___	34/
f. Fails to show concern about child	___	___	___	___	___	35/
g. Is excessively dependent	___	___	___	___	___	36/
h. Other (Specify)_____ _____	___	___	___	___	___	37/

Q22. How would you characterize the quality of the working relationship between the parent and the social worker as it has manifested itself over the past six months? (Check appropriate response for mother and father.)

	Mother 38/	Father 39/
Good	(1)	(1)
Fairly good	(2)	(2)
Mixed or average	(3)	(3)
Fairly poor	(4)	(4)
Very poor	(5)	(5)
No relationship (little or no contact)	(6)	(6)
Other (Specify) _____ _____	(7)	(7)
Not applicable	(8)	(8)
Unknown	(9)	(9)

Q23. Is there any information about the nature of service contacts with the parent(s) which you deem significant and has not been covered by the information already provided? 40-41/

_____
_____
_____
_____
_____
_____
_____
_____

Q24 A. How difficult was it for you to fill out this form? 42/

        Very difficult*
        (Answer Q24 B.) ___(1)___

        Somewhat difficult*
        (Answer Q24 B.) ___(2)___

        Quite easy ___(3)___

        Very easy ___(4)___

*Q24 B. What was the source of difficulty? 43-44/

_____
_____
_____
_____
_____

Name of Rater_____ Telephone_____

Agency Position_____ 45-46/

Highest Professional Degree: 47/

    High school graduate   ___(1)___

    Some college   ___(2)___

    BSW   ___(3)___

    Other Bachelor's degree   ___(4)___

    MSW   ___(5)___

    Other Master's degree   ___(6)___

    DSW or Ph.D. in social work   ___(7)___

    Other doctoral degree   ___(8)___

    Other   ___(9)___

Years with Agency_____ 48-49/

What is the size of your caseload?

    Number of children_____ 50-51/
    Number of families_____ 52-53/

How well do you feel you know the MOTHER of the child? 54/

    Very well   ___(1)___

    Fairly well   ___(2)___

    Slightly   ___(3)___

    Hardly at all   ___(4)___

    Other (*Specify*)_____

    _____ ___(5)___

How well do you feel you know the FATHER of the child? 55/

    Very well   ___(1)___

    Fairly well   ___(2)___

    Slightly   ___(3)___

    Hardly at all   ___(4)___

    Other (*Specify*)_____

    _____ ___(5)___

III Foster Children and Their Foster Parents: Adoption Perspectives

CONTENTS

1 Foster Children and Their Foster Parents 219
Introduction 219
Sampling Methodology 219

2 Characteristics of the Foster Families 223
The Foster Families 223
Foster Family Composition 227
Summary 227

3 The Children in Foster Family Care 229
The Foster Children 229
Summary Comments 232

4 Discharge Objectives and the Issue of Adoption by Foster Parents 238
Introduction 238
Factors Associated with Discharge Plans 238
Approach to the Foster Parents About Adopting the Child 242
Sources of Doubt About Adoption 242
Factors Related to Adoption Planning 245
Three Types of Adoption Planning 245
Summary Comments 250

5 Assessing the Child's Relationships to the Natural Family and to the Foster Family 251
Child's Relationship to Natural Family 251
Child's Relationship to the Foster Family 255
Conflict Over Family Attachments 255
Summary Comments 255

6 What Lies Ahead for the Child? 259
Predicting Status Changes 259
Parental Contact and Projected Changes 259
Earliest Timing of Status Change Events 262

7 Evaluative Ratings of the Foster Parents 264
How the Foster Parents Relate to the Children 264
Understanding and Rapport 264
Quality of Care 271
Coordination of Household 276
The Adjustment of the Children 276
Summary Comments 276

8 Creation of Composite Indexes 279
Factor Analysis 279
Creation of Indexes 279
Summary Comments 282

9 Multiple Regression Analysis of the Index Scores 286
Child's Integration in Foster Home 286
Relationship to Natural Family 286
Evaluation of the Foster Home 290
Conflicted Feelings Over Family Attachments 290
Comments 290

10 Movement Toward Permanency: A Validity Test 293
Introduction 293
Discharge Status 293
Discharge Status and Index Scores 293
Multiple Regression Analyses 295
The Predictions of Social Workers 299
Comments 299

11 Summary of Findings and Implications 302
Introduction 302
Key Findings 302

Notes 305

Appendixes 307

The Questionnaire 311

LIST OF TABLES

Table
1. Agencies Participating in Mini-Project 3: Total Questionnaires Sent and Returned 220
2. Reasons for Failure to Complete Forms for Those Returned Blank 221
3. Characteristics of Foster Homes According to Age of Child 224
4. Composition of Foster Families 228
5. Characteristics of Children According to Age of Child 230
6. Information About Siblings of Subjects Who Are in Foster Care According to Age of Child 233
7. Caseworkers' Replies to the Question: "About How Often Does Child See His Own Mother?" According to Age of Child 234
8. Caseworkers' Replies to the Question: "About How Often Does Child See His Own Father?" According to Age of Child 235
9. Last Time Child Saw Natural Mother According to Age of Child 236
10. Last Time Child Saw Natural Father According to Age of Child 237
11. Discharge Objective by Child's Current Age and Years in Care as of December 31, 1977 239
12. Discharge Objective for Children According to Frequency of Contact with Natural Mother 240
13. Discharge Objectives for Children According to Presence of Siblings in Foster Care 241
14. Information About Whether Foster Parents Had Been Approached to Consider Adoption of the Child According to Age of Child 243
15. Information as to Whether Foster Parents Had Been Approached to Consider Adoption According to Number of Foster Placements Experienced by the Child 246
16. Information Regarding Foster Parents Having Been Approached to Consider Adoption of Child According to Presence of Siblings in Foster Care 247
17. Information as to Whether Foster Parents Had Been Approached to Consider Adoption According to Frequency of Child's Contact with Natural Mother 248
18. Agency Approach to Foster Parents About Adoption and Their Reactions According to Selected Variables 249
19. Caseworkers' Ratings of the Quality of the Foster Child's Relationship to His/Her Natural Mother According to Age of Child 252
20. Caseworkers' Ratings of the Quality of the Foster Child's Relationship to His/Her Natural Father According to Age of Child 253
21. Caseworkers' Ratings of the Quality of the Foster Child's Relationship to His/Her Natural Family as a Whole According to Age of Child 254
22. Child's Integration in Foster Home According to Age of Child 256
23. Acceptance of the Child by Foster Mother According to Age of Child 257
24. Child's Manifestation of Conflict Over Family Attachments According to Age of Child 258
25. Caseworkers' Ratings of the Possibility of Status Changes To Be Experienced by Child. 260
26. Caseworker's Estimate That Child Will Be Adopted by Foster Family in One-to-Two Years According to Frequency of Child's Contact with Natural Mother 261
27. Predicted Status Change Events Likely to Affect the Child Within Three Time Periods. 263
28. Caseworkers' Ratings of the Degree of Affection Shown by Foster Mother to Foster Child by Age of Child 265
29. Caseworkers' Ratings of the Degree of Affection Shown by Foster Father to Foster Child by Age of Child 266
30. Caseworkers' Ratings of the Degree of Affection Shown by Foster Child Toward Foster Mother According to Age of Child 267
31. Caseworkers' Ratings of the Degree of Affection Shown By Foster Child Toward Foster Father According to Age of Child 268
32. Caseworkers' Ratings of the Understanding of the Child Shown by Foster Mother According to the Age of the Child 269

33. Caseworkers' Ratings of the Understanding of the Child Shown by Foster Father According to the Age of the Child 270
34. Caseworkers' Ratings of Rapport Between Foster Mother and Child According to Age of Child 272
35. Caseworkers' Ratings of Rapport Between Foster Father and Child According to Age of Child 273
36. Caseworkers' Ratings of the Characteristics of the Foster Parents According to Age of Child 274
37. Caseworkers' Ratings of the Coordination of the Foster Family's Household 277
38. Caseworkers' Ratings of Adjustment of the Foster Children According to Age of Child 278
39. Items from Questionnaire Included in the Factor Analysis 280
40. Rotated Factor Matrix for Items from Questionnaire 281
41. Index of Child's Integration in the Foster Home 283
42. Index of Child's Relationship to Natural Family 284
43. Index of Worker's Evaluation of the Foster Home 285
44. Correlations Between Independent Variables Used in the Study, Means and Standard Deviations 287
45. Relation of Independent Variables to Index of Child's Integration Within Foster Home 288
46. Relation of Independent Variables to Index of Child's Relationship to the Natural Family 289
47. Relation of Independent Variables in Index of Worker's Evaluation of the Foster Home 291
48. Relation of Selected Independent Variables to the Social Worker's Rating of Child's Manifestation of Conflict Over Family Attachments 292
49. Mean Scores on Index of Child's Relationship to Natural Family According to Discharge Plan and Discharge Status After One Year 294
50. Mean Scores on Index of Child's Integration in the Foster Home According to Discharge Plan and Discharge Status After One Year 296
51. Relation of Selected Predictor Variables to Child's Status on December 31, 1978 for Children with a Discharge Plan of Return to Parents or Relatives 297
52. Relation of Selected Predictor Variables to Child's Status on December 31, 1978 for Children with a Discharge Plan of Adoption 298
53. Social Workers' Predictions of Possibility of Return of Children During Coming Year and Discharge Status of Children One Year Later 300
54. Social Workers' Predictions of Possibility of Adoption of Children by Foster Parents During Coming Year and Discharge Status of Children One Year Later 301

1 Foster Children and Their Foster Parents

Introduction

Foster parents are highly significant actors in the phenomenon of foster care of children. In New York City, foster family homes provide care for over 17,000 children—almost 64 percent of the children in care.[1] Recent reports from Child Welfare Information Services (CWIS) show that children remain in care for very long periods; their foster families often become the only stable families the children have known. This is especially true of children coming into care at very young ages.[2]

That many of the children in foster care have lost contact with their parents is also a well established fact.[3] This phenomenon makes the child's relationship with his foster parents even more crucial than it otherwise might be.

In this monograph, we report on an effort to provide fairly comprehensive information about agency perspectives on the relationship between foster children and their foster parents. The data come from one of the three "mini-projects" designed to provide a trial run of data modules dealing with foster care. They cover new domains of content for possible future expansion of the data base initially included in the CWIS system in New York City and subsequently by CCRS for all of New York State.[4]

The questionnaire employed in this mini-project is shown in the Appendix. As can be seen from the content of the items, much of the information that was elicited from the caseworkers who served as informants sought to establish the agency's perspective with respect to the possibility that the foster parents were, or could become, the permanent parents of the child through adoption. This is obviously a crucial area to pin down in shaping the way a child's case is handled and is at the heart of permanency planning for foster children.

Among the important informational domains included in the questionnaire were the following:

(1) The degree to which the child had contact with his own natural family and the intensity of his identification with his parents and other family members.

(2) The degree to which the child was embedded in his foster family, identified with it as his "real" family and was accepted by his foster parents.

(3) The state of the agency's thinking about discharge plans for the child and the likely changes in his status that would occur within the coming year, within one to two years and within three to five years.

(4) The personal and social characteristics of the foster family including the ages of the foster parents, composition of the household, type of housing, income and occupations of the parents, their ethnicity and religion; also included was the number of years they had served the agency as foster parents and the number of children that had been placed with them.

(5) The evaluation of the foster parents as likely adoptive parents, i.e., the kind of care offered the children placed with them, their capacity to stimulate the children, etc.

(6) Information as to whether the foster parents had ever been approached by the agency to consider adopting the foster child, when this was done, and their reactions to the presentation of this opportunity.

Sampling Methodology

The list of the 33 agencies that participated in the mini-project is shown in Table 1.[5] Because of the heavy demands made upon some agencies in the prior two mini-projects and because there was indication that the agencies were experiencing intense "paper work" pressures, a decision was made to limit the demand upon any agency to 15 cases. By this decision, it was possible to secure cooperation from agencies that were approached after participating in the first two mini-projects even though they had not volunteered for the third project.

The 15 cases were randomly drawn from each agency's CWIS data file. Several agencies required supplementary lists when it emerged that the children designated had already been discharged.

The criteria for selection of cases required that the children were living in foster family care arrangements and had been in their current placements for at least a year. Only one child was selected from a single family. Of 486 forms sent to the 33 agencies, 478 (98.4 percent) were returned. Of these, 92 (19.2 percent) were returned not completed. The reasons for this are shown in Table 2. There were 26 children who were already discharged and 12 who went home on trial discharge. There were also 22 children who had been legally adopted and 13 where this was shortly to take place. Eight children had recently left

TABLE 1

AGENCIES PARTICIPATING IN MINI-PROJECT 3:*
TOTAL QUESTIONNAIRES SENT AND RETURNED

Sent	Agency	Returned	Completed
15	Abbott House	15	15
15	Angel Guardian Home	15	14
7	Astor Home for Children	7	7
1	Brooklyn Home for Children	1	1
26	Brookwood Child Care	26	15
15	Cardinal Hayes Home for Children	15	15
15	Cardinal McCloskey School and Home for Children	15	12
16	Catholic Guardian Society - Brooklyn	16	12
15	Catholic Guardian Society - New York	15	15
15	Catholic Home Bureau	15	11
11	Children's Aid Society	9	8
14	Children's Village	14	13
15	Edwin Gould Services for Children	12	9
17	Greer-Woodycrest Children's Services	17	10
23	Graham-Windham	23	11
15	Harlem-Dowling Children's Services	15	14
9	Inwood House	9	7
15	Jewish Child Care Association	15	12
14	Kennedy Child Study Center	14	10
15	Lutheran Community Services, Inc.	15	9
15	McMahon Services for Children	15	14
15	Mission of Immaculate Virgin	15	11
15	New York Foundling Hospital	15	15
15	Pius XII School	15	15
17	St. Cabrini Home, Inc.	17	14
15	St. Cominic's Home	12	11
15	St. Joseph Children's Services	15	14
15	St. Joseph's Home of Peekskill	15	13
13	St. Vincent's Hall	13	5
17	Salvation Army	17	15
15	Sheltering Arms Children's Service	15	12
17	Spence-Chapin	17	15
14	Talbot Perkins	14	12
486		478	386

*Total of 33 agencies participated in MP-3.

TABLE 2

REASONS FOR FAILURE TO COMPLETE FORMS FOR THOSE RETURNED BLANK*

Discharged	26
On trial discharge	12
Adopted	22
To be adopted (form not completed)	13
Child institutionalized	8
Child placed in new foster home within past few months (not in foster home for one full year)	3
Child AWOL	1
Form not completed (no explanation)	7
TOTAL	92

*A total of 478 questionnaires were returned leaving an N of 386.

their foster homes for placement in institutions.

We are thus left with a sample of 386 cases. While the size of returned forms is more modest than those that were garnered for the prior two mini-projects, the random selection of cases and the large number of participating agencies lend support for the view that the findings from the survey can be accepted as quite strongly representative of the foster family placements extensively used by the system to house foster children. The size is also deemed adequate for the statistical treatment of the data originally contemplated for the study.

2 Characteristics of the Foster Families

The Foster Families

In Table 3, we set forth a number of the characteristics of the foster families based upon data derived from the questionnaire. The data are displayed for the group as a whole and also according to the ages of the children placed with them. Three age classifications of the children are used: 1 to 5 years, 6 to 9 years, and 10 to 13 years.

It should be pointed out that organized information about foster parents is relatively hard to come by.[6] Few agencies have taken the initiative to collect and aggregate information about the families they have recruited to take care of foster children. At the present time there does not appear to be any agency in the country that has the capability of charting changes in the characteristics of its foster parents over time. Considering their importance as major contributers to the foster care system, the lack of accurate and current information must be seen as a weakness in practice.

Age. The mean ages of the foster mothers and the foster fathers as shown in Table 3 are 46.1 and 47.9 years respectively. Those taking care of the older children were two to three years older in age than those whose foster children were in the youngest group. About 12 percent of the foster mothers were 35 years or younger, 53 percent were between 36 and 50 years of age, and 34 percent were 51 years of age or older. Only six percent were 60 years of age or older.

It should be pointed out that 69 of the foster families (17.9 percent) represented family situations in which only a single parent was present. In almost all cases, the single-parent household involved widowed women. In two cases, foster fathers were carrying on as heads of households after the deaths of their wives.

Years with Agency and Number of Children Served. For the 386 foster families, the mean length of time they had served with the agencies was 6.0 years. Those caring for the older foster children had an average tenure of 6.9 years while those with younger children showed a mean of 4.3 years. Sixteen (4.1 percent) of the families had been associated with the agency for ten or more years. Two families stood out as "old timers," each having served 21 years with their agencies.

The families had served close to five children in their experiences with the agencies (mean = 4.7 children). Those caring for the youngest children had served close to six children.

Ethnicity and Religion. The sample was heavily loaded with black foster families (53.6 percent) and the remainder were about equally divided between Puerto Rican (23.1 percent) and white foster families (21.1 percent). The white families tended to be over-represented among the oldest children while the Puerto Rican families had more than their share of children six to nine years of age.

The sample was about evenly divided between Protestants (47.5 percent) and Catholic foster families (46.6 percent). Jews constituted a very small percent of the families (2.8 percent) as was a miscellaneous group classified under "other" (3.1 percent).

Education. About 44 percent of the foster mothers had not completed high school while about 42 percent were identified as graduates. About ten percent of the foster mothers had experienced some college education but only about two percent had graduated from college. The foster fathers showed 46 percent with less than a high school diploma, 33 percent who had graduated and over 16 percent with some college education including about seven percent who had graduated from college.

Housing and Location of Residence. Almost two-thirds of the foster families lived in their own private homes. There was a greater tendency for families caring for the youngest children to be in private apartments than those caring for the oldest children. Almost 19 percent of those caring for children six to nine years of age were in rented apartments in public housing projects while this was true of almost 12 percent of those caring for the older children and less than seven percent of those who had the youngest children in their homes.

The families were about evenly divided between those living in the boroughs and those in suburban counties. Queens was the most frequent location for the city dwellers (22.0 percent) and Manhattan was the least likely location (5.3 percent).

Occupation and Income. Almost a half of the foster fathers were either laborers, service workers or operatives (47.6 percent) while 17.3 percent were craftsmen. About 28 percent were in white collar, managerial or in professional or technical jobs. Homes providing care for the youngest children tended to reflect more service and operative types of employment than those with the older children.

About 30 percent of the families had incomes below

TABLE 3

CHARACTERISTICS OF FOSTER HOMES ACCORDING TO AGE OF CHILD
(N = 386)

Characteristic	1 to 5 Years	6 to 9 Years	10 to 13 Years	Total
Mean Years of Age at Last Birthday of Foster Father	46.4	47.4	49.4	47.9
Mean Years of Age at Last Birthday of Foster Mother	45.5	45.1	47.0	46.1
Intactness of Foster Home				
% Intact	81.8	79.1	84.6	82.1
% One-parent home	18.2	20.9	15.4	17.9
Mean Years with Agency	4.3	5.6	6.9	6.0
Mean Number of Children Agency Has Placed with Foster Family	5.6	4.2	4.7	4.7
Ethnicity of Foster Father:				
% White	20.6	18.1	31.1	24.8
% Black	50.8	41.9	52.3	48.6
% Puerto Rican	28.6	37.1	15.9	25.4
% Other Hispanic	--	2.9	0.7	1.2
Ethnicity of Foster Mother:				
% White	18.2	13.1	28.3	21.1
% Black	57.1	50.8	54.3	53.6
% Puerto Rican	22.1	33.1	16.2	23.1
% Other Hispanic	2.6	3.0	0.6	1.9
% Other	--	--	0.6	0.3
Religion of Foster Father:				
% Protestant	43.6	43.9	51.7	47.5
% Catholic	50.0	49.6	43.0	46.6
% Jewish	1.6	2.8	3.3	2.8
% Other	4.8	3.7	2.0	3.1
Religion of Foster Mother:				
% Protestant	50.6	50.4	51.7	51.1
% Catholic	42.9	45.0	42.0	43.2
% Jewish	1.3	0.8	2.9	1.8
% Other	5.2	3.8	3.4	3.9

(Continued)

TABLE 3 (Continued)

CHARACTERISTICS OF FOSTER HOMES ACCORDING TO AGE OF CHILD

Characteristic	1 to 5 Years	6 to 9 Years	10 to 13 Years	Total
Education Completed - Foster Mother:				
% Less than 5 years grammar school	2.7	3.9	2.3	2.9
% 5-8 years grammar school	12.2	14.7	8.7	11.5
% Some high school	31.1	28.7	29.1	29.3
% High school graduate	37.7	41.0	45.3	42.4
% Some college	12.2	7.8	7.6	8.5
% College graduate	2.7	0.8	2.3	1.9
% Unknown	1.4	3.1	4.7	3.5
Education Completed - Foster Father:				
% Less than 5 years grammar school	--	3.8	--	1.3
% 5-8 years grammar school	24.2	18.1	12.8	16.8
% Some high school	24.2	30.5	27.7	27.9
% High school graduate	29.0	34.3	33.8	33.0
% Some college	9.7	3.8	12.8	9.2
% College graduate	8.1	7.6	6.8	7.3
% Other	--	--	0.7	0.3
% Unknown	4.8	1.9	5.4	4.1
Housing of Foster Family:				
% Own private home	68.4	67.9	79.3	73.2
% Rent private home	6.6	4.6	2.9	4.2
% Own cooperative apartment	3.9	0.8	0.6	1.3
% Rent apartment, public housing project	6.6	19.1	11.5	13.1
% Rent apartment, private	13.2	7.6	5.7	7.9
% Other	1.3	--	--	0.3
Location of Foster Family:				
% Manhattan	6.7	7.0	3.5	5.3
% Bronx	4.0	17.8	12.8	12.8
% Brooklyn	16.0	12.4	14.5	14.1
% Queens	30.6	19.4	20.3	22.0
% Staten Island	--	0.8	1.2	0.8
% Nassau or Suffolk	22.7	17.8	15.7	17.8
% Westchester	4.0	5.4	12.8	8.5
% Other New York State	9.3	17.1	14.5	14.4
% Out of New York State	6.7	2.3	4.7	4.3

(Continued)

TABLE 3 (Continued)

CHARACTERISTICS OF FOSTER HOMES ACCORDING TO AGE OF CHILD

Characteristic	1 to 5 Years	6 to 9 Years	10 to 13 Years	Total
	(Percentaged)			
Occupation of Foster Father:				
Laborer	9.3	10.3	11.5	10.7
Service worker	22.1	20.8	17.5	19.4
Operative	27.7	14.9	15.3	17.6
Craftsman/foreman	13.0	17.3	19.0	17.3
Sales worker	--	--	3.8	1.8
Clerical worker	5.6	9.2	9.2	8.5
Manager	5.6	9.2	5.3	6.6
Professional/technical	9.3	10.3	11.5	10.7
Other	7.4	8.0	6.9	7.4
Percent	100.0	100.0	100.0	100.0
Total	(54)	(87)	(131)	(272)
Approximate Monthly Income of Foster Family (Excluding Foster Care Payments):				
$500 or less	14.5	12.4	11.9	12.6
$500 or over - less than $700	26.3	22.5	11.3	18.2
$700 or over - less than $900	17.1	23.2	19.6	20.4
$900 or over - less than $1100	15.8	9.3	13.1	12.3
$1100 or over - less than $1300	6.6	11.6	16.7	12.9
$1300 or over - less than $1500	7.9	7.8	7.1	7.5
$1500 or over	9.2	10.1	13.7	11.5
Other	1.3	2.3	1.8	1.9
Unknown	1.3	0.8	4.8	2.7
Percent	100.0	100.0	100.0	100.0
Total	(76)	(129)	(168)	(373)

$700 a month whereas close to 21 percent had incomes of $1,100 a month or more. On the whole, the income of the families tended to reflect modest material circumstances. Nevertheless, the majority of families owned their own homes.

Foster Family Composition

The foster families varied in size and composition, ranging from family units in which the foster child was the only child present in three-person households to large families with ten or more persons living in the home in addition to the foster parents. Information about family composition is potentially important since a foster family with many children might feel less motivated to enter into formal adoption arrangements to secure permanency for a child than a family where the foster child is the only youngster in the home. That is, it is conceivable that the strength of attachment of foster parents to children may reflect the number of children available to them. This is stated as a hunch rather than with any sense of certainty.

The composition of the 386 foster families covered in this survey is shown in Table 4. In 24.1 percent of the homes, the foster child was the only person in the family besides the parents themselves. Twenty-eight percent of the families had five or more family members in addition to the foster parents.

Altogether, there were 780 foster children cared for by these families, averaging two foster children per family. In addition, there were 329 own children, 31 nieces or nephews and 15 grandchildren included among the foster families. Parents, grandparents, siblings and others were also reported living with relatively small numbers of the families.

Summary

The characteristics of the foster parents that stand out from these data include the following:

- The foster parents tend to be in their middle years, with an average age in the late 40s.
- The foster parents have been with the agency for an average of six years and have had an average of almost five children placed with them.
- The families are heavily recruited from minority groups, with black families constituting more than half of the sample.
- Almost three-fourths of the families own private homes while 13 percent rent apartments in public housing projects and eight percent rent apartments in private buildings.
- Only five percent of the foster families live in Manhattan while almost 50 percent live in the other boroughs. Almost 45 percent of the families live outside of the city, mainly in surrounding suburbs.
- The families tend to have modest incomes, with the foster fathers concentrated in labor and service occupations.

TABLE 4

COMPOSITION OF FOSTER FAMILIES

a. Number of Family Members in Addition to Foster Parents[a]	Number	Percent
One member only (foster child)	93	24.1
Two members	42	10.9
Three members	63	16.3
Four members	80	20.7
Five members	57	14.8
Six members	31	8.0
Seven members	13	3.4
Eight or more members	7	1.8
TOTAL	386	100.0

b. Types of Family Members	Number	Percent
Foster children (including subjects)	780	66.6
Own children	329	28.1
Step-children	2	0.2
Nieces or nephews	31	2.7
Grandchildren	15	1.3
Parents	4	0.3
Grandparents	3	0.3
Siblings	2	0.2
Aunt, uncle	1	0.1
Other	2	0.2
TOTAL	1169	100.0

[a] Of the 386 foster homes covered by the survey, 69 were single parent households.

3 The Children in Foster Family Care

The Foster Children

The 386 children in our study had been living with their foster families for at least a year at the time our investigation was carried out. As explained earlier, this was a criterion for their inclusion in the study. In this chapter, we provide background information about our subjects as developed from an analysis of their CWIS data files and from the responses of the social workers to the survey questionnaire. Such data are set forth in Table 5.

Age and Time in Care. The mean age of the children at the time of the survey was 9.1 years. It is noteworthy that three-fourths of them entered care as pre-schoolers, i.e., under six years of age, and almost a third came in as infants. Many of the children thus joined their foster families while still young enough to develop deep roots, particularly if their own parents failed to keep in touch with them.

The children had been in care for an average of 5.7 years and at their current agencies for 5.1 years. The children who were 10 to 13 years of age had been with their agencies for an average of 6.3 years while the youngest group were in care for an average of 3.0 years.

Reasons for Placement. The children entered foster care for a variety of reasons; most of these were related to the inability of their parents to carry out their parental responsibilities effectively. For example, about 20 percent of the subjects had come into foster care because of neglect and this was true of even larger proportions of the younger children.

Almost 12 percent of the children were in care because a parent suffered from a drug abuse problem; this was true of 16 percent of the children who were five years or younger. Nine percent of all the children had been abandoned and this was an important category for children 10 to 13 years of age (13.1 percent).

Only 6.6 percent of the children were in care for reasons related to their own behavior. This was noted as a factor for almost ten percent of the older children. It should be kept in mind that, unlike most of the children described here, children who enter foster care because of behavioral problems are apt to be older and placed in institutions rather than in foster family homes.

Ethnicity and Religion. The majority of children in the sample were minority youngsters with about 52 percent black and 30 percent Hispanic. Fifteen percent were white. They were almost evenly divided among Protestants (46.2 percent) and Catholics (48.8 percent). About two percent of the children were Jewish.

Discharge Objectives and Family Contacts. According to the CWIS data files accessed for these children as of December 31, 1977, about half of them (49.6 percent) were slated for adoption and about one-fourth (25.4 percent) were candidates for being returned to their parents or relatives. About ten percent were destined to be discharged to their own responsibility when reaching adulthood. Discharge plans were clearly varied by age with almost twice the proportion of the younger children said to be destined to be returned to their parents as the older. On the other hand, the oldest group was the only one where an appreciable proportion (19.3 percent) was identified as likely to be discharged to their own responsibility.

Adoption loomed large for each of the three age groupings but was particularly outstanding for the children six to nine years of age; 55.6 percent of this group had adoption as the designated plan. This compared with 42.7 percent for the youngest and 48.3 percent for the oldest group.

For the 95 children who had been freed for adoption, the amount of contact with their parents was, as expected, extremely minimal. Almost 92 percent had not seen either of their natural parents during the past six months.

For the 282 children not freed for adoption, almost 50 percent were reported to have had no contact with their natural parents.[7] Almost five percent of the cases involved a failure of the caseworker to report visiting information.

About 40 percent of the children were in contact with their parents on at least two occasions during the past two months and an additional six percent had one such contact. The younger children had the largest proportion with one or more contacts (55.2 percent) and the oldest group came next (46.0 percent).

Court-Adjudicated Status. Very few of the children were in foster care because of child abuse (0.3 percent) but almost a fourth were adjudicated as neglected (23.6 percent). Fully a third of the youngest age group were in the neglected category, at least ten percent more than either of the other age groupings.

A substantial proportion of the children (53.5 percent) had been covered by the court review process mandated by Section 392 of the New York Social Services Law. This law was enacted in 1971 and now provides for judicial

TABLE 5

CHARACTERISTICS OF CHILDREN ACCORDING TO AGE OF CHILD[a]

Characteristic	1 to 5 Years	6 to 9 Years	10 to 13 Years	Total
Mean Age	4.0	8.1	12.0	9.1
Age When First Entered Care:				
% Under 1 year	65.3	29.4	18.7	31.6
% 1 to 2 years	29.3	27.8	15.9	22.6
% 3 to 5 years	5.3	30.9	18.7	20.1
% 6 or more years	--	11.9	46.6	25.9
Mean Years in Care	3.1	5.3	7.1	5.7
Mean Years at Current Agency	3.0	4.8	6.3	5.1
Selected Reasons for Placement:[b]				
% Home behavior	--	6.3	9.7	6.6
% Child abuse	6.7	5.6	5.1	5.6
% Neglect	24.0	24.6	15.9	20.4
% Parent alcoholic	2.7	4.8	8.0	5.8
% Parent drug abuse	16.0	13.5	9.7	12.2
% Abandonment	2.7	7.9	13.1	9.3
Ethnicity of Child:				
% Black	58.7	47.6	51.7	51.7
% White	17.3	8.7	18.7	15.1
% Hispanic	21.3	39.7	26.1	29.7
Religion of Child:				
% Protestant	46.7	43.7	47.7	46.2
% Catholic	44.0	53.2	47.7	48.8
% Jewish	1.3	0.8	2.8	1.9
Discharge Objectives Reported for Child:				
% To parents or relatives	37.3	24.6	21.0	25.4
% Adoption	42.7	55.6	48.3	49.6
% To own responsibility	2.7	1.6	19.3	10.1
% Other, unknown	6.6	8.7	4.5	6.4
% Not reported	10.7	9.5	6.8	8.5

[a] CWIS data file as of December 31, 1977.

[b] Categories are not mutually exclusive and more than one reason can be reported for each child.

(Continued)

TABLE 5 (*Continued*)

CHARACTERISTICS OF CHILDREN ACCORDING TO AGE OF CHILD

Characteristic	1 to 5 Years	6 to 9 Years	10 to 13 Years	Total
Contact with Parents Over Past Six Months: Free for Adoption:				
% None	83.3	97.0	90.0	91.6
% One contact	8.3	--	6.0	4.2
% Two or more contacts	8.3	3.0	4.0	4.3
% Not reported	--	--	--	--
Contact with Parents Over Past Six Months: Not Free for Adoption:				
% None	42.9	50.5	51.6	49.3
% One contact	6.3	2.2	7.9	5.7
% Two or more contacts	49.2	37.7	38.1	40.4
% Not reported	1.6	9.7	2.4	4.6
Court-Adjudicated Status:				
% Abused	--	--	0.6	0.3
% Neglected	33.3	22.2	20.5	23.6
% Court review--foster care reauthorized	29.3	53.2	63.6	53.3
% Court remand	20.0	11.9	7.4	11.4
% No court involvement	16.0	12.7	8.0	11.1
% Not reported	1.3	--	--	0.3
Number of Foster Home Placements Experienced by Child:				
% First placement	76.0	58.1	62.1	63.6
% Second placement	16.0	24.8	26.0	23.6
% Third placement or more	8.0	17.1	11.9	12.8

review of children who have been in foster care continuously for 18 months.

The largest proportion of children receiving reauthorization of the foster care arrangements under this review procedure was in the oldest group (aged 10 to 13 years) where 63.6 percent of the children had been so reviewed. On the other hand, only 29.3 percent of the youngest group had been covered by the judicial review process.

Sequence of Placements. It is of interest to observe that most of the subjects, almost two-thirds of the children (63.6 percent), were in their first foster home placement. About a fourth (23.6 percent) were in their second placements. Despite the widespread view that children in foster care are subject to a great deal of turnover, it turns out that only 12.8 percent of the children in the study had experienced two or more placements. There was some variation by age groupings in this regard but not of a pronounced sort.

Siblings in Care. A factor that is quite important in planning for children in foster care is the matter of the number of children in a given family who require foster care. If an agency has to deal with a family of three or four children, the task of planning for permanent living arrangements can be quite different in character and the challenges presented than if a single child is involved. The presence of several children usually means that at least one or more of the children have received some care at the hands of the natural mother. Single children in foster care are more likely to be the only children of young natural parents whose maternal and paternal careers have hardly gotten off the ground.

Size of sibship systems can also be viewed as important variables when natural parents are completely out of the picture. It is one kind of phenomenon to arrange for the adoption of a single child. It is much more complex—although certainly not impossible—to secure an adoptive placement for a multiple sibling group.

Table 6 shows that over a third of the children in the study were without any siblings in care. The youngest group of children showed a more pronounced tendency in this regard; 48.7 percent of these children were the only children from their families in care.

For 41.5 percent of the cases, the subjects were in sibship systems that contained as many as three children in care. Forty-one of the subjects (10.6 percent) were in family groups involving five or more children in care.

For the children with siblings in care, only 28.3 percent were in foster family care in homes not shared by a sibling. This was much more the case with the grouping of young children (one to five years of age); 41 percent of these subjects were in homes not shared with any of their siblings.

In almost 70 percent of the cases involving siblings in care, the caseworkers indicated that it was the agency's goal to keep the siblings together. There were 75 children (30.7 percent) where this was not the goal. However in about 75 percent of the cases in which siblings were not placed together, the homes in which our subjects were placed were not seen as being able to absorb additional siblings.

Contact with Parents. In the questionnaire prepared for the study, the question was asked: "About how often does child see his own mother?" Table 7 shows that only 25.1 percent of the children saw mothers as frequently as once in three months. Almost a third of the children were said to "never" see their mothers and for another 19 percent of the cases, the mother was out of the picture entirely. Of the three age groups, the oldest children showed the fewest children in contact with their mothers.

Contact with the natural fathers was sparse for all three age groups. For the children taken together, only 12.8 percent saw their fathers at least once in three months. It would appear that only 22.1 percent of the children *ever* saw their father whatever the frequency (see Table 8).

Table 9 shows that only 37.6 percent of the children had seen their mothers within the past year. For the fathers, this figure was reduced to 17.8 percent (see Table 10).

Summary Comments

The children who constitute the subjects of our study have the following characteristics:

- Their average age is about nine years and they have been in care for an average of 5.7 years.
- They are predominantly black and Puerto Rican and have come into care largely because of parental breakdown in functioning. Very few have been placed because of their own behavioral difficulties.
- Many of the children have been known to the courts. A fourth of them have been adjudicated as neglected. More than half have had their status subjected to court review and foster care has been reauthorized.
- More than half of the children have lost contact with their parents and many have not seen their parents in over two years. Their fathers are particularly out of the picture.
- Most of the children—almost two thirds—are in the first foster home in which they were placed when they entered foster care.
- The majority of these children have siblings in care and in many cases the siblings are in the same foster home.
- Almost half the children are said to have adoption as a discharge plan while a fourth are slated to be returned to their parents.

TABLE 6

INFORMATION ABOUT SIBLINGS OF SUBJECTS WHO ARE IN FOSTER CARE ACCORDING TO AGE OF CHILD

Information About Siblings	1 to 5 Years	6 to 9 Years	10 to 13 Years	Total
	(Percentaged)			
A. Does child have any siblings in care?				
None	48.7	32.1	32.7	35.5
One	14.5	26.7	23.8	23.0
Two	23.7	21.4	17.4	20.1
Three	3.9	9.9	14.5	10.8
Four	5.3	6.1	6.4	6.1
Five	1.3	1.5	3.5	2.4
Six or more	2.6	2.3	1.7	2.1
Percent Total	100.0 (76)	100.0 (131)	100.0 (172)	100.0 (383)[a]
B. How many siblings are placed in the same foster family as this child?				
None	41.0	22.5	28.4	28.3
One	30.8	56.2	48.3	48.4
Two	23.1	14.6	13.8	15.6
Three	5.1	5.6	6.0	5.7
Four	--	--	2.6	1.2
Five	--	--	--	--
Six	--	1.1	0.9	0.8
Percent Total	100.0 (69)	100.0 (89)	100.0 (116)	100.0 (244)
C. Does agency have goal of keeping these siblings together?				
Yes	58.3	74.7	68.4	69.3
No	41.7	25.3	31.6	30.7
Percent Total	100.0 (36)	100.0 (91)	100.0 (117)	100.0 (244)
D. Is the home in which the child is placed a potential home for siblings?				
Yes	29.6	29.8	19.2	24.8
No	70.4	70.2	80.8	75.2
Percent Total	100.0 (27)	100.0 (57)	100.0 (73)	100.0 (157)

[a] Excludes 13 children where the information was not provided.

TABLE 7

CASEWORKERS' REPLIES TO THE QUESTION:
"ABOUT HOW OFTEN DOES CHILD SEE HIS OWN MOTHER?"
ACCORDING TO AGE OF CHILD

Reported Frequency	1 to 5 Years	6 to 9 Years	10 to 13 Years	Total
	(Percentaged)			
At least once a month	16.9	16.7	9.5	13.5
At least once in 3 months	15.6	8.3	12.4	11.6
About once in 6 months	11.7	4.5	6.5	6.9
About once a year	2.6	1.5	3.0	2.4
Occasional, but less than once a year	6.5	7.6	9.5	8.2
Never	27.2	33.3	34.8	32.8
Other	3.9	6.1	0.6	3.2
Not applicable (mother deceased, surrendered child, etc.)	6.5	21.2	23.7	19.3
Mother placed with child	9.1	0.8	--	2.1
Percent Total	100.0 (77)	100.0 (132)	100.0 (169)	100.0 (378)

[a] Excludes 8 children where the information was not provided.

TABLE 8

CASEWORKERS' REPLIES TO THE QUESTION:
"ABOUT HOW OFTEN DOES CHILD SEE HIS OWN FATHER?"
ACCORDING TO AGE OF CHILD

Reported Frequency	1 to 5 Years	6 to 9 Years	10 to 13 Years	Total
	(Percentaged)			
At least once a month	7.0	7.9	8.9	8.2
At least once in 3 months	9.9	3.1	3.6	4.6
At least once in 6 months	2.8	1.6	3.0	2.5
About once a year	2.8	3.1	--	1.6
Occasional, but less than once a year	4.2	4.7	6.0	5.2
Never	53.5	47.2	53.6	51.4
Other	4.2	3.1	1.2	2.5
Not applicable (paternity not acknowledged, father deceased, etc.)	15.5	29.1	23.8	24.0
Percent Total	100.0 (71)	100.0 (127)	100.0 (168)	100.0 (366)[a]

[a] Excludes 20 children where the information was not provided.

TABLE 9

LAST TIME CHILD SAW NATURAL MOTHER ACCORDING TO AGE OF CHILD

Last Contact	1 to 5 Years	6 to 9 Years	10 to 13 Years	Total
	(Percentaged)			
Less than 3 months	27.2	29.4	20.2	25.0
3 months but less than 6 months	5.2	2.3	7.8	5.4
6 months but less than 1 year	19.5	2.3	5.4	7.2
1 year but less than 2 years	14.3	6.2	10.2	9.7
2 years but less than 5 years	11.7	20.2	19.2	18.0
5 years or over	2.6	20.9	18.0	15.8
Other	1.3	1.6	1.2	1.3
Not applicable (e.g., never saw mother, mother deceased, etc.)	9.1	16.3	18.0	15.5
Mother placed with child	9.1	0.8	--	2.1
Percent Total	100.0 (77)	100.0 (129)	100.0 (167)	100.0 (373)[a]

[a] Excludes 13 children where the information was not provided.

TABLE 10

LAST TIME CHILD SAW NATURAL FATHER ACCORDING TO AGE OF CHILD

Last Contact	1 to 5 Years	6 to 9 Years	10 to 13 Years	Total
	(Percentaged)			
Less than 3 months	16.2	10.5	12.3	12.4
3 months but less than 6 months	2.9	0.8	1.2	1.4
6 months but less than 1 year	4.4	4.8	3.7	4.2
1 year but less than 2 years	8.8	7.3	5.6	6.8
2 years but less than 5 years	10.3	12.9	8.0	10.2
5 years or over	5.9	20.2	28.4	21.2
Other	5.9	2.4	1.9	2.8
Not applicable (paternity not acknowledged, deceased, etc.)	45.6	41.1	38.9	41.0
Percent Total	100.0 (68)	100.0 (124)	100.0 (162)	100.0 (354)[a]

[a] Excludes 32 children where the information was not provided.

4 Discharge Objectives and the Issue of Adoption by Foster Parents

Introduction

In this chapter, we seek to arrive at better understanding of the plans developed for each child by the agency under whose care he had been placed. In the previous chapter, we showed that about half of the children had adoption as the designated plan and about a fourth were supposed to be returned to their parents or relatives. One child in ten was slated to be discharged to his own responsibility when reaching majority. We explore here some factors associated with this differentiation in discharge planning. We also examine a very specific issue: Has the agency ever approached the foster parents to consider the possibility of adoption of the child placed with them?

Factors Associated with Discharge Plans

In Table 11, we show data derived from the CWIS data file of December 31, 1977, linking the agency's specified discharge objective with the child's age and the length of time he had been in care. Of particular interest is the planning for the older children, i.e., who were currently aged 10 to 21 years. The table shows three subgroups who had been in care two to five years, six to nine years and 10 to 21 years. For the children who had been in care for the shortest period, 27.7 percent had adoption as the discharge plan and 23.7 percent were to be discharged to their parents. For those in care for six to nine years, the group destined to be adopted was quite high, 58.2 percent, while those who were to be returned to their parents constituted only 14.5 percent of the group. Those who had been in care for the longest time period had the highest proportion of children identified as adoption-bound; 71.1 percent of this group were categorized in this way. Only 4.4 percent of the group were considered returnable to their parents.

For children currently 6 to 9 years of age, we again observe that the longer the time spent in care, the more likely was adoption to be identified as the discharge plan. For those in care 2 to 5 years, adoption was the discharge plan for 52.2 percent of the group and for those in care 6 to 9 years, it was the designated plan for 67.4 percent.

The caseworker's designation of a discharge objective is made quite comprehensible when we link discharge planning to the frequency of the mother's contact with the child. This is shown in Table 12. For example, the selection of a plan that calls for the child to be returned to his parents descends with the decrease in frequency of maternal contact. Thus, 55.8 percent of the children who had contact with their mothers about once a month had return to the parental home as a discharge plan. This was true of 38.7 percent of those who saw their mothers once in three months, 12.9 percent of those who saw their mothers occasionally, and 6.5 percent of those who were described as never seeing their mothers.

The same linear relationship between discharge plans and frequency of parental contact applies with respect to the projection of adoption as a likely source of permanency for a child. The percentage of children slated for adoption shows the following progression: 8.5 percent of those seen once a month, 22.7 percent of those seen once in three months, 32.0 percent where the contact was once in six months, 33.4 percent where it took place once a year, 54.8 percent where the encounter with the parent was no more than occasional, and as much as 73.4 percent where contact never took place.

The findings reported here are in line with the writer's previous identification of the importance of visiting as a predictor of a child's future status in foster care.[8] The strong association between discharge plans and parental visiting takes on greater saliency because only a third of the children were reported to see their parents once in six months or more frequently.

Siblings in Care. It was anticipated that the number of children from a given family that might be in foster care would strongly influence the nature of discharge planning. Thus, it would seem more likely that a single child in foster care would be a candidate for adoption than a multiple sibship group. There were two reasons for this expectation: (1) parents of more than one child in care tend to show greater commitment to their children as evidenced by their visiting behavior; and (2) it would seem more difficult to find adoptive homes for several children as opposed to a single child.

Table 13 cross-tabulates information about siblings in care with discharge planning. The table is not easy to interpret because a third factor appears to have some importance in helping to shape the choice of discharge plans: whether the child who is the subject in our study has a sibling in the same foster home as opposed to their being

TABLE 11

DISCHARGE OBJECTIVE BY CHILD'S CURRENT AGE AND YEARS IN CARE AS OF DECEMBER 31, 1977[a]
(N = 377)[b]

Years in Care:	Under Two Years			2 to 5 Years			6 to 9 Years		10 to 21 Years
Current Age:	Under 2 Years %	2 to 5 Years %	6 to 9 Years %	10 to 21 Years %	2 to 5 Years %	6 to 9 Years %	10 to 21 Years %	6 to 9 Years %	10 to 21 Years %	10 to 21 Years %
Discharge Objective:										
Discharge to parents	--	62.5	42.8	--	33.9	19.4	23.7	17.3	14.5	4.4
Discharge to relatives	--	--	14.3	--	1.5	7.5	7.9	--	5.5	--
Discharge to own responsibility										
Adoption	100.0	--	--	--	3.1	3.0	26.3	--	18.2	8.9
Adult custodial care required	--	37.5	--	--	41.5	52.2	27.7	67.4	58.2	71.1
Unknown	--	--	--	--	1.5	--	--	--	--	6.7
Not reported	--	--	14.3	--	6.2	6.0	3.9	11.5	1.8	2.2
	--	--	28.6	--	12.3	11.9	10.5	3.8	1.8	6.7
Percent Total	100.0 (2)	100.0 (8)	100.0 (7)	(0)	100.0 (65)	100.0 (67)	100.0 (76)	100.0 (52)	100.0 (55)	100.0 (45)

[a]The data presented here derive from the CWIS data file of December 31, 1977. The table has the same format as Table 29 (Series A) of the CWIS Special Report Series developed by David Fanshel and John Grundy.

[b]Of the 377 children, 365 were in care, one on suspended payment and 11 on trial discharge. Excluded are 9 children who were included in Mini-project #3 but were discharged by the time of the CWIS report.

TABLE 12

DISCHARGE OBJECTIVE FOR CHILDREN ACCORDING TO FREQUENCY OF CHILD'S CONTACT WITH NATURAL MOTHER*
(N = 385)

Discharge Objective	Once A Month	Once in Three Months	Once in Six Months	Once A Year	Occasionally	Never	Other	Not Applicable
				(Percentaged)				
To parents	55.8	38.7	36.0	11.1	12.9	6.5	16.7	11.1
To relatives	3.4	6.8	8.0	22.2	--	1.6	8.3	4.9
To own responsibility	11.9	13.6	16.0	22.2	3.2	4.8	8.3	13.6
To adoption	8.5	22.7	32.0	33.4	54.8	73.4	50.1	64.3
To institution	1.7	--	--	--	--	2.4	--	--
Not applicable	11.9	6.8	4.0	--	22.6	7.3	8.3	4.9
Unknown	6.8	11.4	4.0	11.1	6.5	4.0	8.3	1.2
Total	100.0	100.0	100.0	100.0	100.0	100.0	100.0	100.0
Number of Children	(59)	(44)	(25)	(9)	(31)	(124)	(12)	(81)

*Does not include 1 case where information was unavailable.

TABLE 13

DISCHARGE OBJECTIVES FOR CHILDREN
ACCORDING TO PRESENCE OF SIBLINGS IN FOSTER CARE*
(N = 381)

Discharge Objective	No Sibling in Care	One Sibling in Same Foster Home	One Sibling in Different Foster Home	Two or More Siblings in Same Foster Home	Two or More Siblings in Different Foster Homes
			(Percentaged)		
To parents	14.9	25.6	14.8	32.1	21.3
To relative	3.0	5.1	14.8	3.6	--
To own responsibility	8.2	6.0	11.1	19.6	12.8
To adoption	58.2	46.1	51.9	32.2	57.3
To institution	1.5	0.9	--	--	--
Not applicable	9.0	10.3	3.7	8.9	4.3
Unknown	5.2	6.0	3.7	3.6	4.3
Total	100.0	100.0	100.0	100.0	100.0
Number of Children	(134)	(117)	(27)	(56)	(47)

*Does not include 5 cases where information for either variable in the cross-tabulation was not provided.

in separate foster family households.

Children who had no siblings in care showed only 14.9 percent where the discharge plan called for them to be returned to parents. In this respect, they were similar to subjects who had a sibling in a different foster home; 14.8 percent of these children were slated to return to their parents. However, where a child had a sibling in the same foster home, a larger proportion had return to parents as the designated discharge plan; 25.6 percent of these children had such a plan. For children with two or more siblings in the same foster home, the proportion slated to return home was even larger, almost a third of the children (32.1 percent). Those subjects with two or more siblings in different foster homes showed only 21.3 percent where return to parents was the discharge plan.

Fully 58.2 percent of the single children had adoption as the discharge plan. But almost as high a proportion of adoption-bound children were to be found where the subjects of our study had one sibling in care and where this child was in a different foster home (51.9 percent), or two or more siblings in care who were located in different foster homes (57.3 percent). The group of subjects with the lowest proportion of cases where adoption was the designated discharge objective were those with two or more siblings in the same foster home; 32.2 percent of these children had a discharge plan calling for adoption.

Approach to the Foster Parents About Adopting the Child

A more concrete approach to the matter of discharge planning is to inquire as to whether the foster parents had ever been approached to consider adoption. This was an important item in the questionnaire prepared for the study. The responses of the caseworkers are shown in Table 14.

It may come as a surprise to the reader that over three-fourths of the foster parents (77.9 percent) had already been approached by the agency as to whether they were interested in considering the adoption of the children who were our subjects. For children who were in the youngest group, i.e., one to five years of age, the proportion of foster parents approached was slightly lower (67.5 percent). However, it is still impressive that the overwhelming majority of cases were considered appropriate for adoption by the foster parents. This fact makes amply clear that the relationship of most foster parents and their wards has, in the eyes of the agencies involved, taken on a quality of permanency. Put another way, whatever has been said about foster care implying that it is a "temporary" arrangement does not seem supported by these data.

It was of interest to learn how recently the foster parents had been approached. Table 14 shows that in a third of the cases, the approach had been recent, within the past six months. Another 22 percent had been spoken to within the past 7 to 12 months. Almost a quarter of the foster parents had been approached over two years earlier. There was some differentiation by the age of the children, with the foster parents of the youngest having tended to be approached more recently.

Of critical importance for the children were the responses of the foster parents. Were they pleased to be given the opportunity to seal the relationships with their foster children through the route of adoption? Were they perhaps intimidated by the prospect of having complete responsibility for the rearing of the children?

Table 14 shows that the majority of foster parents reacted positively to the prospects for adoption. Almost three-fourths were so described. For 52.9 percent of the cases, the reactions were characterized as "very positive" and for 19.5 percent, it was "somewhat positive."

Of interest is the fact that almost a fourth of the foster parents were said to be against adoption with 13.3 percent described as "somewhat against" and 9.9 percent, "very against."

Table 14 shows that the proportion of foster parents who were resistant to the idea of adoption was age-related. Altogether, only 11.6 percent of the foster parents with subjects one to five years of age were described as tending to be against adoption; this was true of 20.2 percent with children 6 to 9 years old, and 29.9 percent of those with children 10 to 13 years of age. Along the same vein, 73.0 percent of the foster parents of the youngest group of children were described as "very positive" compared to 54.8 percent of the middle group and 43.8 percent of the oldest children.

Sources of Doubt about Adoption

Some of the comments written by the social workers who filled out the questionnaires helped to explain why some of the foster parents were reluctant to consider adoption. Some, for example, were concerned about the handicaps suffered by the children placed with them:

- Child is very handicapped, deaf/mute with other medical problems. Although on surface family has integrated him into their group as one of them, idea of permanent commitment to this needy child has caused them to insist on his early removal from the home.
- Billie is a difficult child to integrate into any family. He's very handicapped (Rubella child) and will thrive much better in a facility (medical) which will be able to meet his many medical needs. However, his foster mother is not a warm, responsive person. She demonstrated little affection towards the other children in the home. She does give very good physical care and is cooperative with all appointments.
- George is a slow child. He has health problems. He needs special schooling to prepare for kindergarten. He has recently had T&A. Foster family has had numerous problems. A rather fragile home.
- Child is an abused, neglected, C.P. child. Although she has special needs, these have been beautifully met.
- The extensive scarring of Sally's body and the resulting psychological trauma has been hard for all. Therapy for Sally and supportive casework to family has helped them be less protective and more realistic in goals for Sally.

There were quite a few cases where the foster parents

TABLE 14

INFORMATION ABOUT WHETHER FOSTER PARENTS HAD BEEN APPROACHED
TO CONSIDER ADOPTION OF THE CHILD
ACCORDING TO AGE OF CHILD

Information about Approach to Foster Parents	1 to 5 Years	6 to 9 Years	10 to 13 Years	Total
A. Had Foster Parents Been Approached to Consider Adoption of the Child? (N = 385)				
% Yes	67.5	80.6	80.5	77.9
% No	32.5	19.4	19.5	22.1
B. When Had Foster Parents Been Approached? (N = 295)				
% Within past 6 months	43.2	27.4	32.6	32.6
% Within past 7 to 12 months	19.6	22.6	22.5	22.0
% Over one year ago but less than two years	19.6	25.5	17.4	20.7
% Two years ago or over	17.6	24.5	27.5	24.7
C. Reported Reactions of Foster Parents Who Had Been Approached: (N = 293)				
% Very positive	73.0	54.8	43.8	52.9
% Somewhat positive	13.5	20.2	21.2	19.5
% Somewhat against	5.8	9.6	19.0	13.3
% Very against	5.8	10.6	10.9	9.9
% Other	1.9	4.8	5.1	4.4

had serious questions about adopting the child because of the quite severe emotional problems that had characterized the child's history before coming into the foster home or afterwards:

- Because of the serious psychological past history of child, the parents worry about a stormy adolescence and therefore reserve full commitment.
- Child is presently being tested for hyperkinetic reaction in childhood. He is in constant motion, destructive, and has trouble sleeping.
- Upon original placement, Claude was a severely disturbed child who exhibited autistic-like tendencies, part of which included unrelatedness to others. Since his stay with Mr. and Mrs. M., he has been able to connect with and make attachment with the family, although how much we are unsure of.
- The B.'s have not had natural children of their own and are uncertain about their abilities to meet their future responsibilities based on past and current behavior problems (i.e., enuresis, lying, stealing, extremely poor academic performance). The B.'s had been reconsidering their adoption commitment which further increased S.'s behavior problems. I do not think they have received adequate support services in the past and with such services (which are now underway) such as therapy, tutoring and increased family counseling, they may be helped significantly.

Some of the foster parents were not enthused about the idea of adoption because of relationship difficulties that had arisen between themselves and their foster children:

- Foster parents were very committed to this child and anticipated adoption until about 10 months ago when child began to overtly reject them. She began acting out in school, home and community, finally running away to relatives. Although child is to be discharged to aunt, there are strong possibilities that placement (discharge) will not be lasting.
- Child was placed in current home after removal from previous foster home upon allegations of mishandling of another foster child by previous foster father. Close emotional attachment to previous foster mother continues and is a prominent factor in question of "adjustment" in new foster home.
- There seems to be a problem of Carl's full capacity as a boy. Foster parents verbalized concern about his masculinity. He seems feminine for his nine years and is beginning to realize his ways are not acceptable not just to the foster parents but to others around him. This is affecting his positive relationship with his foster parents.
- Child was placed in this home after having reported being abused by former foster parents. The present foster parents are trying to get to know this youngster, who has some psychological problems.
- Recent sexual precociousness and sexual play have had an effect on the relationship and attitude of foster father to foster child.
- The foster parents did feel positively about adopting. However, they have begun of late to feel that Eugene is unable to understand and give back the affection they have openly given him. They also state that he has tremendous needs which they feel unable to fill, due to the large size of their family and in part due to their own lack of being able to completely accept a child as their own who does not feel the same about them. Eugene's continued strong way of stating that whenever his father returns, he will go with him makes it difficult for the foster parents to adopt.

Some of the foster parents evidently had difficulty in considering adoption because the circumstances did not appear right to them even though they presumably felt positively about the child placed with them. Sometimes it was a matter of their advanced age, own health problems or personal circumstances that served as a barrier to adoption:

- There is evidence that foster parents have some serious health problems which are being currently evaluated by the agency.
- Foster parents love babies and enjoy giving them a good start. Feel they are too old to adopt a young child.
- Terry is a young child who was placed in this home at three weeks of age—mother surrendered child before she was two years. This is only family child has known. Age of foster mother an element in adoptive home study. Foster mother's adult daughter has been made legal guardian for child in the event of her mother's death.
- The foster child in question is a black American in ethnic background while the foster family is white Puerto Rican. Child is not affected by this nor is the foster family in their relationship to the child. However, foster parents show some concern over the child's peers' acceptance of this situation and need occasional counseling in this regard. Thus far they show positive signs of effectively dealing with their feelings concerning this.
- Foster parents have a deep attachment to an older foster child who will be their adopted daughter soon. There is a tendency to give this child second place in all areas to the older child.
- The foster parents have had mixed feelings about adopting Joseph's brother who has cerebral palsy and is retarded.

Some of the foster parents simply lacked sufficient depth of feeling to go "the whole way":

- The foster parents love Regina very much but are skeptical about committing themselves to an irreversible decision like adoption.
- Foster parents do not agree on the adoption. Foster mother wanted to adopt Gilda, but foster father was threatening to separate from foster mother if she went through with the adoption.
- The plan was for Sammy to be adopted by this foster family. Sammy was relatively happy in his former foster home of six years and had to be removed because of an emergency within the foster home. It was a shock to learn that the "new" foster home backed down from their agreement to adopt. The home would never have been used had we known. We would have only selected a pre-adoptive situation.

Factors Related to Adoption Planning

In a further effort to understand why some foster parents had been asked to consider adoption while some had not been approached to do so, a number of cross-tabulations with selected background variables were made. These included: the number of placements the children had experienced before taking up residence in the foster home, the number of siblings of the child in care, the amount of contact the child had with his natural mother, the child's age and years in care, and the intactness of the foster home.

Table 15 considers whether the child's placement in the foster home is his first, second or third placement and relates this information to the issue of the foster parents' having been asked to consider adoption treated as a dichotomy (yes/no). The data show a modest but discernible tendency for children in first placements to more likely be in homes where the foster parents have been asked by agencies to consider adoption. The children in first placements constituted almost 64 percent of all the children in the sample and 80.6 percent of their foster families were asked to consider adoption. This was not much greater than the 76.7 percent of foster families whose wards were in second placements but quite higher than the 64.6 percent of foster families whose children were in their third placements (or more). It should be emphasized that even where children had experienced several prior foster family placements, agencies were prepared in the majority of cases to consider the current foster family as a source of permanency for the child.

Table 16 links the phenomenon of siblings in care with the question of movement to adoption by the foster parents. The largest group of children in the study were those who had no siblings in care; they constituted about 35 percent of the sample. Almost four-fifths of these children (79.3 percent) had foster parents who were approached to consider adoption. This compared with 74.4 percent of children with a single sibling in the same foster home and 69.6 percent of those with two or more siblings in the same foster home. Children involved in split situations, i.e., where children were placed in separate foster homes, were even more likely to be in situations where the foster parents were asked to consider adoption. Thus, where the subject had one sibling in a different foster home, we find that 88.9 percent of the foster parents were asked to consider adoption. This was true of 85.1 percent of subjects with two or more siblings in different foster homes.

While the children in "split" placement situations, i.e., placed in separate foster homes, constitute less than 20 percent of the sample, it is nevertheless a source of possible concern that permanency of living arrangement would be achieved for these children at the possible expense of natural family integrity. There is insufficient information about the circumstances requiring splits in placement to make any authoritative comments about the matter. This is an area that appears in need of greater study.

As might be expected, natural parent contact with the foster child is linked to the question of adoption by foster parents. This is made clear in Table 17. There were 124 children in the sample (32.1 percent) where the social workers indicated that they never had contact with their natural mothers. This group of children showed the highest proportion of situations where foster parents had been asked if they were interested in adoption. Fully 91.1 percent of the foster parents of such unvisited children were approached. By comparison, 35.6 percent of the foster parents were approached where their wards were visited on a monthly basis, 63.6 percent where the visits by mothers took place once in three months and 80.8 percent where the visits were on a once-in-six-months basis.

It is easy to understand why children who never see their natural mothers are likely candidates for adoption. It is perhaps less comprehensible that children who see their mothers once in three months show two-thirds of the group where foster parents have been approached to consider adoption. Similarly, we need to know more about the circumstances which impelled agencies to turn to the foster parents in 35.6 percent of the cases where the natural mother was visiting at least once a month.

Three Types of Adoption Planning

In Table 18, three types of cases are set forth for analysis: (1) situations where the foster parents were not approached to consider adoption (22.3 percent), (2) situations where they were approached but their reactions were somewhat or very negative (22.8 percent), and (3) situations where their reactions were somewhat or very positive (54.9 percent). These three "outcomes" were studied with reference to the following independent variables: the number of years the foster families have been with the agency, the child's age, the years the child has been in care and the intactness of the foster home.

The foster parents who were not approached to consider adoption had been serving with the agency for much shorter periods of time than those who were approached. The mean period of time they had served was 3.98 years compared to 7.69 years for those who had been approached and showed negative reactions to the idea and 6.05 years for those who showed positive reactions. The one-way analysis of variance showed the differences to be statistically significant ($F = 14.011$, $p < .001$).

The data presented in Table 18 also show the time factor just cited in other forms: the child's age and the mean years spent in care. Foster parents tend to be approached to consider adoption when the children are somewhat older and after they have been in care for more

TABLE 15

INFORMATION AS TO WHETHER FOSTER PARENTS HAD BEEN APPROACHED
TO CONSIDER ADOPTION ACCORDING TO NUMBER
OF FOSTER PLACEMENTS EXPERIENCED BY THE CHILD*
(N = 371)

Foster Parents Approached?	First Placement	Second Placement	Third Placement
	(Percentaged)		
Yes, asked to consider adoption	80.6	76.7	64.6
Not approached	19.4	23.3	35.4
Total	100.0	100.0	100.0
Number of Children	(237)	(86)	(48)

*Does not include 15 cases where information for either variable in the cross-tabulation was not provided.

TABLE 16

INFORMATION REGARDING FOSTER PARENTS HAVING BEEN APPROACHED
TO CONSIDER ADOPTION OF CHILD
ACCORDING TO PRESENCE OF SIBLINGS IN FOSTER CARE*
(N = 382)

Foster Parents Approached?	No Sibling in Care	One Sibling in Same Foster Home	One Sibling in Different Foster Home	Two or More Siblings in Same Foster Home	Two or More Siblings in Different Foster Homes
	(Percentaged)				
Yes, asked to consider adoption	79.3	74.4	88.9	69.6	85.1
Not approached	20.7	25.6	11.1	30.4	14.9
Total	100.0	100.0	100.0	100.0	100.0
Number of Children	(135)	(117)	(27)	(56)	(47)

*Does not include 4 cases where information for either variable in the cross-tabulation was not provided.

TABLE 17

INFORMATION AS TO WHETHER FOSTER PARENTS HAD BEEN APPROACHED TO CONSIDER ADOPTION ACCORDING TO FREQUENCY OF CHILD'S CONTACT WITH NATURAL MOTHER
(N = 386)

Foster Parents Approached?	Once A Month	Once in Three Months	Once in Six Months	Once A Year	Occa-sionally	Never	Other	Not Appli-cable
				(Percentaged)				
Yes, asked to consider adoption.	35.6	63.6	80.8	88.9	87.1	91.1	100.0	86.4
Not approached	64.4	36.4	19.2	11.1	12.9	8.9	--	13.6
Total	100.0	100.0	100.0	100.0	100.0	100.0	100.0	100.0
Number of Children	(59)	(44)	(26)	(9)	(31)	(124)	(12)	(81)

TABLE 18

AGENCY APPROACH TO FOSTER PARENTS ABOUT ADOPTION
AND THEIR REACTIONS ACCORDING TO SELECTED VARIABLES

A. Number of Years Foster Families With Agency

	Mean	S.D.	N
Not approached	3.976	3.203	84
Approached--Reaction negative	7.690	5.527	84
Approached--Reaction positive	6.052	4.570	210
TOTAL	5.955	4.714	378

F-test = 14.011
$p < .001$

B. Child's Age Last Birthday

	Mean	S.D.	N
Not approached	8.081	3.535	86
Approached--Reaction negative	9.636	2.881	88
Approached--Reaction positive	8.814	3.245	212
TOTAL	8.492	3.293	386

F-test = 7.109
$p < .001$

C. Years Child Has Spent in Care

	Mean	S.D.	N
Not approached	3.912	1.804	86
Approached--Reaction negative	6.664	3.065	88
Approached--Reaction positive	5.942	3.004	211
TOTAL	5.653	2.963	385

F-test = 23.349
$p < .001$

D. Intactness of Foster Home
    (N = 386)

	Intact Home	One-Parent Home
	(Percentaged)	
Not approached	21.1	27.5
Approached--Reaction negative	24.9	13.0
Approached--Reaction positive	54.0	59.5
Percent	100.0	100.0
TOTAL	(317)	(69)

extended periods of time. The differentiation among the three groups of children is statistically significant for both of these variables.

The differences reported here are in line with a previous finding of the writer that indicated that adoption of children by their foster parents comes rather late in the child's experience in foster care.[9] It was shown that such adoptions tend to take place almost eight years after children enter foster care. The following comment at the time of publication would appear to continue to be pertinent at the present time:

> Why do foster parent adoptions take place so far along in the child's placement experience? Can we undertake in the coming year to reduce the average time in care for such adoptions to 7 years and the following year to 6 years? Such planning may require earlier determination that foster homes are going to become transformed into adoptive homes. Plans for carrying out such adoptions would have to be monitored carefully, with time frames for specified tasks clearly set forth.

Table 18 also shows that there is little differentiation between intact foster families and one-parent homes with respect to approaches by the agency to consider adoption. Slightly more of the intact homes were approached but there was a higher proportion of negative reactions to the idea among them than was true of the one-parent homes.

Summary Comments

Perhaps what stands out most in these data is the degree to which adoption by the foster parents looms as the major avenue to permanency for the foster children who are our research subjects. The following findings are most noteworthy:

- Adoption is by far the discharge plan of choice for children who experienced extended time in care. For example, 71.1 percent of children who have been in placement for ten or more years are said to be slated for adoption.
- Adoption as a discharge plan is closely linked to patterns of visiting by the natural mother. For example, there is a large group of children in the study who are described as "never" seeing their mothers; 73.4 percent of these children have adoption as the designated discharge plan.
- The size of the child's sibling group is a modest predictor of discharge planning. Whether or not the siblings are in one foster home appears to be a fairly important additional variable.
- A very large proportion of the foster parents (77.9 percent) had already been approached by the agencies to consider adoption of the subjects. A majority (52.9 percent) were very positive about the prospect and a sizable group were somewhat positive (19.5 percent). The group who felt negatively about making the commitment reflected 22.2 percent of the sample.
- Foster parents tended to be approached to consider adoption six to seven years after the children had entered care.

5 Assessing the Child's Relationships to the Natural Family and to the Foster Family

The writer once heard a distinguished management expert from a graduate school of business make an address to child welfare agency executives. He compared the task of computerizing information about foster care services with that of providing potential airline passengers with reservations for seats. He saw both operations as simply a reflection of the "queuing" problem long familiar to operations researchers. The audience tittered in amusement because it was clear that the speaker did not fully appreciate the great difference involved in the two phenomena. The placement of children in available living arrangements that are suited for them and in which they are likely to remain for extended periods obviously calls for more demanding and subtle forms of cognitive awareness than does the allocation of airline seats.

The matter of describing a child's ties to his own parents as well as the quality of his integration within his foster family after he has lived with the latter for a few years is probably an even more demanding task than the original selection of the home. The kind of attachments the child has developed are key to case planning perspectives about the most likely sources of permanency for him. In due course after a child's placement in a foster home, an agency is likely to feel compelled to develop a point of view as to whether a child is likely to be returned to his natural parents or whether his future is unquestionably tied to his foster parents.

In this chapter, we seek perspective on the child's attachments to his own parents and to his foster parents as seen by the social worker assigned to the case. The specification of these attachments, or lack of them, provides the matrix within which plans for the child's permanent abode can be made.

Child's Relationship to Natural Family

In Table 19, we present the frequency distributions for the ratings made by the social workers characterizing the child's attachment to the natural mother. It certainly does not portend well for the reunification of families to find that only 11.1 percent of the children are rated as showing a *deep attachment* to their mothers and another 5.7 percent showing a *close attachment*. An additional 15.1 percent of the children are seen as having a more attenuated relationship with their mothers and are rated as only showing *some attachment*. More than two-thirds of the children are rated as having little, if any, sense of relationship to their mothers. Some 15.9 percent of the children were rated as showing *minimum attachment* to their mothers while 39.7 percent were characterized as *devoid of relationship* with their mothers. An additional 12.5 percent of the cases were rated as "non-applicable" because the mother was deceased or had early dropped out of the picture so that no relationship with the parent was possible.

The distributions in Table 19 by age groupings do not show marked differentiation in the assigned ratings on the basis of age although more of the youngest children (48.0 percent) are rated as being devoid of a relationship with the natural mothers than the oldest children (32.2 percent). All three age groups, however, show a minority of children who are rated as having as much as *some attachment* to their natural mothers.

Table 20 provides information about the child's relationship to the natural father. The social workers' ratings reflected even more attenuated relationships with the fathers than was true of the mothers. More than half of the children were rated as being *devoid of a relationship* with their fathers (50.8 percent) and 9.8 percent were characterized as showing a *minimum attachment*. In addition, almost a fourth of the fathers were totally out of the picture (23.6 percent). Only a tenth of the children had anything resembling a meaningful relationship with their fathers, with 5.7 percent rated as having a *deep attachment* and 3.8 percent as having a *close attachment*.

The youngest children had less than five percent who were rated as having a *deep* or *close attachment* to their fathers. The middle group showed less than seven percent with any meaningful relationship with their fathers while the older children had close to 14 percent.

Table 21 shows the distribution of ratings of the child's relationship to the natural family as a whole. One child in five was rated as having some degree of closeness to his family. Some 9.6 percent of the subjects were rated as showing a *deep attachment* to their families while 10.1 percent were seen as having a *close attachment*. Over a fourth of the children were rated as having *some* or a *minimum attachment* to their families. This left over a half of the subjects being rated as *devoid of a relationship* (37.7 percent) or having families totally out of the picture (13.9 percent).

TABLE 19

CASEWORKERS' RATINGS OF THE QUALITY OF THE FOSTER CHILD'S RELATIONSHIP TO HIS/HER NATURAL MOTHER ACCORDING TO AGE OF CHILD

Quality of Relationship to Mother	1 to 5 Years	6 to 9 Years	10 to 13 Years	Total
	(Percentaged)			
Deep Attachment: Deeply conscious of belonging to own parents and/or family, closely identified with blood ties and feels basic attachment. Sense of own roots lies in this relationship.	12.0	10.4	11.2	11.1
Close Attachment: Has clearly evidenced attachments to this relationship. Often shows sense of close identification and indications that the relationship has important meaning. Yet there is evidence of child feeling apartness and occasionally distancing self from the relationship.	2.7	5.6	7.4	5.7
Some Attachment: Gives evidence that the relationship has some meaning. Child occasionally gives sign that some elements of identification exist. But there are also strong pulls away from this relationship.	12.0	12.0	19.1	15.1
Minimum Attachment: Dominant quality evidenced by child indicates minimum sense of attachment. Only occasionally and fleetingly is there sign that parent(s) or family has meaning for him/her and ties are valued. Distancing self from the relationship(s) has become major method of coping with life situation.	12.0	16.8	17.1	15.9
Devoid of Relationship: Feels totally devoid of a relationship with the natural parent and/or family. On a manifest level, they are totally out of consciousness. Shows no sense of identification or rootedness in this relationship.	48.0	44.0	32.2	39.7
Other/Not Applicable	13.3	11.2	13.2	12.5
Percent Total	100.0 (75)	100.0 (125)	100.0 (152)	100.0 (352)[a]

[a] Excludes 14 children where no rating was made.

TABLE 20

CASEWORKERS' RATINGS OF THE QUALITY OF THE FOSTER CHILD'S RELATIONSHIP TO HIS/HER NATURAL FATHER ACCORDING TO AGE OF CHILD

Quality of Relationship to Father	1 to 5 Years	6 to 9 Years	10 to 13 Years	Total
	(Percentaged)			
Deep Attachment: Deeply conscious of belonging to own parents and/or family, closely identified with blood ties and feels basic attachment. Sense of own roots lies in this relationship.	1.5	3.8	9.0	5.7
Close Attachment: Has clearly evidenced attachments to this relationship. Often shows sense of close identification and indications that the relationship has important meaning. Yet there is evidence of child feeling apartness and occasionally distancing self from the relationship.	3.0	2.8	4.9	3.8
Some Attachment: Gives evidence that the relationship has some meaning. Child occasionally gives sign that some elements of identification exist. But there are also strong pulls away from this relationship.	3.0	6.6	7.6	6.3
Minimum Attachment: Dominant quality evidenced by child indicates minimum sense of attachment. Only occasionally and fleetingly is there sign that parent(s) or family has meaning for him/her and ties are valued. Distancing self from the relationship(s) has become major method of coping with life situation.	6.0	11.3	10.4	9.8
Devoid of Relationship: Feels totally devoid of a relationship with the natural parent and/or family. On a manifest level, they are totally out of consciousness. Shows no sense of identification or rootedness in this relationship.	55.2	60.4	41.7	50.8
Other/Not Applicable	31.3	15.1	26.4	23.6
Percent Total	100.0 (67)	100.0 (106)	100.0 (144)	100.0 (317)[a]

[a] Excludes 69 children where no rating was made.

TABLE 21

CASEWORKERS' RATINGS OF THE QUALITY OF THE FOSTER CHILD'S RELATIONSHIP TO HIS/HER NATURAL FAMILY AS A WHOLE ACCORDING TO AGE OF CHILD

Quality of Relationship to Natural Family as a Whole	1 to 5 Years	6 to 9 Years	10 to 13 Years	Total
	(Percentaged)			
Deep Attachment: Deeply conscious of belonging to own parents and/or family, closely identified with blood ties and feels basic attachment. Sense of own roots lies in this relationship.	2.8	9.4	12.7	9.6
Close Attachment: Has clearly evidenced attachments to this relationship. Often shows sense of close identification and indications that the relationship has important meaning. Yet there is evidence of child feeling apartness and occasionally distancing self from the relationship.	7.0	12.8	9.6	10.1
Some Attachment: Gives evidence that the relationship has some meaning. Child occasionally gives sign that some elements of identification exist. But there are also strong pulls away from this relationship.	11.3	15.4	16.6	15.1
Minimum Attachment: Dominant quality evidenced by child indicates minimum sense of attachment. Only occasionally and fleetingly is there sign that parent(s) or family has meaning for him/her and ties are valued. Distancing self from the relationship(s) has become major method of coping with life situation.	8.5	9.4	19.1	13.6
Devoid of Relationship: Feels totally devoid of a relationship with the natural parent and/or family. On a manifest level, they are totally out of consciousness. Shows no sense of identification or rootedness in this relationship.	47.9	45.3	27.4	37.7
Other/Not Applicable	22.5	7.7	14.6	13.9
Percent Total	100.0 (71)	100.0 (117)	100.0 (157)	100.0 (345)[a]

[a] Excludes 41 children where no rating was made.

The overall picture that emerges from Tables 19 through 21 is that of a sample of children in foster care largely abandoned by their natural families. Only about one child in five is seen as having any deep or close involvement with his parents, usually the mother.

Child's Relationship to the Foster Family

Since only a minority of the children seemed well-connected to their own parents, it is a matter of considerable interest to determine whether there is evidence that foster parents are able to fill the void. Table 22 appears to support the view that the future of many of the subjects does indeed lie with their foster parents. Over three-fourths of the children are rated as either being *deeply integrated* within the foster families to the point of experiencing the foster parents as *own* family (52.6 percent) or *quite strongly identified* with them (25.9 percent). Children showing *some reserve* accounted for 16.1 percent of the ratings.

It is of interest that only one percent of the children were rated as *fairly uncomfortable* in the homes and holding themselves quite aloof. The group rated in more absolute terms as *not integrated* accounted for less than one percent (0.8 percent).

The ratings of the youngest group showed them to be the most rooted in their foster homes with 64.9 percent rated as *deeply integrated* compared to 50.0 percent of the children 6 to 9 years of age and 49.1 percent of those 10 to 13 years of age.

Another indication of the child's status vis-a-vis his foster family was the rating made by the social workers with respect to the following instruction: "Rate the foster parent's acceptance of the child, the degree to which he/she is included as part of the family's affairs while his/her difference is also accepted. Or does the foster parent regard the child as an intruder with a strong sense of him/her as a stranger?"

In seven out of ten cases (69.4 percent), the social workers rated the foster mothers as showing *strong acceptance* of the child, incorporating him as a part of the family without reservation. For another 21.5 percent, there was *general acceptance* with acceptance of the child with some reservation. For a smaller group (5.4 percent), there was *acceptance with ambivalence*. Only 2.1 percent of the families were rated as showing a *lack of acceptance* and 0.5 percent displaying open *rejection*.

We again observe from the data in Table 23 that the youngest group is more accepted as part of the foster family than the older children, even though all three groups show a considerable majority where there was strong acceptance attributed to the foster families. Almost ten percent of the oldest group were rated in the least accepted categories compared to less than three percent of the youngest group.

Conflict Over Family Attachments

The potentiality for foster children becoming upset about conflicting loyalties to their own parents and their foster parents seems readily apparent. The caseworkers were given the following instruction: "Rate the degree to which the child is caught up in emotional pulls between own (natural) family and foster family. Is he/she at ease with the present allocation of roles of own family and foster family? Is there evidence of greater pull to one or the other family to which he/she belongs?"

Almost half (49.9 percent) the children were rated as being *at peace* with the current arrangements. A substantial proportion were rated as showing *some anxiety* about where they stood vis-a-vis their own parents and their foster parents.

A minority of the children were rated as having made only a *marginal peace* with their situations (4.7 percent), or were *noticeably upset* (4.2 percent) or *quite upset* (2.6 percent). For 11.7 percent of the children, there was indication that a rating was not applicable, presumably because the natural family was totally out of the picture.

The ratings were distinctly differentiated by age groupings of the children. Thus, 68.8 percent of the youngest children were rated as being *at peace* with the arrangements compared with 41.6 percent of the oldest subjects. More upsetness was reported for the middle and older children. From the other findings reported here, it would appear that the younger children have suffered less from conflicting involvements because they have tended to have little involvement with their natural parents. The older children are more likely to have had extended living experiences with the natural families (Table 24).

Summary Comments

The ratings by the social workers support the view that for a majority of the children, the foster homes have become their real homes. They are apparently not in conflict about their situations. However, there are sizable groups of children, particularly among the older children in foster family care, who experience various degrees of unease with their living arrangements. These children are caught in a tug of war between their foster families and their natural families.

TABLE 22

CHILD'S INTEGRATION IN FOSTER HOME ACCORDING TO AGE OF CHILD[a]

Degree of Integration	1 to 5 Years	6 to 9 Years	10 to 13 Years	Total
	(Percentaged)			
Deeply Integrated: Experiences the foster parents as own family and expects to remain with them; child's removal from home would be extremely upsetting to him/her.	64.9	50.0	49.1	52.6
Quite Strongly Identified. Child is quite strongly identified with foster family although there is some tendency to hold back slightly from total involvement; removal from home would be experienced as quite painful wrench.	15.6	24.6	31.4	25.9
Some Reserve: Child feels fairly much at ease in the home but is quite conscious that this is not own family. Holds self somewhat aloof and there is reserve in showing loyalty to family. Removal would create some problems but recovery would be experienced fairly soon.	9.1	20.1	16.0	16.1
Fairly Uncomfortable: Child is fairly uncomfortable in home and holds himself quite aloof. Times when he joins in with family activities are relatively rare. Removal from home would be fairly easy to take.	--	1.5	1.1	1.0
Not Integrated: Child is not integrated within foster family. Essentially feels a stranger; removal from home would not evoke emotional reaction.	--	1.5	0.6	0.8
Other/Not Applicable	10.4	2.2	1.7	3.6
Percent Total	100.0 (77)	100.0 (134)	100.0 (175)	100.0 (386)

[a] Instruction given the respondents was: "Rate the degree to which the child feels he belongs in the foster home and has sunk his roots with the foster family. Is he strongly embedded in the home, having strong emotional ties with the foster parents?"

TABLE 23

ACCEPTANCE OF THE CHILD BY FOSTER MOTHER ACCORDING TO AGE OF CHILD[a]

Degree of Acceptance	1 to 5 Years	6 to 9 Years	10 to 13 Years	Total
	(Percentaged)			
Strong Acceptance: Shows strong acceptance of child and incorporates him/her as part of family without reservation; no holding back in positive regard.	77.9	68.7	66.1	69.4
General Acceptance: Accepts child in general but does not go "all the way"; shows some reservation in full acceptance but overall tone is quite positive.	19.5	20.9	22.9	21.5
Acceptance With Ambivalence: Tends to accept child but there are areas where child is not fully part of family; there is some ambivalence in acceptance with mixture of positive and negative features.	--	7.5	6.3	5.4
Lack of Acceptance: Predominant tendency is to be caught up with sense of child's difference; not able to accept child but without open rejection.	2.6	0.7	2.9	2.1
Rejection: Child openly resented and rejected by foster parent; not accepted as part of family's inner circle.	--	0.7	0.6	0.5
Other/Not Applicable	--	1.5	1.2	1.1
Percent	100.0	100.0	100.0	100.0
Total	(77)	(134)	(175)	(386)

[a] Instruction given the respondents was: "Rate the foster parent's acceptance of the child, the degree to which he/she is included as part of the family, an intimate partner in the family's affairs while his/her difference is also accepted. Or does the foster parent regard the child as an intruder with a strong sense of him/her as a stranger?"

TABLE 24

CHILD'S MANIFESTATION OF CONFLICT OVER FAMILY ATTACHMENTS
ACCORDING TO AGE OF CHILD[a]

Degree of Conflict	1 to 5 Years	6 to 9 Years	10 to 13 Years	Total
	(Percentaged)			
At Peace: Is essentially at peace with current arrangements; exhibits no distress or concern about balance of relationships between own family and foster family.	68.8	49.6	41.6	49.9
Some Anxiety: Tends to be accepting about current arrangements but occasionally manifests some anxiety about where he/she stands vis-a-vis own parents and/or foster parents.	10.4	27.8	33.5	26.9
Marginal Peace: Has made some adjustment to status situation; not particularly upset about where he/she stands but has made only marginal peace with current arrangements.	2.6	4.5	5.8	4.7
Noticeably Upset: Shows noticeable upset about status but has accommodated self to the situation somewhat.	--	4.5	5.8	4.2
Quite Upset: Is quite upset about current arrangements; keenly aware of lack of resolution of status.	2.6	2.3	2.9	2.6
Other/Not Applicable	15.6	11.3	10.4	11.7
Percent Total	100.0 (77)	100.0 (133)	100.0 (173)	100.0 (383)[b]

[a] Instruction given the respondent was: "Rate the degree to which the child is caught up in emotional pulls between own (natural) family and foster family. Is he/she at ease with the present allocation of roles of own family and foster family? Is there evidence of greater pull to one or more families to which he/she belongs?"

[b] Excludes 3 children where no rating was made.

6 What Lies Ahead for the Child?

Predicting Status Changes

The caseworkers filling out the questionnaire prepared for this try-out of a new data module for a computerized data system were asked to prognosticate what was likely to happen to the child vis-a-vis his status in foster care. They were given the following instruction: "Considering what is known about this case, rate the possibilities of the following events taking place within the coming year, within one to two years, and within three to five years. Take into account your own knowledge of the case and possible future actions of the court. This is a subjective judgment on your part." They were asked to consider the following possibilities: (1) return to own parents, (2) placement with a relative, (3) transfer to another home for adoption, (4) being adopted by present foster parents, (5) remaining in the foster home.

Securing the perspectives of the social workers does not guarantee, of course, that the projected plans will be carried out. However, eliciting their thinking about what lies in store for the child presumably reflects the views of the agency and provides insight about case planning from the most creditable source available. Further, one can test the predictive validity of the projected plans by gathering follow-up data after the passage of a year. Such data are presented in Chapter 10.

In Table 25, we present the caseworkers' ratings of possible status changes involving the children being reported upon. The projections are for the *coming year, within one to two years* and *within three to five years*. It is sobering to observe that for each of these time periods, less than ten percent of the children are seen as having a strong possibility of return to the natural parents. During the coming year, 74.2 percent of the children are flatly rated as having *no possibility* of return home. The prospects improve very little even over longer time projections.

The possibility of placement with relatives is a very minor one with less than five percent of the children ever being rated as having a strong possibility that such a change will eventuate as a reality. Similarly, only modest possibilities are projected that the child will be moved from his present foster home to another home for adoption.

Looming fairly large as a possibility is the prospect of the child being adopted by his foster parents. For the coming year, 36.4 percent of the children are deemed to have a strong possibility that such an event will take place and 7.1 percent a moderate possibility. Within one to two years, more than half the children have strong or moderate possibilities of achieving permanency through such adoptions and the same holds true for the period three to five years from the time of the rating. Only about 31 percent of the children in these two specified time periods are rated as having no possibility of adoption by their foster parents.

During the forthcoming year, the caseworkers project a strong possibility that the children will stay in their present foster homes for 74.6 percent of the subjects. In the second time period, the projection is for 63.0 percent of the sample and for the third time period it is 58.2 percent. The rating of *no possibility* of remaining in the present foster home ranges from 6.6 percent in the first time period to 13.4 percent for the third.

These ratings by the social workers point to the centrality of the foster parents in planning for the future of these subjects. It must be kept in mind, in this connection, that these children had been in foster family care for an average of 5.7 years. Many of them had lost contact with their natural parents and the foster parents provided the only sense of family available to them. Despite this, one still must be impressed with the limited number of natural parent homes still available to the children. The question also rises again: Why does it take so long for foster family homes to be transformed into adoptive homes?

Parental Contact and Projected Changes

One way of obtaining insight about the ratings made by the social workers is to relate them to the frequency of contact between the children and their natural mothers. Such a cross-tabulation is shown in Table 26, where the caseworker's rating of the possibility that the child will be adopted by the foster parents within one to two years is related to frequency of contact between the child and his natural mother.

Where children were said to see their mothers at least every month, only 13.6 percent were rated as having a strong possibility of being adopted by their foster parents while 55.9 percent were seen as having no such possibility. For children seen once in three months, the social workers rated 25.0 percent as having a strong possibility of being

TABLE 25

CASEWORKERS' RATINGS OF THE POSSIBILITY OF STATUS CHANGES TO BE EXPERIENCED BY CHILD[a]

	Within the Coming Year	Within One to Two Years	Within Three to Five Years
	(Percentaged)		
Possibility of Return to Own Parent(s)			
Strong possibility	7.5	7.6	9.3
Moderate possibility	4.3	6.0	4.4
Slight possibility	14.0	15.5	18.0
No possibility	74.2	70.9	68.3
PERCENT	100.0	100.0	100.0
TOTAL	(372)[b]	(367)	(366)
Possibility of Placement With Relative			
Strong possibility	3.5	3.5	4.4
Moderate possibility	2.2	2.2	2.5
Slight possibility	7.0	11.1	11.3
No possibility	87.3	83.2	81.8
PERCENT	100.0	100.0	100.0
TOTAL	(369)	(368)	(363)
Possibility of Transfer to Another Home for Adoption			
Strong possibility	5.6	6.0	5.2
Moderate possibility	2.9	4.4	5.0
Slight possibility	12.3	20.2	18.2
No possibility	79.2	69.4	71.6
PERCENT	100.0	100.0	100.0
TOTAL	(375)	(367)	(363)
Possibility of Being Adopted by Present Foster Parents			
Strong possibility	36.4	40.7	42.3
Moderate possibility	7.1	10.7	8.1
Slight possibility	15.1	17.8	18.0
No possibility	41.4	30.8	31.6
PERCENT	100.0	100.0	100.0
TOTAL	(365)	(354)	(345)
Possibility of Remaining in Foster Home			
Strong possibility	74.6	63.0	58.2
Moderate possibility	9.8	17.8	15.9
Slight possibility	9.0	9.3	12.5
No possibility	6.6	9.9	13.4
PERCENT	100.0	100.0	100.0
TOTAL	(376)	(365)	(359)

[a] For the ratings displayed here, the caseworkers were given the following instruction: "Considering what is known about this case, rate the possibilities of the following events taking place within the coming year, within one to two years, and within three to five years. Take into account your own knowledge of the case and possible future actions of the court. This is a subjective judgment on your part."

[b] The total number of cases for each rating is somewhat less than 386 because no ratings were made by the workers for some cases although the forms were otherwise filled out.

TABLE 26

CASEWORKER'S ESTIMATE THAT CHILD WILL BE ADOPTED BY FOSTER FAMILY IN ONE TO TWO YEARS ACCORDING TO FREQUENCY OF CHILD'S CONTACT WITH NATURAL MOTHER
(N = 386)

Possibility of Adoption by Foster Family	Once A Month	Once in Three Months	Once in Six Months	Once A Year	Occa-sionally	Never	Other	Not Appli-cable	Total
				(Percentaged)					
Strong possibility	13.6	25.0	34.7	44.5	38.7	51.6	58.3	38.2	37.8
Moderate possibility	1.7	11.4	11.5	22.2	9.7	4.8	--	9.9	7.3
Slight possibility	16.9	22.7	19.2	--	22.6	13.7	16.7	13.6	16.1
No possibility	55.9	31.8	23.1	33.3	25.8	19.4	16.7	23.5	28.2
Not applicable	11.9	9.1	11.5	--	3.2	10.5	8.3	14.8	10.6
Total	100.0	100.0	100.0	100.0	100.0	100.0	100.0	100.0	100.0
Number of Children	(59)	(44)	(26)	(9)	(31)	(124)	(12)	(81)	(386)

adopted by their foster parents and 31.8 percent were rated as having no possibility of being adopted in this way.

On the other hand, the very large group of children who never saw their mothers had a majority (51.6 percent) rated as having a strong possibility of being adopted by their foster parents and 19.4 percent who were seen as having no possibility of such an event taking place. The relationship between parental contact and adoption planning appears clearly established here.

Earliest Timing of Status Change Events

In Table 27, we have organized the predictions of the social workers to emphasize the earliest timing of status changes being projected for the children. Thus, if there was indicated a *strong possibility* that a child would be returned to his natural parents during the coming year, the child was located in this earlier period as the time of projected change. Some 83.3 percent of the children slated to be returned to their parents were said to be likely to make such a move during the coming year while 14.8 percent would return home in one to two years. A very small group (1.9 percent) were rated as likely to return to their parents in three to five years.

Where two types of status changes were rated as having the same possibility of happening, the "ties" were resolved by the following preferred order of classification:

	Number of Children	Percent
Return to parents	54	14.0
Adoption by foster family	179	46.3
Adoption with move from foster home	34	8.8
Discharge to a relative	8	2.1
Remain in foster home	106	27.5
Other move (e.g., mental hospital)	5	1.3
TOTAL	386	100.0

The largest group of children slated for a change in status were the 179 youngsters likely to be adopted by their foster parents. They constituted 46.3 percent of the sample. It is also of interest that 95.5 percent of this group were seen as likely to achieve their adoptive status during the coming year.

Adoption entailing a move out of the foster home was designated as a likely possibility for 34 children who constituted 8.8 percent of the sample. Such a move was projected for the coming year for 91.2 percent of the children.

There was a large residual group where the children appeared to be destined to remain in foster care. This group contained 106 children who constituted 27.5 percent of the sample.

TABLE 27

PREDICTED STATUS CHANGE EVENTS LIKELY TO AFFECT THE CHILD
WITHIN THREE TIME PERIODS[a]

Earliest Timing of Status Change Event	Return to Parent	Adoption by Foster Family	Adoption With Move	Discharge to Relative	Remain in Foster Home	Other Move	Total
	(Percentaged)						
Within the coming year	83.3	95.5	91.2	87.5	91.5	80.0	92.0
Within one to two years	14.8	3.4	8.8	--	5.7	20.0	6.2
Within three to five years	1.9	1.1	--	12.5	2.8	--	1.8
Percent (Column)	100.0	100.0	100.0	100.0	100.0	100.0	100.0
Percent (Row) TOTAL	14.0 (54)	46.3 (179)	8.8 (34)	2.1 (8)	27.5 (106)	1.3 (5)	100.0 (386)

[a] The caseworker filling out the form was given the following request: "Considering what is known about this case, rate the possibilities of the following events taking place within the coming year, within one to two years, and within three to five years. Take into account your own knowledge of the case and possible future actions of the court. This is a subjective judgment on your part."

[b] The children were classified for likely status changes by creating an 18-digit field reflecting the six status change events specified for three time periods. The field was scanned by computer to locate the most likely occurrences and resolving ties by the following preferred order of classification: (1) return to parent, (2) adoption by foster parents, (3) adoption by other persons, (4) discharge to relatives, (5) remaining in the present foster home, and (6) other (unspecified) changes. The child's likely change in status was then classified as to timing, with the earlier likelihood of change given precedence.

7 Evaluative Ratings of the Foster Parents

The assessment of the foster families by their social workers included a number of rating scales presented in this chapter. The ratings were usually made separately for the foster mothers and the foster fathers. Taken together, they were designed to provide a portrayal of the quality of the foster home, most particularly, its ability to meet the emotional needs of foster children placed in the home.

The development of the rating scales was undertaken with awareness of the following limitations of the enterprise: (1) There was quite a bit of variation among the social workers with respect to educational backgrounds and experience; some raters had graduate training and considerable child welfare work experience while others were untrained and/or inexperienced. (2) Some of the social workers had long experience with the foster homes they were asked to rate while others were required to make their assessments on the basis of more limited contact. (3) There was variation in the qualities of the children placed with families. Some made great demands on the foster parents because of handicaps related to past experience. They would be a challenge in whatever home they might be placed. On the other hand, many of the children were relatively problem-free and posed little challenge to their foster parents.

Given such sources of variation, it is quite clear that the ratings would have to be probed for their reliability and validity if they are to be included in any routine data collection system as part of the effort to expand the data base for systems such as CWIS. While some effort is made in this direction in the chapters that follow, only a modest beginning is reflected in the steps we have taken. Testing for reliability and validity of measures such as those produced here must be seen as an ongoing task involving repeated trials of these measures.

How the Foster Parents Relate to the Children

The question of how warm and affectionate the foster parents are to the children placed in their care would seem to be a critical judgment in establishing the suitability of the placement as a long-term living arrangement for the child. The rating task posed to the social workers was fairly straightforward: "Rate the foster parent's expression of affection to the child personally. Does the parent manifest a warm, personal affection to the child or a matter-of-fact unemotional attitude, or definite antagonism?"

Table 28 shows the distribution of ratings of the affection shown by the foster mothers. On the whole, they are seen as quite affectionate to the children with 53.6 percent rated as *warm* (loving, expressive and highly demonstrative) and 35.5 percent as showing *quiet warmth* (fondness, positively oriented).

Less than ten percent of the foster mothers were seen as *objective* (6.2 percent), *somewhat cool* (1.6 percent), *avoiding* (0.8 percent) or *hostile* (0.5 percent).

The ratings are age-related to a fairly noticeable degree. As might be expected, the foster mothers are rated as being more loving and expressive to the youngest children; 72.7 percent of those caring for younger children were rated as being *warm* compared to 48.0 percent of those caring for the oldest children. The latter group was more inclined than the other two groups to show *quiet warmth* (38.3 percent), to be *objective* (9.1 percent) or *somewhat cool* (2.3 percent).

The ratings of the foster fathers showed them to be more apt to display *quiet warmth* (41.7 percent) than *warm* affectionate display (28.1 percent). The ratings were also age-related in the same manner as indicated in the ratings of the foster mothers (Table 29).

Tables 30 and 31 cover ratings made by the social workers of the child's showing of affection to the foster parents. They tend to be the mirror-image of what was seen as the tendencies of the adults. On the whole, the sample of children is seen as showing expressive warmth or quiet warmth to their foster parents. The younger children are seen as considerably more expressive than those in the oldest group. The children are also seen as somewhat more restrained in the expression of affection to the foster fathers than to the foster mothers.

The age-related differentiations in ratings may reflect cultural norms which permit greater affectionate display of feeling between adults and children when they are younger and also permit women to be more demonstrative to the giving and receiving of affection.

Understanding and Rapport

Tables 32 and 33 concern the ratings made by the social workers of the degree of understanding shown by the foster mothers and the foster fathers of the children who constituted the subjects of the study. They were given

TABLE 28

CASEWORKERS' RATINGS OF THE DEGREE OF AFFECTION
SHOWN BY FOSTER MOTHER TO FOSTER CHILD BY AGE OF CHILD[a]

Degree of Affection Shown	1 to 5 Years	6 to 9 Years	10 to 13 Years	Total
	(Percentaged)			
<u>Warm</u>: Loving, expressive, highly demonstrative.	72.7	50.1	48.0	53.6
<u>Quiet Warmth</u>: Fondness, positively oriented.	26.0	37.3	38.3	35.5
<u>Objective</u>: Neutral, somewhat inhibited, matter-of-fact.	1.3	5.2	9.1	6.2
<u>Somewhat Cool</u>: Aloof, distant.	--	1.5	2.3	1.6
<u>Avoiding</u>: Annoyed, irritated, bothered.	--	2.2	--	0.8
<u>Hostile</u>: Antagonistic, disliking, blaming, icy.	--	0.7	0.6	0.5
<u>Other</u>	--	1.5	1.1	1.0
<u>No Foster Mother (deceased)</u>	--	1.5	0.6	0.8
Percent Total	100.0 (77)	100.0 (134)	100.0 (175)	100.0 (386)

[a] Instruction given the respondents was: "Rate the foster parent's expression of affection to the child personally. Does the foster parent manifest a warm, personal affection to the child or a matter-of-fact unemotional attitude, or definite antagonism?"

TABLE 29

CASEWORKERS' RATINGS OF THE DEGREE OF AFFECTION
SHOWN BY FOSTER FATHER TO FOSTER CHILD BY AGE OF CHILD[a]

Degree of Affection Shown	1 to 5 Years	6 to 9 Years	10 to 13 Years	Total
	(Percentaged)			
Warm: Loving, expressive, highly demonstrative	45.5	28.8	20.0	28.1
Quiet Warmth: Fondness, positively oriented.	29.9	40.9	47.4	41.7
Objective: Neutral, somewhat inhibited, matter-of-fact.	5.2	3.0	13.1	8.1
Somewhat Cool: Aloof, distant.	--	2.3	1.7	1.6
Avoiding: Annoyed, irritated, bothered.	--	0.8	--	0.3
Hostile: Antagonistic, disliking, blaming, icy.	--	--	0.6	0.3
Other	1.3	4.5	2.3	2.9
No Foster Father (deceased)	18.2	19.7	14.9	17.2
Percent Total	100.0 (77)	100.0 (132)	100.0 (175)	100.0 (384)[b]

[a] Instruction given the respondents was: "Rate the foster parent's expression of affection to the child personally. Does the foster parent manifest a warm, personal affection to the child or a matter-of-fact unemotional attitude, or definite antagonism?"

[b] Excludes 2 children where no rating was made.

TABLE 30

CASEWORKERS' RATINGS OF THE DEGREE OF AFFECTION SHOWN BY FOSTER CHILD TOWARD FOSTER MOTHER ACCORDING TO AGE OF CHILD[a]

Degree of Affection Shown	1 to 5 Years	6 to 9 Years	10 to 13 Years	Total
	(Percentaged)			
Warm: Loving, expressive, highly demonstrative.	80.5	44.8	40.0	49.7
Quiet Warmth: Fondness, positively oriented.	15.6	46.3	39.4	37.0
Objective: Neutral, somewhat inhibited, matter-of-fact.	--	6.0	12.6	7.8
Somewhat Cool: Aloof, distant.	1.3	0.7	4.6	2.6
Avoiding: Annoyed, irritated, bothered.	--	0.7	1.1	0.8
Hostile: Antagonistic, disliking, blaming, icy.	1.3	--	1.1	0.8
Other	1.3	--	0.6	0.5
No Foster Mother (deceased)	--	1.5	0.6	0.8
Percent Total	100.0 (77)	100.0 (134)	100.0 (175)	100.0 (386)

[a] Instruction given the respondent was: "Rate the child's expression of affection to the foster parent personally. Does the child manifest a warm, personal affection to the foster parent or a matter-of-fact unemotional attitude, or definite antagonism?"

TABLE 31

CASEWORKERS' RATINGS OF THE DEGREE OF AFFECTION SHOWN BY FOSTER CHILD TOWARD FOSTER FATHER ACCORDING TO AGE OF CHILD[a]

Degree of Affection Shown	1 to 5 Years	6 to 9 Years	10 to 13 Years	Total
	(Percentaged)			
Warm: Loving, expressive, highly demonstrative.	55.8	28.0	21.7	30.7
Quiet Warmth: Fondness, positively oriented.	22.1	38.6	42.9	37.2
Objective: Neutral, somewhat inhibited, matter-of-fact.	--	8.3	11.4	8.1
Somewhat Cool: Aloof, distant.	1.3	0.8	5.1	2.9
Avoiding: Annoyed, irritated, bothered.	--	--	--	--
Hostile: Antagonistic, disliking, blaming, icy.	--	--	1.1	0.5
Other	2.6	4.5	2.9	3.4
No Foster Father (deceased)	18.2	19.7	14.9	17.2
Percent Total	100.0 (77)	100.0 (132)	100.0 (175)	100.0 (384)[b]

[a] Instruction given the respondents was: "Rate the child's expression of affection to the foster parent personally. Does the child manifest a warm, personal affection to the foster parent or a matter-of-fact unemotional attitude, or definite antagonism?"

[b] Excludes 2 children where no rating was made.

TABLE 32

CASEWORKERS' RATINGS OF THE UNDERSTANDING OF THE CHILD
SHOWN BY FOSTER MOTHER ACCORDING TO THE AGE OF THE CHILD[a]

Degree of Understanding Shown	1 to 5 Years	6 to 9 Years	10 to 13 Years	Total
	(Percentaged)			
Highly Insightful: Shows good understanding of child's inner states.	45.4	36.6	26.4	33.7
Fairly Good Insight: Generally is in tune with the child; often has fairly good sense of what is going on with him/her.	42.9	44.8	44.8	44.4
Moderate Insight: Has good grasp of everyday situations, but often misses the subtle aspects of the child's inner feelings.	6.5	13.4	21.3	15.6
Little Insight: Generally lacks insight into child's inner state; often misses the obvious.	5.2	3.0	4.0	3.9
Devoid of Insight: Completely fails to see the child's viewpoint, capacities, limitations. Expects entirely too much or too little. Fails to meet child on his/her own ground.	--	0.7	2.3	1.3
Other.	--	1.5	1.2	1.1
Percent Total	100.0 (77)	100.0 (134)	100.0 (174)	100.0 (385)[b]

[a]Instruction given the respondents was: "Rate the foster parent's understanding of the child's abilities, needs, point of view, etc. Does the foster parent's behavior indicate a sound appreciation of 'what makes the child tick,' or does it indicate a failure to appreciate the child's capacities and limitations and to fathom the child's inner feelings?"

[b]Excludes 1 child where no rating was made.

TABLE 33

CASEWORKERS' RATINGS OF THE UNDERSTANDING OF THE CHILD
SHOWN BY FOSTER FATHER ACCORDING TO THE AGE OF THE CHILD[a]

Degree of Understanding Shown	1 to 5 Years	6 to 9 Years	10 to 13 Years	Total
	(Percentaged)			
Highly Insightful: Shows good understanding of child's inner states.	32.5	22.0	15.5	21.1
Fairly Good Insight: Generally is in tune with the child; often has fairly good sense of what is going on with him/her.	32.5	35.6	35.1	34.8
Moderate Insight: Has good grasp of everyday situations, but often misses the subtle aspects of the child's inner feelings.	11.7	15.9	23.0	18.3
Little Insight: Generally lacks insight into child's inner state; often misses the obvious.	2.6	3.0	6.9	4.7
Devoid of Insight: Completely fails to see the child's viewpoint, capacities, limitations. Expects entirely too much or too little. Fails to meet child on his/her own ground.	--	0.8	1.7	1.0
Other	2.6	3.0	2.9	2.9
No Foster Father (deceased)	18.1	19.7	14.9	17.2
Percent Total	100.0 (77)	100.0 (132)	100.0 (174)	100.0 (383)[b]

[a] Instruction given the respondents was: "Rate the foster parent's understanding of the child's abilities, needs, point of view, etc. Does the foster parent's behavior indicate a sound appreciation of 'what makes the child tick,' or does it indicate a failure to appreciate the child's capacities and limitations and to fathom the child's inner feelings?"

[b] Excludes 1 child were no rating was made.

the following instructions: "Rate the foster parent's understanding of the child's abilities, needs, point of view, etc. Does the foster parent's behavior indicate a sound appreciation of 'what makes the child tick,' or does it indicate a failure to appreciate the child's capacities and limitations and to fathom the child's inner feelings?"

Most of the foster mothers were seen as being in tune with the foster children. About a third (33.7 percent) were rated as *highly insightful* (shows good understanding of child's inner states) and 44.4 percent were rated as having *fairly good insight* (generally is in tune with the child; often has fairly good sense of what is going on with him/her).

Over 20 percent of the foster mothers were seen as having some limitations in their understanding of the children. Some 15.6 percent were rated as having *moderate insight* (has good grasp of everyday situations, but often misses the subtle aspects of the child's inner feelings). A small proportion of the mothers (3.9 percent) were seen as having *little insight* (generally lacks insight into child's inner state; often misses the obvious). Only an occasional foster mother (1.3 percent) was rated as *devoid of insight* (completely fails to see child's viewpoint, capacities, limitations).

The older children were more apt to be the recipients of lesser insight; 27.6 percent were living with mothers who were rated as only having moderate or less insight. This contrasted with 11.7 percent of the cases involving the youngest children.

Foster fathers tended to be perceived as somewhat less insightful about the children than the foster mothers. Almost a third were rated as showing only moderate or less insight toward the older children placed in their homes.

Tables 34 and 35 concern the state of rapport between the foster mother and child and between the foster father and child. The instruction given to the social workers was: "Rate the closeness of the psychological relationship between the parents and child. Do they show a high degree of rapport, or are they distant and out of touch with each other and lack mutual understanding and shared feelings?"

Over a third of the foster mothers (37.1 percent) were rated as showing the *highest rapport* (complete sharing of intimate thoughts and feelings; implicit trust and confidence in each other). About a third (33.7 percent) were rated as showing *fairly high rapport* (close mutual understanding and sympathy but with occasional relapses). The last third of the sample of foster mothers were rated as showing reduced levels of rapport.

Noticeable differences between the ratings of foster mothers of the youngest children and those with the oldest children is shown in Table 34. We also note that the ratings of the foster fathers show fairly distinct differences from those assigned to their wives. The social workers tended to see the foster mothers as having a higher degree of rapport with the foster children than the foster fathers.

Quality of Care

Table 36 provides a series of ratings of characteristics of the foster parents that relate to the quality of care that can be offered to children placed in the homes. For each characteristic, the ratings range on a five point scale from a "positive factor" (+ +) to its polar opposite "negative factor" (– –). The ratings cover a variety of areas as shown below:

Physical Aspect of the Home (adequacy of home maintenance and quality of care). As pointed out in Chapter 2, almost three-fourths of the foster parents owned private homes. By and large, the ratings by the social workers reflect a view of the foster parents as very able and well organized in their approaches to home care. The homes with older children and those in the middle group were rated somewhat more positively than those with the youngest children. Negative ratings were extremely rare.

Health Care and Health Supervision Offered to Children. In this area, too, the foster parents were seen as having very positive qualities. Most of the ratings were at the positive end of the continuum, with the foster parents of the youngest group of children rated slightly lower than other foster parents. Negative ratings were, again, almost never made.

Capacity to Intellectually Stimulate Children. While most foster parents are seen in positive terms, this is an area in which at least one in five families is rated as either being in the middle (rated '0' instead of '+' or '+ +') or in a few instances in negative terms. Almost six percent of the foster parents caring for the older children are rated negatively while this is rarely the case for the younger and middle groups of children.

Extent of Marital Harmony Prevailing Between Foster Mother and Foster Father. Some social workers may not be at ease in making judgments about the marital relationship of foster parents because it may feel too intrusive. Yet if foster homes are to be considered as permanent homes for children, "permanency planning" must take into account a perspective that the marriages are viable and the family life provided the children is essentially harmonious. The ratings of the social workers shown in Table 36 indicate that most of the marriages are seen positively. About ten percent include the middle range or somewhat negative ratings. Homes caring for older children have a slightly higher proportion of negative ratings.

Adequacy of Foster Family Income. As an issue related to providing permanency, only six out of ten foster families were rated on the positive side of the scale while more than a fourth (26.6 percent) were rated neutrally. For 6.3 percent, the social workers rated this factor as a negative feature indicating that lack of income was a problem in contemplating the possibility of the child remaining in the home permanently.

Age of Foster Parents. Less than ten percent of the foster parents were rated negatively on this factor. They were seen as too old to contemplate that the children could remain with them on a permanent basis.

Stability of Personality of Foster Mother and Foster Father. The ratings show a fairly positive view of the personalities of the foster mothers and the foster fathers. Of the foster mothers, only 7.1 percent were rated negatively and this was true of only 4.0 percent of the foster fathers.

Past Performance with Children. By and large, the social workers had a positive perspective on the parental competence of the foster parents based on their past performance with children. Negative ratings were rarely made. Almost 15 percent of those caring for younger children

TABLE 34

CASEWORKERS' RATINGS OF RAPPORT BETWEEN FOSTER MOTHER AND CHILD
ACCORDING TO AGE OF CHILD[a]

Quality of Rapport	1 to 5 Years	6 to 9 Years	10 to 13 Years	Total
	(Percentaged)			
Highest Rapport: Complete sharing of intimate thoughts and feelings. Implicit trust and confidence in each other.	61.0	36.6	26.9	37.1
Fairly High Rapport: Close mutual understanding and sympathy, but with occasional temporary lapses.	18.2	35.1	39.3	33.7
Moderate Rapport: Moderate degree of rapport in most situations; achieve close confidence in a good many respects, but fail in others.	6.5	17.9	18.3	15.8
Little Rapport: Do not have close rapport but occasionally a close relationship is temporarily established.	1.3	6.0	6.9	5.4
Minimal Rapport: Perfunctory relationship, superficial understanding, interest slight or forced. Tend to be inhibited in each other's presence.	1.3	0.7	5.1	2.8
Lowest Rapport: Isolated from each in feelings. No sharing of confidence or aspirations. No active interest in each other.	1.3	0.7	0.6	0.8
Other	10.4	3.0	2.9	4.4
Percent Total	100.0 (77)	100.0 (134)	100.0 (175)	100.0 (386)

[a] Instruction given the respondents was: "Rate the closeness of the psychological relationship between the parents and child. Do they show a high degree of rapport; or are they distant and out of touch with each other and lack mutual understanding and shared feelings?"

TABLE 35

CASEWORKERS' RATINGS OF RAPPORT BETWEEN FOSTER FATHER AND CHILD ACCORDING TO AGE OF CHILD[a]

Quality of Rapport	1 to 5 Years	6 to 9 Years	10 to 13 Years	Total
	(Percentaged)			
Highest Rapport: Complete sharing of intimate thoughts and feelings. Implicit trust and confidence in each other.	44.1	23.5	16.2	24.3
Fairly High Rapport: Close mutual understanding and sympathy, but with occasional temporary lapses.	18.2	28.8	29.4	27.0
Moderate Rapport: Moderate degree of rapport in most situations; achieve close confidence in a good many respects, but fail in others.	6.5	19.7	22.0	18.1
Little Rapport: Do not have close rapport but occasionally a close relationship is temporarily established.	--	3.0	9.8	5.5
Minimal Rapport: Perfunctory relationship, superficial understanding, interest slight or forced. Tend to be inhibited in each other's presence.	--	1.5	2.9	1.8
Lowest Rapport: Isolated from each in feelings. No sharing of confidence or aspirations. No active interest in each other.	1.3	0.8	1.2	1.0
Other	11.7	3.0	3.5	5.0
No Foster Father (deceased)	18.2	19.7	15.0	17.3
Percent Total	100.0 (77)	100.0 (132)	100.0 (173)	100.0 (382)

[a] Instruction given the respondents was: "Rate the closeness of the psychological relationship between the parents and child. Do they show a high degree of rapport; or are they distant and out of touch with each other and lack mutual understanding and shared feelings?"

TABLE 36

CASEWORKERS' RATINGS OF THE CHARACTERISTICS OF THE FOSTER PARENTS
ACCORDING TO AGE OF CHILD[a]

Characteristic	Age in Years	Positive Factor (++)	+	Neutral 0	-	Negative Factor (--)	Not Applicable	Unknown
		(Percentaged across)						
Physical aspect of the home: adequacy of home maintenance and quality of care. (N=384)	1-5	50.0	25.0	11.2	2.6	--	9.2	1.3
	6-9	67.2	20.9	7.5	3.0	--	1.5	--
	10-13	69.5	20.7	6.9	1.7	0.6	0.6	--
	Total	64.8	21.6	8.1	2.2	0.3	2.6	--
Health care and health supervision offered to children. (N=383)	1-5	56.6	30.3	3.9	--	--	9.2	--
	6-9	73.9	18.7	6.0	--	--	1.5	--
	10-13	72.8	20.2	5.2	0.6	0.6	0.6	--
	Total	70.0	21.7	5.2	0.3	0.3	2.6	--
Foster family's capacity to intellectually stimulate children. (N=382)	1-5	34.2	36.8	15.8	1.3	--	10.5	1.3
	6-9	35.8	40.3	20.1	1.5	--	2.2	--
	10-13	39.5	41.3	12.8	2.9	3.5	--	--
	Total	37.2	40.1	16.0	2.1	1.6	2.9	0.3
Extent of marital harmony prevailing between foster mother and foster father. (N=383)	1-5	36.8	27.6	7.9	3.9	--	22.4	1.3
	6-9	45.9	21.8	5.3	0.8	1.5	21.8	3.0
	10-13	44.8	24.1	6.9	4.0	2.9	14.4	2.9
	Total	43.6	24.0	6.5	2.9	1.8	18.5	2.6

[a] Instruction given the respondents was: "Indicate whether the following characteristics of the foster parents constitute a positive factor or a negative factor in evaluating the home as a potential permanent placement for the child. If situation varies over time, give your judgment about the most typical situation that prevails."

(Continued)

TABLE 36 (Continued)

CASEWORKERS' RATINGS OF THE CHARACTERISTICS OF THE FOSTER PARENTS ACCORDING TO AGE OF CHILD

Characteristic	Age in Years	Positive Factor (++)	+	Neutral 0	-	Negative Factor (--)	Not Applicable	Unknown
		(Percentaged across)						
Adequacy of foster family's income. (N=383)	1-5	24.0	33.3	24.0	4.0	1.3	10.7	2.7
	6-9	32.1	27.6	32.1	3.0	1.5	2.2	1.5
	10-13	27.6	37.4	23.6	5.2	2.9	2.3	1.1
	Total	28.5	33.2	26.6	4.2	2.1	3.9	1.6
Age of foster parents (N=382)	1-5	27.6	21.1	23.7	10.5	5.3	10.5	1.3
	6-9	31.6	35.3	24.8	2.3	3.8	2.3	--
	10-13	31.8	31.2	24.3	7.5	3.5	1.2	0.6
	Total	30.9	30.6	24.3	6.3	3.9	3.4	0.5
Stability of personality of foster mother. (N=381)	1-5	52.0	22.7	6.7	4.0	4.0	9.3	1.3
	6-9	50.0	35.8	6.0	3.7	1.5	3.0	--
	10-13	50.0	31.4	7.6	4.7	3.5	0.6	2.3
	Total	50.4	31.2	6.8	4.2	2.9	3.1	1.3
Stability of personality of foster father. (N=380)	1-5	33.3	26.7	10.7	1.3	1.3	24.0	2.7
	6-9	45.5	22.0	6.1	3.0	1.5	18.9	3.0
	10-13	38.7	28.9	11.6	2.3	1.7	13.9	2.9
	Total	40.0	26.1	9.5	2.4	1.6	17.6	2.9
Evidence of past performance by foster parents with own, foster or adopted children. (N=383)	1-5	46.7	26.7	9.3	1.3	1.3	13.3	1.3
	6-9	55.2	27.6	8.2	2.2	--	4.5	2.2
	10-13	56.3	29.3	7.5	2.9	1.1	2.9	--
	Total	54.0	28.2	8.1	2.3	0.8	5.5	1.0
Quality of discipline of children maintained by foster parents. (N=382)	1-5	34.7	40.0	12.0	2.7	--	9.3	1.3
	6-9	42.9	36.1	11.3	7.5	--	1.5	0.8
	10-13	49.4	33.3	10.9	1.7	3.4	0.6	0.6
	Total	44.2	35.6	11.3	3.9	1.6	2.6	0.8

had ratings indicating the situations were not applicable or unknown, suggesting lack of prior experience with children as a basis for making such ratings.

Quality of Discipline of Children. The ratings tended to reflect a fairly positive view of the capacities of the foster parents to discipline the children. Those with older children included 5.1 percent who were rated negatively.

Coordination of Household

The foster homes were rated as to the coordination of the household and the smoothness of function. The rating was taken from the Fels Behavior Rating Scales first developed by Champney at the Fels Institute and further adapted by Baldwin, Kalhorn and Breese.[10]

Almost nine out of ten of the homes were seen to reflect either *excellent* or *good management.* Only 8.5 percent were rated as showing *fair coordination* ("quite a bit of disorder, but usually can find things . . . things get done but often after fairly long delays"). Less than one percent of the families were described as showing *poor coordination.* None were rated as *chaotic* (Table 37).

The Adjustment of the Children

One final rating was focused upon the adjustment of the child in the foster home. It was a scale developed by the writer in an earlier study of the transracial adoption of American Indian children.[11]

The distribution of ratings shows that about a fourth of the children (25.7 percent) are seen as making an *excellent* adjustment (the outlook for his/her future is excellent). Another 18.7 percent were characterized as showing an *excellent-hopeful* adjustment. Almost a third of the children (35.1 percent) were rated as *hopeful;* they were seen as making an adequate adjustment with their strengths outweighing the weaknesses shown.

Less than 20 percent of the children were seen as having *guarded* outlooks for the future. There was a particular concentration of less optimistic ratings for the older children, covering about a fourth of such youngsters (24.1 percent) compared to about ten percent of the middle group (9.7 percent) and the youngest group of children (10.4 percent) (Table 38).

Summary Comments

In this chapter, we have tapped the perceptions of social workers of important qualities of the foster parents. In the main, they tend to be seen positively in the way they relate to the children placed in their care. Rarely do we find on any given rating scale more than ten percent of the foster parents showing qualities that cause doubt about their ability to relate to the children and provide sound care. In the chapter that follows, we shall see the dimensionality of these ratings to determine how many factors are implicated in the overall perspectives of the social workers.

TABLE 37

CASEWORKERS' RATINGS OF THE COORDINATION
OF THE FOSTER FAMILY'S HOUSEHOLD[a]

Rating	Percent Distribution
<u>Excellent Management</u>: Extremely effective management. Model of efficiency with planning of activities well managed and planned. Confusion unknown.	30.8
<u>Good Management</u>: Smooth-running and efficient on the whole. House kept in order and on schedule most of the time. Meals, finances, education planned ahead. Some superficial disorder.	59.1
<u>Fair Coordination</u>: Quite a bit of disorder, but can usually find things. Buying inefficient but meals fairly adequately planned. Things get done but often after fairly long delays.	8.5
<u>Poor Coordination</u>: Essential rudiments of organization are there, but inefficiency and confusion are common. Often late; off schedule half the time. Home tends to be disorderly.	0.8
<u>Chaotic</u>: Disorganized. No planning. Confusion reigns even in essentials. Home is extremely disorderly and uncared for.	--
<u>Other</u>	0.8
Percent Total	100.0 (386)

[a] Instruction given the respondents was: "Rate the routine functioning of the foster family household as to the smoothness of organization. Is it effectively planned and executed? Or is it uncoordinated and chaotic? Consider care of belongings, coordination of activities, efficiency of home management as it works in practice. Disregard variations in aesthetic standards, style or form."

TABLE 38

CASEWORKERS' RATINGS OF ADJUSTMENT OF THE FOSTER CHILDREN ACCORDING TO AGE OF CHILD[a]

Adjustment Rating	1 to 5 Years	6 to 9 Years	10 to 13 Years	Total
	(Percentaged)			
Excellent: Child is making an excellent adjustment in all spheres of his/her life--the outlook for his/her future is excellent.	37.7	26.9	19.5	25.7
Excellent-Hopeful	24.7	18.7	16.1	18.7
Hopeful: Child is making an adequate adjustment--his/her strengths outweigh the weaknesses shown--the outlook for his/her future is hopeful.	24.7	37.3	37.9	35.1
Hopeful-Guarded	3.9	6.7	9.2	7.3
Guarded: Child is making a mixed adjustment--generally the problems he/she faces are serious and the outlook for his future adjustment is somewhat guarded.	5.2	8.2	12.6	9.6
Guarded-Unpromising	1.3	--	0.6	0.5
Unpromising: Child is making an extremely poor adjustment--the outlook for his future adjustment is unpromising.	--	1.5	1.7	1.3
Other	2.6	0.7	2.3	1.8
Percent Total	100.0 (77)	100.0 (134)	100.0 (174)	100.0 (385)[b]

[a] Instruction given the respondents was: "Considering everything you know about this child, rate his overall adjustment."

[b] Excludes 1 child where no rating was made.

8 Creation of Composite Indexes

Factor Analysis

We have employed a fairly large set of variables in the form of ratings to measure phenomena dealing with the child in the context of his/her foster family. When we examined the product-moment correlations between the variables, we found, as might be expected by those familiar with studies using clinical assessments, a high degree of intercorrelation among the variables. This suggested an underlying structure influencing the choice of responses to the items. We recognized the necessity of developing measures that more parsimoniously reflected the domains embedded in this underlying structure.

As a guide to the selection of items that might be composited into indexes having a common core of content, an exploratory factor analysis was performed for the 42 items shown in Table 39. The method of factor analysis is a statistical technique for examining the relationships between any number of variables in order to reduce the variables into a set of underlying "factors." Factor analysis is a more rigorous approach to discerning patterns that can be found among the variables than could be obtained by visual inspection of the simple correlation matrix.

The principle components method of factor extraction was used with the varimax solution for orthogonal rotation.

The factor analyses were carried for a three, four, five and six factor solution. Upon inspection of the results, the selection of the five factor solution was chosen as the preferred treatment of the data. It accounted for 50.8 percent of the total variance in the unrotated solution. The rotated factors appeared readily interpretable. The factor structure and communalities are displayed in Table 40.

It should be pointed out that the four factor solution produced very similar results to the five factor solution that was accepted. The main difference lies in the fact that information about the social worker's knowledge of the case was found to be combined with variables describing the worker's position in the agency and size of his/her caseload. This information emerged as a single factor in the four factor solution and as two factors in the five factor solution. Common to both solutions were three major factors covering the child's integration in the foster family, his relationship to his/her natural family, and a series of evaluative ratings of the foster family.

The six factor solution was almost identical to the five factor solution but tended to identify a separation dimension covering the foster father's relationship to the child. Among reasons for rejecting it as a solution was that it was less "clean" in that variables loading heavily on the "foster father factor" also tended to load heavily on the first factor covering the child's integration in the foster home.

Creation of Indexes

Each factor can be interpreted in terms of those variables with substantial loadings, say, over .50. It was intended that the factor analysis would serve as a guide to the creation of composite indexes.

The three important factors revealed in the five factor solution presented in Table 40 concern the child's relationship to his/her own natural family and to his/her foster family and the qualities of the foster families. The last two factors are rather trivial in importance and relate to the social worker's self-reported knowledge of the cases they were asked to report on and facts about their position in the agency.

Factor I: Child's Integration in the Foster Home. The variables with the largest loadings on this factor clearly describe the quality and intensity of a child's integration within his/her foster family home. There are about a dozen such variables and they include such information as the affection shown by the foster mother and foster father to the child, his/her affection for them, the rapport between them and the degree of understanding and acceptance of the child by the foster parents. The factor is easy to interpret and appears to have almost no simultaneous heavy loading of items on the other factors.

Factor II: Child's Relationship to the Natural Family. This factor is mainly defined by nine items, three of which involve ratings of the degree of the child's attachment to his/her natural mother, natural father and family as a whole. There are three heavily loaded items which describe the frequency of the child's contacts with his/her mother, father and relatives and three that provide information about the last contact the child has had with these persons. It has previously been shown that many of the children in the sample no longer saw their parents and had not seen them for some years. The interpretation of this factor also seems quite straightforward and the items are not simultaneously loaded on the other factors in a significant way.

TABLE 39

ITEMS FROM QUESTIONNAIRE INCLUDED IN THE FACTOR ANALYSIS

Item

1. Reactions of foster parents to agency inquiry about adoption.
2. How often child sees own mother.
3. How often child sees own father.
4. How often child sees relatives.
5. Last time child saw mother.
6. Last time child saw father.
7. Last time child saw relatives.
8. Rating of physical aspects of foster home.
9. Rating of health supervision offered by foster parents.
10. Rating of foster family's capacity to intellectually stimulate children.
11. Rating of marital harmony in foster home.
12. Rating of adequacy of foster family income as factor in child care.
13. Rating of age of foster parents as factor in adoption of child.
14. Rating of stability of personality of foster mother.
15. Rating of stability of personality of foster father.
16. Rating of foster parent's past performance with children as a factor in adoption.
17. Rating of quality of discipline of foster parents.
18. Rating of child's relationship to natural mother.
19. Rating of child's relationship to natural father.
20. Rating of child's relationship to natural family.
21. Rating of child's conflict of feelings over family attachments.
22. Rating of integration of child in foster home.
23. Rating of affection shown by foster mother to child.
24. Rating of affection shown by foster father to child.
25. Rating of affection shown by child to foster mother.
26. Rating of affection shown by child to foster father.
27. Rating of rapport between foster mother and child.
28. Rating of rapport between foster father and child.
29. Rating of foster mother's understanding of the child.
30. Rating of foster father's understanding of the child.
31. Rating of foster mother's acceptance of the child.
32. Rating of foster father's acceptance of the child.
33. Rating of adjustment of foster home.
34. Rating of coordination of foster family household.
35. Rating of overall child adjustment.
36. Social worker's knowledge of child.
37. Social worker's knowledge of foster mother.
38. Social worker's knowledge of foster father.
39. Position in agency of responding social worker.
40. Highest educational degree of responding social worker.
41. Number of children in the caseload of the social worker.
42. Number of families in the caseload of the social worker.

TABLE 40

ROTATED FACTOR MATRIX FOR ITEMS FROM QUESTIONNAIRE

Item	FACTOR I Child's Integration in Foster Home	FACTOR II Child's Relationship to the Natural Family	FACTOR III Evaluating the Foster Home	FACTOR IV Social Worker's Knowledge of Case	FACTOR V Social Worker's Position in Agency	Communality
1.	.470	-.295	.058	-.017	-.019	.312
2.	.019	.751	-.026	-.014	-.029	.567
3.	.008	.578	.058	.202	.081	.385
4.	-.019	.691	-.003	.042	-.047	.482
5.	.012	.754	-.049	-.044	.028	.574
6.	.048	.594	.078	.164	.168	.417
7.	.011	.660	-.025	-.008	-.041	.438
8.	.045	-.096	-.691	.009	-.009	.488
9.	.144	.033	-.697	.006	.030	.509
10.	.297	.059	-.669	-.015	.044	.541
11.	.166	.079	-.659	.134	-.080	.493
12.	-.031	.055	-.603	.090	.070	.381
13.	-.003	.034	-.527	.072	.184	.318
14.	.325	.115	-.673	.023	-.022	.573
15.	.205	.050	-.612	.239	-.124	.491
16.	.240	.033	-.627	.078	-.020	.458
17.	.289	.055	-.648	.070	-.115	.525
18.	-.178	.699	-.106	-.060	-.011	.535
19.	-.142	.623	-.120	.048	.042	.427
20.	-.205	.711	-.126	-.082	-.007	.570
21.	.487	-.196	-.001	-.137	.116	.308
22.	.627	-.383	-.008	-.001	-.044	.542
23.	.661	.109	-.299	-.034	-.065	.543
24.	.633	.030	-.150	.255	-.160	.515
25.	.693	-.110	-.179	-.028	.068	.530
26.	.725	-.077	-.078	.153	-.051	.563
27.	.744	-.008	-.297	-.019	.125	.657
28.	.724	-.012	-.227	.180	.058	.611
29.	.620	.061	-.477	-.009	.133	.634
30.	.594	-.002	-.387	.233	.055	.560
31.	.736	.042	-.244	-.062	.076	.613
32.	.725	.012	-.079	.154	.021	.556
33.	.526	-.036	-.536	.077	.024	.571
34.	.151	.011	-.552	.058	.002	.331
35.	.648	-.027	-.227	-.006	.072	.478
36.	-.015	.063	-.150	.813	.090	.697
37.	.101	.045	-.157	.801	.129	.694
38.	.180	.072	-.222	.734	-.042	.628
39.	.052	.169	-.063	.023	.640	.445
40.	-.028	-.003	-.081	.066	.634	.414
41.	.055	-.002	-.017	.045	.770	.599
42.	.096	-.032	.115	.002	.598	.381
Sum of Squares	6.879	4.512	5.682	2.268	2.013	21.354

Factor III: Evaluating the Foster Home. This factor clearly involves an evaluation of the foster parents. It is defined by at least ten items and is distinguished from the issue of whether the child is rooted in the foster home as measured by Factor I. The foster parents are seen in terms of the qualities they show as parents.[12]

Factor IV: Social Worker's Knowledge of the Case. This is a minor factor which is defined by three items in which the social worker has characterized his/her knowledge of the child, the foster mother and foster father.

Factor V: Social Worker's Position in the Agency. This is also a minor factor which describes the respondent's position in the agency, agency background and number of children and families in the caseload.

The factor analysis was used as a guide to the creation of indexes as shown in Tables 41, 42 and 43. The Index of the Child's Integration in the Foster Home is composed of nine items. The index emphasizes the foster parents' orientations to the child. Each item is strongly correlated with the corrected total score represented by the sum of all remaining items in the composite set. The internal reliability of the index is also quite well established with a standardized alpha of .88.

The Index of Child's Relationship to Natural Family represents a composite of five items. The frequency of family visitation and information about the last time the child saw a member of his/her family was consolidated into two single items coded to show the maximum and most recent contact of the child with any family member. The correlations of items with the modified total score are relatively modest, ranging from .46 to .63, and the measure of internal reliability is fairly high (standardized item alpha = .79).

The Index of the Worker's Evaluation of the Foster Home is a composite of 12 ratings by the social workers. The corrected item-criterion correlations are also modest, ranging from .43 to .67. The measure of internal reliability shows a high degree of unity of content among the items (standardized item alpha = .88).

The intercorrelation between index scores showed that the relationship between the Index of the Child's Integration in the Foster Home and the Index of the Child's Relationship to the Natural Family was quite minimal (r = −.083). This was also true of the Index of the Worker's Evaluation of the Foster Home and the Index of the Child's Relationship to the Natural Family (r = .118). However, the two indexes measuring the foster home were quite strongly correlated (r = .590; p < .001) and obviously tapped somewhat overlapping domains. Thus, a foster family that was perceived as strongly committed to a child was also perceived as possessing more positive qualities.

Summary Comments

We have consolidated the information obtained from our research booklets into a few important dimensions. They deal with the two relationships that can have deep meaning for the foster child, i.e., his/her ties with his/her natural family and with his/her foster family. Deciding what is the likely source of permanency for a child—the key question in the foster care of young children who experienced extended placements—is obviously closely linked to the agency social worker's perception in these areas.

If a child's natural parents no longer visit him, if the last time they saw him was three or four years ago, and if he never talks about them, all of this information will be reflected in the Index of Child's Relationship to the Natural Family. If he/she is the recipient of affection from his/her foster mother and foster father, if they show rapport with him/her and understanding of him/her, and if an effort is made to integrate him/her in their home, this will likely be reflected in the Index of the Child's Integration in the Foster Home.

Of what use would the gathering of such information be in the management of a child welfare agency? The expectation of the writer is that it will make possible the scanning of caseloads of foster children to establish the important dimensions that are linked to permanency planning. It will hopefully enable an agency to be aware of where it needs to go in planning its activities in behalf of the children in its care.

Planning for the futures of children in foster care is *not* like filling airline seats. We need solid information on the nature of the child's attachments, his connections with his own family and his foster family. Simply put, a nine-item index is a more solid measure of a relationship than a single item.

TABLE 41

INDEX OF CHILD'S INTEGRATION IN THE FOSTER HOME

Items

A. Integration of child in foster home
B. Affection of foster mother to child
C. Affection of foster father to child
D. Rapport between foster mother and child
E. Rapport between foster father and child
F. Foster mother's understanding of child
G. Foster father's understanding of child
H. Foster mother's acceptance of child
I. Foster father's acceptance of child

	Intercorrelations Among Items[a]									Corrected Item - Total Correlation
	A	B	C	D	E	F	G	H	I	
A	--									.88
B	.38	--								.87
C	.19	.27	--							.86
D	.41	.60	.25	--						.86
E	.27	.22	.81	.46	--					.85
F	.31	.58	.22	.67	.30	--				.86
G	.17	.19	.80	.31	.80	.45	--			.85
H	.44	.66	.25	.62	.29	.61	.30	--		.86
I	.32	.29	.72	.31	.70	.31	.74	.55	--	.85

[a]Correlation is between each item and the sum of all other items in the index with the item itself deleted to correct for auto-correlation.

Alpha Measure of Internal Reliability

Item	Alpha if Item Deleted
A	.88
B	.87
C	.86
D	.86
E	.85
F	.86
G	.85
H	.86
I	.85
Total Items	.87
Standardized Item Alpha	.88

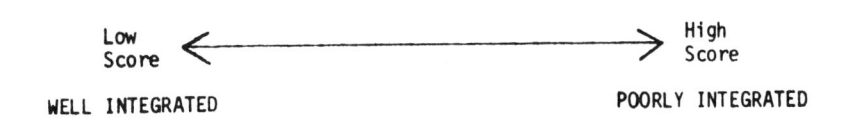

```
       Low    <-------------------->    High
      Score                              Score

WELL INTEGRATED                      POORLY INTEGRATED
```

TABLE 42

INDEX OF CHILD'S RELATIONSHIP TO NATURAL FAMILY

<u>Items</u>

A. Relationship of child to natural mother
B. Relationship of child to natural father
C. Relationship of child to natural family
D. Frequency of family's visits to child
E. Last time family visited child

	Intercorrelations Among Items					Corrected Item - Total Correlation
	<u>A</u>	<u>B</u>	<u>C</u>	<u>D</u>	<u>E</u>	
A	--					.63
B	.54	--				.56
C	.71	.61	--			.62
D	.32	.29	.28	--		.46
E	.38	.34	.36	.49	--	.53

<u>Alpha Measure of Internal Reliability</u>

<u>Item</u>	<u>Alpha if Item Deleted</u>
A	.70
B	.72
C	.70
D	.77
E	.73
Total Items	.77
Standardized Item Alpha	.79

Low Score ←————————————→ High Score

CLOSELY IDENTIFIED   NOT IDENTIFIED

TABLE 43

INDEX OF WORKER'S EVALUATION OF THE FOSTER HOME

Items

A. Rating of physical aspects of foster home
B. Rating of health supervision offered by foster parents
C. Rating of foster family's capacity to intellectually stimulate children
D. Rating of marital harmony in the foster home
E. Rating of adequacy of foster family income as factor in child care
F. Rating of age of foster parents as factor in adoption of child
G. Rating of stability of personality of foster mother
H. Rating of stability of personality of foster father
I. Rating of foster parent's past performance with children as a factor in adoption
J. Rating of quality of discipline of foster parents
K. Rating of adjustment of the foster home
L. Rating of coordination of foster family household

	A	B	C	D	E	F	G	H	I	J	K	L	Corrected Item-Total Correlation
A	--												.59
B	.65	--											.64
C	.45	.51	--										.67
D	.31	.36	.31	--									.50
E	.41	.38	.41	.18	--								.50
F	.34	.34	.45	.13	.52	--							.45
G	.41	.50	.54	.41	.28	.31	--						.66
H	.23	.27	.31	.70	.19	.19	.39	--					.49
I	.38	.37	.49	.24	.31	.34	.57	.30	--				.57
J	.36	.49	.53	.33	.42	.36	.51	.32	.49	--			.65
K	.29	.34	.39	.33	.19	.16	.46	.28	.35	.45	--		.50
L	.44	.34	.31	.28	.26	.68	.28	.22	.20	.34	.44	--	.43

Intercorrelations Among Items

Alpha Measure of Internal Reliability

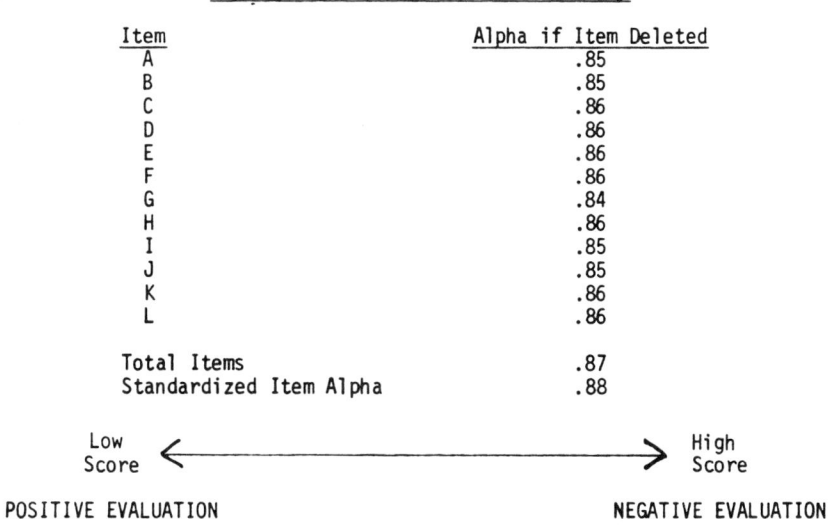

Item	Alpha if Item Deleted
A	.85
B	.85
C	.86
D	.86
E	.86
F	.86
G	.84
H	.86
I	.85
J	.85
K	.86
L	.86
Total Items	.87
Standardized Item Alpha	.88

Low Score ← → High Score

POSITIVE EVALUATION   NEGATIVE EVALUATION

9 Multiple Regression Analysis of the Index Scores

In order to obtain additional perspectives on the indexes created from the items used in this special survey, a series of multiple regressions were undertaken, with each index treated as a dependent variable. The independent variables used as predictors are shown in Table 44, where we show the intercorrelations among the variables as well as their means and standard deviations.

The correlations among the independent variables contain information which is of interest. For example:

- The total number of children the foster parents had cared for in their service to the agency was significantly associated with the number of years they had served (r = .482; p < .001).
- The longer a child had been in care, the more likely was adoption to be the designated discharge plan (r = .313; p < .001).
- Black foster mothers were more apt to be older (r = .194; p < .001) and widowed (r = .197; p < .001).

Child's Integration in Foster Home

Using the Index of the Child's Integration in the Foster Home as the dependent variable, five significant predictors were established. This is shown in Table 45. The child's age was shown to exert a significant effect on the degree of his or her integration in the home. The regression coefficient was .22 (p < .001) and the variable accounted for 5.0 percent unique variance in the index scores calculated for cases. This can be interpreted to indicate that since older children tend to have been in care longer (r = .515, p < .001), usually in the same foster home, they have become more deeply embedded in their foster homes with the passage of time. This coincides with a common sense understanding of the process and the finding can be construed as reflecting a construct validation of the index.

The social worker's self-report of knowledge of the case also showed a strong positive effect, accounting for 5.5 percent of the unique explained variance in the scores. Here, too, the time factor appears to be operative since better known cases presumably involved longer relationships between the social worker and the child.

It is of interest that black children tended to be seen as less integrated within their homes than the other children.

The regression coefficient was .17 (p < .001) and accounted for 3.0 percent of unique variance explained. As shown in Table 44, the black foster homes were more likely to have older foster mothers who tended to be widowed. This information might help explain the greater tenuousness of the black children's placement. As a group, they were not subjected to a greater frequency of placements than the other children.

As might be expected, the more placements reported for a child, the less likely he was perceived to be deeply integrated within the foster home (regression coefficient = .17; p < .001). We also observe that children for whom adoption was being planned were more likely to be seen as integrated in the foster home.

The multiple correlation for the five independent variables cited was .41 and accounted for 17 percent of the variance in the index scores. The variance accounted for was obviously quite modest.

Relationship to Natural Family

In Table 46, we show the results of the multiple regression analysis of the scores developed for the Index of Child's Relationship to Natural Family. The analysis reveals that the fact of having a discharge plan calling for adoption of the child is overwhelmingly the most important item of information descriptive of the child's relationship to his or her natural family. The standardized regression coefficient is .49 (p < .001) and 20.8 percent of unique variance is explained by this information. The meaning of this highly significant predictor is quite clear: agencies move to adoption as the plan of choice when they have totally given up on the natural family as a viable resource for the child. These are very likely to be families who have dropped out of the child's life and have been absent for a number of years.

The number of years that a child has spent in care is also a significant predictor of index scores. The longer the child has been in care the more likely is it that his relationship with his parents has become attenuated. We must bear in mind the fact that children who have been in care a long time reflect the residual groups from previously entering cohorts who have not been able to escape the impermanency of foster care. This has no doubt been due to the lack of commitment of their parents.

TABLE 44

CORRELATIONS BETWEEN INDEPENDENT VARIABLES USED IN THE STUDY, MEANS AND STANDARD DEVIATIONS
(N = 386)

		(1)	(2)	(3)	(4)	(5)	(6)	(7)	(8)	(9)	(10)	(11)	(12)	(13)	(14)
Number of siblings in foster care	(1)	1.000	-.097	-.047	.076	-.072	-.054	-.172***	-.070	-.136**	.162**	.168***	-.076	.010	-.068
Number of years foster family with agency	(2)		1.000	.482***	.188***	.513***	-.052	.342***	-.136**	.006	-.094	-.028	.235***	.036	-.123*
Number of children agency placed with family	(3)			1.000	-.064	.034	.066	.248***	-.016	.025	-.068	.159**	.016	.020	-.157**
Child's age last birthday	(4)				1.000	.515***	.072	.095	-.023	.001	-.116	-.080	-.013	.051	.101*
Child's years in care	(5)					1.000	.076	.235***	-.052	.096	-.106	-.104*	.313***	.075	-.065
Child's number of foster home placements	(6)						1.000	-.003	.061	-.054	-.028	.100	-.025	-.027	.039
Foster mother's age	(7)							1.000	.194***	.296***	-.186**	-.172***	.054	-.021	.072
Intactness of foster home (intact/ONE PARENT FOSTER HOME)	(8)								1.000	.197***	-.110*	-.038	-.018	.003	.017
Foster mother ethnicity: Black (others/BLACK)	(9)									1.000	-.605***	.020	.037	-.020	.128*
Foster mother ethnicity: Hispanic (others/HISPANIC)	(10)										1.000	.011	-.003	.054	-.086
Total children in foster family household	(11)											1.000	-.055	-.011	-.057
Discharge plan: Adoption (others/ADOPT)	(12)												1.000	-.021	.023
Worker's knowledge of foster home/child	(13)													1.000	.092
Worker's agency status	(14)														1.000
MEAN		1.438	5.955	4.696	8.492	5.653	1.491	46.072	1.179	0.528	0.246	3.389	0.497	1.869	2.383
STANDARD DEVIATION		1.578	4.720	4.571	3.298	2.967	0.714	8.785	0.384	0.500	0.431	1.764	0.501	0.771	0.527

*p < .05   **p < .01   ***p < .001

TABLE 45

RELATION OF INDEPENDENT VARIABLES TO INDEX OF CHILD'S INTEGRATION
WITHIN FOSTER HOME
(N = 386)

Independent Variables[a]	Zero-order Correlation	Standardized Regression Coefficient	Percent Unique Variance Explained
1. Child's Age Last Birthday	.25***	.22***	5.0
2. Worker's Knowledge of Foster Home/Child	.24***	.24***	5.5
3. Foster Mother's Ethnicity: Black (others/BLACK)	.16**	.17***	3.0
4. Child's Number of Foster Home Placements	.14**	.14**	1.9
5. Discharge Plan: Adoption	.11*	-.10*	1.1
Multiple R		.41	
Multiple R^2		.17	

*p < .05   **p < .01   ***p < .001

Partial Correlations with Dependent Variable for Variables Not Entered:

Number of Siblings in Foster Care	.01	Foster Mother's Age	-.03
		Intactness of Foster Home	-.08
Number of Years Foster Family with Agency	.01	Foster Mother's Ethnicity: Hispanic	.02
Number of Children Agency Placed with Family	-.03	Total Children in Foster Family Household	.01
Child's Years in Care	-.05	Worker's Agency Status	.04

[a] Independent variables were entered to meet the criterion of "best prediction." The first variable selected was the one with the highest correlation with the dependent variable. The next variable selected is the variable with the maximum partial correlation with the dependent variable, relative to the independent variable that has already been entered into the equation, and so forth. This produces a solution which is "stepwise" in the usual sense, meaning that the best variable was entered at each step.

TABLE 46

RELATION OF INDEPENDENT VARIABLES TO INDEX OF CHILD'S RELATIONSHIP
TO THE NATURAL FAMILY
(N = 386)

Independent Variables[a]	Zero-order Correlation	Standardized Regression Coefficient	Percent Unique Variance Explained
1. Discharge Plan: Adoption	.56***	.49***	20.8
2. Worker's Knowledge of Foster Home/Child	.10	.10*	1.1
3. Child's Years in Care	.28***	.20***	2.6
4. Child's Age Last Birthday	-.07	-.17***	2.1
Multiple R		.59	
Multiple R^2		.35	

*p < .05   ***p < .001

Partial Correlations with Dependent Variable for Variables Not Entered:

Number of Siblings in Foster Care	-.01	Intactness of Foster Home	.04
Number of Years Foster Family with Agency	-.05	Foster Mother's Ethnicity: Black	.01
Number of Children Agency Placed with Family	-.04	Foster Mother's Ethnicity: Hispanic	.07
Child's Number of Foster Home Placements	.01	Total Children in Foster Family Household	-.07
Foster Mother's Age	-.05	Worker's Agency Status	.07

[a] Independent variables entered according to "best criterion."

Older children appear to have maintained closer relationships with their natural families. This is perhaps explained by the following proposition: the older a child when he enters foster care, the more likely he is to experience committed relationships with his parents.

The multiple correlation for the four independent variables is .59 which accounts for 35 percent of the variance in index scores. Most of this can be attributed to the predictor variable dealing with discharge planning.

Evaluation of the Foster Home

Only three variables emerge as significant predictors of scores developed for the Index of Worker's Evaluation of the Foster Home. Accounting for most of the variance is the indication that the social worker feels that he/she has good knowledge of the foster home. The standardized regression coefficient is .32 ($p < .001$) and the variable accounts for 10.2 percent of the variance in scores.

On a more modest level, significant effects are shown for the age of the foster mother and her ethnicity. Older foster mothers and those who are black tend to show lower evaluations. On the other hand, the intactness of the foster home, the number of years the foster family has been with the agency and the number of children cared for show almost no association with the index scores after the three significant predictors have been partialed out. (Table 47).

Conflicted Feelings Over Family Attachments

Previous discussion about the rating scale dealing with manifestations by the child of conflict over family attachments (Table 24) pointed up the fact that almost half the children seemed at peace with the current arrangements while 27 percent showed some anxiety. More severe stress over conflicting pulls between natural parents and foster parents were said to characterize about 11.5 percent of the sample.

Table 48 shows the results of a multiple regression analysis of this scale. Included among the independent variables were the scores reflecting the indexes previously analyzed and discussed in this chapter. As it turned out, five variables were significant predictors with the strongest being the three index scores.

The scores reflecting the Index of the Child's Integration in the Foster Home were, by far, the strongest predictor. The standardized regression coefficient was .50 ($p < .001$) and the scores accounted for 20.3 percent of unique variance in the rating of the child's manifestation of conflicted feelings. We interpret the finding to indicate that the more the child was rooted in his foster family, the less likely he was perceived by his social worker to be in conflict. If his relationship to his foster family was more that of the outsider, the more likely he was viewed as being in conflict.

On the other hand, the scores derived from the Index of the Child's Relationship to the Natural Family showed an opposite significant effect (standardized regression coefficient = $-.28$; $p < .001$). The more a child appeared in touch with and identified with his own family, the more in conflict over his situation in foster care he appeared to his social worker. The index scores accounted for 6.3 percent of unique variance in the dependent variable. Put another way, a child whose own family had essentially abandoned him appears to give greater external evidence of being at peace with his current living arrangement; the foster family had no competition for the child's loyalties.

Also emerging as statistically significant but quite modest predictors were the scores reflecting the Index of the Worker's Evaluation of the Foster Home, the number of years the foster family had served with the agency and the variable indicating whether or not the agency had approached the foster parents to consider adoption.

The direction of seeming influence of these variables was somewhat surprising and difficult to interpret. Foster families that were positively evaluated were also seen as having foster children in conflict in their homes. The positive evaluations of the homes may reflect their tendency not to "take over" completely so that the child could retain some identification with his own family.

Foster families who had experienced long tenure with the agency were also seen as having foster children who were in conflict. This is difficult to explain.

Foster parents who had been approached to consider adoption were in situations where the child was seen as experiencing minimal conflict.

Comments

The index scores we have analyzed here deal with quite central areas of the foster care phenomenon. If the items included in the indexes can be employed in practice on a routine basis, it will be possible to trace the social workers' perceptions of the nature of the child's attachments over time. It will also be possible to determine whether ratings early in the child's experience in foster care can significantly predict the later course of events such as his return to his parents or the securing of adoptive status for him. This is something we examine in a preliminary way in the next chapter.

TABLE 47

RELATION OF INDEPENDENT VARIABLES TO INDEX OF WORKER'S EVALUATION
OF THE FOSTER HOME
(N = 386)

Independent Variables[a]	Zero-order Correlation	Standardized Regression Coefficient	Percent Unique Variance Explained
1. Worker's Knowledge of Foster Home/Child	.31***	.32***	10.2
2. Foster Mother's Age	.20***	.16***	2.5
3. Foster Mother's Ethnicity: Black	.18***	.14**	1.7
Multiple R		.40	
Multiple R^2		.16	

**p < .01   ***p < .001

Partial Correlations with Dependent Variable for Variables Not Entered:

Number of Siblings in Foster Care	-.03	Child's Number of Foster Home Placements	.02
Number of Years Foster Family with Agency	.03	Intactness of Foster Home	.07
Number of Children Agency Placed with Family	-.07	Foster Mother's Ethnicity: Hispanic	.05
Child's Age Last Birthday	.01	Total Children in Foster Family Household	-.04
Child's Years in Care	.03	Discharge Plan: Adoption	.05
		Worker's Agency Status	-.02

[a] Independent variables entered according to "best criterion."

TABLE 48

RELATION OF SELECTED INDEPENDENT VARIABLES
TO THE SOCIAL WORKER'S RATING OF CHILD'S MANIFESTATION
OF CONFLICT OVER FAMILY ATTACHMENTS[a]
(N = 386)

Independent Variables	Zero-order Correlation	Standardized Regression Coefficient	Percent Unique Variance Explained
1. Index of Child's Integration in Foster Home	.45***	.50***	20.3
2. Index of Child's Relationship to Natural Family	-.27***	-.28***	6.3
3. Index of Worker's Evaluation of Foster Home	.04	-.14**	1.5
4. Number of Years Foster Family with Agency	.09	.10*	1.0
5. Foster Family Approached re Adoption (yes/NO)	.09	-.11*	0.9
Multiple R		.54	
Multiple R^2		.29	

*p < .05   **p < .01   ***p < .001

[a] Low score corresponds with minimal conflict.

10 Movement Toward Permanency: A Validity Test

Introduction

One way of assessing the validity of the indexes created from the data elements used in this test run is the procedure employed in the previous studies. With the passage of a year's time since the collection of the data, we attempted to establish the predictive power of index scores in accounting for children moving out of care to a more permanent living arrangement in conformity with the discharge plan of being returned to parents or relatives or being adopted by the foster parents. Since the CWIS data files are updated for all cases every six months, it was possible to determine which children in our sample had been discharged over the course of the year and to identify the discharge destination. For this purpose, the CWIS data file of December 31, 1978 was accessed and a matching program was used to create a sub-file of the study sample.[13]

Discharge Status

Of 372 cases followed up as of December 31, 1978, there were 69 children identified as discharged from the system over the course of the previous year. The information as to destination is as follows:

	Number	Percent
Discharged to parent or relative	19	5.1
Adopted	26	7.0
Trial discharge or suspended payment	24	6.5
Still in care	303	81.4
TOTAL	372	100.0

We thus see that in the course of a year, about 19 percent of the children left care. This provides an opportunity to determine the degree to which the data gathered in the new module is predictive of discharge status. The reader should bear in mind the fact that a single year provides only a limited test since the departure of children is a process that goes on for many years.[14]

In undertaking this analysis of discharged cases, we seek to test the following hypotheses:

(1) Children who are closely identified with their natural families and have maintained contact with them—as measured by the Index of Child's Relationship to Natural Family—are more apt to have a discharge plan calling for return to parents or relatives than children who lack such ties.

(2) Within the group for whom return home is the designated discharge plan, those with closer ties to their parents are more likely to return home in the course of a year.

(3) For children with the designated discharge plan of adoption, it would be expected that those who are more deeply embedded in their foster homes—as measured by the Index of the Child's Integration in the Foster Home—would have their adoption status formalized in greater numbers over the course of a year.

(4) Where foster homes are evaluated more positively—as measured by the Index of Worker's Evaluation of Foster Home—it would be anticipated that there would be greater movement to adoption.

Discharge Status and Index Scores

Child's Relationship to Family. In Table 49, the mean scores reflecting the Index of the Child's Relationship to Natural Family are shown for subjects classified by discharge plan (return to parents or relatives/adoption) and their discharge status on December 31, 1978 (in care/discharged).[15] There is a quite pronounced difference between the mean scores of the children according to the discharge plan. Children destined to be returned to their parents showed a mean index score of 2.40 while those deemed suitable for adoption had a mean of 4.18; the difference was statistically significant ($p < .001$). The differences are easily interpreted to signify that children closely identified with their families—and in contact with them—were scheduled to be returned home. Those who had almost no relationship to their parents were deemed to be in need of adoptive planning.

The difference in mean index scores between discharged children and those still in care on December 31, 1978 was trivial. This can be explained by the fact that the two types of discharge, i.e., return to own family or adoption tended to cancel each other out. The difference is better shown in the interaction variable shown in the analysis of variance table displayed in Table 49. Discharged children returned to own family showed a mean of 2.09 compared to a mean of 2.71 for those whose discharge

TABLE 49

MEAN SCORES ON INDEX OF CHILD'S RELATIONSHIP TO NATURAL FAMILY
ACCORDING TO DISCHARGE PLAN AND DISCHARGE STATUS AFTER ONE YEAR[a]
(N = 329)

Discharge Status		Return to Parents or Relatives is Discharge Plan	Adoption is Discharge Plan	Row Marginals
In Care	Mean S.D. N	2.71 0.90 65	3.84 0.89 200	3.28
Discharged	Mean S.D. N	2.09 0.84 38	4.52 0.44 26	3.31
Column Marginals	Mean	2.40	4.18	3.29

Analysis of Variance

Source	Sum of Squares	DF	Mean Square	F-Test	Significance
(A) Discharge Status	0.044	1	0.044	0.060	N.S.
(B) Discharge Plan	149.251	1	149.251	202.000***	Under .001
A x B	19.512	1	19.512	26.408***	Under .001
Unit	240.132	325	0.739		

[a]Forty-seven cases not included where discharge plan was other than return to parents or relatives or adoption.

plan called for return home but who were still in care. The former had previously been described as more closely identified with their families than those still in care.

For the children who had adoption as the designated discharge plan, the discharged (adopted) children showed a mean index score of 4.52, showing them to be almost devoid of a relationship with their natural families. This compared with a mean of 3.84 for those children not yet adopted, indicating a less pronounced distance from their natural families. The interaction variable was significant in its contribution to the total sum of squares (p < .001).

Child's Integration in the Foster Home. In Table 50, we show a similar analysis of variance approach to the Index of Child's Integration in the Foster Home. Mean index scores are shown for the cells representing the intersection of discharge plans at the time of the survey and discharge status a year later. The differences in mean scores are very modest and only one group stands out as different. The children who had adoption as the designated discharge plan and indeed were adopted in the course of a year had mean scores indicating the deepest embedment in their foster homes. Significant differences were accounted for by the discharge plans (p < .05) but not for the later discharge status for groups. The interaction of the two independent variables was significant (p < .05) and is largely accounted for by the adopted children.

The Index of the Worker's Evaluation of the Foster Home was analyzed in similar fashion to the prior two indexes. No significant differences in means of index scores were found to be associated with discharge plans or later discharge of the subjects. The interaction of the two independent variables also showed no significant effect.[16]

Multiple Regression Analyses

Another way of analyzing the potential use of the index scores in predicting the discharge of our subjects was through their inclusion in a multiple regression analysis of the status of the children on December 31, 1978. This was undertaken separately for children whose discharge plan called for them to be returned to their natural parents and those who were slated for adoption.

Return to Own Family. In Table 51, we display the results of the multiple regression analysis of the one-year status outcomes for children who were supposed to be returned to their parents or relatives. There were 103 children included in this analysis, 65 of whom were still in care on December 31, 1978, while 38 were discharged or on trial discharge to their parents or relatives. The dependent variable for this analysis was a dichotomy reflecting the child's status (0 = in care, 1 = discharged).

We observe the saliency of the Index of Child's Relationship to Natural Family as a predictor of discharge. The standardized regression coefficient is $-.32$ (p < .01) and the scores account for 9.4 percent of unique variance in the discharge status measure. This finding confirms the fact that the children who were most closely identified with their parents and in contact with them were more apt to return home.

A second significant predictor poses more of a challenge for interpretation. The number of years the foster family had been with the agency was inversely related to a child's return to his own family. The standardized regression coefficient is $-.33$ (p < .01) and 7.0 percent of unique variance in the criterion variable is accounted for. The writer's subjective reaction to this finding is that children are more likely to leave care when they are in foster families that have not had long careers of fostering. This raises the possibility that shorter tenure in the role on the part of foster parents is associated with easier egress of the child, either because such homes tend to be used by the agencies for children with viable families or because the behavior of the foster parents influences the discharge planning and activity. This is an interesting area for future research.

A modest but statistically significant predictor of discharge is the number of children placed by the agency with each foster family. The more children placed with the family the more likely is the child to achieve reunion with his own family. Here, too, the causal aspects in the situation need to be better understood. Do agencies use certain families for children who are not going to stay on a permanent basis? Are there types of families who do not need to "hold on" and are facilitative of the child's return to his own family? At issue here is whether agencies are using foster homes differentially according to discharge prospects identified for children or whether the foster families exert a force on the discharge process stemming from their own internal dynamics particularly as related to their motives in caring for foster children.

Two additional predictors we might cite, modest in size and not statistically significant, are the child's age and the intactness of the foster home. Older children tend to return home in greater numbers. This relates to previous speculations of the writer that older children, often having had prior care at the hands of their own parents, have greater claims to the loyalty of those parents than children who came into care as infants.[17] With respect to the issue of whether the foster home was identified as intact or was a single parent home, it appears that the foster children tended to leave care for return more frequently from intact foster families than those containing a single foster parent.

Adoption-bound. Table 52 presents a multiple regression analysis of the status of children on December 31, 1978 who had adoption identified as the designated discharge plan. There were 226 children so identified, more than twice the number where return to own family was the designated plan. There were only two significant predictors of discharge to adoption: the Index of the Child's Relationship to the Natural Family and the variable dealing with the reported reactions of the foster parents to the agency's inquiry about their interest in adoption.

It is clear that the index describing the child's relationship to his own family assumes a high level of importance in our thinking since it is the most important predictor for the two types of discharge we have covered. In the analysis of the movement to permanency of adoption-bound children, the index shows a standardized regression coefficient of .25 (p < .001) and accounts for 5.9 percent of unique variance.

The meaning we attach to the finding can be understood in concert with our previous discussion of Table 49 showing the index scores according to discharge plan and discharge status. A child's identification and contact with his own family not only discriminate between types of discharge

TABLE 50

MEAN SCORES ON INDEX OF CHILD'S INTEGRATION IN THE FOSTER HOME
ACCORDING TO DISCHARGE PLAN AND DISCHARGE STATUS AFTER ONE YEAR
(N = 329)

Discharge Status		Return to Parents or Relatives is Discharge Plan	Adoption is Discharge Plan	Row Marginals
In Care	Mean S.D. N	1.80 0.61 65	1.79 0.65 200	1.78
Discharged	Mean S.D. N	1.90 0.50 38	1.49 0.49 26	1.70
Column Marginals	Mean	1.85	1.64	1.75

Analysis of Variance

Source	Sum of Squares	DF	Mean Square	F-Test	Significance
(A) Discharge Status	0.426	1	0.426	1.118	N.S.
(B) Discharge Plan	2.168	1	2.168	5.687*	Under .05
A x B	1.865	1	1.865	4.893*	Under .05
Unit	123.893	325	0.381		

TABLE 51

RELATION OF SELECTED PREDICTOR VARIABLES TO CHILD'S STATUS
ON DECEMBER 31, 1978 FOR CHILDREN WITH A DISCHARGE PLAN
OF RETURN TO PARENTS OR RELATIVES[a]
(N = 103)

Independent Variables[b]	Zero-order Correlation	Standardized Regression Coefficient	Percent Unique Variance Explained
1. Index of Child's Relationship to Natural Family	-.32***	-.32**	9.4
2. Number of Years Foster Family with Agency	-.09	-.33**	7.0
3. Number of Children Agency Placed with Foster Family	.10	.25*	5.0
4. Child's Age Last Birthday	.16	.20	3.1
5. Intactness of Foster Home	-.11	-.17	2.6
Multiple R		.45	
Multiple R^2		.20	

*p < .05   **p < .01   ***p < .001

Partial Correlations with Dependent Variable for Variables Not Entered:

Number of Siblings in Foster Care	-.07	Index of Worker's Evaluation of Foster Home	.06
Foster Family Approached re Adoption (yes/NO)	.02	Child's Years in Care	-.03
Reaction of Foster Parents to Idea of Adoption (positive/AGAINST)	-.05	Child's Number of Foster Home Placements	-.09
Frequency of Family's Visits to Child	.04	Foster Mother's Age	.10
Last Time Family Visited Child	.03	Foster Mother's Ethnicity: Black	.15
Index of Child's Integration in Foster Home	.04	Foster Mother's Ethnicity: Hispanic	.04
		Total Children in Foster Family Household	.02

[a]Analysis restricted to cases where child's designated discharge plan was return to parents or relatives. Dependent variable is child's status on December 31, 1978 (in care/DISCHARGED).

[b]Independent variables entered according to "best criterion."

TABLE 52

RELATION OF SELECTED PREDICTOR VARIABLES TO CHILD'S STATUS
ON DECEMBER 31, 1978 FOR CHILDREN WITH A DISCHARGE PLAN
OF ADOPTION[a]
(N = 226)

Independent Variables[b]	Zero-order Correlation	Standardized Regression Coefficient	Percent Unique Variance Explained
1. Index of Child's Relationship to Natural Family	.25***	.24***	5.9
2. Reaction of Foster Parents to Idea of Adoption (positive/AGAINST)	-.22***	-.22***	4.7
Multiple R		.33	
Multiple R^2		.11	

***$p < .001$

Partial Correlations with Dependent Variables for Variables Not Entered:

Number of Siblings in Foster Care	-.08	Index of Worker's Evaluation of Foster Home	-.04
Number of Years Foster Family with Agency	-.01	Child's Years in Care	-.11
Number of Children Agency Placed with Family	.08	Child's Number of Foster Home Placements	-.01
Child's Age Last Birthday	-.07	Foster Mother's Age	.01
Foster Family Approached re Adoption (yes/NO)	.01	Intactness of Foster Home	-.02
Frequency of Family's Visits to Child	.04	Foster Mother's Ethnicity: Black	.02
Last Time Family Visited Child	.00	Foster Mother's Ethnicity: Hispanic	.04
Index of Child's Integration in Foster Home	-.04	Total Children in Foster Family Household	.09

[a] Analysis is restricted to cases where child's designated discharge plan was adoption. Dependent variable is child's status on December 31, 1978 (in care/ADOPTED).

[b] Independent variables entered according to "best criterion."

plans being promulgated—return home or adoption—but also, within categories of discharge plan, discriminate between those who stay in care and those who go on to adoption. For our sample, at least, the more removed a child is from his natural family the more quickly can his adoption status be finalized. This fits in with common sense notions of the foster care phenomenon but it is important to pin this down as a fairly firm indication of the predictive validity of the index in question.

The information that the reported reaction of the foster parents to the agency's inquiry about their interest in adoption is a significant predictor of movement to discharge is also a finding that could have been expected. The standardized regression coefficient was −.22 ($p < .001$) and the variable accounted for 4.7 percent of unique variance in the discharge phenomenon.

Of interest is the fact that the Index of the Child's Integration in the Foster Home is not a significant predictor of discharge to adoption. Actually, the Index showed a product-moment correlation of −.15 ($p < .05$) with the outcome variable indicating that the children who were well integrated within their foster homes were likely to be adopted by their foster families. The failure of the index to emerge as a significant predictor is partially accounted for by the fact that it correlated quite strongly with the variable describing the foster parent's reaction to an inquiry about adoption ($r = .50; p < .001$). Foster parents of children described as being well integrated in their foster homes showed a strong tendency to react positively to the agency's overture about adoption. The fact of shared variance between the two phenomena served to suppress the role of the index as a predictor.

The Index of the Worker's Evaluation of the Foster Home showed a low correlation with discharge status ($r = −.08$). Its role as a predictor of events dealing with status change is obviously trivial.

The Predictions of Social Workers

In Chapter 6, we revealed the predictions of the social workers of the changes in status likely to take place for the foster children within the coming year, within one to two years and within three to five years. We now ask: How good were these predictions? This question is tested in Table 53 where we look at the predictions that the children would be returned to parents during the coming year. In Table 54, we test the predictions concerning adoption by the foster parents.

Table 53 shows that 19 children were discharged to parents or relatives during the year following the return of the schedule being tested. Another 20 children were returned home on trial discharge. Three-fourths of the relatively small group of children who were said to have a *strong possibility* of returning to their families did indeed experience such a move; this was true of one-fourth of the children rated as having a *moderate possibility* of such a return. Little more than 11 percent of the children rated as having a *slight possibility* of such a discharge were returned home.

We observe that 266 children— or 72 percent of the sample—were rated as having *no possibility* of return home. Only four percent of these children were returned to their families while 25 of them (9.3 percent) were adopted by their foster families.

The ratings of the social workers about the chances for discharge to family during the year following the filling out of the forms must be seen as predictions that are fairly strong.

In Table 54, the ratings of the social workers about the possibility of adoption by the foster parents within the coming year is tested by the data covering the events that took place. Twenty-six children were adopted by their foster parents and for 22 of them, the workers rated the chance of such an adoption as being a *strong possibility*. Of concern is the fact that 102 children (80.9 percent) who were rated in similar fashion did not in fact get adopted by their foster parents. Evidently, the process of such adoption is slower in most cases than the worker predicted.

Comments

The Index of the Child's Relationship to the Natural Family appears to be potentially useful in developing perspectives on what lies ahead for children included in any agency's caseload. The children who fall on the shoulders of the curve, scoring very high or very low on the index, are apt to experience a change in status in a relatively immediate period. Those who appear closely identified with their families—and in contact with them—are apt to rejoin their parents. Those who seem totally devoid of a relationship with their families are more apt to have their adoptions finalized. From a planning point of view, there is great advantage in being able to anticipate the flow of children toward more permanent living arrangements.

TABLE 53

SOCIAL WORKERS' PREDICTIONS OF POSSIBILITY OF RETURN OF CHILDREN DURING COMING YEAR AND DISCHARGE STATUS OF CHILDREN ONE YEAR LATER[a]
(N = 372)

Discharge Status	POSSIBILITY OF RETURN TO PARENTS							
	Strong Possibility		Moderate Possibility		Slight Possibility		No Possibility		Not Applicable	
	No.	%	No.	%	No.	%	No.	%	No.	%
Discharged to parents or relatives	12	50.0	3	18.8	1	1.9	3	1.1	--	--
Trial discharge to parents	6	25.0	1	6.3	5	9.6	8	3.0	--	--
Adoption by foster family	--	--	--	--	--	--	25	9.3	1	7.1
Adoption by other	--	--	--	--	--	--	--	--	--	--
Other destination	--	--	--	--	--	--	--	--	--	--
Still in care	6	25.0	12	74.9	46	88.5	230	86.6	13	92.9
TOTAL	24	100.0	16	100.0	52	100.0	266	100.0	14	100.0

[a]Discharge Status is provided by CWIS data file dated December 31, 1978. Ten cases are omitted because children were already discharged when questionnaires were returned in 1977. Four cases are omitted of children leaving care on suspended payment.

TABLE 54

SOCIAL WORKERS' PREDICTIONS OF POSSIBILITY OF ADOPTION OF CHILDREN BY FOSTER PARENTS DURING COMING YEAR AND DISCHARGE STATUS OF CHILDREN ONE YEAR LATER[a]

(N = 372)

| Discharge Status | POSSIBILITY OF ADOPTION BY FOSTER PARENTS ||||||||||
| | Strong Possibility || Moderate Possibility || Slight Possibility || No Possibility || Not Applicable ||
	No.	%	No.	%	No.	%	No.	%	No.	%
Discharged to parents or relatives	--	--	--	--	1	1.9	18	12.4	--	--
Trial discharge to parents	2	1.6	--	--	2	3.7	15	10.3	1	4.8
Adoption by foster family	22	17.5	1	3.8	--	--	1	0.7	2	9.5
Adoption by other	--	--	--	--	--	--	--	--	--	--
Other destination	--	--	--	--	--	--	--	--	--	--
Still in care	102	80.9	25	96.2	51	94.4	111	76.6	18	85.7
TOTAL	126	100.0	26	100.0	54	100.0	145	100.0	21	100.0

[a]Discharge Status is provided by CWIS data file dated December 31, 1978. Ten cases are omitted because children were already discharged when questionnaires were returned in 1977. Four cases are omitted of children leaving care on suspended payment.

11 Summary of Findings and Implications

Introduction

Our trial run of the data module has provided a rich amount of information about the relationship of children living in foster family care with their own natural families and with their foster families. These relationships are the key elements in "permanency planning" and any management information system dealing with foster children cannot be considered *comprehensive* in its coverage unless it has descriptive capability in these areas. Basic questions that are addressed by the module include the following:

- How long has the child been in the foster home? Does he regard the foster family as his *own* family?
- Does the child identify with his natural family? When did he last see his parents? How often does he see his parents in the current period?
- What are the agency's discharge plans for the child? What is likely to happen in the coming year: return to parents? Adoption by his foster parents? Adoption by persons other than his foster parents? Staying in the foster home with his status unchanged? What is likely to happen within one to two years? Three to five years?
- Have the foster parents been approached to consider adoption of the child? When did this take place? What was the nature of their reaction?
- How does the social worker evaluate the foster home with regard to its suitability as an adoptive home for the child? What is the strength of their affection, rapport and understanding of the child? What qualities do they as parents show in the areas of home maintenance, health supervision, discipline, and so forth?

These rather profound questions about the child and his foster family have to be filtered through a prior understanding of the child's relationship to his own natural family. There are questions that social workers must address in any foster family care situation in which the issue of providing the child with a permanent living arrangement requires resolution. The children in this study had been in foster care for an average period that was close to six years. The issue of permanency was clearly pertinent to the case planning for almost every child.

The descriptive tasks we have addressed here pose considerable challenge because of the subtle human processes that need to be captured. It is one thing to ask a social worker to provide information about a child's background characteristics, the reasons he is in care, the frequency with which he sees his parents, and the nature of service contacts with his parents. It is a more demanding task to ask social workers to rate the quality of interaction between a child and his foster parents, his identity with his own parents and the degree of conflict he might have about mixed loyalties to both sets of parents.

We are faced with the following key questions: How much of what is regarded as essential information for case planning for children in foster care can be computerized? That is, can the information be put into categorical form? Can it be collected routinely? Does it yield useful perspectives for program managers, systems planners and legislators? At another level, the question arises: To what extent can we replace long narratives in case records now routinely the practice in all agencies with categorical information that lends itself to computerization? The answers to these questions may emerge from an examination of the data gathering experience we report here.

Key Findings

Many different kinds of information have been reported here that appear highly useful and not normally available. The following domains are included:

The Children. Since the children represent a random sample drawn from the CWIS files of each of 33 agencies of children who have been in their foster homes for at least a year, they can be regarded as representative of a much larger group of children in the foster care system. Of interest are the following kinds of information:

- The children averaged about 9.1 years of age at the time of the survey and had been in care for an average of 5.7 years and had been at the particular agency for an average of 5.1 years.
- Over half of the children were black and about 30 percent were Hispanic.
- Less than half the children had seen either of

their parents over the past six months.
- About 64 percent of the children were in their first placement and 24 percent were in their second placement.
- About half the children were identified as having discharge plans calling for their adoption while about a fourth were slated to be returned to their parents or relatives. One child in ten was identified as likely to be discharged to his own responsibility.
- Two-thirds of the children had one or more siblings in care and almost three out of four such children had siblings in the same foster family home. In 70 percent of the cases, the agency had the goal of keeping the siblings together.

The Foster Families:

- The foster families had been with the agencies for an average of 6.0 years and cared for an average of 4.7 foster children.
- The families were spread throughout the boroughs of the Bronx, Brooklyn and Queens and counties outside of New York City.
- Almost three-fourths of the families owned their own homes while 13 percent rented apartments in public housing projects.
- The foster parents were, on the average, in their late 40's, largely of high school education and of modest incomes. The foster fathers tended to be concentrated in unskilled, operative and crafts jobs.

Prospects for Permanency. About eight out of ten of the foster families had been approached by the agency to consider adoption of the child. This points to the centrality of the foster families in the agency's considerations relative to planning for permanency. This coincides with an earlier published report of the writer analyzing the discharge of children from foster care in New York City, which examined the status of all children in care:

> The data . . . clearly reflect the saliency of natural parents as a major resource for their children even when they have been in care for extended periods. Foster parents also loom fairly large, but only after the children have been in care for at least five years; they account for the highest proportion of discharges for children who depart from care after 6 to 10 years of placement.[18]

About three out of every four foster parents approached to consider adoption were reported to react positively. About one in four families were said to show a negative reaction, often related to concern about the child's physical or emotional development or his way of relating to the family. Such cases obviously reflect case planning dilemmas since many of the children had been with the foster families for a number of years and would find a move to a new home traumatic.

Some of the most significant information to come out of the use of the data module relates to the widespread loss of contact between the foster children and their natural families and the simultaneous deep involvement of the children with their foster families. Only about 11 percent of the subjects were seen by their social workers as exhibiting a deep sense of attachment to their mothers and another 20 percent were rated as showing close or some attachment. Forty percent of the children were said to be totally devoid of a relationship with their mothers and another 16 percent revealed a minimum attachment. The ratings describing the relationship of the children to their natural fathers showed an even greater tendency for the children to show no sense of identification with the parent.

The situation of the children with respect to their parents is sobering and is no doubt related to the erosion that has taken place after the many years of separation experienced by a large proportion of the children. We must bear in mind that only 37 percent of the children had seen their mothers during the past year while 33 percent had not seen their mothers in at least two years and 15 percent had never seen their mothers or the mothers were totally out of the picture.

The picture that emerges from an analysis of the social workers' ratings of the relationship of the children to their foster parents provides a counterbalance to the grim picture provided about the natural families. It would appear that many of the children have compensated for their loss of family and many years of separation through taking on the foster family as an *own* family. Almost 53 percent of the children were rated as being deeply integrated within their foster families and 26 percent were rated as quite strongly identified. Many of the ratings of the degree of acceptance of the child by the foster parents were concentrated on the most positive pole of the scale. Mutual displays of affection between the child and his foster family were also frequently reported.

The creation of three composite indexes on the basis of a factor analysis of the items included in the module being tested permits a more parsimonious integration of the information made available. Each of these indexes has been shown to have a fairly high level of internal reliability. We also observe that a measure of predictive validity has been established for the Index of the Child's Relationship to the Natural Family. This index appears quite pivotal to our understanding of why some children returned to their own families in the course of a year while others had their adoption status finalized. In any systematic program to advance the goal of permanency for foster children, an index of this kind would appear to be highly useful in identifying children who should be prime candidates for discharge.

The indexes describing the foster parents were not strongly predictive of changes in the status of the children. Part of the explanation for this may reside in the overwhelmingly positive views of the foster parents reflected in the social workers' ratings. The children had been in care with these families for considerable periods, on the average. It is anticipated that more differentiation in index scores will be shown when ratings are made for groups of children who have been in care for shorter periods.

The module employed in this trial run appears to hold promise for enriching the data base for systems like CWIS. Further work will need to be done in the context of ongoing practice situations to further test the reliability and validity of the measures. Equally important, it will be necessary to test the tolerance of social workers to provide such information routinely.

We close on a final note: this effort to test a data module describing a child's relationship to his natural family and his foster family has depended upon a single informant: his social worker. Future research effort should be extended to the foster children themselves to determine how they perceive their life situations and what they want for themselves in the way of ongoing relationships.[19]

Notes

1. See: David Fanshel and John Grundy, "Quarterly Report Series for New York City for September 30, 1978" (New York: Child Welfare Information Services).

2. It has recently been shown that almost 6,000 children currently in care in New York City entered the system under one year of age and show a mean of 7.4 years in care. See: David Fanshel, "Pre-Schoolers Entering Foster Care in New York City: The Need to Stress Plans for Permanency," *Child Welfare*, LVII: 2 (February 1979), pp. 67-87.

3. David Fanshel and Eugene B. Shinn, *Children in Foster Care: A Longitudinal Investigation* (New York: Columbia University Press, 1978), pp. 85-111, see also: David Fanshel, "Parental Visiting of Foster Children," *Social Work Research and Abstracts*, 13: 3 (Fall 1977), pp. 2-10.

4. The Child Care Review Service (CCRS) was established within the New York State Department of Social Services by an act of the State Legislature in 1976. The system was implemented in 1977, utilizing the design and management expertise acquired by CWIS. See: *Child Care Review Service: Report to the Legislature, May 1977* (Albany, New York: New York State Department of Social Services).

5. Three additional agencies had initially agreed to participate in the study but did not follow through with completed forms. One of these went out of existence while another withdrew from the study because of reservations about the ethics of supplying information about foster families for computerized information systems. The third agency did not fulfill its agreement, with the explanation that a recent increase in work pressures had altered its views about participation.

6. The reader is referred to the writer's earlier work on foster parents: David Fanshel, *Foster Parenthood: A Role Analysis* (Minneapolis: University of Minnesota Press, 1966); and David Fanshel and John Grundy, *Foster Parenthood: A Replication and Extension of Prior Studies* (New York: Columbia University School of Social Work, 1971; mimeographed). See also the material on foster parents in a recent review of the research literature on foster care by Alfred Kadushin in *Social Service Research: Reviews of Studies*, ed. by Henry S. Maas (Washington, D.C.: National Association of Social Workers, 1978), pp. 120-24.

7. Nine children are not included in these data; they could not be located in the CWIS files of December 31, 1977.

8. David Fanshel, "Parental Visiting of Children in Foster Care: Key to Discharge?" *Social Service Review*, 49 (December 1975), pp. 493-514; Fanshel, "Parental Visiting of Foster Children," *op. cit.*

9. David Fanshel, "Children Discharged From Foster Care in New York City: Where to—When—At What Age?" *Child Welfare*, LVII: 8 (September-October 1978), pp. 467-483.

10. Alfred L. Baldwin, Joan Kalhorn and Fay Huffman Breese, "The Appraisal of Parent Behavior," *Psychological Monographs*, 64:4, Whole No. 299 (Washington, D.C.: American Psychological Association, 1949).

11. David Fanshel, *Far From the Reservation* (Metuchen, N.J.: Scarecrow Press, 1972), pp. 365-366.

12. The negative signs in Table 40 for Factor III items have no substantive meaning and simply reflect the direction of items in the codes created by the investigator.

13. In the matching of our computerized research file of 386 cases with the same cases in the CWIS file of December 31, 1978, 10 cases were not included because the children had been discharged somewhat earlier than the year covered. Four additional cases were excluded because the matching program failed to locate the children in the CWIS data file.

14. See: Fanshel, "Children Discharged From Foster Care in New York City," *op. cit.*

15. Forty-seven cases excluded where discharge plan was other than discharge to parents or relatives, or adoption.

16. No table presented.

17. See: Fanshel, "Pre-Schoolers Entering Foster Care in New York City," *op. cit.*

18. See: Fanshel, "Children Discharged From Foster Care in New York City," *op. cit.*, p. 475.

19. Current research by Dr. Trudy Festinger involving interviews with former foster children should provide useful information about how the system of foster care is perceived by those who directly experienced it.

Appendix

APPENDIX A

INFORMATION ABOUT CASEWORKERS WHO PROVIDED INFORMATION FOR THE STUDY

A. <u>Highest Professional Degree:</u>

	No.	Percent
Some college	11	2.9
BSW	14	3.6
Other Bachelor's degree	135	35.2
MSW	177	46.0
Other Master's degree	44	11.5
Doctorate	3	0.8
TOTAL	384	100.0

B. <u>Years with Agency:</u>   Mean = 3.58 years
   S.D. = 3.40

C. <u>Number of Children in Caseload:</u>   Mean = 21.74
   S.D. = 8.54

D. <u>Number of Families in Caseload:</u>   Mean = 12.15
   S.D. = 4.62

E. <u>Respondents' Knowledge of the Foster Child and the Foster Parents</u>[a]

	Foster Child	Foster Mother	Foster Father
	(Percentaged)		
Very well	45.9	48.0	24.7
Fairly well	39.6	41.7	33.8
Slightly	11.6	7.4	18.8
Hardly at all	2.1	2.1	8.8
Not at all	0.8	0.5	5.4
Other (deceased, etc.)	--	0.3	8.5
Percent	100.0	100.0	100.0
Total	(379)[b]	(379)[b]	(352)[c]

[a] The caseworkers were asked: "How well do you feel you know the child? The foster parent(s)?"

[b] Excludes 7 cases where no ratings were made.

[c] Excludes 34 cases where no ratings were made.

APPENDIX B

REPORTS OF SOCIAL WORKERS ABOUT DIFFICULTY IN PROVIDING REQUESTED DATA ACCORDING TO AGE OF CHILD[a]

Degree of Difficulty	1 to 5 Years	6 to 9 Years	10 to 13 Years	Total
	(Percentaged)			
Very difficult	2.6	3.0	1.7	2.4
Somewhat difficult	24.7	25.8	23.3	24.4
Quite easy	58.4	59.1	66.3	62.2
Very Easy	14.3	12.1	8.7	11.0
Percent Total	100.0 (77)	100.0 (132)	100.0 (172)	100.0 (381)[b]

[a] The caseworkers were asked: "How difficult was it for you to fill out this form?"

[b] Excludes 5 cases where no ratings were made.

The Questionnaire

We wish to acknowledge that a number of scales used in our questionnaire derive from the following source:

Alfred L. Baldwin, Joan Kalhorn, and Fay Huffman Breese, "The Appraisal of Parent Behavior," *Psychological Monographs, General and Applied*, Vol., 63, No. 299 (1949). (Published by the American Psychological Association.)

COLUMBIA UNIVERSITY SCHOOL OF SOCIAL WORK

Research and Demonstration Center
622 West 113 Street • New York, N.Y. 10025

EXPANDED DATA BASE FOR CHILD WELFARE

To Child Welfare Social Worker:

    The New York State Department of Social Services has granted funds to Columbia University to conduct research designed to expand the data base of Child Welfare Information Services (CWIS). Your agency has agreed to participate in this research on a limited sample of the agency's children. Other agencies are also participating in this effort. The results of this work will make it possible to determine what kind of information can expeditiously be gathered to add to our knowledge about children in foster care. The aim of this effort is to improve service to children.

    Your cooperation in filling out the enclosed form will facilitate our study greatly. For some of the items, it may be necessary to make an estimate based upon your most informed judgment. Please try to answer every item. You will later be contacted for your advice about the content of items and their wording. If you have any doubt about a reply, place a question mark next to the item.

    The material you provide will be treated in the strictest confidence. Please return the form to _____ _____ who has been designated as your agency's contact person with our project.

Thank you very much for your help in this matter.

                                                       Sincerely yours,

                                                       David Fanshel, D.S.W.
                                                       Director
                                                       Research and Demonstration Center

CONFIDENTIAL

COLUMBIA UNIVERSITY SCHOOL OF SOCIAL WORK
Research and Demonstration Center
622 West 113 Street
New York, New York 10025

Trial Form on the Child's Current Foster Home Placement

     This is a pre-test version of an information form about children placed in foster family homes who have been in the same home for at least one year. The form is designed to secure information about the nature of the child's relationship with the foster family. There is particular interest in obtaining the agency's perspective about the potential use of the foster family home as a permanent placement for the child. The form is being tested for Child Welfare Information Services (CWIS). Your cooperation in filling out the form will make it possible to learn more about the kind of information that needs to be gathered about children in foster care in order to improve the delivery of service.

     Your care in filling out the form will be appreciated. The data will be kept confidential and a report will be made to your agency about the findings.

ID Name_____

SSC Number_____
             1-9/

Worker Code_____

Agency_____
         12-14/

(Card): 10-11/(08)   (MP 3)

> BACKGROUND INFORMATION: We would first like to obtain information about the child and the foster family.

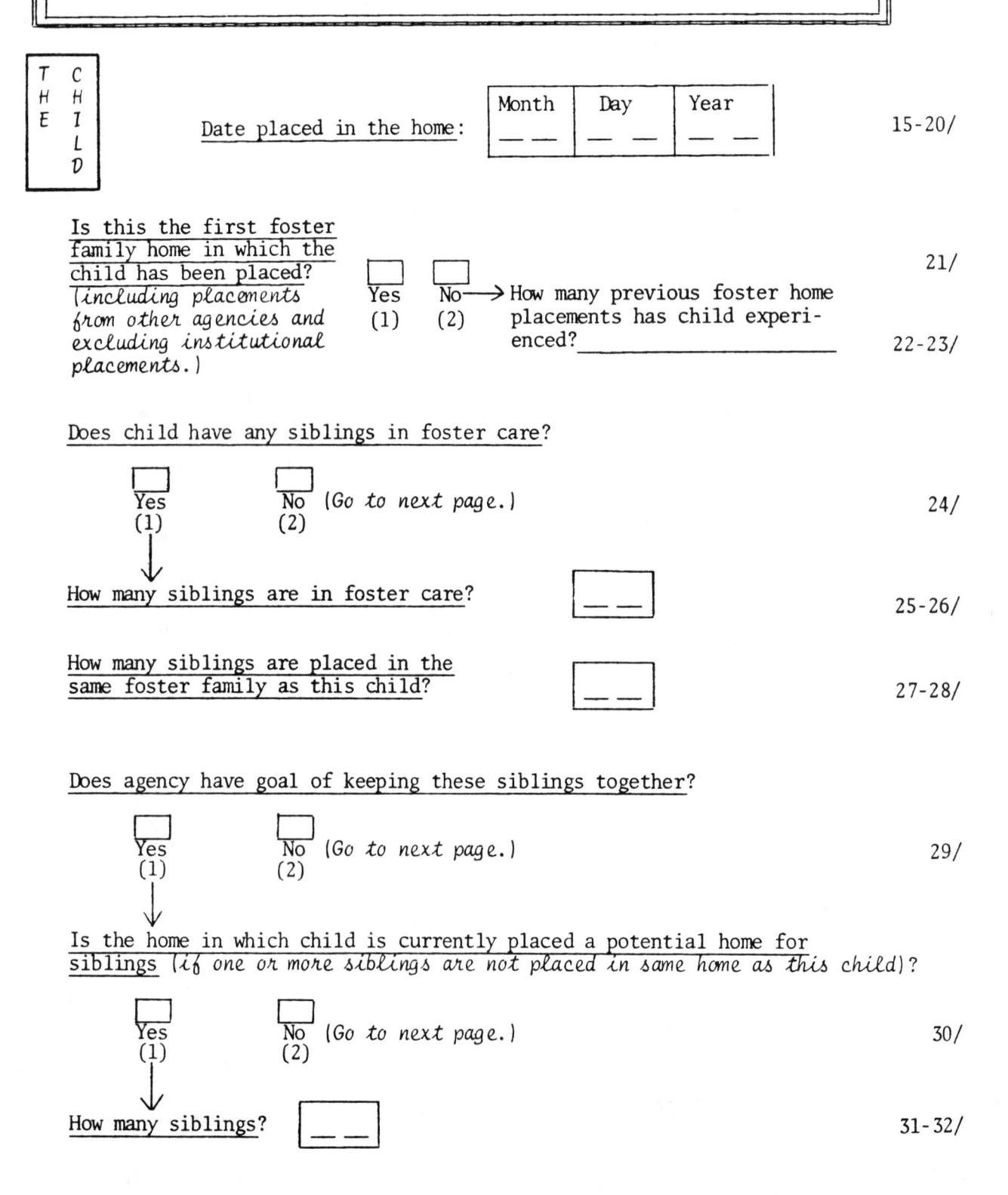

THE CHILD

Date placed in the home: | Month | Day | Year | 15-20/

Is this the first foster family home in which the child has been placed? *(including placements from other agencies and excluding institutional placements.)*

☐ Yes (1) ☐ No (2) → How many previous foster home placements has child experienced? _____

21/

22-23/

Does child have any siblings in foster care?

☐ Yes (1)   ☐ No (2) *(Go to next page.)*

24/

↓

How many siblings are in foster care? ☐☐   25-26/

How many siblings are placed in the same foster family as this child? ☐☐   27-28/

Does agency have goal of keeping these siblings together?

☐ Yes (1)   ☐ No (2) *(Go to next page.)*

29/

↓

Is the home in which child is currently placed a potential home for siblings *(if one or more siblings are not placed in same home as this child)*?

☐ Yes (1)   ☐ No (2) *(Go to next page.)*

30/

↓

How many siblings? ☐☐   31-32/

INITIAL OF LAST NAME _____ Wife _____
                                    (first name)

                                Husband _____
                                         (first name)

[THE FOSTER FAMILY]

Number of years with agency: [__ __]   33-34/

Estimated total number of
children placed with family by agency: [__ __]   35-36/

Housing of Foster Family: 37/   Approximate Monthly Income of   40/
                                      Foster Family (excluding foster
  ☐ Own private home   care payments):
  1
  ☐ Rent private home   ☐ $500 or less
  2   1
  ☐ Own cooperative apartment   ☐ $500 or over - less than $700
  3   2
  ☐ Rent apartment, public   ☐ $700 or over - less than $900
  4 housing project   3
                                        ☐ $900 or over - less than
  ☐ Rent apartment, private   4 $1,100
  5
  ☐ Other (Specify) _____   ☐ $1,100 or over - less than
  6   5 $1,300
    _____
                                        ☐ $1,300 or over - less than
                                        6 $1,500

                                        ☐ $1,500 or more
                                        7
Number of rooms   ☐ Other (Specify) _____
in home: [__ __] 38-39/   8
                                          _____

                                        ☐ Unknown
                                        9

Borough or town/village family lives in _____   41/

Postal zip code _____   42-46/

315

FOSTER MOTHER

Age: ☐☐ 47-48/

Race/Ethnic Background: 49/
- ☐₁ White
- ☐₂ Black
- ☐₃ Hispanic (*Specify*)_____
- ☐₄ Other (*Specify*)_____

Religion: 50/
- ☐₁ Protestant
- ☐₂ Catholic
- ☐₃ Jewish
- ☐₄ Other

Education Completed: 51/
- ☐₁ Less than 5 years grammar school
- ☐₂ 5-8 years grammar school
- ☐₃ Some high school (or AA degree)
- ☐₄ Graduated high school or post-high school certificate
- ☐₅ Some college
- ☐₆ Graduated college
- ☐₇ Graduate or professional school
- ☐₈ Other (*Specify*)_____
- ☐₉ Unknown

Occupation:_____ 52/

FOSTER FATHER

Age: ☐☐ 53-54/

Race/Ethnic Background: 55/
- ☐₁ White
- ☐₂ Black
- ☐₃ Hispanic (*Specify*)_____
- ☐₄ Other (*Specify*)_____

Religion: 56/
- ☐₁ Protestant
- ☐₂ Catholic
- ☐₃ Jewish
- ☐₄ Other

Education Completed: 57/
- ☐₁ Less than 5 years grammar school
- ☐₂ 5-8 years grammar school
- ☐₃ Some high school (or AA degree)
- ☐₄ Graduated high school or post-high school certificate
- ☐₅ Some college
- ☐₆ Graduated college
- ☐₇ Graduate or professional school
- ☐₈ Other (*Specify*)_____
- ☐₉ Unknown

Occupation:_____ 58/

Foster Family Members

Please list below the first names of each household member NOW living at home beginning with the head of the family and check boxes that apply. *(Include child covered by this form.)*

First Names of Household Members	Relationship to Family Head	Sex	Foster Child	Sibling of Child Covered by This Form	Age at Last Birthday
1. _____	Foster Father (1) 59/	[X] M (1) [ ] F (2) 60/		[ ] (1) 61/	___ years old 62-63/
2. _____	Foster Mother (2) 64/	[ ] M (1) [X] F (2) 65/		[ ] (1) 66/	___ years old 67-68/
3. _____ (Child covered by this form)	____ 69/	[ ] M (1) [ ] F (2) 70/	[X] (1) 71/		___ years old 72-73/
4. _____	____ 74/	[ ] M (1) [ ] F (2) 75/	[ ] (1) 76/	[ ] (1) 77/	___ years old 78-79/
5. _____	____ 12/	[ ] M (1) [ ] F (2) 13/	[ ] (1) 14/	[ ] (1) 15/	___ years old 16-17
6. _____	____ 18/	[ ] M (1) [ ] F (2) 19/	[ ] (1) 20/	[ ] (1) 21/	___ years old 22-23/
7. _____	____ 24/	[ ] M (1) [ ] F (2) 25/	[ ] (1) 26/	[ ] (1) 27/	___ years old 28-29/
8. _____	____ 30/	[ ] M (1) [ ] F (2) 31/	[ ] (1) 32/	[ ] (1) 33/	___ years old 34-35/
9. _____	____ 36/	[ ] M (1) [ ] F (2) 37/	[ ] (1) 38/	[ ] (1) 39/	___ years old 40-41/
10. _____	____ 42/	[ ] M (1) [ ] F (2) 43/	[ ] (1) 44/	[ ] (1) 45/	___ years old 46-47/
11. _____	____ 48/	[ ] M (1) [ ] F (2) 49/	[ ] (1) 50/	[ ] (1) 51/	___ years old 52-53/
12. _____	____ 54/	[ ] M (1) [ ] F (2) 55/	[ ] (1) 56/	[ ] (1) 57/	___ years old 58-59/

(Card): 10-11/(09)

Considering what is known about this case, rate the possibilities of the following events taking place within the coming year, within one to two years, and within three to five years. Take into account your own knowledge of the case and possible future actions of the court. This is a subjective judgment on your part. (Respond for each time period.)

Within the Coming Year	Within One to Two Years	Within Three to Five Years	
60/ □1 □2 □3 □4	61/ □1 □2 □3 □4	62/ □1 □2 □3 □4	**That child will return to own parent(s)** Strong possibility Moderate possibility Slight possibility No possibility
63/ □1 □2 □3 □4	64/ □1 □2 □3 □4	65/ □1 □2 □3 □4	**That child will be placed with relatives** Strong possibility Moderate possibility Slight possibility No possibility
66/ □1 □2 □3 □4	67/ □1 □2 □3 □4	68/ □1 □2 □3 □4	**That child will remain in present foster family home** Strong possibility Moderate possibility Slight possibility No possibility

Continued

Considering what is known about this case, rate the possibilities of the following events taking place within the coming year, within one to two years, and within three to five years. Take into account your own knowledge of the case and possible future actions of the court. This is a subjective judgment on your part. (Respond for each time period.) Cont'd.

Within the Coming Year	Within One to Two Years	Within Three to Five Years	
			That child will be transferred to another home for adoption
69/	70/	71/	
☐ 1	☐ 1	☐ 1	Strong possibility
☐ 2	☐ 2	☐ 2	Moderate possibility
☐ 3	☐ 3	☐ 3	Slight possibility
☐ 4	☐ 4	☐ 4	No possibility
			That child will be adopted by current foster family
72/	73/	74/	
☐ 1	☐ 1	☐ 1	Strong possibility
☐ 2	☐ 2	☐ 2	Moderate possibility
☐ 3	☐ 3	☐ 3	Slight possibility
☐ 4	☐ 4	☐ 4	No possibility
			Other event involving status change (Specify) _____
75/	76/	77/	
☐ 1	☐ 1	☐ 1	Strong possibility
☐ 2	☐ 2	☐ 2	Moderate possibility
☐ 3	☐ 3	☐ 3	Slight possibility
☐ 4	☐ 4	☐ 4	No possibility

Has foster family ever been approached by the agency to consider adoption of the child?

☐ Yes   ☐ No   12/
 1   2

(If "No," respond to the following question:)

(If "Yes," respond to the following question:)

Do any of the following reasons account for foster parents not having been approached? (Check all that apply.)

☐ Adoption not identi-   14/
1   fied as a suitable plan for child

☐ Foster parents are   15/
1   not deemed suitable as adoptive parents to this child

☐ Other (Specify)_____   16/
1
_____
_____

How long ago were the foster parents approached?   13/

☐ Within past 6 months
 1
☐ Within past 7 to 12 months
 2
☐ Over one year ago but less than two
 3
☐ Two years ago or over
 4

What was their reaction?   17/

☐ Very positive
 1
☐ Somewhat positive
 2
☐ Somewhat against
 3
☐ Very against
 4
☐ Other (Specify)_____
 5
_____
_____

Is it contemplated that adoption will be arranged on a subsidized basis?   18/

☐ Yes
 1
☐ No
 2
☐ Other
 3

(Card): 10-11/(10)

About how often does child see his own mother, father, sibling(s) or other relatives? (*For siblings and relatives, report on maximum visiting of any individual. Include step-parent with "relatives."*)

Mother 19/	Father 20/	Siblings Outside Foster Home 21/	Relatives 22/	
☐ 1	☐ 1	☐ 1	☐ 1	At least once a month
☐ 2	☐ 2	☐ 2	☐ 2	At least once in 3 months
☐ 3	☐ 3	☐ 3	☐ 3	About once in 6 months
☐ 4	☐ 4	☐ 4	☐ 4	About once a year
☐ 5	☐ 5	☐ 5	☐ 5	Occasional, but less than once a year
☐ 6	☐ 6	☐ 6	☐ 6	Never
☐ 7	☐ 7	☐ 7	☐ 7	Other
☐ 8	☐ 8	☐ 8	☐ 8	Not applicable
☐ 9				Mother placed with child

When was the last time child saw his mother, father, siblings or other relatives? (*For siblings and relatives, report on maximum visiting of any individual. Include step-parent with "relatives."*)

Mother 23/	Father 24/	Siblings Outside Foster Home 25/	Relatives 26/	
☐ 1	☐ 1	☐ 1	☐ 1	Less than 3 months
☐ 2	☐ 2	☐ 2	☐ 2	3 months but less than 6 months
☐ 3	☐ 3	☐ 3	☐ 3	6 months but less than 1 year
☐ 4	☐ 4	☐ 4	☐ 4	1 year but less than 2 years
☐ 5	☐ 5	☐ 5	☐ 5	2 years but less than 5 years
☐ 6	☐ 6	☐ 6	☐ 6	5 years or over
☐ 7	☐ 7	☐ 7	☐ 7	Other (*Specify*) _____
☐ 8	☐ 8	☐ 8	☐ 8	Not applicable
☐ 9				Mother placed with child

Indicate whether the following characteristics of the foster parents constitute a positive factor or a negative factor in evaluating the home as a potential permanent placement for the child. If situation varies over time, give your judgment about the most typical situation that prevails. (Check appropriate category for each item.)

	Positive Factor (++)	+	Neutral 0	-	Negative Factor (--)	Not Applicable	Unknown
	(1)	(2)	(3)	(4)	(5)	(6)	(7)
Physical aspect of the home: adequacy of home maintenance and quality of care	++ ☐	+ ☐	0 ☐	- ☐	-- ☐	NA ☐	UK ☐	27/
Health care and health supervision offered children	++ ☐	+ ☐	0 ☐	- ☐	-- ☐	NA ☐	UK ☐	28/
Foster family's capacity to intellectually stimulate children	++ ☐	+ ☐	0 ☐	- ☐	-- ☐	NA ☐	UK ☐	29/
Extent of marital harmony prevailing between foster mother and foster father	++ ☐	+ ☐	0 ☐	- ☐	-- ☐	NA ☐	UK ☐	30/
Adequacy of the foster family's income	++ ☐	+ ☐	0 ☐	- ☐	-- ☐	NA ☐	UK ☐	31/
Age of the foster parents	++ ☐	+ ☐	0 ☐	- ☐	-- ☐	NA ☐	UK ☐	32/
Stability of personality of the foster mother	++ ☐	+ ☐	0 ☐	- ☐	-- ☐	NA ☐	UK ☐	33/
Stability of personality of the foster father	++ ☐	+ ☐	0 ☐	- ☐	-- ☐	NA ☐	UK ☐	34/
Evidence of past performance by the foster parents with own, foster or adopted children	++ ☐	+ ☐	0 ☐	- ☐	-- ☐	NA ☐	UK ☐	35/
Quality of discipline of children maintained by foster parents	++ ☐	+ ☐	0 ☐	- ☐	-- ☐	NA ☐	UK ☐	36/

> For the scales that follow, indicate which of the categories set forth best describe the child's placement situation, his/her orientation to foster care, and the qualities shown by the foster parents.

Child's relationship to own (natural) family. (Rate the sense of family shown by the child, a feeling of belongingness to each of his parents and family as a whole. Does he/she manifest a consciousness of his parents and his family as a whole with an accompanying sense of identification with them? Or does he/she feel bereft of family--esentially without blood ties?)

	Natural Mother 38/	Natural Father 39/	Natural Family as Whole 40/	
HIGH ATTACHMENT ↑	☐ 1	☐ 1	☐ 1	Deeply conscious of belonging to own parents and/or family, closely identified with blood ties and feels basic attachment. Sense of own roots lies in this relationship.
	☐ 2	☐ 2	☐ 2	Has clearly evidenced attachments to this relationship. Often shows sense of close identification and indications that the relationship has important meaning. Yet there is an evidence of child feeling apartness and occasionally distancing self from the relationship.
	☐ 3	☐ 3	☐ 3	Gives evidence that the relationship has some meaning. Child occasionally gives sign that some elements of identification exist. But there are also strong pulls away from this relationship.
	☐ 4	☐ 4	☐ 4	Dominant quality evidenced by child indicates minimum sense of attachment. Only occasionally and fleetingly is there sign that parent(s) or family has meaning for him/her and ties are valued. Distancing self from the relationship(s) has become major method of coping with life stimulation.
↓ LITTLE OR NO ATTACHMENT	☐ 5	☐ 5	☐ 5	Feels totally devoid of a relationship with the natural parent and/or family. On a manifest level, they are totally out of consciousness. Shows no sense of identification or rootedness in this relationship.
	☐ 6	☐ 6	☐ 6	Other (*Please describe*) _____

Conflicting feelings over family attachments (Rate the degree to which the   41/
child is caught up in emotional pulls between own (natural) family and
foster family. Is he/she at ease with the present allocation of roles of
own family and foster family? Is there evidence of greater pull to one or
the other families to which he/she belongs?)

MINIMUM STRESS ☐ 1   Is essentially at peace with current arrangements; exhibits no distress or concern about balance of relationships between own family and foster family.

☐ 2   Tends to be accepting about current arrangements but occasionally manifests some anxiety about where he/she stands vis-a-vis own parents and/or foster parents.

☐ 3   Has made some adjustment to status situation; not particularly upset about where he/she stands but has made only marginal peace with current arrangements.

☐ 4   Shows noticeable upset about status but has accommodated self to the situation somewhat.

MAXIMUM STRESS ☐ 5   Is quite upset about current arrangements; keenly aware of lack of resolution of status.

☐ 6   Other (*Please specify*)_____
_____
_____

Integration of Child in Foster Home (Rate the degree to which the child 42/
feels he belongs in the foster home and has sunk his roots with the foster
family. Is he strongly embedded in the home having   strong emotional ties
with the foster parents?)

STRONG EMBED- MENT IN FOSTER HOME	☐ 1	Deeply integrated within foster family. Experiences the foster parents as <u>own</u> family and expects to remain with them; child's <u>removal</u> from home would be extremely upsetting to him/her.
↑	☐ 2	Child is quite strongly identified with foster family although there is some tendency to hold back slightly from total involvement; removal from home would be experienced as quite painful wrench.
	☐ 3	Child feels fairly much at ease in the home but is quite conscious that this is not own family. Holds self somewhat aloof and there is reserve in showing loyalty to family. Removal would create some problems but recovery would be experienced fairly soon.
↓	☐ 4	Child is fairly uncomfortable in home and holds himself quite aloof. Times when he joins in with family activities are relatively rare. Removal from home would be fairly easy to take.
WEAK EMBED- MENT IN FOSTER HOME	☐ 5	Child is not integrated within foster family. Essentially feels a stranger; removal from home would not evoke emotional reaction.
	☐ 6	Other (*Please specify*)_____

Affectionateness of Foster Parents Towards Child (Rate the foster parent's expression of affection to the child personally. Does the foster parent manifest a warm, personal affection to the child or a matter-of-fact unemotional attitude, or definite antagonism?) (Select one of the following categories which best reflects the overall situation.)

	Foster Mother 43/	Foster Father 44/	
MOST AFFECTIONATE	☐ 1	☐ 1	Warm, loving, expressive, highly demonstrative.
	☐ 2	☐ 2	Quiet warmth, fondness, positively oriented.
	☐ 3	☐ 3	Objective, neutral, somewhat inhibited, matter-of-fact.
	☐ 4	☐ 4	Somewhat cool, aloof, distant.
LEAST AFFECTIONATE	☐ 5	☐ 5	Avoiding, annoyed, irritated, bothered.
	☐ 6	☐ 6	Hostile, antagonistic, disliking, blaming, icy.
	☐ 7	☐ 7	Other (Please describe) _____

Affectionateness of Child Towards Foster Parents (Rate the child's expression of affection to the foster parent personally. Does the child manifest a warm, personal affection to the foster parent or a matter-of-fact unemotional attitude, or definite antagonism?) (Select one of the following categories which best reflects the overall situation.)

	Foster Mother 45/	Foster Father 46/	
MOST AFFECTIONATE	☐ 1	☐ 1	Warm, loving, expressive, highly demonstrative.
	☐ 2	☐ 2	Quiet warmth, fondness, positively oriented.
	☐ 3	☐ 3	Objective, neutral, somewhat inhibited, matter-of-fact.
	☐ 4	☐ 4	Somewhat cool, aloof, distant.
LEAST AFFECTIONATE	☐ 5	☐ 5	Avoiding, annoyed, irritated, bothered.
	☐ 6	☐ 6	Hostile, antagonistic, disliking, blaming, icy.
	☐ 7	☐ 7	Other (Please describe) _____

Rapport between foster parents and child. (Rate the closeness of the psychological relationship between the parents and child. Do they show a high degree of rapport; or are they distant and out of touch with each other and lack mutual understanding and shared feelings?) (Select *one* of the following categories which best reflects the overall situation.)

	Foster Mother 47/	Foster Father 48/	
HIGHEST RAPPORT	☐ 1	☐ 1	Complete sharing of intimate thoughts and feelings. Implicit trust and confidence in each other.
	☐ 2	☐ 2	Close mutual understanding and sympathy, but with occasional temporary lapses.
	☐ 3	☐ 3	Moderate degree of rapport in most situations; achieve close confidence in a good many respects, but fail in others.
	☐ 4	☐ 4	Do not have close rapport but occasionally a close relationship is temporarily established.
	☐ 5	☐ 5	Perfunctory relationship, superficial understanding, interest slight or forced. Tend to be inhibited in each other's presence.
LOWEST RAPPORT	☐ 6	☐ 6	Isolated from each in feelings. No sharing of confidence or aspirations. No active interest in each other.
	☐ 7	☐ 7	Other (*Please describe*) _____

Understanding of Child Shown by Foster Parents (Rate the foster parent's understanding of the child's abilities, needs, point of view, etc. Does the foster parent's behavior indicate a sound appreciation of "what makes the child tick," or does it indicate a failure to appreciate the child's capacities and limitations and to fathom the child's inner feelings.) *(Select one of the following categories which best reflects the overall situation.)*

	Foster Mother 49/	Foster Father 50/	
MOST UNDERSTANDING	☐ 1	☐ 1	Highly insightful about child; shows good empathic understanding of his/her inner states.
↑	☐ 2	☐ 2	Generally is in tune with child; often has fairly good sense of what is going on with him/her.
	☐ 3	☐ 3	Has good grasp of everyday situations, but often misses the subtle aspects of the child's inner feelings.
↓	☐ 4	☐ 4	Generally lacks insight into child's inner state; often misses the obvious.
LEAST UNDERSTANDING	☐ 5	☐ 5	Completely fails to see the child's viewpoint, capacities, limitations. Expects entirely too much or too little. Fails to meet child on his/her own ground.
	☐ 6	☐ 6	Other *(Please specify)* _____

Acceptance of the Child (Rate the foster parent's acceptance of the child, the degree to which he/she is included as part of the family, an intimate partner in the family's affairs while his/her difference is also accepted. Or does the foster parent regard child as an intruder with a strong sense of him/her as a stranger?) (Select *one* of the following categories which best reflects the overall situation.)

	Foster Mother 51/	Foster Father 52/	
HIGHEST ACCEPTANCE	☐ 1	☐ 1	Shows strong acceptance of child and incorporates him/her as part of family without reservation; no holding back in positive regard.
↕	☐ 2	☐ 2	Accepts child in general but does not go "all the way"; shows some reservation in full acceptance but overall tone is quite positive.
	☐ 3	☐ 3	Tends to accept child but there are areas where child is not fully part of family; there is some ambivalence in acceptance with mixture of positive and negative features.
	☐ 4	☐ 4	Predominant tendency is to be caught up with sense of child's difference; not able to accept child but without open rejection.
LEAST ACCEPTANCE	☐ 5	☐ 5	Child openly resented and rejected by foster parent; not accepted as part of family's inner circle.
	☐ 6	☐ 6	Other (*Please describe*) _____

Adjustment of the Foster Home (Rate the general internal adjustment of the foster family as a whole in its day-by-day relationships. Is the home atmosphere characterized by satisfaction, stability and happy adjustment; or by thwarting, unpleasantness, repression and insecurity? Rate the total configuration--the quality of the home atmosphere.) 53/

BEST ADJUSTMENT
↑
↓
WORST ADJUSTMENT

- ☐ 1 Exceedingly well-adjusted. Characterized by pleasant cooperation, security and full satisfactions throughout.

- ☐ 2 Fundamentally sound adjustment, but with minor conflicts here and there.

- ☐ 3 Fairly smooth on surface but moderate evidence of insecurity and repression exists.

- ☐ 4 Definite evidence of mild maladjustment throughout.

- ☐ 5 Dominated by maladjustment, coloring most family activities.

- ☐ 6 Extreme maladjustment; torn with conflict, repression and insecurity.

- ☐ 7 Other *(Please describe)* _____
  _____
  _____

Coordination of Household (Rate the routine functioning of the foster family 54/
household as to the smoothness of organization. Is it effectively planned
and executed? Or is it uncoordinated and chaotic? Consider care of belongings,
coordination of activities, efficiency of home management as it works in practice. Disregard variations in aesthetic standards, style or form.)

WELL MANAGED
☐ 1 Extreme effective management. Model of efficiency with planning of activities well managed and planned. Confusion unknown.

☐ 2 Smooth-running and efficient on the whole. House kept in order and on schedule most of the time. Meals, finances, education planned ahead. Some superficial disorder.

☐ 3 Fair coordination. Quite a bit of disorder but can usually find things. Buying inefficient but meals fairly adequately planned. Things get done but often after fairly long delays.

☐ 4 Poor coordination; essential rudiments of organization are there, but inefficiency and confusion are common. Often late; off schedule half the time. Home tends to be disorderly.

POORLY MANAGED
☐ 5 Chaotic, disorganized. No planning. Confusion reigns even in essentials. Home is extremely disorderly and uncared for.

☐ 6 Other (*Please specify*)_____
_____
_____

Overall Adjustment Rating (Considering everything you know about this 55/
child, rate his overall adjustment.)

☐ 1 Child is making an excellent adjustment in all spheres of his/her life--the outlook for his/her future adjustment is excellent.

☐ 2

☐ 3 Child is making an adequate adjustment--his her strengths outweigh the weaknesses shown--the outlook for his/her future adjustment is hopeful.

☐ 4

☐ 5 Child is making a mixed adjustment--generally the problems he/she faces are serious and the outlook for his future adjustment is somewhat guarded.

☐ 6

☐ 7 Child is making an extremely poor adjustment--the outlook for his future adjustment is unpromising.

☐ 8 Other (Please specify)_____

Is there any information about the foster parents and the child's relationship to them which you deem significant in planning for the child and which has not been covered by this form?   56-57/

_____
_____
_____
_____
_____
_____
_____

How difficult was it for you to fill out this form?   58/

Very difficult* (Answer next question)	(1)
Somewhat difficult* (Answer next question)	(2)
Quite easy	(3)
Very easy	(4)

What was the source of difficulty?   59-60/

_____
_____
_____
_____

Name of Rater_____ Telephone_____

Agency Position_____ 61-62/

Highest Professional Degree: 63/

    High school graduate   ___(1)___

    Some college   ___(2)___

    BSW   ___(3)___

    Other Bachelor's degree   ___(4)___

    MSW   ___(5)___

    Other Master's degree   ___(6)___

    DSW or Ph.D. in social work   ___(7)___

    Other doctoral degree   ___(8)___

    Other   ___(9)___

Years with Agency_____ 64-65/

What is the size of your caseload?

    Number of children_____ 66-67/

    Number of families_____ 68-69/

How well do you feel you know the child? The foster parent(s)?

	Child 70/	Foster Mother 71/	Foster Father 72/
Very well	(1)	(1)	(1)
Fairly well	(2)	(2)	(2)
Slightly	(3)	(3)	(3)
Hardly at all	(4)	(4)	(4)
Not at all	(5)	(5)	(5)
Other	(6)	(6)	(6)

CONCLUSION

The major argument that can be made to support the utilization of the data modules created in the context of the three field trials described in this volume is quite simple: the findings are obviously highly informative for those interested in promoting permanency for foster children. We have been provided insight to an extent we have not previously experienced in the context of the early phase of the CWIS system about phenomena that simply must be understood if social services to children in foster care are to be rationally managed. We highlight here some of our major findings.

Family Visiting of Children in Care (Mini-Project 1)

The phenomenon of visiting is now illuminated in the following ways:

a. We learned that two out of five of the mothers of children not freed for adoption were out of the picture because they were deceased, their whereabouts were unknown, they had not been seen in two years or they were in a mental hospital. This was true for close to four out of five of the fathers.

b. We found a noteworthy amount of visiting of foster children by persons other than their parents: stepparents, grandparents, siblings, other relatives and friends of the family. For children not freed for adoption, almost 15 percent had no visiting from parents but had contact with relatives or friends; the proportion of such children deprived of visits of any kind—totally unvisited children—was reduced to 17 percent.

c. For children not freed for adoption, almost three out of ten had not had contact with their mothers since birth (or since placement) or had otherwise not seen them within the past two years.

d. For the entire sample, some 55 percent of the mothers were characterized by the social workers as tending never to visit their children; this was true of almost 42 percent of the mothers of children not freed for adoption.

e. For children not freed for adoption, it was reported that almost 32 percent had mothers whose visiting frequency had been declining. On the other hand, almost 20 percent had mothers whose visiting was increasing.

f. There was a fair amount of contact between mothers and children by way of telephone calls, letters, cards and gifts. Where parents of children failed to visit children not freed for adoption, the situation was ameliorated in some 16 percent of the cases because the parent wrote or telephoned.

g. Only about 27 percent of the mothers of children not freed for adoption were rated as responsible in their visiting behavior while 36 percent were rated as irresponsible. Some of the remaining mothers were deemed to be unable to visit because of circumstances beyond their control.

h. About 12 percent of the mothers of children not freed for adoption were identified as being candidates for termination of parental rights because of their visiting behavior. For unvisited children, almost a third of the cases were identified as likely requiring termination of parental rights.

i. For those mothers who did visit their children (not freed for adoption), 26 percent were characterized as showing problems during visits because they related to their children in a superficial manner. About 6 percent of the mothers were also said to visit too briefly, 11 percent created disturbances, 10 percent were either intoxicated or under the influence of drugs, and 9 percent appeared bizarre. Almost half of the visiting mothers showed at least one behavioral problem when visiting and over 20 percent showed two or more problems. The behavioral difficulties shown by the small group of visiting fathers was similarly distributed.

j. Of 707 children not freed for adoption, 415 children received visiting from the mother or father or both. A little less than half were said to show enjoyment in being visited. Almost two out of five children were cautious, uncomfortable or embarrassed, or even anxious or upset when visited.

k. Children who experienced absolutely no visiting of any kind from any family-connected person appeared to be more resigned to the failure of their mothers to keep in touch with them. Only about 19 percent showed some form of negative reaction. The children who retained some contact with their families, but not with their mothers, included 53 percent who appeared to show overt negative reaction to the absence of their mothers. We considered this a provocative finding.

l. Factors affecting visitation by the mothers were identified for cases in which the children were visited by their mothers and those where they were not visited. The factors most constraining the visiting behavior of mothers who were in some form of contact with their children were low motivation to visit (54 percent), distance from the child's placement address (46 percent), mental illness (39 percent), physical illness (35 percent), lack of funds for carfare or babysitter (27 percent), and other child care responsibilities (27 percent). For unvisited children, factors negatively affecting visitation by the mothers included low motivation to visit (79 percent), mental illness (59 percent), distance from the child's placement address (44 percent), and other child care responsibilities (32 percent).

m. In about 40 percent of the cases involving children not free for adoption, agencies reported that some effort to stimulate visiting by the mothers had achieved modest returns; however, more mothers were non-responsive than those who came forth with improved visiting.

n. About six percent of the cases involved agency restriction of parental visiting by the mothers and about eight percent had been constrained in the past.

These findings constitute the essential elements in the rather complex phenomenology of family visiting of children in foster care. The determination of how much of this information can be incorporated in a management information system such as CWIS or CCRS cannot be resolved with any sense of scientific rigor. Seasoned observers of the foster care phenomenon can easily scrutinize the data elements involved and rely upon pooled judgments about which to include in an expanded system. As one such observer, the writer feels motivated to recommend the entire group of elements as being potentially useful in moving children toward permanency.

The Availability and Capacities of Parents for Service Involvement (Mini-Project 2)

We again look at the major findings of one of the miniprojects as a way of conjuring with the complex question: Are these data elements worthy of inclusion in a management information system so that the information can be routinely collected? The test is the subjective disposition of the reader regarding the worthwhileness of the information.

a. For almost 1,300 cases included in the study, we find that in six out of ten cases the mother or father was available. To be more exact, in 52 percent of the cases the mother was available and in an additional eight percent, the father was available in her absence. In 40 percent of the cases, the mother was either deceased, her whereabouts unknown, she had not been seen in two years or she was in a mental hospital. The longer the children were in care, the less likely was the mother to be available.

b. For the mothers who were available, all but about 15 percent had been seen by a social worker within the past three months. Twenty-one percent had been seen on six occasions or more. The social workers characterized the pattern of contact between the mothers and social workers as follows: 11 percent were never seen—no contact whatever, 25 percent were occasionally seen, and 11 percent were seen about every other month. About 44 percent of the available mothers were seen at least once a month.

c. In 27 percent of the cases where mothers were available, service contacts were declining; in 29 percent they were on the increase. In 35 percent of the cases there had been no change in patterns of service contact.

d. A major need identified by the social workers who were surveyed was counseling to help the parents clarify their feelings about resumption of care of the children. In 47 percent of the cases such need was described as being "very much" the case and for 23 percent the category chosen was "somewhat."

e. The factor most tending to lower the frequency of contact between social workers and available parents was the latter's low motivation to see the social workers. For the mothers, this was identified as being "very much" a factor in 30 percent of the cases and "somewhat" in 24 percent. Distance from the agency was said to hinder the participation of the mother ("very much" or "somewhat") in 32 percent of the cases. Other identified factors were mental illness (24 percent), and other child care responsibilities (22 percent).

f. Major and minor factors affecting the mothers that tended to keep children in foster care were: child rearing or child care practices (47 percent major and 22 percent minor); parent-child relationship problems (46 percent major and 20 percent minor); severe personal adjustment problems in the form of depression (28 percent major and 15 percent minor); mental illness (25 percent major and 6 percent minor); inadequate housing 21 percent major and 26 percent minor); alcoholism (19 percent major and 5 percent minor); home management problems (22 percent major and 22 percent minor); and physical health problems (18 percent major and 14 percent minor).

g. Social workers reported a fairly high degree of difficulty in engaging the available mothers in an ongoing service contact because of the following factors: resistance to seeing the social worker (22 percent very much and 29 percent somewhat); failing to keep appointments (22 percent very much and 25 percent somewhat); lack of ability to discuss personal problems (21 percent very much and 32 percent somewhat); defensiveness about self (30 percent very much and 30 percent somewhat); and failing to show concern about the child (18 percent very much and 22 percent somewhat).

h. The referral of the available mothers to other agencies offering service took place on a modest scale. Service contacts were already established to meet the following problems: inadequate housing (nine percent), health problems (15 percent), severe depression (13 percent), parent-child relationship problems (13 percent); mental illness (14 percent), child rearing or child care practices (12 percent), and inadequate income (8 percent). The mothers were unwilling to use the service of other agencies in the following problem areas: child rearing or child care practices (19 percent), management of home (11 percent), alcoholism (10 percent), severe depression (12 percent), and parent-child relationship problems (18 percent).

i. The agency's perspective on the possiblity of the child being returned home was, overall, rather dismal. In 50 percent of the cases where the mother was available, the social worker chose the category "no prospect" for such return; in 16 percent of the cases the category of "slight prospect" was chosen. In only 15 percent of the